# INTERPRETING MAIMONIDES

Moses Maimonides (1138–1204) was arguably the single most important Jewish thinker of the Middle Ages, with an impact on the later Jewish tradition that was unparalleled by any of his contemporaries. In this volume of new essays, world-leading scholars address themes relevant to his philosophical outlook, including his relationship with his Islamicate surroundings and the impact of his work on subsequent Jewish and Christian writings, as well as his reception in twentieth-century scholarship. The essays also address the nature and aim of Maimonides's philosophical writing, including its connection with biblical exegesis, and the philosophical and theological arguments that are central to his work, such as revelation, ritual, divine providence, and teleology. Wide-ranging and fully up-to-date, the volume will be highly valuable for those interested in Jewish history and thought, medieval philosophy, and religious studies.

CHARLES H. MANEKIN is Professor of Philosophy at the University of Maryland. He is the author of *On Maimonides* (2005) and *The Logic of Gersonides* (1991), and the editor of *Medieval Jewish Philosophical Writings* (Cambridge, 2008).

DANIEL DAVIES is Research Associate for the PESHAT project at the University of Hamburg. He is the author of *Method and Metaphysics in Maimonides' Guide for the Perplexed* (2011).

# INTERPRETING MAIMONIDES

## *Critical Essays*

EDITED BY

### CHARLES H. MANEKIN

*University of Maryland*

### DANIEL DAVIES

*University of Hamburg*

CAMBRIDGE
UNIVERSITY PRESS

# CAMBRIDGE
## UNIVERSITY PRESS

University Printing House, Cambridge CB2 8BS, United Kingdom

One Liberty Plaza, 20th Floor, New York, NY 10006, USA

477 Williamstown Road, Port Melbourne, VIC 3207, Australia

314–321, 3rd Floor, Plot 3, Splendor Forum, Jasola District Centre, New Delhi – 110025, India

79 Anson Road, #06–04/06, Singapore 079906

Cambridge University Press is part of the University of Cambridge.

It furthers the University's mission by disseminating knowledge in the pursuit of
education, learning, and research at the highest international levels of excellence.

www.cambridge.org
Information on this title: www.cambridge.org/9781107184190
DOI: 10.1017/9781316875483

© Cambridge University Press 2019

First published 2019

Printed and bound in Great Britain by Clays Ltd, Elcograf S.p.A.

*A catalogue record for this publication is available from the British Library.*

*Library of Congress Cataloging-in-Publication Data*
NAMES: Manekin, Charles Harry, 1953– editor. | Davies, Daniel, 1977– editor.
TITLE: Interpreting Maimonides : critical essays / edited by Charles H. Manekin, Daniel Davies
DESCRIPTION: Cambridge ; New York, NY : Cambridge University Press, [2018] | Includes
bibliographical references and index.
IDENTIFIERS: LCCN 2018033429 | ISBN 9781107184190
SUBJECTS: LCSH: Maimonides, Moses, 1135–1204. | Maimonides, Moses, 1135–1204. Dalālat al-
Ḥā'irīn. | Jewish philosophy.
CLASSIFICATION: LCC B759.M34 I58 2018 | DDC 181/.06–dc23
LC record available at https://lccn.loc.gov/2018033429

ISBN 978-1-107-18419-0 Hardback

# Contents

# Tables

# Contributors

HERBERT A. DAVIDSON is Professor of Hebrew (Emeritus) and Research Professor at the University of California, Los Angeles. His books include *Moses Maimonides: The Man and His Works* (2005) and *Maimonides the Rationalist* (2011).

DANIEL DAVIES is Research Associate for the PESHAT project at the University of Hamburg. He is the author of *Method and Metaphysics in Maimonides' Guide for the Perplexed* (2011).

DIANA DI SEGNI is Research Associate in the Faculty of Philosophy at the Thomas-Institut, University of Cologne, and the author of *Moses Maimonides and the Latin Middle Ages. Critical edition of Dux neutrorum I, 1–59"* (2016).

YEHUDA HALPER is Senior Lecturer in the Department of Jewish Thought at Bar Ilan University and the author of numerous studies in medieval Jewish and Islamic philosophy. He is the editor of the forthcoming *The Pursuit of Happiness in Medieval Jewish and Islamic Thought.*

WARREN ZEV HARVEY is Professor of Jewish Thought (Emeritus) at the Hebrew University of Jerusalem. He has written numerous articles on Maimonides and is the author of *The Physics and the Metaphysics of Hasdai Crescas* (1999).

HANNAH KASHER is Professor of Jewish Thought (Emerita) at Bar Ilan University. Her most recent book is *"High Above All Nations" (Deut. 26:16): Milestones in Jewish Philosophy on the Issue of the Jewish People* (2018).

SARA KLEIN-BRASLAVY is Professor of Jewish Philosophy (Emerita) in the Department of Hebrew Culture Studies at Tel-Aviv University. Her books include *Maimonides as Biblical Interpreter* (2011), *"Without any Doubt": Gersonides on Method and Knowedge* (2011), and *Gersonides'*

*Interpretation of the Stories on the Creation of Man and the Story of the Garden of Eden* (2015).

Y. TZVI LANGERMANN is Professor of Arabic at Bar Ilan University and specializes in the history of science and philosophy (Jewish and Islamic) and the thought of Maimonides. He most recently co-edited *Texts in Transit in the Medieval Mediterranean* with Robert G. Morrison (2016).

CHARLES H. MANEKIN is Professor of Philosophy at the University of Maryland. He is the author of *On Maimonides* (2005) and *The Logic of Gersonides* (1991), and the editor of *Medieval Jewish Philosophical Writings* (Cambridge, 2008).

JAMES T. ROBINSON is the Caroline E. Haskell Professor of the History of Judaism, Islamic Studies, and the History of Religions at the University of Chicago Divinity School. He is the author of *Samuel Ibn Tibbon's Commentary on Ecclesiastes, The Book of the Soul of Man* (2007) and several critical editions of Hebrew commentaries on Scripture.

KENNETH R. SEESKIN is the Philip M. and Ethel Klutznick Professor of Jewish Civilization in the Department of Philosophy at Northwestern University. He is the author of several books on Maimonides, including *Searching for a Distant God: The Legacy of Maimonides* (2000) and *Maimonides on the Origin of the World* (2007).

JOSEF STERN is William H. Colvin Professor of Philosophy (Emeritus) at the University of Chicago. His most recent book, *The Matter and Form of Maimonides' Guide* (2013), won the 2014 Book Prize of the *Journal of the History of Philosophy*.

DAVID WIRMER is Assistant Professor of Arabic and Jewish Philosophy in the Philosophy Department at the University of Cologne. His publications include *Averroes: Über den Intellekt* (2008) and *Vom Denken der Natur zur Natur des Denkens: Ibn Bāǧǧa's Theorie der Potenz als Grundlegung der Psychologie* (2014).

# *Acknowledgments*

The Editors would like to thank Hilary Gaskin, Sophie Taylor, Marianne Nield, and Bret Workman of Cambridge University Press, as well as Sunantha Ramamoorthy of Integra Software Services, for their patient shepherding of the text to its publication.

The editing was completed when Manekin was on a funded research leave from the University of Maryland for which he thanks Samuel Kerstein, Professor and Chair of the Philosophy department, and Bonnie Thornton Dill, Professor and Dean of the College of Arts and Humanities. Davies thanks Giuseppe Veltri, Professor of Jewish Philosophy at Hamburg University, for the opportunity to pursue the research for this volume.

# Note on the Text

Unless otherwise indicated, page references to Maimonides's works are to the following editions and translations:

*Commentary on the Mishnah* = *Perush ha-Mishnah*, 7 vols., ed. and tr. J. Kafah (Jerusalem: Mosad Harav Kook, 1963–1968). *Introduction to the Commentary on the Mishnah, Introduction to Chapter Ḥeleq, Sanhedrin*, and *Introduction to Avot* (*Eight Chapters*) in *Haqdamot ha-Rambam la-Mishnah*, ed. and Hebrew tr. I. Shailat (Maaleh Adumim: Maaliyot, 1992), or according to the Kafah edition.

*Code of Law* = *Mishneh Torah*, ed. Z. Frankel, 14 vols., (Jerusalem, 1975–2007).

*Guide* = *Dalālat al-Ḥā'irīn,* ed. S. Munk and I. Joel (Jerusalem: Junovitch/ Azriel, 1930/31) (Ar.); *Moreh Nevukhim*, tr. S. Ibn Tibbon and ed. Y. Even Shmuel (Jerusalem: Mossad Ha-Rav Kook, 1981) (Heb.); *The Guide of the Perplexed*, tr. S. Pines (University of Chicago Press, 1963) (Eng.).

*Letters* = Either *Iggerot ha-Rambam*, ed. I. Shailat (Jerusalem: Maaliyot, 1988) or *Iggerot ha-Rambam: Maqor ve-Targum*, ed. Y. Kafih (Jerusalem: Mossad ha-Rav Kook, 1987) or *Iggerot ha-Rambam*, ed. D. Baneth (Jerusalem: Magnes Press, 1946).

*Responsa* = *Teshuvot ha-Rambam*, ed. and tr. J. Blau (Jerusalem: Mekitsei Nirdamim, 1957–1961).

# Introduction

### Daniel Davies and Charles H. Manekin

Moses Maimonides is the prism through which medieval Jewish philosophy is often viewed and a reference point or inspiration for much Jewish philosophy today. Despite the abundance of Maimonides studies that regularly emerge, there is room for a new volume that addresses issues bearing on his philosophy and its varied interpretation, which continue to develop in sometimes surprising ways. This volume collects essays that are relevant particularly to interpretations of Maimonides's philosophical arguments and legacy.

Maimonides was born in 1137/8 in Cordoba, a city that was taken in 1148 by the Almohads, under whose rule Maimonides lived for much of his early life. Along with his family, he moved for a time through Spain and North Africa, and no doubt learned much about the surrounding culture. Scholars disagree about the exact impressions Almohad thought left on Maimonides and the ways in which his own writing reflects that impact, if at all. Herbert Davidson is one of the major protagonists in this debate, and his contribution focuses mainly on an ongoing discussion with Sarah Stroumsa. He states his opposition to the methodological assumption that Maimonides was aware of all major works of his time and that he read closely everything available. Davidson considers some of the particular ways in which Stroumsa has argued that Almohad influence can be detected in a number of Maimonides's legal rulings and philosophical presentations. In each case, he argues, there are more plausible candidates for Maimonides's sources.

Y. Tzvi Langermann raises doubts concerning another recently popular candidate for influencing Maimonides, al-Ghazālī. As well as questioning or refuting particular instances of supposed influence, Langermann calls for clarity about what "influence" amounts to in historical scholarship. He denies that Maimonides's arguments or phrasing must always have a prior source, and he also argues that particular attempts to make the case for Ghazālī's direct influence are unconvincing and, as in Davidson's essay, can be given more plausible interpretations. While Langermann agrees that comparing the two thinkers can be useful and can help to clarify possible meanings, these two chapters present a powerful case for caution in identifying Maimonides's sources too confidently.

During his time in Morocco, Maimonides began writing his Mishna commentary, which began a project of halakhic writings that he continued after settling in Egypt. Hannah Kasher includes material from these works to address an important question about the status of some particular outsiders in Maimonides's thought, women and gentiles, about whom Maimonides makes some disparaging remarks. Kasher acknowledges that Maimonides would have been molded by attitudes in the texts and traditions to which he was committed. For example, his views of women's inferiority are based in biological notions of the time, even though Maimonides does not apply this judgment to all women. However, Kasher points out that he sometimes justifies his negative legal rulings by considering their practical ramifications rather than by "natural inferiority." She argues that while Maimonides thought that women and gentiles are capable of reaching human perfection, they are disadvantaged either by their biology or the circumstances of their birth.

By the time he completed his major halakhic works, Maimonides was already a man of great renown throughout the Jewish world, and his fame would grow far greater, but the work for which he is most noted specifically as a philosopher was to be written later in life. *The Guide for / of / to the Perplexed* was completed toward the end of the twelfth century and has been scrutinized ever since. Even after centuries of such study, in many different contexts, Kenneth Seeskin can still fruitfully ask about the *Guide*'s subject matter. He argues that Maimonides insists on the need to use theoretical speculation in order to reach human perfection, but that such reasoning does not always lead to certain conclusions. Through analyses of Maimonides's approach to the *via negativa*, creation, prophecy, and providence, Seeskin argues that the *Guide* encourages its readers to approach deep matters with the humility that enables them to recognize truth when it is possible, and to act and inquire appropriately when it is not. Seeskin's article exemplifies how the *Guide* is still to give up more of its secrets.

The contributions by the volume's editors offer interpretations of some doctrines that have proven particularly difficult for readers to accept. In both cases, the most common approaches in academic studies today assume that Maimonides's explicit positions cannot be his real positions. Charles Manekin explains Maimonides's take on the Mosaic revelation, in which Moses is assigned the rank of a "scribe" who reports God's words.

However, there is a trend in recent scholarship that makes Moses the Law's author, according to Maimonides, since divine authorship is said to be opposed to some of Maimonides's philosophical principles. Manekin argues that Maimonides presents the divine authorship of the Law as a natural event that is perfectly compatible with the requirements of reason, as he understood them, and there is therefore no reason to deny that his statements are genuine. Daniel Davies addresses another aspect of Maimonides's writing that is generally considered to be inconsistent, God's knowledge and providence. Whereas many scholars argue that Maimonides implicitly limits God's knowledge when he limits God's providence to species, despite his claim that God's knowledge is not limited at all, Davies argues that there is no conflict between the two doctrines. Instead, although Maimonides connects them by arguing that the reasons that lead some to deny God's knowledge of individuals actually indicate that God is not provident over particulars, they are two separate doctrines. Therefore, regarding these doctrines also, there is no need to claim that Maimonides's stated opinions are not genuine.

David Wirmer argues that there does appear to be an inbuilt conflict, or to be precise, a contradiction, in Maimonides's treatment of the question of final causality. When writing in the context of creation, Maimonides denies that the world or even a part of it has an end beyond the pure will of God. Yet when writing in the context of providence, Maimonides's purposive deity seems to differ from the Aristotelian intelligent principle from which the world proceeds in only one respect, and that is its lack of necessity. Wirmer argues that while *Guide* iii.25 is helpful in establishing that the search for ends is not a futile one, and hence relieves the perplexity of the perfect men on this question in *Guide* iii.13, in other respects the two chapters are at cross purposes, which may be due to a contradiction between Maimonides on creation and on providence.

Theological issues such as these connect with religious praxis in Maimonides's works, and Yehuda Halper explores the relationship between the binding of Isaac and ritualistic prayer. Halper looks at the different kinds of trials discussed in the *Guide* and argues that they perform a similar function to parables, which are designed to teach. Contrasting Abraham's trial with that of Job, Halper identifies two kinds of tests corresponding to the two resulting beneficiaries, the examiner or the appraised. However, Abraham's test differs as it benefits neither. Instead, like prayer and temple rituals, the purpose is to teach foundations of the Torah to its readers. Arguing that prayer performs the same function as trials allows Halper to explain how Maimonides links ritual with belief.

Halper's interpretation of Maimonides's reading of the Binding of Isaac story serves as a reminder that Maimonides the philosopher cannot be separated from Maimonides the Biblical exegete; for one thing, Maimonides was convinced that scriptural terms and parables encode metaphysical truths; for another, he desired in the *Guide* to provide the key that unlocks these truths, and to reduce the perplexity of those students who were confused by the apparent contradiction of philosophy and the Law. Although Maimonides did not innovate the philosophical reading of Scripture, even within his Andalusian rabbinical milieu, his attempts to "combine the Law with the intelligible" had an enormous impact on the history of Jewish exegesis, both rationalist and kabbalist. James T. Robinson traces the movement of Maimonides's interpretations of Jacob's ladder over the course of several centuries. That Maimonides offers more than one interpretation underscores the difficulty of taking his philosophical exegesis of Scripture as authoritative, which may explain why some interpreters of Maimonides's philosophy continue to pay little attention to his scriptural exegesis. Sara Klein-Braslavy, who has published several volumes decoding Maimonides's Biblical exegesis in the *Guide*, considers some of that ambiguity deliberate and alluring. She asks here why the *Guide* continues to fascinate readers today. Her answer is that the work's enigmatic nature, especially in its Biblical interpretations, but also in its philosophical doctrines, challenges its readers to decipher the work's intent, a challenge that brings with it intellectual rewards.

As well as its colossal impact on different streams of Jewish thought, the *Guide* left its mark on the Latin scholastics, most famously through Dominican theologians. Diana Di Segni's contribution presents the latest scholarly research into the story of Maimonides's reception in the Latin world, which is wider than usually acknowledged. Based on the three Latin versions that circulated in the thirteenth century, Di Segni assesses the main philosophical and theological questions on which Maimonides was considered authoritative and uncovers use of the *Guide* in some early works in which its author is unnamed. Additionally, she shows that the complete Latin translation of the *Guide* was available before the halfway point of the thirteenth century in Northern Italy, not only in Paris, as had previously been thought.

The last two essays consider the interpretations of Maimonides offered by Leo Strauss and Shlomo Pines, the scholars whose work has dominated the last half century of interpreting Maimonides. Anyone who studies Pines's 1963 classic translation of the *Guide* encounters the two scholars' introductory essays. It is therefore fitting that the final two chapters of the volume are dedicated to Pines and Strauss, respectively, as interpreters of Maimonides. Josef Stern compares aspects of Pines's introductory essay on the philosophical sources of the *Guide* to a highly influential article that Pines wrote in 1979, which argued that Maimonides emphasized the limitations of the human intellect and the inability of humans to acquire metaphysical knowledge. It is commonly believed that Pines began to read Maimonides as a "proto-Kantian" only in or shortly before 1979. But Stern recounts that the essays set different agendas, both of which have been followed up in scholarship on Maimonides: a political agenda, on the one hand, and a "critical" or skeptical one, on the other. In the earlier essay, Pines adopted a "meta-philosophical" approach, asking about the relationship between religion and philosophy: The later essay focused on a "philosophical" question of the goal of human life. Stern expounds the two agendas and suggests why Pines pursued them at different times.

In a much-needed interpretation of a particularly enigmatic essay, Warren Zev Harvey deciphers some of Strauss's introductory essay. As well as being a contribution to understanding Strauss on Maimonides, Harvey's chapter reflects some of the author's own developing understanding and appreciation of Strauss's grasp of the *Guide*'s intricacies. He explains particular passages and hints in Strauss's essay, including Strauss's treatments of Maimonides's arguments about God's existence and nature, and also considers aspects of the literary character of the essay. Furthermore, Harvey argues that, in his later works, Strauss was not bound by the Athens-Jerusalem dichotomy that anchors the ways in which he is usually understood.

Despite their differences, both Strauss and Pines situated Maimonides squarely within the world of the Muslim Aristotelian philosophers. Strauss's essays on the *Guide* set scholars off on a hunt (some would say a wild goose chase) for Maimonides's esoteric doctrines, which were more compatible with the Muslim philosophers than his explicit views. Pines's essays in the history of Jewish philosophy, with their emphasis on viewing Jewish thinkers within their non-Jewish intellectual environment, set scholars off on a hunt for Maimonides's philosophical and intellectual antecedents and sources. Several articles in this volume challenge both these approaches, which are still very much alive in the field.

Maimonides died in 1204 after an enormously productive life, rich in events and controversy. His *Nachleben* continues to reverberate, and this volume presents some of the exciting new directions it is currently taking in academic studies, with contributions that further develop previous approaches and others that challenge widely held assumptions.

# CHAPTER I

# Maimonides and the Almohads

## Herbert A. Davidson

There is no reason to doubt that Maimonides was acquainted with all the writings of Aristotle known in Moslem Spain, i.e., practically the whole *Corpus Aristotelicum.*

S. Pines, "Translator's Introduction" in *Guide of the Perplexed*

There is clear evidence that Maimonides received the most comprehensive education available in al-Andalus and Fez both from his explicit statements and from our knowledge of the educational curriculum, religious as well as philosophical, of the educated Jews in Islamic Spain.

I. Dobbs-Weinstein, "Maimonides' Reticence toward Ibn Sīnā"
in *Avicenna and His Heritage*

My own working hypothesis is that Maimonides . . . read all he could find.

S. Stroumsa, *Maimonides in His World*

Maimonides certainly lived a full life. He was born in Andalusia and witnessed the Almohads' conquest of most of the country and the havoc they wreaked on the Jewish communities. In his early twenties, he dwelt for a time in Fez but soon bade goodbye to Morocco and its intolerant rulers, visited Palestine, and in his late twenties settled in Egypt, where he remained until his death. In his early period he composed a commentary on two-thirds of the Babylonian Talmud, which he did not publish, and three works that he did: a Commentary on the entire Mishnah corpus; the *Book of Commandments*; and the *Mishneh Torah*, a comprehensive code of Jewish law on which, he says, he labored day and night for ten years. The introduction to the *Mishneh Torah* lists the sources from which he drew: the Babylonian Talmud, the Jerusalem Talmud, Sifra, Sifre, Tosefta, and the commentaries, responsa, and halakhic compilations of the Geonim. He writes that he mastered "all of these books" and employed them in determining norms for the entire range of scriptural and rabbinic law.[1]

In addition to his rabbinic studies he found time for secular science. Al-Qifṭī's biographical dictionary, which dates from shortly after Maimonides's time – but is not always reliable – reports that he "read philosophy [i.e., he read texts, likely with a teacher] in Andalusia, mastering mathematics [which would include astronomy] and acquiring a smattering of logic. He also read medicine there, excelling in its scientific side."[2] Independently of al-Qifṭī we know that in his early period, Maimonides studied medicine with Jewish and Arabic physicians and discussed difficult diagnoses with them;[3] that he attained expertise in astronomy and in the mathematics needed for making complicated astronomical calculations;[4] and that he acquired a knowledge of at least the basic features of the Arab-Aristotelian picture of the universe.

In his later period, he was no less industrious. He composed his *Guide for the Perplexed*, in the course of which he cites five works of Aristotle and one falsely attributed to him, Ptolemy's *Almagest*, works of Alfarabi and Ibn Bājja, and a pair of compositions ascribed to Alexander Aphrodisias. He drew from al-Ghazālī, whose name he never mentions.[5] Two letters written by him that cast light on his medical practice have been preserved. The first, which now exists as part of a single long letter dated 1191, relates that he had achieved fame as a physician, that his patients included members of the Muslim aristocracy, and that after he finished dispensing care, he spent the remainder of the day searching the medical literature for whatever might be pertinent to his patients. He found no time to look at "anything scientific" apart from medicine.[6] The second letter is dated 1199, by which time his practice extended to the Sultan and his family. He describes traveling to Cairo every morning and meeting with the Sultan. At the earliest, he returned to Fustat in the afternoon where in his words "I find my courtyard full of Jews and Gentiles of every class." He attended to

---

[1] Maimonides, *Code of Law, Introduction*, ed. Z. Frankel, p. 4.

[2] H. Davidson, "Ibn al-Qifṭī's Statement Regarding Maimonides' Early Study of Science," *Aleph*, 14 (2014), 245–258, 256.

[3] Maimonides, *On Asthma*, ed. and tr. G. Bos (Provo: Brigham Young University Press, 2002), chapter 13, §§33, 38; *Medical Aphorisms, Treatises 6–9*, ed. and tr. G. Bos (Provo: Brigham Young University Press, 2007), chapter 8, §69; *Pirqei Mosheh* (medieval translation of the *Medical Aphorisms*), ed. S. Muntner (Jerusalem: Mossad Harav Kook, 1959), ch. 22, §35; ch. 24, §40.

[4] Maimonides, *Commentary on the Mishnah, Rosh ha-Shanah* ii.7; *Code of Law, Sanctification of the New Month*.

[5] H. Davidson, *Maimonides the Rationalist* (Oxford: Littman Library, 2011), pp. 99–172.

[6] Maimonides, *Letters*, ed. D. Baneth, pp. 69–70.

their medical needs, and "they are not gone before nightfall and sometimes
... until two or more hours after dark .... When night falls I am so weak
that I can no longer talk."[7] As many as twelve medical texts by Maimonides
have been preserved, all or the majority of which come from the late
period. The most comprehensive, known in English as the *Medical
Aphorisms*, bears witness to the years spent in studying the medical literature. In the main, it consists of excerpts from ninety of Galen's medical
works.

That he could accomplish so much is a marvel. Nonetheless, there are
writers whose admiration for him is such that they deem his actual
accomplishments insufficient. Books are attributed to him without any
adequate evidence and sometimes contain statements that he could not
possibly have made. Scholars have portrayed him as holding the highest
communal office, although he is never seen to perform the duties of the
office and could not have performed them during the decade in which he
worked day and night on the *Mishneh Torah*, the year when he was
incapacitated with depression after hearing of his brother's death, and
the years in which his medical practice demanded all of his time. And he
has been credited with a much broader knowledge of the philosophic
literature than I have described.

I start with a couple of examples of this last sort.

S. Pines writes: "There is no reason to doubt that Maimonides was
acquainted with all the writings of Aristotle known in Moslem Spain, i.e.,
practically the whole *Corpus Aristotelicum* .... It is moreover abundantly
clear that, from an early age, Maimonides had lived with these texts and
that they formed a notable part of his intellectual makeup."[8] Not a scrap of
evidence is furnished to justify these broad pronouncements. In actuality,
apart from a few questionable tidbits, there are no grounds for imagining
that Maimonides read a single line of Aristotle in his early period. As
already mentioned, he read and used five works of Aristotle in his later
period; there is little reason to suppose that he read more. In the instance of
one of the key Aristotelian works, the *Metaphysics*, solid evidence can be
marshalled to show that he did not consult it in either period.

Pines further writes: "It may be taken as certain that Maimonides made
extensive use of the commentaries [on Aristotle]. This may be inferred not
only from the reference to them in the letter to Ibn Tibbon [where
Maimonides wrote that Aristotle cannot be understood without the

---

[7] A. Marx, "Texts by and About Maimonides," *Jewish Quarterly Review*, 25 (1935), 376–377.
[8] *Guide of the Perplexed*, "Translator's Introduction," p. lxi.

commentary of Alexander, Themistius, or Averroes. H. D.], but also from the fact that the Spanish Aristotelians, whose philosophic education was probably similar to Maimonides', held the commentaries in high esteem."[9] Since Maimonides recommends Averroes's commentary on Aristotle, although he himself did not use it when he wrote the *Guide*,[10] he would have been quite capable of recommending the commentaries of Alexander and Themistius, although he did not use them when writing it. As Pines concedes, the Greek commentaries on Aristotle have left no discernible mark on Maimonides's writings. A work attributed to Alexander that is not a commentary – the *Principles of the Universe* – was used by Maimonides and may have been considered by him as good as a commentary. Otherwise, far from its being taken as certain that Maimonides made extensive use of the Greek commentaries on Aristotle, there is no evidence to support the supposition that he ever looked at them.

I. Dobbs-Weinstein writes: "There is clear evidence that Maimonides received the most comprehensive education available in al-Andalus and Fez both from his explicit statements and from our knowledge of the educational curriculum, religious as well as philosophical, of the educated Jews in Islamic Spain. At the very least, we can be reasonably certain that he would have read all those Arabic works of Ibn Sīnā available in al-Andalus, Fez, and Cairo after 1138."[11] Since she does not identify the "explicit statements" that she had in mind, we cannot judge that part of her contention. As for the inclusion of philosophy in an educational curriculum of educated Jews in twelfth-century Islamic Spain, no such curriculum is known to have existed. The odd rare bird who wanted to study philosophy had no institutional framework to help him. He was on his own.

Maimonides furnishes a glimpse of how philosophy would be taught in his time. When Joseph ben Judah arrived in Egypt from the West he wrote a flattering note to Maimonides saying that he wished to study secular texts with him. Although he had no preparation and would have to start with ABCs, Maimonides accepted him as a pupil. The two read mathematics and astronomy and only then turned to philosophy proper. They started with logic and had not progressed to metaphysics when Joseph left Egypt for Syria.[12] Maimonides is not known to have read philosophic texts with anyone else. He did train a nephew in medicine,

[9] Ibid., p. lxiv.   [10] Ibid., p. cviii; Davidson, *Maimonides the Rationalist*, p. 166.
[11] I. Dobbs-Weinstein, "Maimonides' Reticence toward Ibn Sīnā" in J. Janssens and D. De Smit (eds.), *Avicenna and His Heritage* (Leuven University Press, 2002), pp. 281–296, on p. 283.
[12] *Guide*, Dedication, ed. Munk-Joel, p. 2a.

and when he occasionally refers to other students, the subject of study is rabbinic texts.[13]

Dobbs-Weinstein concedes that Avicenna's "influences ... cannot be directly traced or attributed to a specific text" in the *Guide*. But she asserts that Avicenna's "clearest influences upon Maimonides' thought are evident in the latter's development of the following, closely related distinctions and problems: (1) the origin of the universe or, more precisely, the specific formulation of emanation in a manner such that emanation could be reconciled with creation, (2) the distinction between possible and necessary existence, (3) the nature of acquired, specifically prophetic human intellect."[14] She discovered these three distinctions and problems in her reading of the *Guide for the Perplexed* and at best they would only speak to a possible impact of Avicenna on Maimonides in his later period. They would have no bearing on Maimonides's years in Andalusia and Fez and the first decade or more of his life in Egypt.

The terms *necessarily existent* and *possibly existent* go back to Avicenna, but by Maimonides's time they had become common coin; they have, for instance, a prominent place in al-Ghazālī. As for the first and third points, they turn out to be subtle trains of reasoning that Dobbs-Weinstein supports by a dozen references to the *Guide*. Whether the dozen texts she refers to do bear out her re-creation of Maimonides's thinking may be questioned. Her conclusions regarding Avicenna's "influences" lose their cogency, however, on more conclusive grounds: Not a single quotation of, or reference to, any work of Avicenna's is offered in order to establish that the reasoning she ascribes to Maimonides was suggested by Avicenna or more generally that Avicenna had a direct impact on Maimonides's thought.

As far as the evidence offered goes, there are thus no grounds for concluding that Maimonides read anything written by Avicenna or indeed that he knew anything about Avicenna's philosophic thinking at any point in his writing career. (He was familiar with at least one of Avicenna's medical works.) In fact, there are substantial Avicennan threads in the *Guide for the Perplexed*. But they are at least as likely to have come to Maimonides through an intermediary as to have come directly from Avicenna, the most probable candidate being al-Ghazālī's summary of the views of the "philosophers."[15]

---

[13] H. Davidson, *Moses Maimonides, the Man and His Works* (New York: Oxford University Press, 2005), pp. 65–66.
[14] Dobbs-Weinstein, "Maimonides' Reticence," pp. 282, 287.
[15] In a forthcoming publication, I give textual evidence for Maimonides's having used Ghazali's *Maqāṣid* and *Tahāfut* when writing the *Guide*.

The foregoing is a prelude. My primary interest is a recent attempt to identify an impact on Maimonides's thought of a somewhat different sort. S. Stroumsa submits a methodological guideline, which many would challenge if it were put forward as a general rule for intellectual studies. It is particularly questionable in regard to Maimonides, since it fails to take into account how monumental, and hence time absorbing, an accomplishment his mastery of the rabbinic corpus was.

The guideline reads:

> [Among some scholars,] suggestions that Maimonides might have had access to a specific non-Jewish source encounter resistance and are expected to be accompanied by a positive proof that this was indeed the case. My own working hypothesis is that Maimonides, who only rarely cited his sources, read all he could find, and that he had no qualms about perusing the theological or legal works of non-Jews, and even less so when he respected their author. A priori, therefore, and until proven otherwise, my assumption is that he was generally familiar with major books of his period.[16]

What will concern us will be Stroumsa's application of her hypothesis to the possible impact on Maimonides of the Almohads. The name *Almohads* is a Westernization of Arabic *al-muwaḥḥidūn*, which means those who affirm and uphold unity. The *Muwaḥḥidūn*, or Almohads, were self-styled affirmers and upholders of the unity of God, of Allah. The ideologue of the movement was Ibn Tumart, who died a few years before Maimonides's birth. There exists a compilation of seventeen opuscules in Arabic, which are attributed to Ibn Tumart and encapsulate various aspects of Almohad belief and practice. Much is uncertain, including the date at which the compilation began to circulate, whether all the components come from Ibn Tumart himself, and whether they were originally written in Arabic or whether some or all are translated from Berber, that being the native tongue of Ibn Tumart and his immediate circle. The modern editors of the collection speak of it as Ibn Tumart's "Book," and I shall use similar phraseology without any intent to prejudge the issues.

Maimonides never names the Almohads or alludes to them except in an oblique reference to persecution of Jews in the West, and he never names or refers to Ibn Tumart. There is no way of telling whether the seventeen opuscules were accessible to him in Arabic, should he have wanted to peruse them. Stroumsa thinks, nonetheless, that she can recognize

---

[16] S. Stroumsa, *Maimonides in His World* (Princeton University Press, 2009), p. xii.

"Almohad influence in many of Maimonides' innovations, both on the large scale as also in the details."[17]

1.   Stroumsa writes: "It appears that in his decision to compose a relatively short compendium of law as well as in the principles that guided him. . . (namely, going back to the *uṣūl,* presenting a final ruling, and dispensing with the scaffoldings that traditionally accompanied it), Maimonides was closely following the Almohad example."[18] I address the matter of *uṣūl* first.

*Uṣūl* means *roots.* In an extended and metaphorical sense, the roots of a field of knowledge are the fundamentals – the principles, sources, doctrines, rules, criteria, and the like. To take an instance with which Maimonides was surely familiar: Euclid's *Elements* was translated into Arabic as his *Roots.* Sezgin, whose catalogue of Arabic literature stops at about a century before Maimonides's birth, lists more than fifty books that have *uṣūl* in their titles,[19] and writers of course did not lay down their pens where the catalogue stops. A number of genres of Arabic literature are represented, two of which are pertinent for us: *uṣūl* of *dīn* and *uṣūl* of *fiqh.* Kalam theologians concerned themselves with the roots of religion (*dīn*), that is, with the principles, or doctrines, of the Islamic faith; Muslim legists concerned themselves with the roots of jurisprudence (*fiqh*), that is, with the sources of Islamic law. The Quran, traditions handed down about Muhammad and his associates, and the consensus of the Muslim community, were commonly recognized as valid sources of law, and analogy with established cases was often added as fourth valid tool for deciding legal issues that could not be otherwise adjudicated.

The Arabic Aristotelians, and especially Avicenna[20] and al-Ghazālī, likewise speak of roots of one sort or another. For example, al-Ghazālī's account of the views of the philosophers, which Maimonides may have read in his early period and did read and use in his later period, lists six roots – criteria – for rating pleasures; four roots – principles – of physics; and three roots – categories – of miracles.[21]

*Uṣūl* appear as well in Judeo-Arabic literature prior to Maimonides. Dāwūd al-Muqammiṣ's chief work was known under two names, one of

[17] Stroumsa, *Maimonides in His World,* p. 61.   [18] Ibid., p. 67.

[19] F. Sezgin, *Geschichte des Arabischen Schrifttums,* 13 vols. (Leiden: Brill, 1967–2000), Index.

[20] See Avicenna, *Shifā': Ilāhiyyāt,* ed. and tr. M. Marmura (Provo: Brigham Young University Press 2005), p. 4, line 5; p. 115, line 6; p. 256, line 1; p. 287, line 6; p. 350, line 7; p. 351, line 8; and indices of the Cairo edition of the *Shifā'.*

[21] Ghazali, *Maqāṣid* (Cairo), pp. 171–175, 263, 314. See also Bouyges's index to his edition of Ghazali's *Tahafot al-Falasifat* (Beyrouth: Imprimerie Catholique, 1927), s. v. *uṣūl.*

which was *On the Roots of Religion (Uṣūl al-Dīn)*.²² Saadia wrote a treatise in which he treated the roots *(uṣūl)* of inheritance law.²³ One of Samuel ben Ḥofni's many books is an Arabic work, which has been lost, entitled *On the Roots of Religion (Uṣūl al-Dīn) and its Branches*.²⁴ Baḥya ibn Paquda's *Duties of the Heart* is divided into ten chapters, each of which is devoted to one of the ten roots *(uṣūl)* that together make up the book's subject matter. In Chapter One, Baḥya treats "the firmest of the cornerstones and roots *(uṣūl)* of our religion," which he identifies as the unadulterated belief in the unity of God.²⁵ Maimonides knew and refers to works of Saadia and Samuel ben Ḥofni, and I think that a strong argument can be made for his familiarity with Baḥya's composition.

Towards the beginning of the *Commentary on the Mishnah*, Maimonides digresses concerning a problem in the thesis that God punishes sinners; he writes that the solution to the problem rests on several propositions on which "expert philosophers and the [ancient] rabbis" agree. He thereupon explains why he turned away from the legal matters that are the bread and butter of the Mishnah and allowed himself the digression: "Whenever there is a whiff of a discussion involving belief, I shall provide some explanation; for giving instruction on one of the roots [*aṣl min al-uṣūl*] is more worthwhile than any other instruction that I may give."²⁶ It would have been helpful if he had made explicit the sense in which he was employing the term *roots*, since he usually employs it in a different sense in the Commentary. Nevertheless, although he fails expressly to say so, *roots* in the passage quoted are clearly doctrines to be believed. He deemed giving instruction on the doctrines of the Jewish religion more worthwhile than giving instruction regarding legal matters, which was his main occupation in the Commentary.

There are a few additional instances in the *Commentary on the Mishnah* where *uṣūl* has the sense of theological and philosophical doctrines of the Jewish religion.²⁷ Usually, though, *uṣūl* in the Commentary are general legal rules that govern the individual regulations in a given subrealm of

---

²² Dāwūd al-Muqammiṣ, *Twenty Chapters*, ed. and tr. S. Stroumsa (Leiden: Brill, 1989), p. 22.

²³ Saadia, *Sefer ha-Yerushot*, ed. Y. Miller (Jerusalem, 1967/1968), pp. 1, 9.

²⁴ D. Sklare, *Samuel ben Ḥofni Gaon and His Cultural World* (Leiden: Brill, 1996), p. 27.

²⁵ Baḥya ibn Paquda, *Ḥovot ha-Levavot*, Arabic text, ed. A. Yahuda (Leiden: Brill, 1912), pp. 25, 35; Ibn Tibbon's medieval Hebrew translation, ed. A. Zifroni (Jerusalem, 1928), pp. 19, 25.

²⁶ *Commentary on the Mishna, Berakhot* ix.7.

²⁷ Maimonides, *Commentary on the Mishna*, Introduction, p. 4 ("mighty roots" upon which "the religion" rests); p. 11 ("roots" for evaluating the authenticity of a prophet); *Sanhedrin* x:1 (opening statement; Maimonides says he will discuss "numerous, very valuable roots of [Jewish] beliefs"); ibid., p. 210 ("the roots and fundamentals of our Law are thirteen fundamentals").

Jewish law. For instance, Maimonides calls attention to the roots (*uṣūl*)
governing the permissibility of sowing seeds of different species next to one
another; roots whereby atonement can be made for different classes of sins;
four roots governing the laws of levirate marriage; three roots of inheritance
law; sundry roots regarding meal offerings; roots the understanding of
which will prepare readers for the study of the laws of ritual impurity.[28] I
have a list of over sixty passages in the *Commentary on the Mishnah* that
speak about legal roots in the sense of general rules, and the list is far from
complete.

Two and a half decades after completing the *Commentary on the
Mishnah*, Maimonides recalls what his aim had been in his rabbinic
works. Speaking specifically of the *Mishneh Torah* but casting light on
the *Commentary* as well, he writes: He had endeavored to state all the
"religious [*dīnī*] and jurisprudential [*fiqhī*] roots" so that "those who are
called scholars or geonim or whatever you want to call them can build their
branches [i.e., the individual legal regulations] on jurisprudential roots,"
and place "all of that" – the jurisprudential roots and the regulations that
branch off from them – "on religious roots."[29]

His intent was thus to lay down the doctrinal basis of the Jewish
religion, to organize the myriad regulations of Jewish biblical and rabbinic
law under general roots, or rules, and to set the legal roots and their
branches on the doctrinal underpinning. He especially intended to educate
the rabbinic scholars of his day on roots in both senses; his opinion of
scholars of the day was not high and he did not hesitate to offer them
unsolicited instruction.

Stroumsa tells us that in using the term *uṣūl* as he does, Maimonides
was "closely following the Almohad example." The Ibn Tumart compilation does have a section on *uṣūl*. It begins: "*Roots* are of two sorts,
lexicographical and legal (*sharʿī*)." A root of the lexicographical sort is
that in the expression "root of a tree," in other words, the original
concrete sense of the term. A "legal root is the [sacred] Book, the tradition
[about Muḥammad and his circle], and the consensus [of the entire
Muslim community]," in other words, one of the three sources of
Islamic law.[30]

---

[28] Maimonides, *Commentary on the Mishna, Kilayim* iii.1; *Yoma* x.6; *Yevamot* i.1; *Bava Batra* viii.2; *Menaḥot* ix.9; introduction to the Order *Ṭohorot*, p. 32.

[29] Maimonides, *Treatise on Resurrection*, Arabic original and medieval Hebrew translation, ed. J. Finkel (New York: American Academy for Jewish Research, 1939), p. 4.

[30] *Le livre de Mohammed Ibn Toumert*, ed. I. Goldziher and J. Luciani (Algiers: Imprimerie orientale Pierre Fontana, 1903), p. 18.

We are faced with the choice between alternative explanations of Maimonides's use of the term *roots*: Either the widespread use of the term in Arabic and Judeo-Arabic literatures, notably for the roots of religion and the roots of jurisprudence, furnished him with a convenient tool for formulating his conception of the Jewish religion, to wit: Theological and philosophical roots, or doctrines, constitute the under-pinning of the religion; each area of law has roots and branches, that is to say, general rules and individual laws; the legal edifice, comprising hundreds of roots and thousands of branches, rests on the doctrinal under-pinning. Or else his conceptualization of the Jewish religion was inspired by Ibn Tumart's nth iteration of the notion that the sources, or roots, of Islamic law are the Quran, tradition, and the consensus of the Muslim community.

2.    Stroumsa writes that Maimonides was "closely following the Almohad example" in his decision "to compose a relatively short compendium of law as well as in the principles that guided him . . . (namely, going back to the *uṣūl*, presenting a final ruling, and dispensing with the scaffoldings that traditionally accompanied it)."[31]

She is talking about the *Mishneh Torah*. Her characterization of it as a "relatively short compendium" is hardly accurate, seeing that it contains no less than fourteen books, 982 chapters, and fifteen thousand rulings. None of the seventeen opuscules in the Ibn Tumart compilation nor the seventeen taken together is even remotely similar in nature or scope. Maimonides's use of the term *uṣūl* clearly was not dependent on the compilation. Stroumsa's implication that Maimonides was the first Jewish writer to produce a code consisting of rulings without what she calls "scaffolding" – without recording the ruling's original source and context in the ancient rabbinic corpus – is incorrect. One or two codes prior to Maimonides are known that do the same thing.[32] The uniqueness of his Code lies not in its recording of rulings without scaffolding but in its comprehensiveness.

In short, the Ibn Tumart compilation contains nothing that could have served as an example for the writing of the *Mishneh Torah*, nor was any such example needed, since the *Mishneh Torah* is a natural, albeit significant, stage in the evolution of rabbinic literature.

---

[31] Stroumsa, *Maimonides in His World*, p. 67.
[32] *Halachot Kezuboth*, ed. M. Margulies (Jerusalem: Hebrew University Press, 1942). Arabic abridgement of Saadia's *Sefer Yerushot*; see Sh. Abramson, *Inyanot bi-Sifrut ha-Geonim* (Jerusalem: Mossad Harav Kook, 1974), pp. 232–233.

3.   A key text in the Ibn Tumart volume is a creed (*'aqīda*). If Maimonides
wanted to examine Muslim creeds, over a dozen circulated in his day, but
Stroumsa believes that out of this pool, Ibn Tumart's is the one having a
decisive impact on him. She writes: "The Almohad catechism, the *'aqīda*,
must have served as an important model for" Maimonides when he
decided to include "a noncorporeal perception of God" in his list of
thirteen fundamental principles of the Jewish faith.[33]

My analysis of the creed goes into some detail because the creed stands
at the center of our subject and because it has been badly misread in recent
studies. It opens with a proof that the world came into existence and from
the world's having come into existence, it infers the existence of a creator,
God. In the *Guide for the Perplexed*, Maimonides distinguishes two proce-
dures for proving the existence of God. The Kalam procedure consists in
first proving that the world came into existence after it did not exist and
then inferring the existence of an agent who brought it into existence. The
alternative procedure undertakes to establish the existence of God without
taking a stand on whether the world came into existence after not existing
or has always existed. In the *Guide*, Maimonides rejects the Kalam path for
a pair of reasons: First, the existence of God is more fundamental than the
creation of the world and should be given precedence. Secondly, a more
certain thesis should not be made to depend on one that is less so; and
although creation can be established by "proofs approaching demonstration," by "theoretical, philosophical proofs free of falseness,"[34] the proofs
are not watertight, whereas the existence of God can be demonstrated
apodictically. In his rabbinic works, Maimonides does not yet make his
rejection of the Kalam procedure explicit. But when the *Mishneh Torah*
proves the existence of God as the First Mover of the heavens and not as the
creator of the world, he intimates his position.

In a word, he rejects the procedure that the Almohad *'aqīda* follows for
proving the existence of God.

As for the creed's proof for creation, it molds Quranic motifs into the
most primitive of Kalam arguments. The proof was by no means original
with Ibn Tumart. It goes back at least to al-Ash'arī, and is recorded by
Shahrastānī. When Maimonides wrote the *Guide*, he put it at the head of
the list of Kalam arguments for creation, all of which he rejected.[35] There

---

[33] Stroumsa, *Maimonides in His World*, p. 71.
[34] *Guide for the Perplexed* ii.19, p. 40a; ii. 21, p. 47b.
[35] Ash'arī, *K. al-Luma'* ed. and tr. R. McCarthy as *The Theology of al-Ash'arī* (Beyrouth: Imprimerie
catholique, 1953), §§3–4. H. Wolfson, *The Philosophy of the Kalam* (Cambridge: Harvard University
Press, 1976), pp. 383–385 (overlooks the passage in *K. al-Luma'*).

he cites it in the name of "one" or "several" Kalam thinkers, perhaps feeling that fairness prevented him from holding the school as a whole responsible for the shaky reasoning.

In the Almohad creed the argument goes: From a man's coming into existence after not existing, the existence of a maker who brought him into existence can be inferred. The same inference can be drawn for each stage in the development of the human fetus – from the transformation of sperm into blood, from blood into flesh, from flesh into bone; each stage needs a maker to effect it. The inference can further be drawn from other things that come into existence – from night, day, domesticated and wild beasts, birds, and so on; each needs a maker who brought it into existence. And the inference can be drawn with regard to the heavens and earth. For once we know that one body comes into existence, we can generalize and conclude that all bodies do, because they all resemble each other in occupying place, in undergoing change, and in similar respects. Seeing that they all came into existence, each needs a maker who brought it into existence.

The creator and maker in all instances cannot be a created being, for we see that intelligent animals, which are the highest level of created being, are incapable of replacing even a missing finger. The creator of everything that comes into existence must be uncreated.[36]

The creed proceeds to an argument, after a sort, for the creator's not having a partner. The gist is: If another being shared dominion with the creator, that being would have to be separate from Him. But the creator is neither joined to anything nor separate from anything, since if He were describable as joined or separate He would belong to the class of created beings.[37] No proof of the incorporeality of the creator is offered.

Concerning the relation of the creator to His creation, the creed teaches: God is the "creator of everything." Whatever occurs has been predetermined by Him, and is known to Him, from eternity. He causes all created beings to appear at the moment predestined for them and brings them forth at that moment without an intermediary, from nothing. (We

---

[36] *Livre de Mohammed Ibn Toumert*, pp. 230–232. French translation: H. Masse "La profession de foi (*'aqîda*) et les guides spirituels (*morchida*) du mahdi Ibn Toumert," in *Mémorial Henri Basset* (Paris: Librairie orientaliste Paul Geuthner, 1928), pp. 107–109. F. Griffel has observed that the creed has some philosophic sounding terminology, for example: *necessity of His existence, knowledge of His existence absolutely*, and he conjectures plausibly that it derives from Avicenna and came to Ibn Tumart via Juwaynī. See F. Griffel, "Ibn Tumart's Rational Proof for God's Existence and Unity, and his Connection to the Niẓamiyya Madrasa in Baghdad," in *Los Almohades: Problemas y Perspectivas*, ed. P. Cressier, M. Fierro, and L. Molina (Madrid: Casa de Velázquez, 2005), pp. 753–813. Such embellishments do not succeed in masking the primitive Ashʿarite reasoning.

[37] *Livre de Mohammed Ibn Toumert*, p. 234; French translation, pp. 111–112.

thus have an endorsement of Ash'arite occasionalism and a negation of the laws of physics.) Things survive exactly as long as was predestined for them. God leads some persons in the straight way and misleads others, destines some from their mother's womb for a happy existence, and destines others for hellfire. Yet God is just and beneficent.[38]

As the creed continues, it embraces the Ash'arite dogma that takes literally the tradition of God's being seen on Judgment Day:[39] "Belief in the visibility [of God on Judgment Day] is obligatory. God will be seen without resemblance [to anything else] and without an explanation of how [*takyīf*]." True, the Quran declares that human vision is incapable of attaining perception of God. But Ibn Tumart or whoever the author was qualifies that declaration, explaining: Human vision cannot attain perception of God "in the sense" that it cannot place a limit on Him, include Him, link Him to anything, or separate Him from anything.[40]

And at an especially illuminating juncture, the creed warns about a doctrinal Scylla and Charybdis. It brands both the "attribution of a body [to God]" (*tajsīm*), on the one hand, and "denial [that divine attributes have a real existence superadded to God's essence]" (*ta'ṭīl*), on the other, as "absurd."[41] The negation of the first member of the pair, *tajsīm*, has the effect of asserting that God is not a body. The negation of the second member, *ta'ṭīl*, has the effect of asserting that divine attributes are something real superadded to the divine essence.

The first assertion represents the view of late Ash'arite writers, who joined the more rationalist wing of Kalam in endorsing the incorporeality of God.[42] It is compromised, however, by the assurance that at the Last Judgment, God will – although we cannot say how – be seen; Maimonides's thirteen principles of faith for its part stresses that the incorporeality of God entails the impossibility of seeing any "manner of form" of God.[43]

The second assertion endorses a theory of divine attributes that is distinctively Ash'arite.[44] In his early period Maimonides probably did not know that it was the Ash'arites who viewed divine attributes as superadded

[38] *Livre de Mohammed Ibn Toumert*, pp. 235–236; French translation, pp. 113–114.
[39] Ash'ari's creed, in D. MacDonald, *Development of Muslim Theology* (New York: Russell and Russell, 1965), p. 295. See Quran 75: 22–23.
[40] *Livre de Mohammed Ibn Toumert*, pp. 237–238; French translation, p. 116.
[41] Wolfson, *Philosophy of the Kalam*, pp. 112–113, 127–128.
[42] See H. Davidson, *Proofs for Eternity, Creation, and the Existence of God, in Medieval Islamic and Jewish Philosophy* (New York: Oxford University Press, 1987), pp. 171–172.
[43] Maimonides, *Commentary on the Mishnah, Sanhedrin* x.i, third principle.
[44] See Davidson, *Proofs*, pp. 171–172.

entities of some sort. His *Commentary on the Mishnah*, the work with which he was occupied during his stay in Almohad Morocco, once refers to another distinctively Ash'arite position and makes the revealing statement that he had "heard" that such was the position of Kalam thinkers.[45] At the time, he evidently had only limited knowledge of Kalam and, it would seem, no awareness of distinct Kalam schools.

He was, nevertheless, familiar with the theory of attributes as real entities. In the *Mishneh Torah*, he writes that whereas in the case of man, life and knowledge [as well as other attributes] are distinct from the human essence, there is no such distinction in God. God's life and knowledge are identical with His essence. "For were God to live by virtue of an attribute, *life* [which is superadded to His essence], and were He to know by virtue of an attribute, *knowledge* [superadded to His essence], there would be multiple Gods, namely He, His life, and His knowledge."[46] By the standard of the *Mishneh Torah* the creed of the self-styled upholders of the unity of God is polytheistic.

Later, in the *Guide for the Perplexed*, Maimonides would express himself even more pointedly. He writes in the *Guide*: "I say ... that he who ascribes attributes to God ... removes the existence of God from his belief without realizing it."[47] Since it had been demonstrated that God is absolutely simple, the notion *God possessed of superadded attributes* is a contradiction in terms and does not refer to anything that can exist. By the standard of the *Guide*, the creed of the upholders of divine unity is Godless.

If Maimonides read the Ibn Tumart creed, he would, then, have found: the ill-advised Kalam procedure for proving the existence of God; the feeble argument for creation of al-Ash'arī that, later, in the *Guide*, he would put at the head of the list of rejected Kalam arguments for creation; predestination, with some of the unborn marked by the beneficent God for good fortune and others marked for hellfire; Ash'arite occasionalism (which, together with the previous doctrine, he anathematizes in the *Commentary on the Mishnah*[48]); the assertion that God is not a body, compromised by insistence that He will be seen at the end of days; a theory of divine attributes that the *Mishneh Torah* condemns as tantamount to polytheism and the *Guide* would condemn as tantamount to failure to have any belief in the existence of God.

---

[45] Maimonides, *Commentary on the Mishnah, Avot*, introduction (*Eight Chapters*), chapter 8. The doctrine in question is Ash'arite occasionalism. See Davidson, *Proofs*, p. 399.

[46] Maimonides, *Code of Law, Fundamentals of the Torah* ii.10.     [47] *Guide* i.60, p. 76b.

[48] Maimonides, *Commentary on the Mishnah, Avot*, introduction (*Eight Chapters*), Chapter 8.

We are asked to imagine that this document, which is woven entirely out of doctrines advocated by the fundamentalist wing of Islamic Kalam and which Maimonides would have viewed as an unremitting litany of errors, "must have served as an important model" for him when he drew up his thirteen principles of faith.

4.   Stroumsa writes: "When Maimonides rules against the enjoyment of musical entertainment, he carefully buttresses the ruling with citations from the Jewish sources. And yet it is hard to read his fierce objection to the use of musical instruments in weddings without being reminded of Ibn Tumart's display of puritanical zeal in the streets of Almoravid Tlemcen."[49] Some background is necessary here too.

Mishnah tractate *Soṭah* states: "When the Sanhedrin ceased to operate, song ceased at drinking parties." The passage in tractate *Soṭah* of the Babylonian Talmud that comments on the mishnaic statement consists of miscellaneous condemnations of music, for example: "May the ear that listens to song be torn out"; "when there is song in a house, the house goes to ruin."[50] There are two possible ways of construing the intent of the talmudic comment – or, to be precise, the intent of the redactor of the talmudic tractate. The comment may be understood as supporting the Mishnah's edict that song is forbidden as an expression of grief over the historical disaster. Alternatively, it may be understood as a corrective, according to which song is forbidden in its own right and not as a reaction to a historical event.

In his *Commentary on the Mishnah*, on which he was working during and immediately after his stay in Almohad territory, Maimonides is led at one point to consider the case of a person who suffers from clinical melancholia. He writes that such a person may treat his condition by "listening to songs and melodies, strolling in gardens and handsome buildings, sitting in the presence of handsome drawings, and similar activities that soothe [*yabsuṭ*] the soul and dispel melancholia."[51] Maimonides evidently found nothing intrinsically detrimental in music and on the contrary understood that it soothes the soul. (The rabbinic edict

[49] Stroumsa, *Maimonides in His World*, p. 61. Stroumsa read the responsum in *Letters*, ed. I. Shailat, pp. 425–431. Shailat conjectured that this responsum and another originally formed a single responsum and he printed the two together as one piece. As a consequence, the character of each is distorted. I quote from Maimonides, *Responsa*, ed. and tr. J. Blau, §269.
[50] *Mishnah: Soṭah* ix.12; BT Soṭah, p. 48a.
[51] Maimonides, *Commentary on the Mishnah, Avot*, introduction (*Eight Chapters*), chapter 5, ed. Kafaḥ, p. 388.

against listening to music would be waived if listening to music was indicated for medical reasons.)

In his *Code of Law*, which he composed a decade or so later, he assembles a number of rabbinic enactments that react to events connected with the destruction of the Holy Temple and codifies them under the heading: "After the Temple was destroyed, the rabbis of that generation decreed . . . " One of the enactments is "not to play music. It is forbidden to enjoy and listen to all forms of music . . . because of the destruction. Even singing over wine [without instrumental accompaniment] is forbidden . . . It is nevertheless the custom in all Israel to recite praises of God and sing songs of thanks to Him, and the like, over wine."[52] Maimonides thus codified the ruling of the Mishnah and prohibited music as an expression of mourning for the Temple, side by side with other expressions of mourning. He adds without a hint of disapproval that custom softens the prohibition. There is no fierce objection to the use of musical instruments in weddings.

The code popularly known as the *Tur* similarly rules that, as a sign of mourning for the loss of the Temple, the rabbis forbade both instrumental and vocal music. The *Tur*'s author knew of the responsum purportedly issued by Maimonides, which we shall consider in a moment, and he evidently saw nothing out of the ordinary in it. The main significance that he attaches to it is this: Maimonides's code prohibits instrumental music whether or not wine is being drunk but seems to prohibit singing only where there is drinking; the responsum adds that singing is prohibited whether wine is drunk or not. The *Tur* further notes: The responsum makes clear that there is no difference between songs in Hebrew and those in Arabic and it restricts the prohibition to secular songs.[53] The *Shulḥan 'Arukh* subsequently copies the language of the ruling in Maimonides's Code.[54]

We come to the responsum itself. It has been preserved in two manuscripts, one of which has the heading: "a question from Aleppo," while the other lacks even that. The response begins: "It is known that all music and melodies are forbidden even when not accompanied by words, for the rabbis said: 'May the ear that listens to song be torn out.'" The responsum goes on to maintain that the prophets "censured the use of musical instruments [even] for worship," while it concedes that the Geonim permitted "putting songs and praises [of God] to music." No mention is

---

[52] Maimonides, *Code of Law, Fasts* v.14.     [53] Jacob ben Asher, *Ṭur: Oraḥ Ḥayyim*, §560.
[54] J. Caro, *Shulḥan 'Arukh: Oraḥ Ḥayyim*, §560:3.

made of weddings. As for the reason for the prohibition: "The Talmud explains . . . everything that occasions equanimity or turbulence of the soul [including unaccompanied singing] is prohibited. The reason is quite plain: The human appetitive faculty should be reined in . . . and not let loose." The last sentences are plainly a misrepresentation, for the Talmud knew nothing about a human appetitive faculty. Reining in of the appetitive faculty is a motif found in Maimonides's *Guide for the Perplexed*.[55]

The responsum proceeds: It is "a . . . demonstrated . . . truth" that the purpose of "our" existence is to be a "holy nation" and that all our actions and speech should be manifestations of human "perfection" or should lead to human perfection, as "we explained in Part Three of the *Guide*." Towards its end, the responsum refers to something that "we explained too in the *Guide*," and it contains at least one additional echo of the *Guide*, which it does not, however, mark as such.[56]

Much is irregular here, and the irregularity lies not in the result arrived at but in the route by which it is reached. The responsum comes to more or less the same result as Maimonides's *Code*, with the addition of the one stricter rule that the *Ṭur* points out. But it allows itself the anachronistic misrepresentation of the Talmud. Without mentioning the *Code*, it alters the rationale given there for the prohibition of music by maintaining that music is prohibited not in reaction to a historical event but because of its very nature and the deleterious effect it has on the human soul. Now, when a rabbinic judge is asked a ritual question that was expressly treated in a mishnah, standard protocol requires that he quote the mishnah even if he has grounds for not ruling in accordance with it. When Maimonides was asked a legal-ritual question on which he had ruled expressly in his *Code*, it was hardly thinkable that his answer would make no mention of the relevant ruling in his *Code*. A rabbinic judge was further expected to answer legal questions on the basis of legal, not philosophic sources, and apart from the ostensible present instance, no responsum of Maimonides' cites the *Guide for the Perplexed*. The responsum breaks one rule after another. In all likelihood it is not authentic.

But let us assume that it is authentic and see where Stroumsa's supposition would lead.

Her supposition entails the following series of events. When the young Maimonides was still living in Andalusia or Morocco he heard reports about Ibn Tumart's having smashed musical instruments decades earlier.

[55] Maimonides, *Guide* i.5, p. 16a.
[56] In legislating, the Torah does not take rare situations into account. See *Guide* iii.34.

He was scarcely attracted to Ibn Tumart's beliefs and certainly not to his intolerance or any philosophic acumen that the man displayed. The tales nonetheless caught his fancy, and he stored them away in his memory. In the *Commentary on the Mishnah*, on which he was working at the time, the deleterious effect of music and the admiration of Ibn Tumart's fanaticism lay dormant; Maimonides even credited music with having a soothing effect on the soul. In the *Code of Law*, which he composed about a decade later, the memory remained dormant, and he codified the prohibition against listening to music strictly in accordance with the mishnaic source. Twenty years or so still later, that is, thirty years after he left Morocco and seventy after Ibn Tumart's reported smashing of musical instruments, someone in Aleppo asked for a legal opinion on the permissibility of listening to music. The conscious or unconscious memory of tales of Ibn Tumart's smashing musical instruments finally had its day. It had little effect on the practical result that the responsum arrives at; the result differs at most from the ruling of the Code in the detail pointed out by the *Ṭur*. Yet the long-dormant memory, which had at last awakened, convinced Maimonides that music does have a deleterious effect on the human soul and must be prohibited for that reason. He repeatedly quotes and cites the *Guide for the Perplexed*, pretending thereby to buttress his new position on music but actually intending to create a smokescreen for concealing the foreign source of his inspiration.

5. Stroumsa writes:

> As noted by Joel Kraemer, Maimonides' depiction of the Messiah is characterized by an overwhelming insistence on his military role. One suspects that the frequent military campaigns of the Almohads, in which they were accompanied by a magnificent copy of the Qur'ān and advancing under the banner of the *Mahdī*, offered Maimonides a Messianic model that went well with his reading of the *Laws of Kings*, both in Deuteronomy and the Talmud.[57]

When Scripture describes the future ideal king, it foresees his waging war and emerging victorious. It tells us: "A scepter shall rise out of Israel and shall smite through the corners of Moab and break down all the sons of Seth." "He shall smite the land with the rod of his mouth and with the breath of his lips shall he slay the wicked." "I will give the nations of the earth for thine inheritance . . . Thou shalt break them with a rod of iron. Thou shalt dash them in pieces like a potter's vessel." "In his days, Judah

---

[57] Stroumsa, *Maimonides in His World*, p. 78.

shall be saved and Israel shall dwell safely."[58] Saadia Gaon, in his account of
the messianic age depicts the warfare that the messiah will engage in.[59] The
Talmud has more than one conception of the messianic age, and
Maimonides endorses the most naturalistic conception. According to it,
"the only difference between the present day and the days of the messiah is
Israel's ceasing to be subject to the Gentile kingdoms";[60] the words can be
read as implying that the messiah will employ military means in order to
free his people. Jewish sources were fully able to inform Maimonides that
the messiah will engage in warfare on behalf of his people, and there was no
need of a foreign model.

And although Maimonides did foresee a military role for the Messiah,
it is not at all the case that he overwhelmingly insists on it. On the contrary,
he understands the Messiah's historical function to be the establishment of
conditions whereby mankind can attain the true goal of human existence.
He assures readers that "the prophets and the rabbis were eager for the days
of messiah not in order to rule the world, to subjugate the nations, and to
be raised up by them ... but in order to be free for Torah and science ...
and thereby gain the life of the world to come ... In that time there will be
no famine and warfare, no jealousy and competitiveness, ... The whole
world will busy itself solely in knowledge of God ... and achieve knowledge of God to the extent that it is in man's power."

6.   Stroumsa writes:

> Maimonides sees the duty of the righteous king ... "to proclaim the true
> religion, to fill the world with justice, to break the arm of evil, and to fight
> the wars of the Lord ..." In describing the role of the king as spreading
> justice, Maimonides' Hebrew here ("to fill the world with righteousness"
> [my translation of the Hebrew; H.D.]) is strikingly reminiscent of the
> Arabic formula for describing the role of the *Mahdī* ("that he should fill
> the world with justice as it was full of injustice" [my translation from the
> Arabic; H. D.]). The formula is prevalent in both Shiite and Sunni texts and
> was also used to describe the *Mahdī* Ibn Tumart.[61]

The resemblance to the Muslim formula is indeed striking. At most,
however, it would suggest that Maimonides adapted a standard formula
that Muslim authors used to describe the *mahdi*; it would say nothing

[58] Numbers 24:17; Isaiah 11:4; Psalms 2:8–9; Jeremiah 23:6.   [59] Saadia, *Emunot ve-De'ot* viii.6.
[60] BT *Sanhedrin*, p. 99a, and parallels; Maimonides, *Code of Law, Kings* xii.2.
[61] Stroumsa, *Maimonides in His World*, p. 78; Maimonides, *Code of Law, Kings* iv.10. For the Arabic
     formula, see *Encyclopaedia of Islam*, second ed., s. v. *al-Mahdi* (Madelung). For the application of the
     formula to Ibn Tumart, see *Livre de Mohammed Ibn Toumert*, p. 10. (There is a typographical error
     in Stroumsa's reference.)

about a specifically Almohad influence on Maimonides. And the resemblance might be no more than a coincidence.

The Hebrew Bible is fond of the notion that the earth is full, or will be filled, with one thing or another. More than two dozen biblical verses employ the figure of speech, and they could have helped suggest the qualities of the righteous king to Maimonides. Much of what fills or is to fill the earth according to the Bible is inauspicious, for example: "violence," "idols," "lewdness," "blood," and "guilt." But the Bible also announces: "The earth is full of His praise." "He loveth righteousness and justice; the earth is full of the loving kindness of the Lord." "The earth, O Lord, is full of Thy mercy." "Let the whole earth be filled with His glory." "The earth shall be filled with the knowledge of the glory of the Lord." Maimonides found one of the verses so attractive that it serves him as motto both for his account of the days of the Messiah and for the entire Code of Law: "For the earth shall be full of the knowledge of the Lord as the waters cover the sea."[62]

**Concluding note.** The situation of Averroes vis à vis the Almohads and Ibn Tumart was different from Maimonides's situation, inasmuch as Averroes had personal and professional connections with the Almohad regime as well as knowledge of Ibn Tumart's doctrines. If he was familiar specifically with Ibn Tumart's *'aqīda*, as he likely was, concern for his personal safety prevented him from expressing his opinion of it openly. Nevertheless, considering his attitude to the Kalam, we may be certain that if he was indeed familiar with the *'aqīda*, he viewed it as an unmitigating litany of errors.

---

[62] Maimonides, *Code of Law, Kings* xii.4–5, quoting Isaiah 11:9. The point is important enough for him to spell it out fully twice in the *Code*. See *Code, Repentance* ix.2.

# CHAPTER 2

# Al-Ghazālī's Purported "Influence" on Maimonides
## A Dissenting Voice in Trending Scholarship

### Y. Tzvi Langermann

## Introduction: The Conundrum of Influence Peddling in Academic Scholarship

Did al-Ghazālī influence Maimonides and, if so, what does this mean? How does one prove influence and assess its impact? Can influence be measured? Should we actively be looking to uncover the influence of al-Ghazālī on Maimonides? Is there any way to show that Maimonides was *not* influenced by him?

These are just a few of the questions that have been hounding me for the past few years, as I try to make sense of the spate of publications arguing for al-Ghazālī's influence.

Some of the studies on al-Ghazālī's purported influence may be seen to take their place in the venerated tradition of *Quellengeschichte*, tinged perhaps with traces of modern thoughts on intertextuality. Any given statement in Maimonides must have a "source," and, when it comes to religious thought, especially where "reason" appears to clash with "faith," what better place to look for influence than the writings of al-Ghazālī? Others appear to latch onto the surge in interest in al-Ghazālī. Once accused of putting an end to philosophy and science in Islamic civilization, al-Ghazālī is now seen as a brilliant thinker, an incisive critic rather than a dumb fanatic; close reading of his oeuvre reveals that he was not at all as hostile to philosophy as once thought; and the decline for which he was once blamed is seen to be a construct of Western ignorance and prejudice.[1] That reassessment, in turn, cannot be divorced from the reconsideration of the role of Islam – al-Ghazālī was dubbed, after all, *ḥujjat al-Islām*, the

---

[1] Two recent reassessments are M. A. Al-Akiti, "The Good, the Bad and the Ugly of Falsafa: Al-Ghazālī's *Madnūn*, *Tahāfut*, and *Maqāṣid*, with Particular Attention to the Falsafī Treatments of God's Knowledge of Temporal Events," in Y. Tzvi Langerman (ed.), *Avicenna and His Legacy: A Golden Age of Science and Philosophy* (Turnhout: Brepols, 2009), pp. 51–100, and F. Griffel, "Al-Ghazālī's Cosmology in the Veil Section of His *Mishkāt al-Anwār*," pp. 27–50 in the same volume.

"proof" of Islam – in world history. These developments, I submit, have led academic research to depict Maimonides anew in a more Islamic light, with al-Ghazālī supplying much of the color.

So, if "contextualizing" Maimonides means, in effect, finding the imprint of the heroes of the civilization within which he worked in his writings, then, clearly, one task of scholarship today is to uncover, or construct, Ghazalian influences on Maimonides.

We are all products of our time; but, apparently, only those coming after us can appreciate how this applies to our efforts. We are today aware of how the work of great scholars such as Ignaz Goldziher and Gershom Scholem was influenced (that word again!) by currents moving through their times and places; we ourselves are carried no less by those swirling through the waters in our own age. Those in the mainstream hardly notice. My perch on the margins affords me the outsider's look, which I will share with the readers of this essay.

I am highly skeptical of most of the claims that I have seen for al-Ghazālī's influence, and the bulk of the present offering will consist of an attempt to challenge, if not debunk or utterly refute, some of the claims that have appeared in print. However, my criticism goes beyond the specific passages or issues where al-Ghazālī's influence has been suggested. My malaise is not limited to the social and political undercurrents that seem to me to be in part responsible for the claims that I wish to challenge. I am troubled no less by the absence of any discussion of influence as a category of historical scholarship; none of the people whose papers I critique bother to tell me how influence can be proven, how it is measured, and what it means.

My paper asks whether it is the task of the historian of philosophy or religious thought to look for influences. If the answer is positive, then I ask, is this a primary task, or an ancillary project to the investigation into issues such as the debate over the world's creation in time? Of course, the answers to those questions depend on how one chooses to define influence. For the purpose of this paper, let me say that I regard the influence of thinker A on thinker B – perhaps I should add, the influence that is of interest to me – to be the presence in B of an idea expressed by (or ascribed) to A – in a manner, usually a close textual correspondence, which indicates that B derived the idea from A, either directly – when we have concrete, specific proof that B read A, or met A, or indirectly, when we have similar evidence that B read someone else who can be shown to have read or heard from A. In general, I hold that it is not the historian's primary task to uncover sources of influence; that task is often helpful, at times pivotal, but also dangerous: We can sometimes conflate the thought of our subject with that of his presumed source.

With specific reference to al-Ghazālī and Maimonides, I have as yet seen no evidence at all that Maimonides was influenced by al-Ghazālī. It is critical to separate as best we can the question of how Maimonides's views on a given subject measure up with those of al-Ghazālī, and the question of actual historical influence. Historians of philosophy often view influence "as a matter of explicit argumentation and persuasion between philosophers with different positions . . . This picture is of a sort of grand philosophical colloquium conducted in the Elysian fields among dead giants of the past. From a purely philosophical point of view such exercises can be very informative and illuminating."[2] The fact that the two figures of interest to this paper were religious leaders grappling with the similar issue of tradition versus Aristotle (to grossly over-simplify) is enough to warrant a comparison; and from that perspective, I agree that we can learn a lot about both figures from a comparative study. But influence is another matter entirely.

Many have chosen to base their claims for actual influence – meaning, so I must interpret, that Maimonides was not simply addressing the same issues dealt with by his illustrious predecessor, but reacting in one way or another to something he encountered in the writings of Abū Ḥāmid – on the strength of sweeping generalizations. Most often one hears that al-Ghazālī was so famous or prominent that Maimonides "must have" read his works, as we shall see.[3] An observation of that sort is so all-encompassing as to be of no value to the historian. If everyone was influenced by al-Ghazālī, what do we gain by pointing out that Maimonides too shared in this influence?

Others point to specific influences; these will be the main focus of my critique. Though the passages, or phrases, in which al-Ghazālī's influence is said to be present are certainly found in Maimonides, the arguments for their dependence on al-Ghazālī are not always clear. In any event, they are as a rule not falsifiable; this is certainly not a scientific enterprise. The best one can do is to point to weaknesses in the argument for influence. At times one can also suggest a more plausible source of influence. However, I am hesitant to do that too often, because I do not hold to any doctrine of intertextuality, and I do not believe that every remark or turn of phrase in Maimonides has a source in some earlier literary creation.

[2] A. Gopnik, "Could David Hume Have Known about Buddhism? Charles François Dolu, the Royal College of La Flèche, and the Global Jesuit Intellectual Network," *Hume Studies*, 35 (2009), 5–28.
[3] On this point see C. Manekin's review of S. Stroumsa, *Maimonides in His World: Portrait of a Mediterranean Thinker.* H-Judaic, H-Net Reviews. January, 2011.

Studies on al-Ghazālī's purported "influence" on Maimonides follow a fairly consistent pattern. There is a statement to the effect that Maimonides "must have" been familiar with the writings of al-Ghazālī, and along with this statement, a frank acknowledgment that Maimonides never mentions al-Ghazālī by name.[4] This, in turn, leads to a parade of parallels and similarities between Maimonides and al-Ghazālī, with regard to selected passages in their respective writings. This generates – for me anyway – the methodological crunch. To begin with, there are differences as well as similarities, usually acknowledged as such by the scholars who adduce them. But how much difference is needed in order to show that a "parallel" does not indicate "influence"? Moreover, given the universally admitted fact that the two thinkers worked within the same "cultural tradition," are not "parallels" to be expected? What parameters must then be set for the parallel in order to conclude that it cannot be explained simply in terms of a common cultural tradition, but instead proves a direct influence of one thinker upon another? I cannot accept the bare claim that differences reflect influence, no less so than similarities; the differences are in this case explained by Maimonides's adapting the source to his purposes. This is circular reasoning; the claim rests on the statement that needs to be proved, namely that Maimonides borrowed from al-Ghazālī, and all that remains to clarify is why the two do not say precisely the same thing.

## A Likely Suspect for Influence

Al-Ghazālī's rules for the interpretation of Scripture offer an important point of comparison, one which has not yet been addressed in print, as far as I know.[5] Whether or not Maimonides actually read al-Ghazālī's *Qānūn al-Ta'wīl* is the lesser question; the greater one is, does Maimonides's own

---

[4] One possible, though highly unlikely, exception is found in some variants to Maimonides's correspondence with Samuel Ibn Tibbon, in which Maimonides praises al-Ghazālī without citing a specific work or referring to a particular doctrine. See Doron Forte, "Back to the Sources: Alternative Versions of Maimonides' Letter to Samuel Ibn Tibbon and Their Neglected Significance," *Jewish Studies Quarterly*, 23 (2016), 47–90, on pp. 64–66, who, along with the other scholars who have noticed this variant, does not take it to be authentic (though Forte hesitates to reject it completely). Note that none of those arguing for influence cite this variant; they seem comfortable with the lack of any reference in a Maimonidean writing to Abū Ḥāmid. This letter or series of letters is likely to be the most splintered Maimonidean document of all, and even Forte, in his painstaking study, missed one shard, concerning which see Y. Tzvi Langermann, "A Mistaken Anticipation in Samuel Ibn Tibbon's Translation of Maimonides' *Guide of the Perplexed*" *Daat*, 84 (2017), 21-34 (Heb.), note 17.

[5] In a discussion carried out over Skype as part of a workshop on al-Ghazālī held at Marquette University in the summer of 2016, Frank Griffel mentioned *Qānūn al-Ta'wīl* as the most likely candidate for al-Ghazālī's influence on Maimonides.

approach reflect that of al-Ghazālī in a manner so close that influence must be acknowledged. We must be very careful. The allegorization of Scripture in the Jewish tradition, and the formulation of general rules for interpretation, did not begin with Maimonides. There are some clear statements in Saadia Gaon, and before him, in ancient rabbinic texts. Philo of Alexandria cannot be ignored, even if there is scant evidence that his works were accessible to medieval Jews.[6] Of course, if we must allow for al-Ghazālī's indirect influence on the grounds of the tremendous impact of his thought, then, if we are to be fair, we ought to allow for a similar impact of Philo's allegorizations on al-Ghazālī and other Muslim thinkers, as well as upon the exegesis of his coreligionists. However, I will not pursue that line at present, and will limit my comments to Saadia, much closer to Maimonides chronologically, like him arabaphone and – I trust all will agree this to be relevant – someone whose writings Maimonides undoubtedly studied. Indeed, I may be so bold as to suggest that in the handling of Scripture, Maimonides would have given priority to Jewish sources.

Maimonides states his "rule" as the first of two reasons that he has *not* chosen to interpret figuratively the biblical verses that assert that the world has been created in time.[7] His decision follows a similar one taken with regard to the verses that indicate that the deity is a body: "That the deity is not a body has been demonstrated; from this it follows necessarily that everything that in its external meaning disagrees with this demonstration must be interpreted figuratively, for it is known that such texts are of necessity fit for figurative interpretation." Briefly, whenever the plain sense of a verse contradicts something that has been demonstrated to be true, then that verse is "of necessity (*ḍarūratan*) fit for figurative interpretation (*ta'wīl*)." Since there is no demonstration for eternity, Maimonides does not apply his rule here.

On the face of it, this resembles the rule of figurative interpretation stated by al-Ghazālī in a number of places, and elaborated in a separate monograph bearing the title *Qānūn al-Ta'wīl*. Here it is in his *Faṣal al-Maqāl* (*Decisive Criterion*), in the translation of Frank Griffel: "They[8] also agree that allowing [a reading that deviates from the literal meaning]

---

[6]  The late Bruno Chiesa ("Dawud al-Muqammiṣ e la sua opera," *Henoch*, 18 (1996), 121–156) uncovered evidence that Saadia and David al-Muqammiṣ, as well as Jacob al-Qirqasānī, were familiar with Philonic writings; only the last of the three refers to him directly. S. Lieberman, *Midreshei Teiman: Harẓa'ah 'al Midreshei Teiman 'al mahutam ve-erkam* [*Yemenite Midrashim: A Lecture on the Yemenite Midrashim Their Character and Value*] (Jerusalem: Bamberger and Wahrmann, 1970), detected the influence of Philo's "school," if not of Philo himself, in the philosophical allegorization of Scripture popular among medieval Yemenite Jews.

[7]  *Guide* ii.25, tr. Pines, pp. 327–328.     [8]  The different schools of thought within Islam.

depends upon the production of a demonstration (*burhān*) that the literal meaning (*al-ẓāhir*) is impossible."[9] Has al-Ghazālī influenced Maimonides here?

I have generously cited from a formulation of al-Ghazālī that resembles that of Maimonides most closely. There is no supporting evidence that Maimonides read *Faṣal al-Maqāl*, as indeed, there is no proof that he read any of al-Ghazālī's writings – a fact that cannot be overemphasized. Al-Ghazālī formulated his rule in other places, notably in his monograph on the rules of interpretation, where the text and context are much more removed from Maimonides. Perhaps rather than looking for a source in one particular passage or book by al-Ghazālī, we ought to content ourselves with the connection that al-Ghazālī draws between a contradiction between a demonstrated fact and the plain sense of Scripture, which is the situation that demands allegorization; perhaps this is the idea that resonated strongly through the generations and informed Maimonides's statement. We may further strengthen the case for al-Ghazālī's influence by observing that Maimonides joins his remarks – in this context, the decision *not* to allegorize those verses that speak of creation – with an attack on the "esotericists," *ahl al-bāṭin*. Al-Ghazālī wrote an entire treatise in condemnation of the same approach, *Faḍā'iḥ al-Bāṭiniyya wa Faḍā'il al-Mustaẓhiriyya*.[10]

After trying to make a good case for influence in this matter, let me proceed to show that it is certainly not necessary to do so in order to explain Maimonides's position – again, assuming that we must look for a source, a premise that I deny. Saadia provides detailed guidelines for the appeal to a figurative reading in his *Doctrines and Beliefs*, beginning of book V:

> I declare in the first place that one of the things of which we can be certain is that every statement found in the scriptures must be taken in its plain sense. Only for one of four reasons is it not permitted to take a statement in its plain sense. (1) If sense perception rejects the plain sense of the passage ... (2) in case Reason ('*aql*) repudiates it ... (3) in case there exists some clear text that renders the plain meaning of the passage impossible ... (4) if to the statement of Scripture is attached some tradition which modifies it ... There are only these four reasons which necessitate the interpretation of

---

[9] F. Griffel, *Al-Ghazālī's Philosophical Theology* (Oxford University Press, 2009), pp. 111–112.

[10] Note that al-Ghazālī pegs his denunciation of the esotericists to an endorsement of the literalists; I do not know that Maimonides would take the same "binary" view. Richard McCarthy's abridged English version of the Mustazhiriy is freely accessible on the web at http://ghazali.org/works/bati .htm.

the plain meaning of the Scriptural passages in an allegorical sense; there exists no fifth reason ... "

In my view, of the three authorities just cited, the two that are in closest agreement are Saadia and al-Ghazālī; this is no surprise, given that both are, at least in some sense, *mutakallimūn*. The statements of both are occasioned by the issue of the resurrection of the dead, rather than creation, which is what spurs Maimonides to state his view. It seems to me to be of capital importance that al-Ghazālī, and before him, Saadia, were concerned above all to put *limits* on the allegorization of Scripture. Their main concern was to stem the radical allegorization that they encountered among co-religionists while, at the same time, to allow figurative interpretation where it could not be avoided, as in the case of a contradiction between verses, or where it was the preferable alternative for some other reason. For al-Ghazālī, the problem was more acute, given that the Baṭiniyya were unrestrained in their application of *ta'wīl* wherever they chose to in the Quran. Saadia had the more limited problem of people attempting to explain away the belief in the resurrection and its scriptural support. In contrast to those two theologians, Maimonides, the philosopher (though perhaps also in a loose sense only), is apologizing for *not* allegorizing a verse that his reader – the philosophically adept intended reader of the *Guide* – would have expected him to subject to figurative interpretation.

Maimonides belongs to a tradition where difficult philosophical texts no less than Scripture were subjected to *ta'wīl*. Earlier on in his *Guide* he cites a *ta'wīl* of al-Fārābī on a passage in Aristotle in which the Stagirite indicates that he has no demonstration for the eternity of the world: "However, you know Abū Naṣr's [al-Fārābī's] interpretation (*ta'wīl*) of this example, what he made clear with regard to it, as well as the fact that he considered disgraceful (*shinā'a*) the notion that Aristotle could have doubted the eternity of the world."[12] Similarly, in the introduction to his commentary on Hippocrates's *Aphorisms*, Maimonides notes Galen's *ta'wīl* on Hippocrates's *Mixtures* (*Kitāb al-Akhlāṭ*), a non-literal reading that was

" A. Altmann, *Saadya Gaon; the Book of Doctrines and Beliefs. Abridged Edition, Translated from the Arabic, with an Introduction and Notes by Alexander Altmann* (Oxford: East and West Library, Phaidon Press, 1946), pp. 157–158. The comparandum with Saadia is noted by Rabbi Joseph Qafih in his Hebrew translation of *Guide* ii.25, *Moreh ha-Nevukhim, Dalālat al-Ḥā'irīn* (Jerusalem: Mossad Harav Kook, 1972), p. 357, n. 6). Altmann adds (p. 158, n. 4) that the "same exegetical canon, but in a slightly less elaborate form" is found in the "Leningrad recension."

[12] *Guide* ii.15, tr. Pines, p. 292. I cite from the extensive literature on this problematic passage and offer some insights of my own in "Maimonides and Galen," in P. Bouras-Vallianatos and B. Zipser (eds.), *Brill's Companion to the Reception of Galen* (Leiden: E. J. Brill, forthcoming).

necessary because the book, as it stands, looks to be the work of an alchemist.[13] This tradition attaches, if not sanctity, then, at least, a deep reverence for the works of Greek sages, which, like Scripture, cannot be suspected of conveying falsities or nonsense. I find it hard to imagine that al-Ghazālī would share that attitude in any way.

In short, then, though the influence of al-Ghazālī cannot be ruled out, it is clear that Maimonides's approach to allegorization is fundamentally different from that of al-Ghazālī. He is working within a tradition of philosophical allegorization – allegorization by philosophers of philosophical no less than of prophetic texts. Maimonides scrupulously avoids allegory as a way out of the difficult problem of creation. His finesse of the issue of resurrection involves the allegorization of some, but not all, biblical verses. In his rule he likely follows Saadia; with regard to its application, or lack thereof, he is his own man.

## Survey of Claims for Influence

It may well be that the first person to suggest some connection between the work of the two thinkers was none other than Ibn Taymiyya, a theologian rather than an historian, and someone who was hostile towards both. In his *Dār al-Taʾāruḍ* he observed: "Moses ben Maimon, author of *Guide of the Perplexed* – he was for the Jews what Abū Ḥāmid al-Ghazālī was for the Muslims – combined prophetic views with philosophic views by interpreting the former according to the latter." Ibn Taymiyya wisely did not go beyond noticing a spiritual kinship.[14]

Shlomo Pines discusses the possibility of al-Ghazālī's influence in the section of his masterful essay on the philosophical sources of the *Guide* devoted to the *mutakallimūn* because, in his judgement, al-Ghazālī was "the most outstanding Mutakallim of the period before Maimonides and perhaps of all times."[15] Focusing on the *Tahāfut*, he cautiously begins by saying that "no absolutely certain answer can be given," but avers that in all probability Maimonides had read the book. After citing some passages from the *Guide* that match well with al-Ghazālī's opinions, Pines offers

---

[13] My translation is from the text in Moses Maimonides, *Iggerot: Maqor ve-targum*, ed. and tr. J. Kafih (Jerusalem: Mossad Harav Kook, second printing, 1987), pp. 143–144.

[14] I learned of this reference from Joel Kraemer; see Y. Tzvi Langermann, "My Truest Perplexities," *Aleph: Historical Studies in Science and Judaism* 8 (2008), 301–317, on p. 316. Ibn Taymiyya has anticipated contemporary scholarship in another way, by acknowledging that al-Ghazālī's relationship to philosophy was one of involvement, and not complete rejection.

[15] "Translator's Introduction: The Philosophic Sources of *The Guide of the Perplexed*," pp. cxxvi–cxxix.

a characteristically penetrating comparison between the two thinkers: "However, the probability that it is, at least in part, because of al-Ghazālī's apologetics that Maimonides realized the true issue between philosophy and religion, or religious law, does not mean that he, like al-Ghazālī though for different reasons, chose religion." This amazing sentence by one of the greatest historians of philosophy packs in three important lessons:

a) caution: "the probability that it is, at least in part"
b) identification of the key issue where the interaction takes place: "the true issue between philosophy and religion, or religious law"
c) restricting – a double restriction – the conclusions naturally suggested by this interaction: "does not mean that he, like al-Ghazālī though for different reasons, chose religion"

In short, Pines thinks it likely that Maimonides read the *Tahāfut*, but admits that he has no proof for this. He clarifies that "we may entertain the supposition that the antithesis established by Maimonides between the God of religion ... and the God of the Aristotelian philosophers ... owes a great deal to al-Ghazālī." Pines hints further that, the purported influence notwithstanding, Maimonides, unlike al-Ghazālī, chose philosophy.

Pines suggests the influence of the *Tahāfut* alone; his only argument is that "no philosopher who wished to keep abreast of the intellectual debate of this period could have afforded" not to read the *Tahāfut*. This is a version of the "must have read" claim mentioned above. Pines's comparison between the two thinkers yields significant insights, especially regarding differences. His discussion seems to me of the sort described at the beginning of this paper: a hypothetical engagement of two thinkers that sheds light on the stance taken by the later of the two, regardless of whether, in reality, he ever read the book of the earlier one.

About twenty-five years after Pines's essay appeared, Michael Schwartz published his masterful two-part essay on the kalam sources utilized by Maimonides. Al-Ghazālī has a minor presence there, far less than one would expect for the "most outstanding" representative of the school. He is mentioned in connection with the second, sixth, and tenth principles.[16] Here too the *Tahāfut* stands out. Schwartz is looking only for instances where doctrines and arguments mentioned by Maimonides are found in the literature of the kalam; he is careful not to make any claims of "influence." Nonetheless, the very limited role al-Ghazālī plays in the

---

[16] M. Schwarz, "Who Were Maimonides' Mutakallimun?" *Maimonidean Studies* 2 (1995), 159–209, and 3 (1995), 143–172; see pp. 174, 196, 200 in part one and pp. 163, 166–167 in part two.

most detailed study to date on Maimonides's engagement with the kalam is remarkable. In my view, it mitigates considerably the earlier claims of Professor Pines.

Professors Pines and Schwartz were both great experts in the kalam; their work that I have just cited is scholarship on Maimonides. Now let us look at a short paper written by a great expert on al-Ghazālī, the late Hava Lazarus-Yaffe.[17] What she means by influence is not clear; her study is a search for "parallels" in the writings of the two. Should such parallels be found, then presumably one can argue for influence; I have already voiced my unease with this idea. After stating, as so many others have done, that it is hard to imagine that Maimonides was unfamiliar with the writings of al-Ghazālī, she presents some "parallels" between the writing of the two; "parallels" that, as she is well-aware, are not complete matches; nor are Maimonides and al-Ghazālī the only two thinkers to share in those views. This last point bears repetition; Maimonides and al-Ghazālī must have shared quite a bit, but in order to make a case for "influence," one should also demonstrate that these shared items are not part of a wide cultural phenomenon in which many or all share. Professor Lazarus-Yaffe's conclusion is cautious and wise: "In any event, neither the approach nor the language of al-Ghazālī are recognizable in the words of Maimonides, even in the noteworthy examples that I adduced above. The starting points of al-Ghazālī and his overall approach are also very different from those of Maimonides. For this reason we will have to find additional and more convincing examples than those brought here in order to prove direct influence of the great mystic and anti-philosophical Muslim on Maimonides."

I will now move on to more recent contributions; these as a rule involve other books by al-Ghazālī and lead me to some different methodological observations. The Ghazalian writings at play here are *The Revival of the Religious Sciences* (*Iḥyā' 'Ulūm al-Dīn*) and *The Deliverance from Error* (*al-Munqidh min al-Ḍalāl*). The suggestion that the *Revival* in particular impacted any Jewish author requires especially close inspection. If "must have read" is a legitimate argument for influence, then, I submit, it is also legitimate to ask which writings in particular Maimonides "must have read." Al-Ghazālī was without a doubt one of the towering figures of Islamic thought, and some of his work was very influential in medieval

---

[17] H. Lazarus-Yafeh, "Was Maimonides Influenced by Alghazali?" in M. Cogan, B. L. Eichler, and J. H. Tigay (eds.), *Tehillah le-Moshe: Biblical and Judaic Studies in Honor of Moshe Greenberg* (Winona Lake: Eisenbrauns, 1997), pp. 163–169(Heb.).

Jewish thought. His *Maqāṣid al-Falāsifa* (*Intentions of the Philosophers*) was extremely influential; had anyone advanced a claim for its influence on Maimonides, I would not have been skeptical from the start – though, of course, I would still check any specific claim.[18] However, most of his writings were entirely unknown.

Steinschneider has nothing to say about the *Revival* in his book on the Hebrew translations, an invaluable resource even for strictly Arabic texts studied by Jews; it is not even mentioned in the index. His silence carries much weight. However, in the century that has passed, perhaps new evidence has come forth.[19] Other than the claims regarding Maimonides, to be discussed below, I know only of the paper of S. J. Pearce, which purports to find an unacknowledged citation from the *Revival* in a Hebrew text of Judah Ibn Tibbon.[20] However, the Hebrew maxim in question is a distant paraphrase of al-Ghazālī; it is, however, a literal translation of a widely known hadith. Pearce's claim, then, cannot be accepted.

As for the *Deliverance*, while no traces were to be found in the usual databases, further searching turned up some pieces that were identified by Paul Fenton: one in Oxford, Bodl. Ms. Heb.d.58 (Neubauer 2658), 64–72, and an extract in Cambridge Univ. Lib. T.-S. 8 Ka 1.3.[21] Fenton also detects the influence of the Sufi sections of the *Revival* on the Sufi-inspired writings of Maimonides's descendants. However, I am not prepared to make a blind leap of faith, and decide that Maimonides "must have" utilized the same books as did his offspring; all the more so, since the

---

[18] I can still do no better than to refer to the extensive, detailed account in M. Steinschneider, *Die hebraeischen Uebersetzungen des Mittelalter* (Berlin: Kommissionsverlag des bibliographischen Bureaus, 1893), pp. 298–326.

[19] Two very rich databases must be mentioned: the online catalogue of the Institute of Microfilmed Hebrew Manuscripts, Jerusalem, and the Friedberg Genizah project (https://fjms.genizah.org/). The only trace of the *Revival* found in either is an anti-Sufi treatise, transcribed into Hebrew letters and found in New York JTS ENA (4195.19–20), which merely mentions the *Revival*. No copies of the *Revival* have been identified. See below for some traces of the *Revival* that may be present in writings of Maimonides's descendants.

[20] S. J. Pearce, "The Types of Wisdom Are Two in Number: Judah ibn Tibbon's Quotation from the Iḥyā' 'ulūm al-Dīn," *Medieval Encounters* 19 (2013), 137–166. The maxim that Pearce ascribes to al-Ghazālī states that there are two sciences, the science of bodies and the science of religions. For the hadith see, e.g., F. Rosenthal, *The Classical Heritage in Islam*, reprint, London: Routledge, 1992, p. 67. For a more detailed refutation, see my video: https://www.youtube.com/watch?v=Cgrc_45Ebls.

[21] P. Fenton, "Les traces d'Al-Hallag, martyr mystique de l'islam, dans la tradition juive," *Annales Islamologiques* 35 (2001), 101–127, 106. The IMHM identifies the Oxford text only as "*ḥibbur be-filosofiya be-aravit*" ('Arabic composition in philosophy.') Fenton's paper has some important additions to the catalogue of Ghazaliana in Hebrew letters; however, I fear that he too tends to exaggerate the impact of Ghazalian writings. Fenton's findings have been further explored by N. Hofer, "Scriptural Substitutions and Anonymous Citations: Judaization as Rhetorical Strategy in a Jewish Sufi Text," *Numen*, 61 (2014), 364–395.

passages identified in the *Revival* as having influenced Maimonides come from sections of the *Revival* other than those said to have exerted influence. To sum up, this background research reinforces my suspicion concerning Maimonides's acquaintance with these two books.

I will discuss first the *Deliverance*. Only one scholar, Sarah Stroumsa, has suggested that Maimonides knew of this work. Moreover, she has been diligent enough to provide precise references, and cautious enough not to make too much of them. I will present her argument and my suggestion for a more likely "source," and leave it to the reader to decide:

> An even clearer borrowing of al-Ghazālī's usage of divine attributes is found in Maimonides' "Epistle to Yemen," where he describes the Torah as God's book "which *Guides* us and delivers us from error (*al-munqidh lanā min al-dalāla*) and from erroneous opinions." This formulation echoes, in all likelihood, the title of al-Ghazālī's spiritual autobiography, *al-Munqidh min al-ḍalāl*, and although Maimonides probably neither intended nor expected his Yemenite readers to recognize the allusion, it does betray his own familiarity with the work.[22]

The best one can say about this evidence is that is highly speculative. Note Maimonides's use of the feminine form, *dalāla*, rather than *ḍalāl*, which is found in al-Ghazālī's title. Is this significant? It is, indeed, because it supports my counter-suggestion for a "source" for this phrase. *Dalāla* is used in the Quran three times to signify the opposite of *huda*, "guidance" (2:16; 2:185; 16:36); exactly the same contrast features in the passage by Maimonides under scrutiny here. Hence I would prefer to say that Maimonides's phrase is based on Quranic usage, rather than on al-Ghazālī. Maimonides's use of Quranic phrasing is well-documented, whereas he never mentions nor cites *al-Munqidh*.[23]

Now to the suggestions made concerning al-Ghazālī's *Revival*. Steven Harvey begins his paper with the oft-heard remark: "It is hardly conceivable that he [Maimonides] was not familiar, indeed intimately familiar, with al-Ghazālī's various works."[24] Our old friend, "must have," has been upgraded; now Maimonides "must have" been *intimately* familiar. However, this necessarily amplifies our surprise that Maimonides never

---

[22] S. Stroumsa, *Maimonides and his World* (Princeton University Press, 2009), pp. 25–26.

[23] See my "*Sharh al-Dalala*: A Commentary to Maimonides' *Guide* from Fourteenth Century Yemen," in C. Fraenkel (ed.), *Traditions of Maimonideanism* (Leiden and Boston: Brill, 2009), pp. 155–176 and the literature cited there for Maimonides's use of Quranic phrases.

[24] S. Harvey, "Alghazali and Maimonides and their Books of Knowledge," in J. M. Harris (ed.), *Be'erot Yitzhak; Studies in Memory of Isadore Twersky* (Harvard University Press, 2005), pp. 99–117. I am most grateful to Prof. Harvey for some helpful comments.

mentions al-Ghazālī. Among possible solutions Harvey suggests that Maimonides was repelled by al-Ghazālī's "perfidious betrayal of philosophy."[25] Harvey provides a very thorough survey of earlier discussions, all of which are based one way or another on an anticipated influence, which is then said to be supported by textual parallels. Following this, he presents his own contribution: a comparison of the educational methods prescribed by the two thinkers in the "Book of Knowledge" that stands at the head of their respective codices.

Many similarities can certainly be found. Harvey, however, is well aware that these are not enough to settle the question of "influence." Significant differences can also be pointed out, and he proceeds to do just that. Moreover, Jewish sources can be identified for Maimonides; why, then, ought we to prefer ascribing his pronouncements to al-Ghazālī's influence? Harvey asks some very pertinent questions in this regard. Nonetheless, some way must be found to make "influence" the most compelling option.

So, what to do? Let us make a list of the obligations of teacher and student. Maimonides does not make any such list, but Joseph Ibn 'Aqnīn, whom Maimonides knew in his Moroccan sojourn, does make one; that should be close enough. Harvey boldly asserts that it is "certain that Ibn 'Aqnin had al-Ghazālī's account of the duties of the teacher and the student in front of him when he wrote this chapter."[26] In his note to this remark, however, I see no certainty, only the standard fare of parallels and suppositions. Even here, the parallels between Ibn 'Aqnīn and al-Ghazālī are not perfect, but some misfits on the part of Ibn 'Aqnīn match Maimonides quite well! According to Harvey, Ibn 'Aqnīn certainly relied on al-Ghazālī, though he has Judaized his text. Can we say the same about Maimonides? Of course, Jewish sources cannot be dismissed out of hand. However, the circuitous, speculative, and potholed route by way of Ibn 'Aqnīn confronts us with some of the same ideas in al-Ghazālī's "Book of Knowledge," the opening section of his *Revival*. Hence, "we must begin to consider influence." I see nothing compelling or enticing in this train of argument; and Harvey too maintains only that he has shown that mountains of parallels – even when they can be explained without recourse to al-Ghazālī – lead us only to "begin to consider influence."

In his penultimate footnote, Harvey quotes the late Isadore Twersky to the effect that the "most important source is Maimonides' fertile mind and skill of analysis and synthesis," adding that the "argument for the influence of the *Revival* does not question this emphasis." If so, then, what is the

---

[25] Harvey, "Books of Knowledge," 100.    [26] Ibid., 115 and note 74.

place of influence in the total picture, how does it come into play, and why is it important? Is al-Ghazālī merely a source of raw materials, to be crafted into a literary masterpiece by Maimonides's genius? Should one not argue, not simply "for" influence, but rather, as I think one must, for influence in the sense of a significant formative factor? Is not al-Ghazālī's purported influence made redundant and unnecessary, given Maimonides's originality and the body of Jewish sources that are at least equally plausible sources of influence? I am troubled by these questions, but troubled much more by the fact that neither Harvey, nor any other influence-hunter, bothers to raise them. The hunt for "influences" does not take place within a framework of reasoned explanation for the formation of Maimonides's thought. Instead, it seems to be almost a game, conducted with no end in mind beyond aggrandizing the list of influences and, especially, including in that list "trending" intellectual figures.

Amira Eran's study, the longest to date on our topic, begins with a review of articles by Dov Schwartz and Sarah Stroumsa, both of which aim to show the influence of Ibn Sīnā on Maimonides's views of the afterlife.[27] They both list similarities and differences between Maimonides and Ibn Sīnā, arguing that the former indicate Maimonides's dependence on his predecessor. Eran's critical reading leads her to remark that "the textual resemblance ... made scholars ignore the differences in their doctrines." The Hebrew adage states: Would that your ears hear what your own mouth has said! Eran presumes that Avicennian teachings reached Maimonides by way of al-Ghazālī, "who had a direct influence" on Maimonides. Al-Ghazālī both conveyed directly Ibn Sīnā's teaching, serving as his "mouthpiece," and "disguised" his own views as critiques of his predecessor. Maimonides "imitates the fascinating intellectual maneuvers of his Muslim predecessor."[28]

What do we have here? In order to prove "direct influence" we must take note of differences as well; presumably some (or any?) rule out direct influence. Yet the thinkers in question, both al-Ghazālī and Maimonides, are engaged in "fascinating maneuvers" aimed at disguising their own radical views. What does this mean? It seems to me that we must ferret out the true teachings of both the presumed influencer and the influenced, and compare them; after ascertaining that there are no differences, we can be satisfied that there is influence. Can we ever agree on the true teachings that lurk behind the maneuvers? Decades of scholarship on both al-Ghazālī and Maimonides

---

[27] A. Eran, "Al-Ghazālī and Maimonides on the World to Come and Spiritual Pleasures," *Jewish Studies Quarterly*, 8 (2001), 137–166.

[28] Ibid., 143.

suggest that this is simply too tall of an order to be filled.[29] Can one imagine that only similarities exist, and no differences? Or shall we conveniently explain away differences as camouflage?

Ibn Sīnā may be the ultimate "source" of these ideas, or at least as far back as one can go without leaving Islamic civilization. Al-Ghazālī is credited with creatively adapting Ibn Sīnā; but, in keeping with her critique of Schwartz and Stroumsa, Eran will not allow the possibility that Maimonides too adapted Ibn Sīnā, which seems to me no less reasonable. However, Maimonides is allowed to alter al-Ghazālī somewhat – this is obviously necessary, so that whatever differences that may emerge between the two should not call into question al-Ghazālī's "influence."

I have intimated throughout this paper, and will restate the point again more forcefully here, that claims of influence are in no way falsifiable, especially in the case before us, where Maimonides's "maneuvers" are acknowledged, consequently, in my view, making the argument for influence weaker and the need for substantive evidence stronger. The best one can do is to suggest alternative "sources" that can replace al-Ghazālī in a given topic. But is the identification of sources the primary task of the historian? Is the first and most important question to ask, when studying a passage from Maimonides, "Where did he get this from?" My answer, you may guess, is a resounding "no." The search for sources becomes critical only when the identification of a source is needed to clarify a particular point.

I profess my discomfort at being forced to look for alternative "sources," especially when even a successful search cannot falsify a non-falsifiable claim. History is not an exact science and its claims need not always be formulated in a manner that allows for falsification. Still, historians ought to think about the questions they pose, and what is to be gained by providing an answer. My search for plausible alternatives is conducted under protest.

Eran places great stock in a textual comparison between three "parables" found in both writers. The first concerns the role of reward in education.[30] She discusses a parable that reveals a "gradation of pleasures" offered to the

---

[29] Almost every study on Maimonides's philosophy aims at presenting his "true" views on a given topic, but these "truths" are far from agreed upon. Ever since the demise of his image of the brute who quashed philosophical thinking in Islam, studies on al-Ghazālī's "true" views have flourished; no consensus exists. Since the "true" view is, by definition, not stated explicitly, there will always be some uncertainty as to what this "true" view is, or if, indeed, the "true" view is not the one stated explicitly.

[30] Eran, "Al-Ghazālī and Maimonides," 146–147.

child as he matures: at first sweets (Maimonides) or sports (al-Ghazālī), then clothing (both), then money followed by honor (Maimonides), or sexual gratification followed by power and wealth (al-Ghazālī). The differences are obvious. In part they are due to the contexts: Maimonides is addressing mainly the rewards offered to a young pupil and hence he would not dare introduce sexual satisfaction. But let us not trifle over details. What the two "parables" have in common is something they share with a myriad of ethicists around the medieval world: a moral based on the so-called "ages of man"; these ages – childhood, youth, early manhood, etc. – are the real "gradations" at play. I see no argument for influence from the two passages Eran presents here.[31]

Google, however, seems to agree with Eran. A search for the terms "Maimonides" and "theory of education" (carried out 19 March 2017) yielded little information on "sources." However, the "related searches" suggested by Google all refer to al-Ghazālī. Google is convinced: If you want to know something about Maimonides's theory of education, look to al-Ghazālī! This seems to me a clear indication of the impact of studies such as that of Eran, which cannot go unanswered.

Next comes "The King and the Ball Game Parable."[32] Those fortunate enough to enjoy the intellectual delights of the hereafter would no more decline them for the bodily joys they once enjoyed in this world than would a king give up his power and prestige so as to return to his boyhood ball games. This is Maimonides, explaining why intellectual pleasures are to be to be preferred – not how they are presented to the believer. Al-Ghazālī, however, is explaining why the spiritual pleasures are conveyed in fables when he explains that the child, in his early stage of development, is rewarded by a game of chess or a bird: He is incapable of grasping the true pleasure of political position, which is the reason he is being given his education. Eran sees here a "striking" dependence of Maimonides on al-Ghazālī. I do not. I may feebly suggest, by way of "alternate sources," Galen's small essay on "The exercise with the small ball," which Maimonides cites and which, I think, is responsible for the references to ball games in his work.[33]

---

[31] Note that a fifteenth-century Yemeni writer and commentator on Maimonides cites al-Ghazālī by name in connection with the "ages of man"; see Langermann, "Sharḥ al-Dalāla," pp. 168–170.

[32] Eran, "Al-Ghazālī and Maimonides," 148–149.

[33] The medical benefits of exercise with the ball are mentioned in *Guide* iii.25. Excerpts from Galen's monograph are given at the beginning of book eighteen of Maimonides's *Medical Aphorisms*; Maimonides, *Medical Aphorisms, Treatises 16–21*, ed. and tr. G. Bos (Provo: Brigham Young University Press, 2015), pp. 37–40.

In section C of her paper, which deals with "the eunuch metaphor," Eran cites at length from the *Revival*.[34] Two evident miscues in her translation call into question her understanding of that text. She writes, "that the pleasure of the king, which is an internal [pleasure/sense] is stronger in perfected people who possess all the pleasures of the senses, and that this kind of [i.e. ruling] does not exist in animals, and in young or insane people." I think that "[i.e. ruling]" must be replaced by "[i.e. pleasure].".[35] Later on she writes, "only those who have achieved the rank of the [pleasure of the] knowledge of Allah and the taste of it can possess it, since it is absolutely impossible to convince [in its delighted taste] those who have no heart, for the heart is the origin of this capacity [i.e. ruling in general, and the power of Allah in particular]." Al-Ghazālī is referring to the heart in this last sentence; "[i.e. ruling . . .]" must be replaced by "[i.e. to experience 'taste']" – "taste" being used here in its Sufi sense of unmediated experience.[36]

In this section Eran does not cite from Maimonides. Following the long quote from the *Revival*, she observes: "Maimonides' choice to follow al-Ghazālī by making a 'little boy' the center of his main parables implies that the failure to identify the true end of man's life and the true reward of the service of God can be remedied through devoted education and the attainment of maturity." I doubt that Maimonides is following al-Ghazālī; and maturity does not remedy ignorance, it only (hopefully) makes one willing to take the necessary action that may cure ignorance. But let's not argue over that; let me simply ask, does Maimonides need al-Ghazālī in order to suggest that the failure to understand the meaning of life, and the true reward for the service of God, can be remedied by education that hopefully accompanies maturity?

This should suffice. I cannot here go through Eran's thirty-page paper section by section; were I to do so, my criticisms would look much like those offered already. Those who are on board the influence bandwagon will accuse me of quibbling. All differences between al-Ghazālī and Maimonides are due to the latter's creative adaptation; all similarities, real or imagined, constitute solid evidence for influence. Such is the nature of this debate.

Interest in Maimonides's theory of education, and its sources, was a matter of interest before the Ghazalian connection came into fashion.

---

[34] Eran, "Al-Ghazālī and Maimonides," 149–150.    [35] Ibid., 149.
[36] The passage is on page 150; I comment only on the two instances where Eran erroneously sees an allusion to "ruling," apparently in order to bolster her imagery of the king and the delight he takes in ruling.

Michael Rosenak looks to Plato and his "mythic lie"; tellingly, he also points to the "Rambam-Maimonides dissonance."[37] Recall that Harvey's paper ended in a draw between the influence of al-Ghazālī and Maimonides's – here answering to the name Rambam – creative adaptation of Jewish sources. We may then entertain the thought that the surge of papers on al-Ghazālī's influence is another chapter in this dissonance, with the twist that, given the current zeitgeist, Maimonides (should I say Ibn Maymūn?) draws on Islamic rather than Greek sources.

Indeed, medieval philosophers, or philosophically literate theologians, drew upon a large bank of parables and images, which they interpreted in manners convenient to the points that they wished to make. In some cases, the meaning of the parable is quite obvious. In others, the parable provides a mere skeleton upon which thinkers can build a wide variety of lessons. Let us look briefly at two examples, each of which is utilized by both al-Ghazālī and Maimonides. As far as I know, these have not (yet) been adduced as examples of "influence," nor should we muddy the comparison by looking for influence. Both thinkers make use of the tale of the attempt to describe an elephant to someone who has never seen one, commonly known as the tale of the elephant and the blind men, which is said to be Buddhist in origin.[38] The tale serves to illustrate "the apparent contradiction between 'knowability' and 'unknowability' of God."[39]

By contrast, the parable of the sultan's palace features in radically divergent ways in the writings of the two thinkers. Maimonides (beginning of *Guide* iii.51) uses it as a critical prologue to the culmination of the *Guide* and a discussion of humanity's highest purpose. Al-Ghazālī utilizes it in several places, but never in so climactic a fashion.[40] For Maimonides, the parable presents the classes of humans; for al-Ghazālī, it displays the cosmic hierarchy. In al-Ghazālī's parable, the stars and their influence are a key feature; Maimonides did the best he could to sanitize all forms of Jewish thought from astrology and its aftertastes. Finally, the "throne"

---

[37] M. Rosenak, *Roads to the Palace: Jewish Texts and Teaching* (Providence and Oxford: Berghahn Books, 1995), p. 67.

[38] This story is famous enough to have its own Wikipedia entry: https://en.wikipedia.org/wiki/Blin d_men_and_an_elephant (accessed April 13, 2017). Al-Ghazālī's use of the tale is discussed briefly by H. Landolt, "Ghazālī und 'Religionswissenschaft'," *Asiatische Studien* 45 (1991), 19–72, 27–28; Maimonides alludes to it near the end of *Guide* i.60.

[39] Landolt, "Ghazālī und 'Religionswissenschaft'," 27.

[40] Ibid., 46–47, citing from the *Kīmiyā-yi Saʿadat*, which is in Persian and presumably cannot be taken as an influence on Maimonides, along with one place in the *Revival*. In fact, I find that al-Ghazālī appeals to the parable of the palace more than once in the *Revival*.

in al-Ghazālī's parable is the seat of *al-Muṭāʿ*, "the obeyed one."[41] Maimonides speaks not of the "obeyed one" but of the king; the pinnacle reached by prophets is a court session (*majlis*) with the king. The "throne" is not mentioned (though of course it is discussed in detail elsewhere in the *Guide*) and even a mighty leap of faith cannot succeed in identifying Maimonides's king with al-Ghazālī's *al-Muṭāʿ*.

Mind you, there is no problem here: Two thinkers, each loyal to his own tradition, each building on this own experience and education, and each advancing his personal agenda, will surely find different literary applications, and widely divergent interpretations, for the same skeleton model. The "problem" arises when we presume influence, deep influence of the type several scholars have argued for. So when Maimonides says that he has "invented" (*ibtakaratu*) his parable of the Sultan's palace, is he nodding to al-Ghazālī? My question is not as wild as it sounds. Sarah Stroumsa asserts that Maimonides is not claiming originality, but rather notifying the reader that this parable is not one of the prophetic parables mentioned at the beginning of the *Guide*, and whose proper interpretation is one of its main goals.[42] True, the palace served as a useful parable for others; Maimonides did not invent the palace-as-model. However, I see no reason to deny the originality of its application.

## Conclusions: Zeitgeist, Social Negotiation, and the Writing of History

I am no theorist. My attitude towards theory is that of the folk musician who, when asked if knows any music theory, replied, "Not enough to hurt my playing!" The search for connections between Maimonides and al-Ghazālī surely appears to be a sign of the times: the surge in interest in Islam, the transformation of al-Ghazālī from the villain responsible for the decline of Islamic culture into one of its most brilliant paragons, and, of course, the appreciation that Maimonides and his *Guide* cannot be detached from their Arabic, and Judeo-Arabic, contexts.

---

[41] On this important concept see Griffel, *Al-Ghazālī's Philosophical Theology*, pp. 252–263.

[42] S. Stroumsa, "Citation Tradition: On Explicit and Hidden Citations in Judaeo-Arabic Philosophical Literature," in Joshua Blau and David Doron (eds.), *Heritage and Innovation* (Ramat Gan: Bar Ilan, 2000), pp. 167–178, p. 178, n. 52. Her claim is highly questionable; why doesn't Maimonides take the same care with the other parables brought in the *Guide*? Why does he use, when discussing the parable of the palace, two verbs in the first person, *aḍrabu* and *ibtakaratu*? Thankfully, Stroumsa does not look for a "source."

I participate in all of the above but am concerned not to be swept away; to display the necessary critical acumen even when studying Maimonides in his contexts, with full awareness of the achievement of al-Ghazālī. I stubbornly insist that claims for influence must meet some standards for evidence. There may be no avoiding the judgment that "evidence" is in some way socially constructed; but this, I maintain, should prod us to examine our arguments all the more closely.

Historians of early modern and modern Jewish thought are clearly aware of the problematical nature of "influence," not merely the difficulty of proving influence, but also the weightier question of what it means to be influenced. Two examples will suffice. Speaking of various influences that have been said to have operated on the Ba'al Shem Tov, Moshe Rosman writes:

> even if there is a correlation with regard to the characteristics ... theorizing a causative relationship ... is a case of falling into very common logical fallacy ... The elusive concept of zeitgeist gains meaning when applied to this combination of like circumstances and like, yet diffuse reactions. One can find parallels between the contemporaries Judah Hasid and Francis Assisi in the twelfth century, or Muslim Ayatollahs and certain ultra-orthodox rabbis in the twentieth, but there are no direct links that prove flow of influence.[43]

There is no question that Rabbi Joseph B. Soloveitchik was influenced by Hermann Cohen; after all, he wrote his dissertation on Cohen. Nonetheless, Lawrence Kaplan insists that his study of this particular influence go beyond a superficial stock-taking of similarities. Instead, the real question is:

> What are the internal problems and issues with which the thinker is confronted, what are the basic structures and dynamics of his thought that allow him, indeed compel him, to absorb certain influences and reject others? A truly great thinker is more than the sum total of intellectual influences operating upon him. Rather, he draws upon these influences in a creative and innovative way, always maintaining his own identity, uniqueness, and originality.[44]

Unfortunately, historians of medieval Jewish philosophy have not always thought carefully about the way questions are phrased, evidence weighed, and conclusions drawn, especially when writing about influence. I hope that this essay will serve as a useful corrective.

[43] M. Rosman, *Founder of Hasidism: A Quest for the Historical Ba'al Shem Tov* (University of California Press, 1996), p. 59.

[44] L. Kaplan, "Hermann Cohen and Rabbi Soloveitchik on Repentance," *Journal of Jewish Thought and Philosophy*, 13 (2004), 213–258, 240.

CHAPTER 3

# Maimonides on the Intellects of Women and Gentiles

## Hannah Kasher

Women and gentiles represent the "other" in Maimonides's thought.[1] His works – which were written in Judeo-Arabic and Hebrew – were certainly not addressed to gentiles,[2] nor, it would seem, to Jewish women. However, we will open this discussion with a word of reservation: The status of women[3] and gentiles[4] in Maimonides's thought is not necessarily exclusively the product of his personal perspective. Maimonides considered himself bound by the Jewish tradition, especially its system of commandments, their status already established to a large degree in Jewish law. Therefore, the analysis below cannot rely on those laws cited in his writings that are not the product of his independent ruling. However, it is possible to draw inferences as to his worldview from the reasoning that he provides for these laws, such as, for example, his ruling that only a Jewish man may be crowned as king or appointed to a position of authority:

> No king is appointed . . . unless his mother is a Jewess by descent [. . .]. This rule applies not only to the office of king, but also to other positions of

[1] See G. Blidstein, "The 'Other' in Maimonides' Law," *Jewish History*, 18 (2004), 173–195.

[2] This can be demonstrated by Maimonides's use of the term '*adam*', lit., 'man', when referring only to a Jewish male, "It is permitted for a man (*adam*) to rent his vineyard to a gentile" (*Code of Law, Sabbath* vi.14). See also A. Melamed, "Maimonides on Woman: Formless Matter or Potential Prophet?" in A. L. Ivry, E. R. Wolfson, and A. Arkush (eds.), *Perspectives on Jewish Thought and Mysticism* (Amsterdam: Harwood Academic Pub., 1998), 99–134, esp. 128, n. 27.

[3] See A. Grossman, *Ve-hu yimshol bakh?: ha-ishah be-mishnatam shel ḥakhmei Yisrael bi-yeme ha-benayim* (And He Shall Rule Over You? Medieval Jewish Sages on Women) (Jerusalem: Zalman Shazar Center, 2011), 97–142; M. M. Kellner, "Philosophical Misogyny in Medieval Jewish Philosophy – Gersonides v. Maimonides," in A. Ravitzky (ed.), *Me-Romi li-Yerushalayim: Sefer zikaron le-Yosef-Barukh Sermoneṭah* (Joseph Baruch Sermoneta Memorial Volume), *Jerusalem Studies in Jewish Thought*, 14 (1998), 113–128.

[4] The important and central contributions of M. M. Kellner to this subject should be noted. See especially his latest book, *Gam hem qeruyim adam: ha-nokhri be-'einei ha-Rambam (They, Too, are Called Human: Gentiles in the Eyes of Maimonides)*, (Ramat Gan: Bar Ilan University Press, 2016). See also M. M. Kellner, *Maimonides Confrontation with Mysticism* (Oxford, England: The Littman Library of Jewish Civilization, 2006), 216–264.

authority [. . .] unless one is an Israelite by descent, as it is said: "One from among your brethren" (Deut 17:15) [. . .].

No woman is appointed to be a monarch, for it states "king" (ibid.) not "queen." So too, whenever the appointment to an office is made in Israel, one only appoints a man.

The following may not be set up as king or High Priest: a butcher, a barber, a bathhouse keeper, or a tanner. This is not because they are unqualified but, rather, [because] the people will always disparage them, since they have a base occupation.[5]

Maimonides counts the prohibition against appointing a king who is not of Jewish extraction among the 613 commandments that are of biblical origin. He provides the rationale for this prohibition in the *Guide*: "For no individual has ever been the chief of a nation to whose race he did not belong, without doing it great or small injury,"[6] as Maimonides assumes that there is a sort of human compassion that is rooted in blood relation.[7] In other words, there is no claim here of the inferiority of non-Jews. Rather, the issue is that they are foreigners. It follows that, in principle, Maimonides would consider a prohibition against appointing a Jew to a position of authority in another nation justified.

As mentioned, Maimonides also rules that one may not appoint a woman to a position of authority, even though he does not count this prohibition among the 613 commandments. The explanation for this ruling may be deduced from the rationale he offers for the prohibition against other appointments, mentioned later in the text cited above: "not because they are unqualified; but, rather, [. . .] the people will always disparage them." Among the general public, the status of women is inferior, whether or not Maimonides personally viewed this as justified.

This perspective is apparently also the basis for Maimonides's ruling that "A woman may not read the Torah publicly, out of the respect for the congregation."[8] It is likely that the prohibition depends upon the attitude of the congregation in that time and place, for although he uses the same language in his *Code* against reading from the Torah from a parchment scroll that had not been properly processed,[9] he allows in a responsum that one says the blessings before and after such a scroll, and they are not

[5] *Code of Law, Kings* i.4–6. The translation, with some modification, is taken from Maimonides, *The Code of Maimonides: Mishneh Torah*. Vol. 14, *The Book of Judges*, tr. I. Klein, Yale Judaica Series (Yale Univ. Press, 1949).

[6] *Guide* iii.50, tr. Pines, p. 615. Unless otherwise noted, page references to the *Guide* are to the Pines translation.

[7] Ibid., iii.41.     [8] *Code of Law, Prayer* xii.16.     [9] Ibid., xii.22.

considered to be said in vain, despite the fact that the scrolls are themselves unfit:

> And those in the West relied on this inference [. . .] and no one ever raised an objection, as they were all wise, and their wisdom was level-headed and accurate, and they knew that the blessing was not contingent on the scroll [. . .] but, rather on the reading itself.[10]

In other words, since the general public believed that reading from a Torah scroll made properly of parchment was more dignified, Maimonides ruled in the *Code of Law* that it is preferable to act in accordance with "the respect for the congregation." However, this is not a substantive obligation of Jewish law. For obvious reasons, we will not deal with the practical ramifications of the question of whether the laws instituted concerning the status of women because of "respect for the congregation" are, according to Maimonides, also contingent on time and place.

It is reasonable to assume that the scientific and social views of Maimonides's time, especially those concerning the characteristics of women, did not fail to influence his thought. Maimonides uses a metaphor, which he attributes to Plato, to refer to the status of women relative to men, comparing them to matter and form respectively.[11] Given that matter is the source of all deficiency, including all evil that afflicts the world, in contrast to human form, which is the divine image and the source of immortality, the metaphor clearly expresses the inferiority of women relative to men. Following his Platonic source, Maimonides incorporates allegorical interpretations of biblical texts into his explanation: Eve, alongside the serpent, caused Adam's passions to control him, preventing him from attaining perfection. Also, Proverbs' description of the ideal woman, as opposed to the harlot, represents the ultimate matter, which is subservient to the form, in contrast to the inferior matter, which controls and subjugates.[12] Alongside the influence of Greek philosophy, one can, to a certain degree, distinguish Maimonides's position by comparing it to the views of other Jewish thinkers close to his time, who also accepted the authoritative religious tradition, and who also were subject to the influence of the scientific and social views of their time.

Our concern here is with the question, "What are the consequences of Maimonides's views about the inferior status of the 'other' (women and

---

[10] *Teshuvot ha-Rambam,* ed. and tr. J. Blau, 2: 550–553, responsum 294.
[11] Melamed, "Maimonides on Woman," 100.   [12] *Guide* i.int., 13–14; Ibid., iii.8, p. 431.

gentiles)" rather than the question, "How should male Jews relate to the 'other'?" The inferior status of the "other" may cause discrimination and painful injury, but not necessarily. A paternalistic relationship may be realized in a loving or caring way, especially when the "other" is a woman.[13] It may express compassion, when the woman or gentile is perceived as emotional and suffering. It may even be caring, when the inferior serves as a life partner or an essential worker. On the other hand, the relationship may be hostile when the "other" is a member of an enemy population or another religion.

In order to illustrate the consequences of Maimonides' thought, it is useful to cite an extreme case in which the statuses of gentile and woman converge in one individual, a gentile woman. In this case Maimonides's ruling is not compelled by a binding source in Jewish Law:

> If, however, an Israelite has intercourse with a gentile woman, whether she is a minor of three years and one day old or an adult, whether she is married or unmarried, even if the Israelite is only nine years and one day old, when he does so intentionally, she should be executed. She is executed because she caused an Israelite to be involved in an unseemly transgression, like an animal.[14]

In this context, the life of the gentile woman has no inherent worth as a human being. She is to be executed "because she caused a Jew to be involved in an unseemly transgression," i.e., because she was a "stumbling-block." Even so, to reach meaningful conclusions concerning this issue, one must examine the components of the example cited. Is she dealt with in the same way as an animal because she is a woman, or a gentile, or a female gentile? Or perhaps there is another reason besides her being in the category of female and gentile.

In any case, this source suggests that, according to Maimonides, not every human offspring is deemed a human being in every respect. Indeed, in the *Guide of the Perplexed*, it is possible to find characterizations of people who are not considered humans: He "is not a man, but an animal having the shape and configuration of men."[15] "The status of those is like that of irrational animals."[16] According to Maimonides, attaining "the true human form," which is by way of "human perfection," is achieved by study that leads to the actualization of the intellect. The pinnacle of this study is knowledge of God, within man's ability. This is acquired by means of a progression of knowledge, especially of metaphysics.

---

[13] See Grossman, *Ve-hu yimshol bakh?*, pp. 99, 139.

[14] *behema*, lit. 'beast'. *Code of Law, Prohibited Intercourse* xii.10.     [15] *Guide* i.7, p. 33.

[16] Ibid., iii.51, p. 618.

Therefore, we must ask the following: Is there anything that fundamentally blocks a woman or gentile from attaining "the true human form"; and if so, how is it connected to one's status as a woman or a gentile, if at all? In one of the chapters of the *Guide*, Maimonides describes a congenital defect that prevents a person from acquiring the necessary knowledge:

> For it has been explained, or rather demonstrated, that moral virtues are preparation for the rational virtues, it being impossible to achieve true, rational acts, I mean perfect rationality, unless it be by a man thoroughly trained with respect to his morals and endowed with the qualities of tranquility and quiet. There are, moreover, many people who have received from their first natural disposition a complexion of temperament with which perfection is in no way compatible. Such is the case of one whose heart is naturally exceedingly hot, for he cannot refrain from anger, even if he subjects his soul to very stringent training [. . .] This is also the case of one whose testicles have a hot and humid temperament [. . .] for it is unlikely that such a man, even if he subjects his soul to the most severe training, should be chaste. Similarly, you can find among people rash and reckless folk [. . .] Perfection can never be perceived in such people.[17]

In this context, the requisite knowledge is metaphysics. Corporeal factors can prevent a person from achieving this knowledge, even if they only affect his character, and do not directly harm his ability to learn. However, since a tranquil disposition is a prerequisite for learning, a very hot and extremely reckless temperament does not allow a person to attain his desired goal, and indeed, it is almost impossible to rid himself of this character trait.[18]

People's physical constitutions (temperaments) directly impact their ability to acquire intellectual virtues and rid themselves of intellectual vices:

> For example, if one person's temperament tends more towards dryness, and the essence of his brain is pure and his moistures are few, it is easier for such a person to remember and to understand matters, than it is for a person controlled by white liquid, and whose brain contains many liquids [. . .] if one teaches a person whose nature is coarse and who possesses many liquids, and explains to him, he will learn and understand, but only with difficulty and through great effort.[19]

---

[17] *Guide* i.34, p. 77. Cf. *Guide* ii.36, p. 369. See G. Freudenthal, "Maïmonide: La détermination biologique et climatologique (partielle) de la félicité humaine," in T. Lévy and R. Rashed (eds.), *Maïmonide: Philosophe et Savant* (1138–1204) (Leuven: Peeters, 2004), pp. 81–129.

[18] This stands in contrast with Maimonides's claim in *Commentary on the Mishnah, Introduction to Avot (Eight Chapters)*, viii, that "Except for his being disposed by temperament so that something is easy or difficult for him [. . .] In no way is any action compelled or prevented."

[19] Ibid.

Here, the physical trait directly affects an individual's ability to learn. According to the accepted perspective of that time, a woman's temperament is colder and moister than a man's.[20] This moisture interferes with a woman's ability to understand and to remember; however, with a great effort, it can be overcome.[21]

In another context, Maimonides characterizes women's qualities: "How quickly they are affected and, speaking generally, how feeble are their intellects."[22] In general, "a female in all species is more defective than the male."[23] To be sure, Maimonides does not characterize women in general as possessing the aforementioned defect of excessive heat, which absolutely prevents one from attaining equanimity. And the claim regarding the weakness of their intellect is not a comprehensive one, but rather, only "speaking generally." Still, it is difficult to find a basis for the assumption that Maimonides held women's intellectual inferiority to stem only from socio-cultural circumstances. Their moist corporeal temperament makes it more difficult to attain intellectual achievements than for men, although it does not prevent it entirely.

Maimonides's perception of women's intellectual limitations finds expression in his approach to female education. He posits that women can certainly learn what actions are required of them according to Jewish Law in order to maintain a proper society:

> knowledge in detail of what is prohibited and what is permitted and the like in terms of the other commandments [...] For the knowledge of these things gives primarily composure to the mind [...] And it is possible for all to know them, adult or minor, man or woman, one with much intelligence and one whose intelligence is limited.[24]

---

[20] See *Commentary on the Mishna, Yoma*, viii.4, *Medical Aphorisms*, ch. 25, pt. 2. Cf. G. E. R. Lloyd, "The Hot and the Cold, the Dry and the Wet in Greek Philosophy," *The Journal of Hellenistic Studies*, 84 (1964), 92–106.

[21] Maimonides's "deterministic" statement on the impact of temperament on moral traits appears in the *Guide*, whereas his more "libertarian" statement on the impact of temperament on intellectual traits appears in the *Commentary on the Mishnah*. On Maimonides's alleged determinism in the *Guide*, see S. Pines's excursuses on free will and determinism in the Appendix to his "Studies in Abu'l-Barakāt al-Baghdādī's Poetics and Metaphysics," *Scripta Hierosolymitana*, 6 (Jerusalem, 1960), 120–98, reprinted in *The Collected Works of Shlomo Pines. Vol. I: Studies in Abu l-Barakāt al-Baghdādī. Physics and Metaphysics* (Jerusalem, 1979). Yet notice should be taken of the different contexts: In the *Commentary*, the context is the discussion of the human ability to act, whereas in the *Guide*, the context is the discussion of obstacles to achieving metaphysical knowledge.

[22] *Guide* iii.37, p. 546.     [23] Ibid., iii.46, p. 587.

[24] *Code of Law, Foundations of the Law* iv.13. The translation is adapted from *Mishneh Torah: The Book of Knowledge*, ed. and tr. M. Hyamson (New York, 1937), 39b.

Since even someone "whose intelligence is limited" can understand and know how to act, there is no reason that a woman should not study them.[25] At the same time, the Jewish tradition has ruled that women are not obligated in the study of the Law, and one would not expect Maimonides to deviate from that norm. However, his personal view can be inferred from the explanations that he gives for the Sages' position on this matter and for their reasoning:

> A woman, who studied the Torah, has a reward for it; but her reward is not like that of a man, as she was not commanded [. . .] And even though she has a reward for it, the Sages commanded that a man shall not teach his daughter the Torah (M. *Sotah* 3,3); because most women have no set mind to being taught and they turn the words of the Law into nonsense due to their poor intelligence. The Sages stated: "If one teaches his daughter the Torah, it is as if he taught her vacuousness (*tiflut*)" (ibid.). To what does this apply? To the Oral Torah. However, in terms of the Written Torah, he should not teach it to her *ab initio*; but if he taught her, it is not as if he taught her vacuousness.[26]

Maimonides was bound to the Jewish law and ruled accordingly: The study of the Torah is incumbent on men, and *ab initio* it is exclusively their responsibility to study and to teach the Torah specifically to their male offspring. However, *post factum*, a woman who is learned is assured of her reward. Therefore, a father who has already taught his daughter the Written Torah has not done so in vain. Nonetheless, the wording of Maimonides's rationale may express his personal perspective: "because most women have no set mind to being taught and they turn the words of the Law into nonsense due to their poor intelligence." His explanation regarding the comprehensive prohibition is based on an assumption concerning "most women." If so, what is it about a woman's intellect that makes it unsuitable for Torah study?[27] It is, therefore, reasonable to assume that – as opposed to male children who are capable of being taught – most girls are unable to concentrate sufficiently for this purpose, and learning Torah may even cause harm: "And they turn the words of the Torah into nonsense due to their poor intelligence." Maimonides allows for the possibility

---

[25] See W. Z. Harvey, "The Obligation of Talmud on Women According to Maimonides," *Tradition*, 19, 2 (1981), 122–130.

[26] *Code of Law, Study of the Law* i.13. I have used W. Z. Harvey's translation in Harvey, "The Obligation of Women," p. 123.

[27] The phrase "impoverished intellect" apparently expresses the quality described by the Sages in their statement, "Women are light-minded." (BT *Shabbat* 33b).

that "their intellect will increase."[28] However, as mentioned before, Maimonides is not dealing here with exceptional individuals. His concern relates to the potential harm caused by most of them. As Maimonides writes in his *Commentary on the Mishna (Sotah* 3:3), "He taught her vacuousness, i.e., nonsense and folly." The 'Oral Torah' that women are forbidden to study is apparently not Jewish Law as codified by people like Maimonides, since he explicitly says that such law can be known by "great and small, man and woman, of great or little intelligence."[29] It might refer to the text of the Talmud, which includes rabbinical dialectics, as well as non-legal passages of the Talmud. Elsewhere, Maimonides warns against "wasting time on debate in the Talmud."[30] He may also be concerned with the non-legal (aggadic) sections, which may be misinterpreted by an uneducated public, misinterpretations that could result in dire consequences.[31] Nonetheless, it should be emphasized again that Maimonides is referring to "most women" and "speaking generally"; as will be clarified below, at least one woman actualized fully the divine image with which she was born.

According to Maimonides, human perfection at its pinnacle may be realized in one of two ways: (1) by individuals attaining the level of prophecy during their lifetime, or (2) by individuals attaining intellectual immortality after their day; the latter is his interpretation of the rabbinic notion of "The World to Come." It seems that these two forms of human perfection are not the exclusive domain of men. One can find historical precedents for women attaining the former of these perfections.

For instance, Maimonides may have considered all the women who left Egypt to be prophetesses; he writes that "the least of their wives was compared to Ezekiel b. Buzi as the Sages noted,"[32] and Ezekiel was, of course, a prophet. This assumption is compatible with R. Judah Halevi's perspective that "all of them [the men] reached such a level that they were worthy of hearing the divine speech, and this property passed over to their wives, and some of them became prophetesses."[33] For according to the *Kuzari*, the entire Jewish people attained divine revelation at Sinai, after

---

[28] *Code of Law, Repentance* x.2
[29] *Code of Law, Foundations of the* Law iv.13: "I say that one should not amble about in the 'orchard' [physics and metaphysics] until he has filled his stomach with 'bread and meat'. Now, 'bread and meat' is to know the forbidden and the permitted, and similar things pertaining to the commandments."
[30] *Letter to Joseph* in *Iggerot ha-Rambam*, ed. I. Shailat, pp. 254–259, esp. 258.
[31] See *Commentary on the Mishnah, Introduction to Chapter Heleq, Sanhedrin; Guide* i.int, p. 6.
[32] *Eight Chapters* iv. The reference to the sages is found in *Deuteronomy Rabbah, Ki Tavo*, 8, passim.
[33] *Kuzari*, i.95.

a very short period of preparation: "The people prepared themselves for the level of prophecy [. . .] it took place after three days."[34] On the other hand, Maimonides holds that not everyone present at the Gathering at Mount Sinai heard the articulations of the divine voice, or that if they did, they heard and understood only the first two of the Ten Commandments.[35] Perhaps Maimonides emphasized in the earlier work the exalted level of the people leaving Egypt for rhetorical purposes, and he did not intend to imply that they were prophets. Or it may be that he changed in his mind regarding the level of the generation of the wilderness and the qualifications requisite for attaining prophecy.

In any case, Maimonides does consider Miriam, the sister of Moses and Aaron, one woman who attained both prophecy as well as life in the World to Come.[36] The description of Miriam's departure from this world (alongside that of Moses and Aaron) is presented as "salvation from death"; in this context of the eternity of the true-life, "the other prophets and excellent men are beneath this degree." One might infer from this that Miriam, like Aaron, attained the highest level of human perfection. However, one should note that in that same chapter, the three Patriarchs of the nation are specifically mentioned alongside Moses, as those who maintained their exalted level even when involved in mundane matters. It therefore seems that the ranking here is context-dependent: The Patriarchs were superior to all other prophets insofar as their level was not diminished by involvement in communal activities; Miriam and Aaron's superiority, by contrast, stemmed from dying at the height of intellectual activity. In any case, one cannot see in any of these achievements a true comparison to the prophetic level of Moses, who belonged to both groups. Maimonides clearly declares that Moses was superior to both Aaron and Abraham. Still, according to Maimonides, there was at least one woman in history who attained the level of prophecy, and merited immortality of the soul on the highest level.

* * *

As was mentioned, gentiles are also the "other" in Maimonides's thought. Here, in contrast to the perspective of R. Judah Halevi, there is no indication of a fundamental, "quasi-genetic" difference between Jews and non-Jews. However, Maimonides also shared the view of his time that

---

[34] *Guide* i.87.    [35] *Guide* ii.33.
[36] He adds to her name the epithet by which she is referred to in the Bible, "Miriam the prophetess" (*Code of Law, Impurity of Leprosy* xvi.16)

a certain population possessed a defective physical temperament, which could impair their intellectual ability. This is described by him in *Medical Aphorisms*, in which he cites Alfarabi, whom he greatly respected:

> Abu Nasser Alfarabi, in his *Book of Elements* has already mentioned that people living in temperate climate are more perfect in their intelligence [. . .] than people living in the far northern or southern climates.[37]

Those who speak Greek, Hebrew, Arabic, Persian, and Aramaic are counted among the populations of the temperate climates. Unlike Halevi, Maimonides did not believe that Greek wisdom had originated with Jews, or that the Greek nation had initially come from the north.[38] He also provides a different account of the beginning of human distribution in different climates. He assumes that, starting in the time of the Biblical figure Enosh, "Sabian" paganism began to emerge and later extended over the whole earth. However, through the influence of Abraham and his followers this idolatry was pushed from the center of civilization to "the extremities of the earth, [. . .] the Turks in the extreme North and the Hindus in the extreme South."[39] There is, therefore, a correlation between the presence of paganism in extreme climates and people in these regions being inferior and lacking temperate natures. Maimonides even describes these people and a cultural "missing link" between man and apes:

> Such individuals as the furthermost Turks found in the remote North, the Negroes found in the remote South, and those who resemble them from among them that are with us in these climes. The status of those is like that of irrational animals. To my mind, they do not have the rank of man, but have among the being a rank lower than the rank of man, but higher than the rank of apes.[40]

It may be that paganism did not disappear in the earth's extremities because the climatic conditions therein produced people of such inferior mental and emotional capacities that they were unable to grasp the scientific and theological enlightenment coming from the peoples of the temperate zone. In any case, even if the extreme climates, with their

---

[37] Maimonides's *Medical Aphorisms,* ch. 25, §58, tr. F. Rosner, cited in A. Melamed, *The Image of the Black in Jewish Culture: A History of the Other* (London: Routledge/Curzon, 2003), p. 140.

[38] See A. Melamed, *Raqaḥot ve-tabaḥot: ha-mitos 'al meqor ha-ḥokhmot (Apothecaries and Cooks: The Myth of the Source of the Sciences)* (Jerusalem: University of Haifa and Magnes Press, 2010), pp. 113–119.

[39] *Guide* iii.29, p. 515; for Enosh, see *Code of Law, Idolatry* i.1.

[40] *Guide* iii. 51, p. 618. In general, humans are no different from animals if they fail to actualize their human (i.e., intellectual) potential. See *Guide* i.7, p. 33.

deficiencies, do not contain Jews, their population is not coextensive with all gentiles. Maimonides holds that there is nothing in the non-Jew's physical or emotional makeup that bars them from attaining both prophecy and immortality.

In various writings addressed to different audiences, Maimonides explicitly characterizes prophecy as the perfection that typifies humanity as a whole, not just Jews:

> The sixth principle [of the Law] is prophecy, i.e., that one should know that there are individuals of the human species who possess exceedingly virtuous natures and great perfection, . . . .[41]
> One of the foundations of religion is to know that God bestows prophecy on human beings.[42]
> Our disbelief in the prophecies of Omar and Zayd is not due to the fact that they are not Israelites, as the unlettered folk imagine, [. . .] for Job, Zophar, Bildad, Eliphaz and Elihu are all considered prophets by us, despite the fact that they were not Israelites[. . .] but we give credence to a prophet, or disbelieve him, because of his claim not because of his descent.[43]

Balaam is not included in the list of gentile prophets, although he is presented by the Sages as being a prophet on par with Moses, or even greater than him (*Numbers Rabbah* xiv.20). This is not surprising, given that Maimonides considers Moses's prophecy to be sui generis:

> Thus, it has been made clear that his apprehension is different from that of all those who came after him in Israel, which is "a kingdom of priests" (Exod. 19:6) and all the more of all who came from other nations.[44]

That Scripture characterizes the Jewish people as "a kingdom of priests and a holy nation" is explained by Maimonides as a function of their "knowledge of Him, may He be exalted,"[45] meaning comprehension of God to the extent humanly possible. Since the Bible states that no prophet arose among the Jewish people like Moses, the possibility that a prophet like him could arise among lesser nations is certainly ruled out. The implicit assumption upon which this claim seems to rest is that there is a relationship between the achievements of a given prophet and the society to which he belongs. I will return to this below. Balaam – who, according to the aforementioned rabbinic source, may be considered the

---

[41] *Commentary on the Mishna, Introduction to Chapter Ḥeleq, Sanhedrin*, pt. 6.

[42] *Code of Law, Foundations of the Law* vii.1.

[43] "Epistle to Yemen," in *Crisis and Leadership: Epistles of Maimonides*, tr. A. S. Halkin, with essays by D. Hartman (Philadelphia: Jewish Publication Society of America, 1985), pp. 111.

[44] *Guide* ii.35, p. 368.     [45] *Guide* iii.32, p. 526.

greatest of gentile prophets – is described in the *Guide* as being on a sub-prophetic level even "when he was righteous."[46] Even those gentile prophets listed by Maimonides in his *Letter to Yemen* were not particularly successful. On the one hand, Job is presented in the *Guide* as a sub-prophet.[47] On the other hand, he is presented as being a merely fictional character, as Maimonides apparently favored the approach that his story is only an allegory.[48] Even so, as mentioned, Maimonides clearly states that fundamentally there is nothing preventing a non-Jew from attaining the level of prophecy.[49]

Together with prophecy, immortality is also presented by Maimonides as not limited to Jews:

> But each and every individual of those who came into the world whose spirit moved him and whose knowledge gave him the understanding to set himself apart in order to stand before God to serve Him, to worship Him, and to know God, and walked upright as God had made him [. . .] – he is sanctified as holy of holies, and God will be his share and inheritance forever and ever.[50]

Aside from these demands made of the elite, Maimonides also offers a less demanding entrance fee for the World to Come. For gentiles, who are not obligated in the 613 commandments, the fulfillment of a mere seven is sufficient: The prohibitions of idolatry, sexual immorality, murder, theft, eating the limb of a living creature, and the obligation to establish courts. Maimonides enumerates:

> He who accepts them is referred to as a resident alien[51] in all contexts [. . .] Anyone who accepts the seven commandments and is meticulous in their observance is one of the "pious gentiles"[52] and has a share in the World to Come, provided, that he accepts them and performs them because the Holy One, blessed be He, commanded them in the Law, and informed us through Moses, our teacher, that descendants of Noah had been commanded to observe them. However, if his observance is based on a reasoned conclusion, he is not a "resident alien,"

---

[46] *Guide* ii.45, p. 398. His wickedness is already spelled out at length in Maimonides's *Commentary on the Mishna, Sanhedrin*, X, pt. 2 and *Commentary on the Mishnah, Avot*, v.17.
[47] *Guide* ii.45, p. 398.     [48] *Guide* iii 22.
[49] See J. Levinger, "Prophecy as a Universal Human Phenomenon," in *Ha-Rambam ke-filosof u-khe-poseq* (*Maimonides as Philosopher and Codifier*), (Jerusalem: Bialik Institute, 1989), pp. 21–28 (Heb.).
[50] *Code of Law, Sabbatical and Jubilee* xiii.13.
[51] *ger toshav*. See Y. Blidstein, "On the Status of the Resident-Alien in Maimonides' Thought," *Sinai*, 101 (1988), 44–52 (Heb.)
[52] *ḥasidei umot ha-olam*.

nor one of the "pious gentiles,"; but [alternative reading: nor] one of
their wise persons.[53]

A gentile who accepts upon himself observance of the seven Noahide
Laws has the right to dwell in the land of Israel and is, therefore, called "a
resident alien," even if he does not exercise his right. If he is also
meticulous in observing what he has undertaken, he is considered
a "pious gentile" and has a share in the World to Come. However,
there is a further condition: He must accept it "because the Holy One,
blessed be He, commanded them in the Law, and informed us, by means
of Moses, our teacher, that Noahides had been commanded to observe
them," meaning, by the authority of the Mosaic Law. Such a person may
not remain an idolatrous Christian; nor may he remain a Muslim who
believes in the innovative teachings of the Quran and accepts its content
as authoritative Scripture.

Still, the relationship between the categories "resident alien," "pious
gentile," and "member of the world to come" is not entirely clear.
"Resident alien" is a legal category that obtains, according to Maimonides,
when the law of the Jubilee is in effect; when the Jubilee is not in effect, only
actual converts to Judaism are accepted.[54] Moreover, the category of "resident alien" may apply to gentiles only in the age of the King Messiah, "when
there will be a return to the days of old," and "the Sabbatical Years and
Jubilees will be observed as per the commandments written in the Law."[55]
Maimonides perhaps could allow for the situation where a Noahide becomes
a pious gentile without acquiring the legal status of a resident alien before
a Jewish court. And some have understood him as saying that gentile sages
who are not counted among the pious can obtain immortality. Yet he is
silent about this in his major writings.[56]

As many have emphasized, for Maimonides, the distinction between
someone who belongs to the Jewish people and one who does not is based
solely on one's being a member, either by birth or by choice, of a society
that accepts the binding character of Jewish law, or not. When an individual gentile accepts the yoke of the commandments upon himself as
a convert, he is a Jew, in every sense.

---

[53] *Code of Law, Kings* viii.10–11. See M. M. Kellner, *Confrontation*, pp. 241–250, and the rich
bibliography there.
[54] *Code of Law, Idolatry* x.6; Ibid., *Prohibited Intercourse*, xiv.1–6.     [55] *Code of Law, Kings* xi.1.
[56] In the *Letter to R. Ḥasdai Ha-Levi* (whose authenticity is disputed), Maimonides writes that gentiles
"certainly" have a portion in the World to Come "if they apprehend of the knowledge of the
Creator, may He be exalted, what is fitting to apprehend, and if they establish good traits in their
soul." See *Iggerot ha-Rambam*, ed. I. Shailat, pp. 673–684, esp. p. 681.

\*\*\*

Is the status of an ordinary gentile lower than that of an ordinary Jew? The answer is given in various contexts. In one place, Maimonides implies that the Jewish soul is of greater value inasmuch as the Jews believe in the principles of religion, irrespective of conduct: "And the Law concerned itself with the souls of the Israelites – whether wicked or righteous – because they accompany God, and believe in the foundation of the religion."[57] It would seem that in this context the "and" in the phrase "and believe" should be interpreted as a clarification: All Jews accompany God insofar as they believe in the foundation of the religion. The explanation for their superiority in this context is very similar to the statement mentioned above: Jews are considered to be "'a kingdom of priests and a holy nation' (Exod. 19, 6), through their knowledge of Him."[58]

In another context, the special status of the majority of Israelites is apparently characterized as the product of their actions alone. This can be seen in the category "the multitude of the adherents of the Law (*jumhūr ahl al-sharī'a*),"[59] which is meant to describe ordinary Jews. This population would seem to include Jewish women, as well, as they are only exempt from a small portion of the commandments. As will be discussed below, the path of advancement is not blocked off for them in principle even if, due to their nature, they typically have learning disabilities that make it hard for them to acquire metaphysical knowledge. The status of one who is in this category of "the multitude of the adherents of the Law" is described in the famous parable of the palace presented in the conclusion of the Guide.[60] According to this parable, humanity is ranked based on its degree of closeness to, or distance from, the king, who is located in the innermost chamber of the palace. This "multitude of the adherents of the Law" seek to reach and enter the palace but never see it, although they appear to be facing it. The groups within the population who are in a better state – much closer to the king – consist of those who have acquired knowledge in natural and in Divine science. A person's rank, in terms of his position relative to his goal, is determined by the amount of knowledge he has accumulated in these areas. Even so, aside from a person's position, there is an additional parameter that determines his rank: the realistic possibility that he will approach his goal. As will be clarified below, such a parameter

---

[57] *Code of Law, Murderer and Preservation of Life* xiii.14.    [58] *Guide* iii.32, p. 526.
[59] *Guide* iii.51, p. 619.    [60] Ibid.

exists among "the multitude of the adherents of the Law." This parameter consists of two components: The first is that they are in the city, rather than outside of it, and are facing the palace. The second is that since they are apparently facing the palace, every step that they take brings them closer to the king. As will be clarified below, these advantages distinguish the general Jewish public from others.

There is one group that is remote and located outside the regions of human civilization. It has already been mentioned above:

> Such individuals as the furthermost Turks found in the remote North, the Negroes found in the remote South, and those who resemble them from among them that are with us in these climes. The status of those is like that of irrational animals. To my mind, they do not have the rank of man, but have among the being a rank lower than the rank of man, but higher than the rank of apes.[61]

The position of the next group in the parable appears to be better, as they are located inside the city. However, although they "have opinions and are engaged in speculations," they "have adopted incorrect opinions," which led them to turn their backs on the palace. It is clear that Maimonides has in mind "deniers," i.e., heretics. As opposed to "ignorance," which connotes failure to know that which should be known, "denial" is expressed by "belief about a thing that is different from what the thing really is,"[62] i.e., error, albeit of a weighty sort. Those who believe that they know something are actually "far worse than the first" for two reasons: (1) the more they advance, the further they move from the truth and (2) they pose a threat to others: "They are those concerning whom necessity at certain times impels killing them [...] lest they should lead astray the ways of others."[63]

As mentioned above, those who primarily dwell in the North and South of the inhabited world are remnants of the ancient pagans. On the other hand, the heretics who err, who comprise the population of the central region, are civilized people who are not counted among the believers in the true religion. They are either heretical Jews or Christians, who are characterized by Maimonides as "worshippers of wood and stone," and not monotheists.[64] By contrast, the status of Muslims is different: "These Arabs are not idolaters, at all [...] and they are proper and impeccable monotheists."[65] Granted, the Quran is not divine Law, but that is not due

[61] Ibid., pp. 618–619.    [62] *Guide* i.36, p. 83 (and see n. 15).    [63] *Guide* iii.51, 619.
[64] See *Commentary on the Mishna, 'Avoda Zarah,* i.1–4 and *Guide* i.50, p. 50.
[65] *Letter to Ovadyah,* in *Iggerot ha-Rambam,* ed. I. Shailat, 231–241, esp. 238.

to its content. Rather, Muhammad was incapable of attaining prophecy and being God's messenger because of his ethical limitations, and he plagiarized Mosaic Law. Maimonides characterizes the Muslims as a monotheistic community, whose behavior is uncontrolled. But Muslims would not be considered "the multitude of the adherents of the Law"; on the contrary, both Muslims and Christians are deniers of the Law, because they claim that parts of it have been abrogated.[66]

One way or another, Maimonides frequently implies that the status of gentiles in certain legal areas is no different from that of animals. This finds expression in the rationales that Maimonides provides for several laws. One instance is where Maimonides notes "that the dwelling of a gentile is not considered a dwelling; rather, he is considered like an animal."[67] The other is where he deals with the prohibition against anointing someone using the anointing oil: "One who anoints vessels, an animal, and gentiles who are compared to animals, or the dead with it, is exempt, as it states: 'And you shall not anoint a man's flesh' (Exodus 30:32)."[68]

Aside from these instances, the most significant example for our current topic is the one cited in the beginning of this discussion, in which the status of the hybrid "other" is described: "a gentile + a woman = a gentile woman." The discussion concerns the prohibition against sexual relations between Jews and gentiles. Jews who violate this prohibition receive thirty-nine lashes, if they intended to marry, as, in such a case, they have violated a biblical prohibition. If, however, they have no intention of getting married, then they are only punished by receiving lashes for rebelling against a Rabbinic proscription. In a case in which the man is Jewish and the woman is a gentile, another punishment is added to that meted out by the court: If the act was performed publicly, the man may be killed by zealots. In any case, he is subject to excision at God's hand. Maimonides clarifies the severity of the harm inflicted in such a case:

This sin, despite the fact that it is not subject to capital punishment in court, should not be taken lightly. For it involves harm that has no parallel in any of the prohibited sexual acts. For a son who is born of a woman who is prohibited by virtue of forbidden sexual relations is his son in every respect, and is considered a Jew, despite the fact that he is a bastard. However, a son from a gentile woman is not his son, as it states: "For they will turn your son away from Me" (Deuteronomy 7:4), i.e., remove

---

[66] *Code of Law, Repentance* iii. 8. Cf. H. Kasher, *'Al ha-minim, ha-epikorsim, ve-ha-koferim be-mishnat ha-Rambam* (*Heretics in Maimonides' Teaching*) (Tel-Aviv: Hakibbutz Hameuchad, 2011), 165–167.
[67] *behemah*. See *Code of Law, Eruvim* ii.9.     [68] *Code of Law, Vessels of the Temple* i.6.

him from following God. And this causes him to attach himself to the
gentiles, whom God separated us from, and to turn away from God and to
betray Him.[69]

The serious consequence that might result is the birth of a gentile in
place of a Jew. The description of the transition from "following God" to
"turn[ing] away from God and to betray[ing] Him" corresponds, to
a certain degree, to the description that was mentioned above, to the effect
that Jews are superior to gentiles because "whether wicked or righteous –
because they accompany God, and believe in the foundation of the
religion."[70] In other words, to be born as a gentile rather than as a Jew is
considered to be a very significant "loss," and the Jew who is responsible for
it is severely punished.

What is the law concerning the gentiles involved in such a case? If it is
a situation of "a gentile who had relations with a Jewish woman, if she is
married he is put to death because of her; and if she is single, he is not put
to death."[71] In other words, his sentence corresponds, to a large degree, to
that of a Jew who had relations with a Jewish woman who is not his wife.
As mentioned, in this case, the product of these relations is a Jew in every
sense. However, the result is entirely different when a gentile woman is
involved, and her causing the "loss" makes her punishment more severe:

> If, however, an Israelite has intercourse with a gentile woman, whether she is
> a minor of three years and one day old or an adult, whether she is married or
> unmarried, even if the Israelite is only nine years and one day old, when he
> does so intentionally, she should be executed. She is executed, because she
> caused an Israelite to be involved in an unseemly transgression, like an
> animal. And this is explicit in the Law, as it states: "Yet they are the very ones
> who, at the bidding of Balaam, induced the Israelites [. . . .] and slay also
> every woman who has known a man carnally" (Numbers 31:16–17).[72]

The gentile woman is sentenced to death, regardless of whether she is an
adult or a child (three years and a day old), single or married. These factors
are relevant in terms of the punishment of a Jewish female: She is not
punished at all if she is a child, and is not put to death if she is single.
The criterion here is whether or not the Jewish man "enters into relations
with a gentile woman, when he does so intentionally." However, it makes
no difference that in terms of the gentile woman the act occurs under
duress. The explanation is "because she caused a Jew to be involved in an

[69] Code of Law, Prohibited Intercourse xii.6
[70] Code of Law, Murderer and Preservation of Life xiii.14.    [71] Ibid.
[72] Code of Law, Prohibited intercourse xii.1–10.

unseemly transgression, like an animal." This characterization ("like an animal") is explained in the following context:

> If a minor of nine years enters into relations with an animal or caused it to enter into relations with him, it is put to death because of him, and he is exempt [...] If one has relations with an animal unintentionally, or if a woman unintentionally caused an animal to enter into relations with her, the animal is not put to death because of them, despite the fact that they are adults.[73]

Stoning the animal is purely a function of its having caused a Jew to sin deliberately, even in a case where the sinner is not subject to punishment and is exempt himself. The same is true of a gentile woman. Like an animal, she is also considered an object in every sense, and is to be eliminated if she was the cause of a significant sin. The biblical precedent cited by Maimonides deals with the Midianite women who ensnared the Israelites: "Yet they are the very ones who, at the bidding of Balaam, induced the Israelites [...] and slay also every woman who has known a man carnally" (Numbers 31:16–17); which the Sages interpret as: "The text refers to those who were suitable to enter into relations with" (BT *Yevamot*, 60b). Maimonides relies on the biblical precedent of the Midianite women, despite the fact that he was not bound by Jewish law to comply with any earlier ruling concerning this principle. Maimonides's ruling can be understood in light of a statement of his which was already cited in another legal context, in which he raised a hypothetical question concerning discrimination against gentiles, in terms of damage that they cause:

> Do not be troubled by this matter and do not be shocked by it, just as you aren't shocked by the slaughter of animals, even though they did nothing wrong. For one whose human characteristics are not perfected is not truly a human being, and its telos is only for human beings.[74]

\* \* \*

In conclusion: As we have shown, Maimonides apparently did not see any fundamental impediment standing in the way of the "other" wishing to attain human perfection. Nonetheless, there seems to be a significant inequality of opportunity between Jewish men, on the one hand, and women or gentiles, on the other. The source of this inequality is biological,

---

[73] Ibid., i.16–18.
[74] *Commentary on the Mishna, Bava Kamma,* iv.3. See Levinger, "Prophecy," p. 25.

in the case of women, and historical-social, in the case of gentiles. A woman's moist temperament is the main cause of her learning disabilities, while the Jewish people's extraction from Abraham and Moses, who brought about intellectual and legal revolutions, respectively, is the cause of their superiority over the other nations. Therefore, "In terms of the gentile who did not stand at Sinai and was not given the Law, his chance of attaining human perfection is infinitely weaker than those of a Jew."[75] In any case, it would seem that the status of the average Jewish woman is closer to the status of "ignoramuses who involve themselves with the commandments" than to those "who are considered to be like animals."

[75] Ibid., p. 27.

# CHAPTER 4

# *What the* Guide of the Perplexed *Is Really About*

## Kenneth R. Seeskin

It may seem odd to ask what the *Guide of the Perplexed* is about given that Maimonides states his intention right from the start: to explain the meanings of certain terms occurring in the prophetic books.[1] He enlarges on this by saying that some terms are equivocal in the sense that they have several meanings, some are derivative in the sense that several meanings are derived from an original one, while some are equivocal in the sense that there are times when they are thought to be univocal and others when they are thought to be equivocal.

Maimonides also makes clear that the *Guide* is not for everyone. Those excluded include "the vulgar," who have not engaged in speculation, and those who have not studied the Law in any but its legal sense. That the book is not for the vulgar is hardly surprising. But by eliminating those who have not studied the Law in any but its legal sense, Maimonides could be writing off large numbers of traditional Jews in rabbinic academies.[2] In the Parable of the Palace, he will maintain that people who make no inquiry whatever regarding the rectification of belief "come up to the habitation and walk around it" but do not enter it.[3] In this way, they are inferior to those who have engaged in speculation even if the opinions they hold are true.

Although Maimonides does not say exactly what he means by "speculation" (*nazar*), the context leaves little doubt that it is the kind of reasoning that derives from the Greek philosophic tradition. So understood,

---

[1] *Guide* i.int, tr. Pines, p. 5. Unless otherwise noted, page references to the *Guide* are to the Pines translation.

[2] This calls into question L. Strauss's claim in his introductory essay to the Pines translation of the *Guide*, "How to Begin to Study *The Guide of the Perplexed*," p. xiv, that the *Guide* is not a philosophic book but "a book written by a Jew for Jews." Strauss allows that a Jew may still make use of philosophy and that Maimonides makes ample use of it. But he adds that "as a Jew, he [Maimonides] gives his assent where as a philosopher he would suspend his judgment." The question is whether "Judaism" and "philosophy" are monolithic. I hope to show that they are not.

[3] *Guide* ii.51, p. 619.

speculation can exist with or without a sacred text to guide it. Though Maimonides opens the *Guide* by talking about the conflict and resulting perplexity that arises between the Law and the intellect, one does not have to probe very far to see that the problem is more complicated, for neither adherents of the Law nor those who engage in speculation speak with a single voice.

Some of those who engage in speculation, e.g., the Mutakallimūn, think God exercised free choice in creating the world, and some, e.g., the Aristotelians, think that the world proceeds from God by necessity. Some think God has knowledge of individuals, others that he knows them only to the degree that they instantiate universal laws.[4] Even in regard to language, there are disagreements. Some argue that the terms we use to describe God are true by analogy in the sense that God's power or knowledge are more perfect and more permanent than ours; others argue, as Maimonides does, that they are completely equivocal.[5]

The situation is just as complicated if we turn from the philosophic tradition to the prophetic. The parables and metaphors that make up so much of the prophetic books have always been subject to competing interpretations. What does Jacob's ladder represent? Did Isaiah really think that lions and lambs would lie down together? In what way is the voice from the whirlwind an answer to Job? What is the meaning of the sexual imagery that permeates Song of Songs? Jewish tradition offers a variety of alternatives.

The problem Maimonides faced is this. On the one hand, speculation is needed to achieve the intellectual perfection that he thinks Judaism requires, the skills needed to enter the inner court of the ruler. On the other hand, experience shows that speculation is not always foolproof. We have seen that the philosophic tradition was anything but monolithic. For example, Maimonides claims that philosophers have been debating the subject of creation for 3,000 years and still not resolved the issue with any degree of certainty.[6]

In the Introduction, he expresses caution on how much truth any one person can grasp, saying that "Sometimes truth flashes out to us so that we think that it is day, and then matter and habit in their various forms conceal it so that we find ourselves again in an obscure night, almost as we were at first."[7] This raises the possibility that a person exposed to the give and take of speculative reasoning, seeing truth one moment and losing it another, might become disheartened and wind up distrusting reason altogether.

---

[4] *Guide* iii.20.    [5] *Guide* i.56.    [6] *Guide* i.71, p. 180.    [7] *Guide* i.int., p. 7.

To prevent speculation from going off the rails, Maimonides tells us that the *Guide* is intended for "a religious man for whom the validity of our Law has become established in his soul and has become actual in his belief."[8] In other words, it is intended for someone who is not going to be shaken by the fact that certainty on a wide range of issues may be beyond our reach. Even on those issues where it is within our reach, Maimonides questions whether a person will always be able to explain with total clarity what he has apprehended.[9]

To complete the picture, Maimonides goes on to say that the *Guide* has a second purpose: the explanation of obscure parables occurring in the books of the prophets but not explicitly identified as such. The ignorant think that such parables have only an external sense and no internal one. But, he continues, even those who possess knowledge may be inclined to interpret them according to their external sense and feel perplexity. I take this as further evidence that knowledge and perplexity are not necessarily incompatible. To repeat: Even the wisest among us are only capable of seeing a portion of the truth.

We may conclude, as Maimonides does, that the *Guide* is not intended to resolve every difficulty. Nor is it to set forth a complete exposition of every subject in a manner appropriate to a textbook. "For my purpose," Maimonides tells us, "is that the truths be glimpsed and then again concealed."[10] I suggest that the reason for concealment is not as Leo Strauss argues, that Maimonides is in possession of dangerous truths that he does not want to divulge in public, but that (1) some truths that can be known to be true but can only be understood by those with the proper training, and (2) owing to the nature of the subject matter, some disputes are beyond the ability of the human intellect to resolve.[11] In regard to (2), Maimonides tells us: "You should not think that these great *secrets* are fully and completely known to anyone among us. They are not."[12]

On my reading, the main purpose of the book is to tell us how to cope with this situation – how to identify truth in those instances when it flashes out and how not to lose one's way in those instances when it does not. Rather than a textbook, it is exactly what its name implies: a guide through

---

[8] Ibid., p. 5.    [9] Ibid., p. 8.    [10] *Guide* i.int, pp. 6–7.

[11] See L. Strauss, "The Literary Character of the *Guide of the Perplexed*," in *Persecution and the Art of Writing* (Glencoe, IL: The Free Press, 1952), pp. 55 ff. For the things that must be hidden from the multitude, see *Guide* I. 35, p. 80, but note that this list does not include the incorporeality of God, the fact that God is immutable, the fact that God is not subject to affections, or the fact that there is no likeness between God and any part of creation.

[12] *Guide* i.int., p. 7.

a difficult and complicated subject matter. As Alfred Ivry put it: "Maimonides is one of the perplexed for whom the *Guide* is written; his writing the book is his attempt to work his way out of conundrums he shared with the best minds of his time."[13]

## The Via Negativa

The first part of the *Guide* consists of 42 chapters, most of which are a lexicon of biblical terms that seem to imply that God has bodily features, e.g., "see," "stand," "touch," or "dwell." Maimonides's goal is to show that even if one limits one's horizon to Scripture, these terms are equivocal and allow for a variety of meanings. In chapter after chapter, he argues that words that seem to attribute bodily features to God are really ways of talking about intellectual apprehension or metaphysical perfection. On these issues, the philosophic tradition was monolithic, and Maimonides thought he spoke with complete certainty: A corporeal God is impossible because nothing material can be eternal, infinite, or logically simple.

In his opinion, the philosophic tradition was also monolithic on another point: that God cannot be defined.[14] According to Aristotle, definition proceeds by genus and specific difference. If a monotheistic God is absolute in the sense that he cannot be conditioned by anything, then there is no wider category under which God can be subsumed and thus no possibility of a cause prior to God as *living thing* is prior to *mammal*. While this may seem like an obvious point, its consequences are far reaching because if no definition can be given of God, then strictly speaking neither Maimonides nor anyone else can know what God is. Thus the conclusion: "None but He Himself can apprehend what He is."[15]

We should not underestimate the seriousness of this predicament because most sciences, e.g., Euclidean geometry, begin with rigorous definitions of their terms. If a circle is a set of points equidistant from a given point, then given certain postulates, we can deduce those properties that follow from the nature of circularity. But if God is not susceptible to definition, then metaphysics – or what Maimonides calls divine science – must proceed in a different manner.

Maimonides's first response is to follow the *via negativa*: If we cannot say what God is, we can at least say what God is not – in particular, anything

---

[13] A. Ivry, *Maimonides' Guide of the Perplexed* (The University of Chicago Press, 2016), p. 4.
[14] *Guide* i.52, p. 115. Cf. i.58, p. 135.    [15] *Guide* i.59, p. 139.

that implies finitude, divisibility, or temporality. The reason for this is that what Maimonides calls "attributes of negation" do not give us any knowledge of a thing's essence. As Aristotle explains in *Metaphysics* Z.4, an essence tells us what something *is*, not (we might add) what it is not. To say, for example, that God is *not* divisible may be true and important for mastering divine science; but it is not a definition.

Maimonides also raises doubts about predicates like "exists," "lives," or "knows," because as normally understood, they could lead one to think that God exists *through* or *by means* of existence, life, or knowledge. But this cannot be true. If God's existence were joined to God's essence, then there would have to be a cause superior to God that brought the two together. So rather than say "God exists" or "God knows," it would be better to say "God does not lack existence" or "God does not lack knowledge." Although Maimonides offers several arguments for the existence of God, by avoiding the positive formulation, we counter our normal tendency to think of existence or knowledge as attributes.

Even this has to be modified because according to Maimonides, there is a respect in which attributes of negation are still attributes and consign God to a wider category, e.g., the category of those things that are not divisible. Once God is in a wider category – even a category of which he is the only member – we run the risk of thinking that God possesses a property that must be added to his essence to give a complete description. How then can we say anything about God that is not misleading?

Maimonides answers by saying that "the bounds of expression in all languages are very narrow indeed, so that we cannot represent this notion [divine simplicity] to ourselves except through a certain looseness of expression."[16] Accordingly, even terms like "one" or "eternal" exhibit a certain degree of looseness: the former if it is understood as an accidental quality, the latter if it implies that God exists for all time rather than being outside of time altogether.

It is well known that ultimately Maimonides comes to regard Psalm 65:2 ("Silence is praise to Thee") as "the most apt phrase concerning this subject" and recommends that we limit ourselves to silence and the apprehensions of the intellect.[17] Yet for all its imperfections, metaphysical discourse does have a role to play – to "give the mind the correct direction toward the true reality of the matter"[18] or "conduct the mind toward the utmost reach that man may attain."[19]

---

[16] *Guide* i.57, pp. 132–3.   [17] *Guide* i.59, pp. 139–40.   [18] Ibid., p. 133.   [19] *Guide* i.58, p. 135.

Note how both of these descriptions are qualified: not the true reality of the matter but the correct direction in which to search for it, not the utmost reach but the utmost reach that *we* can achieve. Such discourse frees us from erroneous ways of thinking and helps us recognize our own limitations. But neither of these functions implies that it culminates in a body of propositions that stand to God in the way that the theorems of Euclidean geometry stand to circularity.

The only exception that Maimonides recognizes is the Tetragrammaton (YHWH), the proper name of God as revealed to Moses in Exodus 3:14. Maimonides interprets God's proclamation "I AM THAT I AM" to mean that the subject (God) is identical with the predicate (exists) rather than an attribute added to it. In his words: "This name is not indicative of an attribute but of simple existence and nothing else."[20]

Can we say, then, that simple or necessary existence constitutes the essence of God? It would simplify matters if we could, but as Maimonides insists several times, the meaning of terms when applied to God has nothing in common with their meaning when applied to us.[21] When applied to everything other than God, "exists" is an accident that attaches (or is superadded) to the thing that exists.[22] That is why the existence of everything other than God requires an external cause.

Because God's existence is not an accident, there is no possibility of beginning with existence as we normally understand it and trying to extrapolate to existence in God.[23] As Maimonides expresses it: "There is accordingly an existent whom none of the existent things that He has brought into existence resembles, and who has nothing in common with them in any respect."[24] And again, in connection with Exodus 33:23 ("My face shall not be seen): "The true reality of My existence as it veritably is cannot be grasped."[25] In light of this, the Tetragrammaton, which conveys the idea of necessary existence, leaves us in the dark as to what the nature of that existence is.

It follows that while "God exists" constitutes what Maimonides calls "the foundation of foundations," we cannot give a positive account of either of its terms.[26] In the words of Aquinas, we are "united to Him as to

---

[20] *Guide* i.63, p. 156.      [21] For example, *Guide* i. 35, p. 80, i. 56, p. 130, and i.58, p. 137.
[22] *Guide* i.57, p. 132.
[23] Cf. J. Stern, *The Matter and Form of Maimonides' Guide* (Cambridge: Harvard University Press, 2013), p. 157, who suggests that when it comes to God, we should write "necessarily exists" so as not to confuse God's manner of existing with ours.
[24] *Guide* i.58, p. 137.      [25] *Guide* i.37, p. 86.      [26] *Code of Law, Foundations of the Torah*, i.1.

one unknown."[27] This does not mean that either thinker would have questioned the truth of God's existence; in fact both offer multiple arguments in support of it. It would be better to say that "God exists" is foundational in the sense that it conducts the mind toward the utmost reach that we may attain and provides the cornerstone for an entire worldview. But anyone who thinks that the logical form of "God exists" resembles that of "Giraffes exist" or even "I exist" is seriously mistaken.

What then should we say about Maimonides's demonstrations of the existence of God? If we take Maimonides at his word, his most explicit demonstration takes the form of a constructive dilemma.[28] If the world was created, there must be a creator, in which case God exists. If the world is eternal, there must be something responsible for the eternal motion of the spheres, in which case God exists. Therefore in Maimonides's words "there can be no doubt" that God exists – or that he is one and incorporeal.

Let us assume that the dichotomy created/eternal is exhaustive so that the demonstration is valid. If so, it establishes God's existence without making any positive claim about the nature of God. Following Aristotle, it would be a demonstration of the fact (*to hoti*) rather than the reasoned fact (*to dihoti*).[29] The difference is that while the former tells us *that* something is the case, the latter tells us *why*. For Aristotle, to know a thing in the true sense of the term, we need to know what it is, why it is, and why it cannot be otherwise than what it is.

Consider an analogy. Suppose I showed you a black box that generated predictable amounts of light at regular intervals. You would conclude that there must be a mechanism in the box that is responsible for what comes out. But suppose that when you asked what this mechanism is, I told you that there is no way to know. Under these circumstances, while you could be certain that a mechanism must be present for light to appear, you would lack a scientific understanding of its appearance because you would be unable to provide a causal explanation for what is happening.

The problem is that we can never provide a causal explanation for the existence of God for the simple reason that there is nothing prior to God on which his existence depends. In view of this, a demonstration of the fact may be all we can hope for. Josef Stern accounts for this by saying that while we can have certainty about God's existence, we cannot have

---

[27] *Summa Theologica*, 1.12.13.

[28] *Guide* i.71, pp. 181–2. Pines renders *burhan* as "demonstration" and *burhān qāṭi'* as "cogent demonstration." Both are to be distinguished from "proof" (*dalīl*), which is a weaker form of argument. The distinction can be found at ii.18, p. 299.

[29] *Posterior Analytics*, 71b21–23.

knowledge of it.[30] At *Guide* i.50, Maimonides defines certainty (*yaqīn*) as belief in something together with the realization that a contrary belief is impossible and that no basis can be found for a different belief. Note, as Stern does, that Maimonides's understanding of certainty is not as rigorous as Aristotle's understanding of knowledge because nowhere does Maimonides say that to have certainty, one must be able to answer the question *why*.

Against this Charles Manekin argues that in the Arabic Aristotelian tradition, certainty or certain knowledge came to replace knowledge in Aristotle's sense of *episteme* as the end of demonstration.[31] In the case of Alfarabi, the distinction between an explanatory and a causal demonstration still stands as does the Aristotelian ideal of full explanatory knowledge. But, continues Manekin, from the standpoint of the certainty that demonstrations are supposed to provide, demonstrations of the fact are not inferior to explanatory demonstrations. Thus, both could legitimately be termed *knowledge*.

Spatial limitations prevent me from examining the historical background that informs Maimonides's arguments. As we saw, he is confident that his demonstration of God's existence yields certainty about which there can be no doubt. But this does not obscure the fact that the conclusion of his demonstration still incorporates a large measure of unknowing, for not only are we unable to give a positive account of *what* God is, we are unable to give a positive account of the *nature* of his existence.

Suppose I told you that it is absolutely certain that *x F*'s. But when you asked me to explain what *x* is or to characterize the precise way in which it *F*'s, I told you that the limitations of human knowledge prevent me from saying anything positive. Given the general tendency of philosophers over the ages to relax Aristotle's stringent standards for knowledge, we can imagine situations in which it might be appropriate to credit me with knowing that *x F*'s. But even for us, the limitations under which I am working make a difference. While I may have a kind of knowledge, it would be a knowledge manqué, not science.

If we cannot have positive knowledge of God or the manner of his existence, then there will be severe limits on knowledge of the way in which

---

[30] Ibid.

[31] Manekin, "Maimonides and the Arabic Aristotelian Tradition of Epistemology," in D. M. Freidenreich and M. Goldstein (eds.), *Beyond Religious Borders* (Philadelphia: University of Pennsylvania Press, 2012), pp. 78–91. Manekin bases some of his argument on the work of Deborah Black, "Knowledge (*'Ilm*) and Certitude (*Yaqīn*) in Al-Fārābī's Epistemology," *Arabic Sciences and Philosophy*, 16 (2006), 11–45.

God confers existence on other things. To be sure, God is not responsible for the world in the way that an acorn is responsible for an oak tree or a chicken is responsible for an egg. In fact, Maimonides concludes his discussion of the Book of Job by saying: "Our intellects do not reach the point of apprehending how these natural things that exist in the world of generation and corruption are produced in time."[32]

As we will see in the next section, neither do our intellects reach the point of understanding how things are produced in the heavenly world. Again from Maimonides: "Matter is a strong veil preventing the apprehension of that which is separate from matter as it truly is . . . Hence whenever our intellect aspires to apprehend the deity or one of the intellects, there subsists this great veil interposed between the two."[33]

## Creation

We turn now from God to the production of the world from God. The three alternatives Maimonides discusses are that of Moses, according to which creation is both *de novo* and *ex nihilo*, that of Plato, according to which creation is *de novo* but not *ex nihilo*, and Aristotle, according to which it is neither.[34] So the Aristotelian position is committed to an eternal world whose structure is explained by the continuous information of matter through the process of emanation. Such emanation is not the result of a divine decision but follows by necessity from the nature of the divine essence.

The fact that there are three alternatives and intelligent people who defend them means that the discussion cannot proceed by way of demonstration. As Maimonides tells us, "In all things whose true reality is known through demonstration there is no tug of war and no refusal to accept a thing proven."[35] Moreover, the fact that there is give and take in Maimonides's treatment of creation, including his partial acceptance of the Platonic position, is a clear sign that demonstration has given way to something else, in particular the process of examining each alternative and choosing the one that generates the fewest doubts.[36]

---

[32] *Guide* iii.23, p. 496.    [33] *Guide* iii.9, pp. 436–7.
[34] By creation *de novo*, I mean that there was a first instant in time or, alternatively, that the age of the universe is finite. By creation *ex nihilo*, I mean that the act of creation did not involve a material cause. For more detailed discussion of these alternatives and Maimonides's whole treatment of creation, see K. Seeskin, *Maimonides on the Origin of the World* (New York: Cambridge University Press, 2005).
[35] *Guide* ii.25, pp. 328–29.
[36] *Guide* ii.3, p. 254; ii.23, p. 321. For more on this point, see Manekin, "Maimonides and the Arabic Aristotelian Tradition of Epistemology," pp. 89–95.

Maimonides's arguments regarding creation take two forms. The first group tries to show that the creation of the world *de novo* is possible. The second tries to show that the creation of the world *de novo* is the best explanation of the evidence we have. I take it as uncontroversial that even if these arguments are valid, Maimonides would not have demonstrated creation *de novo*. All he would have done is show that the eternity of the world, though logically possible, is not the most attractive option. If this is right, then despite the problems that acceptance of eternity would raise for the traditional understanding of Genesis 1, it cannot be ruled out completely.

At *Guide* ii.14, Maimonides divides the arguments in favor of eternity into two groups: those derived from the nature of God and those derived from the nature of the world. Given the fact that God's essence is beyond human comprehension, no argument that begins with the nature of God and moves to the production of the world from God can be known with certainty. In deference to Aristotle Maimonides claims that even he did not regard the arguments for eternity as demonstrations.[37]

The other strategy is to prove eternity based on the nature of the world. Because everything in the sublunar realm is subject to generation and destruction, the obvious place to look for support is the heavenly realm. We have seen that here too Maimonides believes that the limits of human knowledge prevent us from understanding things as they truly are. Maimonides will elaborate on this point by saying that both in Aristotle's day and his own, astronomy falls far short of what would be required of a rigorous science. Therefore any attempt to construct a demonstration of eternity from observation of the heavenly bodies is perilous at best.

Before getting to astronomy, Maimonides adds a further argument to the effect that the creation of the world as a whole need not resemble changes that take place within it.[38] According to Aristotle, change involves three principles: act, potency, and an underlying substratum. This led to the claim that before the world was created, it would have to have the potential to be created and the only way for this to happen is if there were an underlying substratum: prime matter. In short, creation of the world – or anything – *ex nihilo* is impossible.

Against this Maimonides points out that the principles that explain change in a perfected creature need not resemble those that explain its genesis or creation. He concludes that we cannot draw inferences from the way the world is now to the way it was first produced. If so, then any

---

[37] *Guide* ii.13, pp. 291–2.    [38] *Guide* ii.17.

attempt to treat creation along the lines associated with change amounts to speculation.

Having shown that eternity cannot be demonstrated so that some form of creation is at least possible, Maimonides sets out to show "by means of arguments that come close to being a demonstration" that, based on everything we know, the best option, i.e., the one to which the fewest number of doubts are attached, is that God created the world by an act of will rather than a necessary process.[39]

This takes us back to astronomy. If the existence of the world could be explained by a necessary process, we would expect there to be a satisfactory account of the motion of the heavenly bodies. Unfortunately the current state of astronomy shows that no such account is available and that there is little hope of ever finding one. Maimonides goes on to show that not only is the motion of the heavenly bodies perplexing but their existence and separate identities are as well. According to the philosophers, nothing but a single simple thing can proceed from a single simple thing.[40] If we assume that God is single and simple, how can we account for multiple intellects that are not simple and multiple spheres that are composites of matter and form? Maimonides concludes that everything that Aristotle has said about the sublunar realm is "indubitably correct," but that everything he says about the sphere of the moon and above is "something analogous to guessing and conjecturing."[41]

Here as elsewhere, Maimonides never passes up an opportunity to stress the limits of human knowledge. Quoting Psalm 115 ("The heavens are the heavens of the Lord, but the earth He has given to the sons of Man"), he maintains that the heavens are too far away and too high in place and rank for us to resolve the issues that confront us. Accordingly the goal of astronomy is not to tell us the way things actually are but to offer a mathematical model that preserves the idea of natural motion and does a good job of predicting the observable phenomenon. In the end, Maimonides sides with the Mosaic account of creation not because it can be known with certainty but for two reasons, neither of which is decisive: (1) it avoids many of the problems that beset the Aristotelian account, in particular its inability to explain planetary motion, and (2) by preserving will and purpose in God, it allows one to hold on to things like miracles and divine promises and therefore comes closest to preserving the traditional interpretation of Genesis 1.[42]

[39] *Guide* ii.19, p. 303.　　[40] *Guide* ii.22, p. 317.　　[41] Ibid., pp. 319–20.
[42] Note, however, that Maimonides himself departs from the traditional understanding of Genesis 1 at ii.30, though not by opting for eternity.

## Prophecy

Like his discussion of creation, Maimonides's discussion of prophecy begins with three alternatives: that God can turn anyone into a prophet by an act of will, that prophecy represents the perfection of human nature and can be achieved only by rigorous training, and that while God cannot turn anyone at all into a prophet, he can prevent someone from becoming a prophet who is otherwise suited for it. The first alternative makes prophecy a miracle, the second makes it a purely natural phenomenon, and the third represents a compromise.

Maimonides is sharply critical of the first position, attributes the second to the philosophers, and describes the third as "the opinion of our Law and the foundation of our doctrine." Note that if the third view is correct, then while prophecy might not always come to one, when it does, it would be a natural phenomenon in the sense that God is not giving the prophet anything above and beyond what his own faculties are capable of providing.

It is obvious that Maimonides must address several problems. The first is that Scripture does not seem to follow a consistent pattern on who does and who does not receive the gift of prophecy. On a literal reading, Hagar and Balaam hear the voice of God, while Baruch, who is much better qualified, does not. In the latter case, why would God want to deny someone a perfection to which he was otherwise suited?[43] The second is the uniqueness of Mosaic prophecy and the Sinai experience. The third is that sometimes God addresses people directly, sometimes in a dream or by means of an angel.

Finally, there is the general problem that we encountered in the previous section. Naturalistic explanations work well when we are dealing with sublunar phenomena that can be observed up close over a period of time. Neither God nor the creation of the world fit these criteria. Though prophecy might seem to be a better fit, it still faces difficulties. How exactly does a human intelligence, which is anchored in the material realm, gain a glimpse of the metaphysical realm? How can a one-time event like revelation at Sinai be studied scientifically?

With respect to Sinai, Maimonides argues that the first two commandments – the acceptance of monotheism and rejection of idolatry – can be known by speculation (or demonstration) alone. Thus: "Now with regard

---

[43] It is possible that Jeremiah's reply to Baruch ("Seekest though great things for thyself? Seek them not," 45:4–5) may indicate that despite all his training, Baruch was not suited for prophecy after all.

to everything that can be known by demonstration, the status of the prophet and that of everyone else who knows it are equal; there is no superiority of one over the other."[44] From a legal perspective, this means that with respect to the first two of the Ten Commandments, a prophet is not necessary; it is only with respect to the last eight that we need a prophet. Earlier in *Guide* i.2, Maimonides maintained that matters that pertain to good and bad behavior are not based on demonstration but on "generally accepted opinions and those adopted in virtue of tradition." Why then is the prophet's superior talent needed? Why, for example, should an ordinary person not be able to figure out that murder, lying, and stealing are wrong?

These questions become central when Maimonides takes up the prophecy of Moses in Book Two, chapters 34–5. According to Maimonides, prophecy consists of an overflow from God "through the intermediation of the Active Intellect, toward the rational faculty of the prophet and then to his imaginative faculty."[45] This implies that both faculties must achieve a degree of perfection for prophecy to occur.

Maimonides insists, however, that this definition applies to every prophet *except* Moses.[46] For present purposes, the chief difference between Moses's prophecy and that of the others are: (1) Moses's prophecy was purely intellectual and did not involve the imagination, and (2) Moses's prophecy did not involve an angel or intermediary because with him alone, God spoke "mouth to mouth" (Numbers 12:8).[47]

If Moses's prophecy was purely intellectual and did not involve the imagination, why does the record of his prophecy – the Torah – contain 611 commandments based on generally accepted opinions and a host of parables and metaphors that bespeak not just *an* imagination but a particularly lively one?[48] This is not to say that the commandments themselves are parables but that the narratives that surround them often are. We can accept Maimonides's claim that not everything that reached Moses also reached the rest of Israel.[49] But we are still left with the question of why the Torah appeals to the imagination so readily and effectively.

It is possible that a perfected intellect might stimulate the imagination if both faculties are at work. It is also possible that a perfected imagination might help a prophet grasp an intellectual truth intuitively rather than discursively. Either way, we are left wondering what exactly Mosaic prophecy involved and what it means to say that no intermediary was required.

---

[44] *Guide* ii.33, p. 364.   [45] *Guide* ii.36, p. 369.   [46] *Guide* ii.35, p. 367.   [47] *Guide* ii.34; ii. 37.
[48] Cf. Strauss, "How to Begin," p. xxxix.   [49] *Guide* ii.33, p. 363.

Did Moses bypass the Agent Intellect or does the lack of an intermediary refer once again to the absence of imagination?[50] Although both interpretations are possible, the former would play havoc with the philosophic conception of prophecy by making Moses superior to the heavenly intelligences.

Given the immediacy of Moses's prophecy, Maimonides maintains that even though the people could demonstrate the truths embodied in the first two commandments, Moses's apprehension of them was still superior. As to what exactly Moses apprehended and what the people did, Maimonides takes refuge in the fact that we are dealing with something whose true nature is beyond our grasp and identifies the Sinai experience as one of the mysteries of the Torah: "The true reality of that apprehension and its modality are quite hidden from us, for nothing like it happened before and will not happen after."[51]

All this leaves open the question of what God contributed to the Sinai experience and what Moses did. To return to the Introduction to Book I, was Moses able to apprehend more or brighter flashes of light than anyone else because of a superior level of apprehension or is it that God intervened by producing flashes that were denied to everyone else? Was the voice that the people heard at Sinai an actual sound (albeit not words), or is this too a metaphor for some form of apprehension?[52]

Howard Kreisel is right to say that while Maimonides's general tendency is to move in a naturalistic direction regarding prophecy, he leaves open the possibility that some sort of supernatural element or divine volition is involved as well.[53] Note, for example, that if it is true that God can prevent someone from becoming a prophet who is otherwise suited for it, then divine volition would have to play a role in every case of prophecy if only to decide *not* to interfere with what natural forces would bring about on their own. This does not mean that God would make a separate decision for each possible prophet but that God's eternal will would have to have consequences that apply in every case.

---

[50] For an extended discussion of this question, and the difficulties in trying to resolve it, see Howard Kreisel, *Prophecy: The History of an Idea in Medieval Jewish Philosophy* (Dordrecht: Kluwer Academic Publishers, 2001), 215 ff. Note, as Kreisel does, that the intermediary or "angel" that played no part in Moses's prophecy could refer to either the Active Intellect based on i.49 or to the imagination based on ii.34 and ii.37.

[51] *Guide* ii.33, p. 366.

[52] For further discussion of this issue, see Benjamin D. Sommer, "Revelation at Sinai in the Hebrew Bible and in Jewish Theology," *Journal of Religion*, 79 (1999), 422–451.

[53] Kreisel, *Prophecy*, pp. 307–8.

Once again we do not have a firm enough understanding of the phenomenon in question to be able to formulate a demonstration, which means that despite the clarity Maimonides has brought to the discussion of prophecy, we still have an intellectual tug of war. In this way, the discussion of prophecy plays a pivotal role in the book. Like creation, the Sinai experience will never be repeated. Also like creation, it raises the question of how much knowledge an earth-bound creature (even one whose prophecy does not involve the imagination) can have of the heavenly realm. Evocative as it is, the metaphor of flashes of light across a dark sky leaves the question unanswered.

Looking ahead to providence, Maimonides's account of prophecy raises the question of how far into the earthly realm God's governance and knowledge extend. Was God aware of the specific features that made Jeremiah a legitimate candidate for prophecy at an early age but stood in the way of Baruch's candidacy even at maturity? Was this the product of a decision or was it something that nature brought about on its own? It is to the subject of providence that we now turn.

## Providence

Where creation and prophecy presented us with three options, providence presents us with five, ranging from the Aristotelian view, according to which providence extends only to things that are permanent and changeless, to the Ash'arite view, according to which providence extends to everything in the universe down to the smallest and most trivial things.[54] Although Maimonides has more sympathy with the former than with the latter, he points out that even the Aristotelian view creates problems. Because my existence as an individual is neither permanent nor changeless, on the Aristotelian view, I would not participate in God's providence in a direct or immediate way.

By contrast the species *humanity* is permanent and changeless, from which it follows that God is aware of the faculties that I possess and what it would mean for me to perfect them. To take a simple example, God knows that I need food to survive but not what I am going to eat for dinner tonight. This coheres with *Metaphysics* Z.15, where Aristotle argues that because definition is always of the universal, an individual cannot be known in its individuality. Thus anything that pertains to it *qua* individual comes about by chance.

---

[54]  *Guide* iii.17.

Maimonides criticizes Aristotle on the grounds that if he is right, there would be no difference between the fall of a leaf from a tree and the drowning of excellent people on a ship because neither pertains to anything permanent and changeless. He therefore feels duty bound to incorporate some of the traditional view (i.e., the opinion of the Law), which holds that people are rewarded or punished according to what they deserve.

With his usual modesty, he prefaces his opinion with a disclaimer: "I am not relying upon the conclusion to which demonstration has led me." Simply stated, his opinion amounts to this: In the sublunar realm, providence varies according to the degree to which things participate in the divine overflow and the species with which it is united.[55] Thus, God watches over every plant and animal species and endows them with the faculties they need to survive.[56] This is a manifestation of divine justice and insures the continued existence of the species but not of the individuals who embody it.

Because humans are the only species endowed with reason, they are the only species where divine providence reaches down to individuals. But here too, providence reaches individuals only to the degree that they have perfected their reason; if they have not, their status is no different from that of the rest of the animal kingdom.

To complete the picture, we must add that according to Maimonides, a person who perfects his reason would come to see, as Job does on Maimonides's reading, that perfecting one's reason and worshipping God are the noblest things a person can do and the only things valuable as ends in themselves.[57] Accordingly: "He [Job] knew God with a certain knowledge, he admitted that true happiness, which is the knowledge of the deity, is guaranteed to all who know Him and that a human being cannot be troubled in it by any of all the misfortunes in question."[58]

It is not that God puts a protective shield around excellent people but that their view of what is important in life and what is not has undergone a fundamental change: Such a person comes to realize that the normal things people devote themselves to and complain about, e.g., loss of property, loss of social standing, or loss of health, pale into insignificance compared to the perfection of reason. In this way, excellent people emulate God by focusing their attention on things that are permanent and unchanging rather than things that come about by chance.

---

[55] *Guide* iii.17, pp. 471–2.    [56] *Guide* iii.12, p. 447; iii.17, p. 473; iii.25, p. 503.
[57] This becomes clear at *Guide* iii.24, p. 497; iii.27, p. 511; iii.54, pp. 634–5.
[58] *Guide* iii.23, pp. 492–3.

The merit of this view is that it frees Maimonides from saying that God takes special notice of Susan's intellectual progress but has disdain for John's lack of it. But problems remain. As Maimonides recognizes, God is perfect in every way, which means that God's knowledge must be perfect. Thus: "It is almost a primary notion that ignorance with regard to anything whatever is a deficiency and that He . . . is ignorant of nothing."[59] In fact, God's knowledge of the world is of a different order than ours because while we know things by looking at them, God knows them according to the special knowledge that comes to the one who has produced them. As Genesis 1.31 tells us: "And God saw everything that He had made, and, behold, it was very good."[60]

The problem is: What does it mean to say that God is ignorant of nothing? Does it mean that God is not ignorant of anything *knowable* so that he knows everything that is necessary and eternal or does it mean that God knows everything that ever has or will happen? The former fits well with Maimonides's modified Aristotelianism, and in a later age will be taken up and defended by Gersonides; the latter fits with the traditional view of providence. Although my own predilections are with the former, Maimonides stresses that unlike human knowledge, God's knowledge that a possible thing will come into existence does not rob it of its status as possible.[61] If God's knowledge extends to things that are merely possible, then it must reach beyond the realm of the eternal verities.

The obvious way to resolve this question would be to inquire into the nature of divine knowledge. But this possibility is blocked for a familiar reason. As Maimonides puts it: "The selfsame incapacity that prevents our intellects from apprehending his essence also prevents them from apprehending His knowledge of things as they are."[62] Or, more fully in regard to the Book of Job:

> The purpose of all these things is to show that our intellects do not reach the point of apprehending how these natural things that exist in the world of generation and corruption are produced in time and of conceiving how the existence of the natural force within them has originated them. They are not things that resemble what we make. How then can we wish that His governance of, and providence for, them . . . should resemble our governance of, and providence for, the things we do govern and provide for?[63]

If we cannot know the nature of divine causality, then we cannot say for sure how far God's knowledge of creation extends. While Maimonides's

---

[59] *Guide* iii.19, p. 477 also see *Guide* iii.21, p. 485.   [60] Cf. *Guide* iii.25, p. 503.
[61] *Guide* iii.20, p. 482.   [62] *Guide* iii.20, p. 482.   [63] *Guide* iii.25, p. 496.

practical message ("Focus your attention on what is necessary and eternal") remains intact, the nature and extent of divine providence is still problematic.

The issue at stake here is the same one that we encountered in the discussions of creation and prophecy: a distant God governed by metaphysical necessity versus a God who acts for a purpose and has some degree of involvement in human affairs. To this day, scholars are not sure which one represents Maimonides's considered view. As with creation, both sides of the dispute give rise to doubts. In the next section, I will argue that the normal question that scholars raise, "Which side is Maimonides on?" is misplaced. The question should be, "Why does Maimonides want us to work through these problems?"

## Conclusion

Putting everything together, we face the following predicament: (1) Although we have demonstrations showing that God is a single, simple thing, we cannot give a definition of God. (2) Although we can be certain that God exists, we cannot give a positive account of the nature of his existence. (3) Although we have good grounds for believing that God created the world from will and purpose, we must concede that eternity is still a possibility. (4) Although we have a workable definition of prophecy, we cannot assume that what is true of Moses and Sinai is also true of other prophets. (5) Although we have grounds for believing that God exercises some form of providence over his creation, we cannot say for sure how far his providence extends. (6) We have 611 commandments setting the boundaries of good and bad behavior as determined by generally accepted opinions.

There will always be people who want to suspend judgment on anything that admits of the slightest possibility of doubt. To these people Maimonides has a ready answer: If all we accept are demonstratively certain truths, human life as we know it would be impossible. Some things must be accepted on the basis of factual demonstrations, some on the basis of the weight of the evidence, some on the basis of practical necessity. By the same token, there will always be people who accept what Scripture says in a literal fashion without asking whether it makes rational sense. Neither group can enter the ruler's palace as described at *Guide* iii.51.

What then do we need to get inside? First, one has to adopt correct opinions. Next comes speculation. While speculation may lead to certainty, we have seen that there are important cases where it does not. Some people would suggest that when speculation does not yield certainty, we have no choice but to rely on faith. Maimonides makes clear, however, that true opinions based on traditional authority are not enough. To enter the palace, one must have an honest assessment of what reason can establish and what it cannot:

> He, however, who has achieved demonstration, to the extent that that is possible, of everything that may be demonstrated; and who has ascertained in divine matters, to the extent that that is possible, of everything that may be ascertained; and who has come close to certainty in those matters in which one can only come close to it – has come to be with the ruler in the inner part of the habitation.[64]

This passage should be read in light of a similar one at i.32:

> For if you stay your progress because of a dubious point; if you do not deceive yourself into believing that there is a demonstration with regard to matters that have not been demonstrated; if you do not hasten to reject and categorically to pronounce false any assertions whose contradictories have not been demonstrated; if, finally you do not aspire to apprehend that which you are unable to apprehend – you will have achieved human perfection and attained the rank of Rabbi Akiba.[65]

Taken together these passages ask for a cautious attitude toward human knowledge. Some things, e.g., that God is incorporeal, can be known with certainty and should be taught to the multitude. But on many of the questions Maimonides raises, all we can do is come close to certainty. Maimonides's point is that on those questions, we should be satisfied with what we have and not claim to have achieved anything more. So far from getting us closer to God, dogmatism about matters that exceed human understanding pushes us further away. To the question "How should one cope with the limits of human knowledge?" Maimonides has another answer: Accept them for what they are and recognize why they cannot be exceeded. For Maimonides, achieving such recognition is not just a good thing to do; it is a sacred mission in its own right. When it is completed, "the souls will find rest . . ., the eyes will be delighted, and the bodies will be eased of their toil and their labor."[66]

This takes us back to the suggestion that Maimonides's purpose in writing the *Guide* was to conceal a doctrine too destructive of the traditional view of Judaism to be put before the average reader. The main problem with this view is that even if we ignore the "average" reader and

---

[64] *Guide* iii.51, p. 619.     [65] *Guide* i.32, p. 68.     [66] *Guide* i. Intro., p. 20.

focus on the elite, centuries of commentary on the book reveal that there is no consensus on what Maimonides's real opinion was.

In a recent work, Moshe Halbertal offers four interpretive possibilities: the skeptical, the mystical, the conservative, and the philosophical.[67] Each is internally consistent, each has textual support, and each has had proponents over the centuries. If the purpose of the book were to communicate to the elite a fixed doctrine, then history shows it was a failure. If, however, the purpose of the book is twofold – first, to clear up confusions where they exist, and second, to explore the various alternatives that arise in the discussion of speculative matters, to raise questions about them, and to stimulate further investigation – then history shows that it was an unparalleled success, for no other book in Jewish philosophy has aroused so much discussion at so advanced a level.

---

[67] M. Halbertal, *Maimonides: Life and Thought* (Princeton University Press, 2014), 279 ff. Note Halbertal's conclusion (p. 357), "It seems to me undeniable that the *Guide of the Perplexed* leaves multiple possibilities open to the reader, and that may well have been Maimonides' intention." Also see Kreisel, *Prophecy*, p. 211: "in the case of Maimonides the author clearly *intended* that different readers understand his position in different ways in their quest for attaining enlightenment from his work."

# CHAPTER 5

# On or above the Ladder? Maimonidean and anti-Maimonidean Readings of Jacob's Ladder

## James T. Robinson

Some philosophers do their best thinking in the margins of other peoples' texts. This was the motto of Harry Wolfson, the pioneering historian of religion and philosophy. His idea was that medieval philosophy, as distinct from ancient and modern, did its best thinking in the form of commentary. The medievals did write systematic works, this is true. What better examples can one find in any era than Thomas Aquinas's *Summa Theologia*, Gersonides's *Wars of the Lord*, and Hasdai Crescas's *Light of the Lord*? But in Wolfson's opinion the most creative work was done through commentary – commentary on Aristotle, commentary on Averroes, and most importantly, commentary on the Bible. It was the Bible in particular that provided a framework for discussion, a forum for controversy, and a virtual classroom of sorts for the teaching and dissemination of novel opinions. Scripture was read and re-read in relation to the intellectual currents of the time, the latest philosophical ideas.

An excellent example of this distinctive method of learning – what Wolfson thought of as scriptural philosophy – is the story of Jacob's ladder. For here a very short text from the Bible, a brief enigmatic description of Jacob's vision in a dream and its setting, served as the focal point for discussions about science and philosophy, about the role of science and philosophy within the religious community, and about the capacity of the human mind to grasp intelligible wisdom. The ladder – an architectural symbol of ascent – would become the favorite metaphor for ideas about spiritual, mystical, and philosophical aspiration. From the twelfth century – with the work of Moses Maimonides – through the fifteenth, Jacob's ladder was explained again and again in light of the changing, competing, and sometimes contradictory ideals of individual exegetes and philosophers.

What I will do in this chapter is introduce several distinct readings of Jacob's ladder, representing a period of some three hundred years, from

Maimonides in his *Guide of the Perplexed* (completed by 1191) to the
exegetical and homiletic works of Isaac Arama and Isaac Abarbanel, who
wrote during the generation of the 1492 expulsion from Spain. All of the
interpretations follow, in one way or another, the original contribution of
Maimonides, but they develop his ideas in new directions, whether philosophical, Kabbalistic, Sufi, or even anti-philosophical.

## The Vision

I will start with the relevant passage from the Bible. Here is Genesis 28:
10–22, according to the King James Version:

> 10. And Jacob went out from Beer-Sheba, and went toward Haran. 11. And
> he lighted upon a certain place, and tarried there all night, because the sun
> was set; and he took of the stones of that place, and put them for his pillows,
> and lay down in that place to sleep. 12. And he dreamed, and behold a ladder
> set up on the earth, and the top of it reached to heaven: and behold the
> angels of God ascending and descending on it [*bo*]. 13. And, behold, the
> Lord stood above it [*'alav*], and said: I am the Lord God of Abraham thy
> father, and the God of Isaac: the land whereon thou liest, to thee will I give
> it, and to thy seed. 14. And thy seed shall be as the dust of the earth, and thou
> shalt spread abroad to the west, and to the east, and to the north, and to the
> south: and in thee and in thy seed shall all the families of the earth be
> blessed. 15. And, behold, I am with thee, and will keep thee in all places
> whither thou goest, and will bring thee again into this land; for I will not
> leave thee, until I have done that which I have spoken to thee of. 16. And
> Jacob awaked out of his sleep, and he said: Surely the Lord is in this place;
> and I knew it not. 17. And he was afraid, and said: How dreadful is this place!
> This is none other but the house of God, and this is the gate of heaven. 18.
> And Jacob rose up early in the morning, and took the stone that he had put
> for his pillows, and set it up for a pillar, and poured oil upon the top of it. 19.
> And he called the name of that place Bethel: but the name of that city was
> called Luz at the first. 20. And Jacob vowed a vow, saying: If God will be
> with me, and will keep me in this way that I go, and will give me bread to
> eat, and raiment to put on, 21. So that I come again to my father's house in
> peace; then shall the Lord be my God: 22. And this stone, which I have set
> for a pillar, shall be God's house: and of all that thou shalt give me I will
> surely give the tenth unto thee.

The text and context in Genesis seems clear enough: Jacob fled from his
brother Esau, stopped briefly to spend the night near Beer Sheba, had
a dream, and through his dream learned about the holiness of the place
where he had slept. In this short text, however, there are several textual

problems and ambiguities. In fact, there are at least seven problems and ambiguities in the first four verses alone.

For example, Jacob went out from Beer Sheba, but according to the previous verses he was not in Beer Sheba but in Hebron. According to the language, Jacob seems to have left Beer Sheba and arrived immediately in Haran, a journey of three days. The English expression "and he alighted upon a certain place" conceals an equally awkward Hebrew locution, which means, literally: and he met something or someone (which is unstated) in that place. But whom did he meet and at what place? And while he took stones of the place as a pillow, when he awoke there was only one stone: What happened to the others?

Most important for us are the ambiguities in the vision itself: The angels of God were ascending and descending, but shouldn't celestial beings first descend into the physical world and then ascend? Finally, two of the remarks in the story have unstated referents: "Behold the angels of God ascending and descending *on it*" and "Behold, the Lord stood *above it.*" Both seem to refer back to the ladder. But, according to rules of grammar, they could also refer back to Jacob, or to any other masculine referent.

All of these difficulties are eliminated by the English translators; their main concern was to provide a fluid, readable, and generally accurate text. In contrast, the ancient and medieval exegetes and philosophers preferred to bring out the difficulties; they preferred not to hide them or eliminate them but to emphasize them. For they considered textual difficulties an opportunity rather than a problem, an opening of sorts in which they could discover – or introduce – new ideas and interpretations. The first to fully realize a philosophical reading of the text in the medieval Jewish tradition was Moses Maimonides.

## The Ladder as Cosmos: The Chain of Existence

The history of medieval Jewish philosophy, as a mature, fully developed field of learning, begins in a sense with Moses Maimonides and his *Guide of the Perplexed*; and his *Guide of the Perplexed*, a difficult and infinitely complex work of philosophy and exegesis, begins with Jacob's ladder. Thus, this biblical text could not but have played an important role in the later developments of Jewish philosophy. That Maimonides's discussion of Jacob's ladder is ambiguous made the text even more appealing to later disciples and enthusiasts.

Maimonides's reference to the ladder appears in the preface to the *Guide*; it is introduced as an example of biblical parables or allegories, and reads as follows:

> Know that the prophetic parables are of two kinds. In some of these parables each word has a meaning, while in others the parable as a whole indicates the whole of the intended meaning . . . . An example of the first kind of prophetic parable is the following text: "And behold a ladder set up on the earth and the top of it reached to heaven; and behold angels of God ascending and descending on it; and behold the Lord stood above it" [Gen 28:12–13]. In this text, the word "ladder" indicates one subject; "set upon the earth" indicates a second subject; "and the top of it reached to heaven" indicates a third subject; "and behold the angels of God" indicates a fourth subject; the word "ascending" indicates a fifth subject; "and descending" indicates a sixth subject; "and behold the Lord stood above it" indicates a seventh subject. Thus every word occurring in this parable refers to an additional subject in the complex of subjects represented by the parable as a whole.[1]

Thus, according to Maimonides, the vision of the ladder has seven distinct meanings. But this is all he says. What could these seven subjects be?

In order to understand Maimonides's explanation, one needs to search through the chapters of the *Guide* for relevant information. In various chapters he explains the possible meanings of the biblical terms "angel," "God," "earth," "heavens," "ascend," "descend," and "stand upon."[2] By collecting information and then rewriting and reconstructing the text, remapping it according to Maimonides's allegorical lexicon, one is left not with a ladder but with the cosmos as a whole, extending from the earth to the outermost sphere, with God, the first cause or prime mover, setting everything in motion. What one sees is not a "ladder" in any ordinary sense but the "chain of existence": the entire world and all its connections presented in symbolic form.

This is how the medievals reconstructed the text following Maimonides's directions. An example is Moses Narboni, a fourteenth-century commentator on the *Guide*. He explains as follows:

> "ladder" indicates the chain of existence and order of its parts; "set upon the earth" indicates the world of elements, which is everything encompassed by

---

[1] See *Guide* i.int, tr. Pines, pp 12–13. Unless otherwise noted, page references to the *Guide* are to the Pines translation. For background on Maimonides's readings of the ladder in general, see S. Klein-Braslavy, "Maimonides' Interpretations of Jacob's Dream about the Ladder," *Bar-Ilan Year Book*, 22–23 (1988), 329–349 (Heb.).

[2] See *Guide* i.2, i.10, 1:15, i.21, ii.6–7, ii.10, ii.30.

the lunar sphere; "and the top of it reached to heaven" indicates the world of spheres; "and behold the angels of God" indicates the world of separate intelligences; "ascending" indicates that they are causes; "and descending" indicates that they are effects . . . ; "and behold the Lord stood above it" indicates that He, may He be exalted, is the first cause, and He is above the ladder ['*alav*] separate from any corporeality; He is not in the ladder [*bo*] . . .[3]

This is how the cosmological reading of Jacob's ladder began, with a few enigmatic remarks by Maimonides at the beginning of the *Guide*. Not all commentators explained the ladder exactly as Narboni did. They differed in details, based on their own inclinations and in light of current scientific theory. What Maimonides did, therefore, was to create an open tradition of sorts; he singled out Jacob's ladder as a "strategic research site" (to use modern terminology) where Jews could pursue their cosmological investigations. He created a safe place for the study of philosophy.

### Ladder and Cave: Philosophy and Social Responsibility

The cosmological reading of the ladder was popular. But it was not the only reading of the text. In the *Guide* itself Maimonides suggested another interpretation, not cosmological but political.

This second explanation of the ladder turns on a textual problem: Who are these "angels of God," he asked, who originate below rather than above? Through a philosophical-philological investigation of the Bible, Maimonides discovered that the term "angel," *malakh* in Hebrew, can refer not only to celestial beings but to prophets, messengers, and spiritual or celestial forces of any sort.[4] He discovered also that the words "ascending" and "descending" can refer not only to changes in place but to changes in status or being.[5] Thus, Jacob's vision of the ladder can teach not only cosmology but the ascent and descent of the prophet: He ascends the ladder of wisdom to God, and then returns to the earth, armed with divine wisdom, to rule or govern the religious community.

Maimonides's political explanation of the ladder, as it appears in *Guide* 1:15, reads as follows:

> To stand [*naṣob* or *yaṣob*]. . . . The term is equivocal. Sometimes it has the meaning of rising and standing straight up. . . . The term has also another meaning: to be stable and permanent. . . . In all cases where this term occurs with reference to the Creator, it has this meaning. Thus: "and, behold, the

---

[3] *Be'ur Narboni*, ed. J. Goldenthal (Vienna, 1852), fol. 2a.   [4] See *Guide* ii.6–7.
[5] See *Guide* i.10.

Lord stood upon it" [Gen. 28:13], that is, was stably and constantly upon it – I mean upon the ladder, one end of which is in heaven, while the other end is upon earth. *Everyone who ascends does so climbing up this ladder, so that he necessarily apprehends Him who is upon it,* as He is stably and permanently at the top of the ladder. It is clear that what I say here of Him conforms to the parable propounded. For the "angels of God" are the prophets with reference to whom it is clearly said: "and he sent an angel" [Num. 20:16; referring to Moses]; "and an angel of the Lord came up from Gilgal to Bochim" [Judg. 2:1; referring to Moses]. How well put is the phrase "ascending and descending," in which ascent comes before descent. For after the ascent and the attaining of certain rungs of the ladder that may be known, comes the descent with whatever decree the prophet has been informed of, with a view of governing and teaching the people of the earth. As we have made clear, it is on this account that this is called "descent."[6]

This political interpretation of Jacob's ladder has more in common with Plato's parable of the cave than the great chain of existence. It is a lesson in social or political responsibility, teaching the requirement of the leader to become a philosopher and the requirement of the philosopher to return to the cave, or descend from the ladder, in order to use his wisdom to lead or govern the community. The passage italicized, however – *everyone who ascends does so climbing up this ladder, so that he necessarily apprehends Him who is upon it* – will have implications for the developing debate around the possibility of achieving metaphysical knowledge: Does one necessarily apprehend God when ascending the ladder or is something more required?[7] Or to state it differently, is God on or above the ladder?

## The Ladder of Wisdom[8]

The political interpretation of the ladder – more Plato's cave than "great chain of being" – was very important. It was a dominant theme in the *Guide* and had considerable influence in the later tradition. But one very important question was not answered: How does the angel, the philosopher, the prophet rise up the ladder to God? Is there some program to

---

[6] See *Guide* i.15, pp. 40–41.

[7] This subject, as is well known, has been central in modern Maimonidean scholarship at least since S. Pines's article, "The Limitations of Human Knowledge according to Al-Farabi, Ibn Bajja and Maimonides," in I. Twersky (ed.), *Studies in Medieval Jewish History and Literature* (Cambridge: Harvard University Press, 1979), pp. 82–109. As will be seen below, and as was already apparent from the citation of Narboni above, it was a subject of contention in the Middle Ages as well.

[8] See, in general, A. Altmann, "The Ladder of Ascension," in E. E. Urbach, Z. Werblowsky, and C. Wirszubski (eds.), *Studies in Mysticism and Religion Presented to Gershom G. Scholem on His Seventieth Birthday by Pupils, Colleagues and Friends* (Jerusalem: Magnes Press, 1967), pp. 1–32.

follow, a curriculum of study, a spiritual practice that helps one achieve this ideal? These questions led to two very different interpretations of the ladder: one philosophical and one mystical.

### The Philosophical Curriculum

The philosophical explanation was first introduced by Samuel Ibn Tibbon, the translator of Maimonides and his first major disciple. According to Ibn Tibbon, the ladder represents the Aristotelian curriculum of sciences – physics, mathematics [which includes astronomy], and metaphysics. Thus ascending the ladder meant mastering the sciences, one after the other, in proper order. Ibn Tibbon's interpretation, in Chapter 11 of his extended philosophical-exegetical treatise *Ma'amar Yiqqavu ha-Mayim*, reads as follows:[9]

> He said that [the ladder] is "set up on the earth." That is, the legs of the ladder are on the earth ... What this means is that the beginning of the apprehension of God's ways is "on the earth" and from the earth. These are the first things that can be apprehended by man.... This is what the philosophers call "natural science" [physics] ... He continued: "the top of it reaches to heaven." That is, the top of the branches [*nofe*] of the Tree of Life reach to the firmament above the Hayyot and to the likeness of the Throne upon it [see Ezek 1:26]. This is what the philosophers call astronomy.

Ibn Tibbon then continues, from physics and astronomy to metaphysics, and then concludes as follows, connecting the study of the Aristotelian cosmos to real knowledge of the cosmos. He writes:

> in order to grasp these things according to proper order, a man begins at the feet of the ladder that is "set up on the earth," and intellectually cognizes the true reality of ... everything ... that extends from the [legs of the] ladder to the lower part of the lunar sphere. After that he can know the true reality [of everything extending] ... from the lowest part of the lunar sphere to the highest part of the highest sphere. After that, he will intellectually cognize, no matter what [*'al kol panim*], the Lord standing on the top of the ladder, ... which is the highest part of the highest sphere. For then he would have ascended the ladder, and from the ladder to its top, and would have seen the Lord, together with the Seraphim, standing on the ladder.

But one problem still remained, even for Ibn Tibbon. Mastering the sciences is one thing, but knowing God is another. Does one really

---

[9] *Ma'amar Yiqqavu ha-Mayim*, ed. M. Bischeles (Pressburg, 1837), ch. 11.

*necessarily* know God by mastering all the sciences – as Maimonides seemed to maintain? Does a complete knowledge of the world necessarily mean knowledge of God? Although Ibn Tibbon does seem quite confident that this is true, at least in this text, in some passages he is less certain. In fact, in one important digression he provides a different explanation for the angels ascending and descending: The angels ascending are the prophets ascending, through study, toward knowledge of God; but the angels descending are something else, not the prophets descending to lead the people, but the separate intellects descending in order to help the individual human intellect reach its final goal. The human intellect can only reach so far, so Ibn Tibbon suggests, before it requires "divine assistance," apparently a connection with the active intellect, which is required to enter into full knowledge of the metaphysical realm. One doesn't go it alone at the highest level of wisdom; one requires, as it were, a celestial guide.

## Contemplative Practice

A different approach to this problem, a more practical approach, was provided by Joseph Ibn Gikatilla, one of the great kabbalists of the later thirteenth century; he introduced what seem to be Sufi ideas in order to resolve this problem. In an early work of his, "Critical Glosses on the *Guide of the Perplexed*," Gikatilla admits the need to master the philosophical sciences, but only as a preliminary step – as a necessary but not sufficient condition for knowing God. But after achieving this first goal, he maintains, one must then isolate oneself, free one's mind of all material fantasies, and contemplate the eternal mysteries. This contemplative practice, introduced into, or rather, on top of the philosophical system, reads as follows:

> Know that Jacob's and all the prophets' prophecy did not descend on them until they had understood all of the wonders of the world according to the correct order, after which they would isolate themselves [*mitboded*] in order to apprehend the supernal intellectual forms in order to conjoin with the supernal world. They would empty their thoughts [*poneh mi-mahashavotav*] from the sensible world and conjoin with the supernal intelligibles. Then the rational soul could be combined with the separate intellects, each individual according to the degree his soul is separate. When the soul of him who apprehends is conjoined above, prophecy overflows on it [the soul] and it sees the eternal fates [? Heb: *sefarim*] of all human beings, and apprehends the past, the present, and the future; each soul reaches a level according to the pure power of its apprehension. These are the levels of prophecy. But the important principle is that no prophet apprehends the intelligibles and the

supernal forms until he has studied and grasped all of the orders of the world below them. Thus it was necessary in the Torah to explain this with regard to Jacob; it describes the order of any prophet that apprehends supernal apprehensions, and it says that no prophet can apprehend any supernal mystery except by way of [what is contained in] this verse.[10]

Why do I say this text shows Sufi influence? The two keys terms used by Ibn Gikatilla are not standard Hebrew. Instead, they seem to be literal and awkward translations of Sufi technical terms: *mitboded* perhaps a Hebrew version of Arabic *khalwa* and *poneh mi-mahashavotav* as Arabic *fanā'*.[11] And in fact in the earlier work of Abraham Maimonides, for instance, Jacob, along with Elijah and other Biblical figures, had become a model for the Sufi mystic, who would isolate himself and go out in the wilderness in order to commune with God.

### Ladders across Cultures

Aristotelian cosmology and curriculum, Platonic ideas about politics and philosophy, and Sufism were not the only sources from which post-Maimonidean Jews drew inspiration in their readings of the ladder. There is evidence of Islamic Neoplatonic influence as well; and there seems to be influence of Christian scholasticism too.

The influence of Islamic Neoplatonism was discovered by Alexander Altmann, another of the pioneering historians of Jewish thought from the generation of Harry Wolfson. Altmann identified the importance of a late eleventh- or early twelfth-century Islamic text entitled the "Book of Gardens" (*Kitāb al-Ḥadā'iq*) or, in Hebrew translation, the "Book of Imaginary Circles" (*Sefer ha-'Agulot ha-Ra'yoniyot*), for Jewish discussions of Jacob's ladder. In this work the author, Ibn al-Sid al-Baṭalyawsī (1052–1127), uses the image of a "ladder of ascents" [*sullam al-ma'ārij*], to describe the ascent of the purified soul from the body to the celestial realm, and the descent of divine inspiration into the corporeal realm below.[12]

This "Book of Gardens" was translated into Hebrew three separate times, and was used, most explicitly, in a Hebrew text by Joseph Ibn

[10] Joseph ibn Gikatilla, *Sefer ha-Hassagot,* printed in *Sheelot u-teshuvot le-he-ḥakham Sha'ul ha-Kohen* (Venice, 1574), pp. 21c–21d.
[11] See M. Idel, *Studies in Ecstatic Kabbalah* (SUNY Press, 1988), Chapter 7, p. 106, citing al-Ghazālī, and cf. the rest of chapter 7, arguing that *hitbodedut* in Abulafia and others is used as "concentration."
[12] More recently the work has been edited with Hebrew translation and full discussion by A. Eliyahu, "Ibn al-Sid al-Batalyawsi and His Place in Muslim and Jewish Thought," unpublished PhD thesis, The Hebrew University of Jerusalem (2010) (Heb.).

Kaspi, a fourteenth-century Jewish philosopher and devotee of Maimonides. Ibn Kaspi's discussion of Jacob's ladder, which moves us from the ladder as cosmos, cave, or Aristotelian curriculum, to the Neoplatonic ascent of the soul, reads as follows, in his *Menorat Kesef*:

> Likewise, there is transmitted in the Torah with the utmost brevity and by way of allusion a parable-like story from Jacob, peace be upon him, namely, the vision of the ladder. Ptolemy [Baṭalyawsī] also mentions in the first chapter of the "Book of Circles" the ladder of ascent [*sullam ha-hagorot, sullam ha-higerut*]; what he says is stolen from our book of Torah. He said there: "Through it prophecy conjoins with the pure particular soul, and on it the purified spirits ascend to the supernal world, and on it the angels descend." Hence it seems to me highly probable that this ladder was the thing which Jacob conceived, in that he conceived the perfect soul mentioned by Ptolemy [Baṭalyawsī].... in my view this is exactly the meaning of this vision.[13]

Ibn Kaspi was not completely comfortable using non-Jewish sources. But he solved this with an appeal to an old motif: Whatever is good must have originated with the Jews.[14]

Rabbi Nissim b. Reuben Gerundi, writing in Barcelona in the later fourteenth century, was much more reserved about mentioning his sources, but he seems to have been equally influenced by non-Jewish thought. In his sermon on Jacob's ladder (Sermon 5 in *Derashot ha-Ran*), he develops the notion that the soul has two faces: one theoretical and one practical. When occupied with philosophy and spiritual matters the soul is facing above, striving toward God; when occupied with material necessities, with the needs of the body, the soul is facing downward, toward the earth. The way he applies this notion to Jacob's ladder reads as follows:

> This was alluded to in Jacob's vision when he said: "and behold the angels of God ascending and descending on it" [Gen. 28:12]. It was shown him in this vision that that place was predisposed toward prophecy, and there [in that place] people can ascend in order to perfect themselves. But he showed him that as long as you live this life of yours, it is impossible that this spiritual ascent be continuous; rather, one can ascend only so long as one is occupied with the needs of the soul, but will descend so long as one is not occupied with the soul but rather occupied with the needs of the body. The vision, therefore, is in the form of an exhortation: that you strive, as much as possible, to occupy yourself with all things that help achieve the ascent, and

---

[13] I cite the translation of Altmann with some modifications; see "Ladder of Ascension," pp. 23–24.

[14] For this motif see, e.g., N. Roth, "The Theft of Philosophy by the Greeks from the Jews," *Classical Folia* 32 (1978), pp. 52–67.

eliminate, as much as possible, things that cause descent. It is impossible for any man who is occupied with the necessary things of this world to be facing above; it is all the more impossible when one is completely overcome by evil dispositions and superfluous desires for the material life.[15]

Nissim does not cite his sources. He does not even allude to the fact that he might be borrowing from any source, Jewish or non-Jewish. But his idea of the two faces of the soul, which appears here in Hebrew for the first time (as far as I know), was a popular notion in Franciscan psychology, and probably borrowed by them from the Latin Avicenna;[16] and the Franciscans, as is now well known, had an active study house in Barcelona, not far from the Jewish quarter where Nissim lived, studied, and taught in the yeshivah.[17]

## God above the Ladder: Anti-Aristotelianism in the Fifteenth Century

The philosophical reading of Jacob's ladder had a remarkable history. It influenced philosophers, kabbalists, and Sufis. It persisted for some three hundred years, and took many forms: cosmological, political, epistemological, spiritualistic, mystical, and psychological.

In the fifteenth century, however, the strongly philosophical tradition came to a sudden end; for several exegetes, preachers, and communal leaders, primarily in Spain, devoted themselves to undoing what the philosophers had done. Influenced by renaissance historicism, and a growing skepticism of the Aristotelian system, they sought to free religion – and scripture – from philosophy and science. They did this in at least two ways: they tried to undermine philosophical readings of the biblical text; and they tried to construct new readings, not philosophical but anti-philosophical. I will give one example of each.

### Isaac Abarbanel

Isaac Abarbanel was the last great Jewish intellectual of Spain; he was expelled in 1492 and resettled in Italy, where he wrote most of his works, including voluminous commentaries on the Bible.

---

[15] *Derashot ha-Ran*, ed. L. Feldman (Jerusalem: Mossad ha-Rav Kook, 2003), Sermon 5, pp. 168–172.

[16] For the Franciscans, note especially Alexander Hales, John of La Rochelle, and Matthew of Aquasparta, as discussed by Obi J. Oguejiofor, *The Arguments for the Immortality of the Soul in the First Half of the Thirteenth Century* (Leuven: Peeters, 1995).

[17] See Warren Zev Harvey, "Nissim of Gerona and William of Ockham on Prime Matter," *Jewish History*, 6 (1992), pp. 88–98.

In his commentary on Genesis 28:10–22, he presents a lengthy survey of all the possible meanings of the Ladder. But he rejects them all for two simple reasons: First, a philosophical dream is inconsistent with the context of the story. Why would God teach Jacob cosmology precisely in that place and that time? Why would he teach him something he did not teach Abraham or Isaac? Second, a philosophical explanation of Jacob's dream is inconsistent with philosophy itself. For dreams, according to the philosophers, are not a legitimate source of theoretical knowledge. This final criticism, which is decisive in Abarbanel's opinion, reads as follows:

> To sum up: we find that the Master Guide [Maimonides] has three opinions regarding the interpretation of this dream, but this is not the place to distinguish which of them is straighter and truer. What is very difficult for me, however, is what he seems to suggest regarding Jacob's apprehension itself: that it was not prophetic but philosophical and theoretical. For what [Jacob] apprehended, according to all of the interpretations suggested by the Master, could have been apprehended by the Greek sages in their philosophizing without the help of prophets. And if his opinion is that this was in fact the level of Jacob, that he reached the philosophical theoretical level and not the prophetic – as is the opinion of the commentators on his book, who were caught in this trap – it is difficult to understand why the Torah provided the following testimony: "and he dreamed." For it is known that the sciences cannot be apprehended in a dream ... As explained in the *Parva Naturalia*: the dream is a specific activity of the imagination and the things [the imagination] produces through combination. It is not a place for intellectual investigation and its apprehensions.[18]

### Isaac Arama

Isaac Arama, Abarbanel's older contemporary and fellow countryman, chose a different path. In his sermon on Jacob's ladder he attempted not to undermine the philosophical reading of the text, but to replace it with an anti-philosophical reading. He did this by shifting emphasis from the ladder itself to God above the ladder, and from the pursuit of knowledge and wisdom to the limitations of knowledge and wisdom. This he does by presenting a lengthy discussion of the ways in which reason is inferior to prophecy: just as imagination is shown false by reason, he maintains, so

---

[18] See Isaac Abarbanel, *Commentary on va-yetse*, Genesis 28:10f, in *Perush ha-Torah le-Rabbenu Yitzhak Abrabanel*, ed. Y. Shaviv (Jerusalem: Horeb, 2007), pp. 561–566, on p. 563. The reference to the *Parva Naturalia* is probably to the Hebrew translation of Averroes's paraphrase of the Arabic version of the *Parva Naturalia*.

reason is shown false by prophecy. His main example is Jacob's ladder. For Jacob thought he had understood the world perfectly through his philosophical investigations, but his dream taught him something he could not have learned through reason: That God can choose a single nation, that God can govern and exercise providence over individual human beings, and that God can be in a place, something the philosophers deny completely. The prophetic dream, therefore, disproves the pretensions of reason.

In addition to shifting attention from the ladder to God above the ladder, Arama also introduces a very odd rabbinic text, which, as far as I can tell, was not cited in the exegetical or philosophical literature before the fifteenth century. In his explanation of this rabbinic text, Arama's real distaste for the philosophers is clear. This is the last text I will cite before finishing with some concluding remarks.

> This is the meaning of the Sages in their dictum: "It may be compared to an infant prince sleeping in his cot on whom flies were settling; when his nurse came she bent over and suckled him, and they flew away. Similarly, at first, 'and behold the angels of God ascending and descending on it.' But when the Holy One, blessed be He, revealed Himself to him, they fled from him. This is the meaning of: 'And behold the Lord stood over him'." [Gen. Rabb. 69:3].
>
> For up to this point, although Jacob had recognized his Creator by way of speculation – he had apprehended God's governance of the world – still there remained a few flies of death that had come into existence from the putrid matter of his human intellect. His philosophical speculations were settling upon him, separating him from the real truth. . . . This was until the infant's nurse came. For she represents divine prophetic guidance [*haysharah*] . . . And the divine prophetic intellect is above the human intellect; it guides it in all areas where it can err, and makes it ascend to places it cannot reach on its own.[19]

With this, the Maimonidean philosophical tradition was coming to an end; the optimistic pursuit of wisdom, represented by the ladder of ascent, was subordinated to the divine intellect, to God above the ladder. The Middle Ages was coming to an end; science and religion were renegotiating their relationship in new ways.

## Conclusion

My main goal in this chapter has been fairly simple: to show the diversity of philosophical and anti-philosophical approaches to Genesis 28, building

---

[19] *Aqedat Yizhaq*, gate 25 (Warsaw, 1904), vol. 1, pp. 203b–211b, on 209b–210a.

on and responding to the foundational insights of Maimonides in the *Guide of the Perplexed*. It was also to show the surprising correspondence between philosophy and exegesis, and the remarkable ease with which ideas could pass from culture to culture so long as they were attached to an authoritative text. But I would like to suggest two additional ideas as well.

First: Arama and Abarbanel were transitional figures, very much between medieval and modern. In fact, there is a direct link between them and Spinoza, who is often considered the father of modern critical study of the Bible, and who contributed a great deal to the modern separation of philosophy from scripture. Arama, Abarbanel, and other like-minded critics of Aristotle paved the way for the emergence of science as an autonomous discipline, independent of religion; and for the emergence of Bible study as an autonomous field, separate from philosophy and science. But it is worth mentioning that, despite this undermining of the scientific or philosophical basis for Jacob's ladder, the motif of ascent on Jacob's dream continued to be cited and used in various ways, even into the modern period. The Hasidim connected Jacob's ladder with the spiritual ascent of the Zaddiq as intercessor. Jacob's ladder appears in ethical manuals and in philosophical works, connected with Kantian ideas about cognition and the limits of reason. Jung singled it out as an archetype, and under the influence of Jung and Freud, Jacob's ladder has become a common symbol of self-transformation and personal fulfillment in our own time.

Second: In all the sources we have looked at, it is remarkable how easy it is to identify the ideology of the exegete or philosopher; each exegete reads the text exactly as one would expect him to read it; the text becomes really a mirror. Modern critical scholarship has aimed to eliminate this approach to the Bible through scientific study, by trying to understand the Bible on its own terms and in ancient near-eastern context through historical, archaeological, and philological research. But has it really reached independence? Is the Bible no longer a mirror? Have we penetrated to the true meaning of the text, or are we simply reproducing our own modern ideals in the text? Are the modern critics no less philosophical exegetes, in a manner, than the premoderns? I think we will not really know until we have some distance from these latter developments. But even now these are questions that are being asked, as contemporary scholars and students of the Bible are becoming more sensitive to their own personal ideological influence on their readings of the text. Perhaps a fuller study of the premodern philosophical reading of Scripture, the Maimonidean in particular, can help put this complicated negotiation in still greater relief.

# CHAPTER 6

# *Reading the* Guide of the Perplexed
## *as an Intellectual Challenge*
### Sara Klein-Braslavy

Why do we keep rereading the *Guide of the Perplexed?* The accepted answers to this question are, of course, those that derive from looking into the book from a historical perspective and from a cultural concern: We wish to familiarize ourselves with the inalienable assets of Jewish thought, and we are curious to know a book that was written by one of medieval Jewry's greatest thinkers, a book that had an enormous influence on Jewish philosophy in both the medieval and modern periods.

But my question is: What is the secret of the book's allure for us? It is not just the desire to understand the book in its historical and cultural context, for when we read it we become fascinated with it, even today, when we disagree with Maimonides's worldview and the philosophical and scientific assumptions at the foundation of his book. This question can obviously be answered in a number of ways, but it seems to me that underlying each one of these answers is the fact that the *Guide* presents its readers with an extraordinary intellectual challenge. Reading this book is a thrilling spiritual adventure, and many of its parts read like a riddle that demands deciphering.

There are two prominent layers of the discussion in the *Guide*: biblical exegesis and theoretical discussion about philosophical and philosophical-logical questions. I wish to present a number of aspects of the intellectual challenge that is present in each one of them without, of course, presuming to exhaust them all and encompass the whole of the book's complexity. I begin with biblical exegesis.

## Biblical Exegesis

One of the most visible characteristics of the *Guide* is that it is not arranged as a systematic composition, but rather possesses its own overall logical structure. Such a structure entails that Biblical passages and topics that

ordinarily would be considered together appear in different places
throughout the book. Such scattered placement is not necessarily motivated by a desire for esotericism,[1] but is dictated by the book's structure and
the dominant tendency of the discussion in different places.

## Open and Closed Texts

The *Guide* is not a closed text. It does not represent Maimonides's final
word on the topics that occupied him. In this regard, it is unlike, for
example, Saadiah Gaon's *Book of Beliefs and Convictions*, in which the
author examines beliefs and convictions for the sake of his contemporaries, whose beliefs are not purified and some of their convictions
incorrect. He offers a system of beliefs and opinions that he establishes
using reason.[2] In a similar manner, at the end of the middle ages, Ḥasdai
Crescas presents an orderly and structured framework of the roots of the
Jewish faith, along with their justifications, in his book *The Light of the
Lord.* Texts like these can be characterized as "closed texts," in which the
author arranges a message and expects the reader to understand and
accept this message. That is, of course, not to say that such texts do not
require explanation, and sometimes even great elucidatory work, on the
part of the reader.[3]

The *Guide* can be characterized as an "open text." Open texts are texts
that do not impart an organized, ordered, clear, teaching to the reader, but
to a large extent leave the reader to construct the texts and understand their
messages. The openness of this text is manifested in different ways, and
that is what creates the great intellectual challenge of the *Guide*. It is
written from the beginning, on the exegetical plane, as an open rather
than a closed text. The readers must be active, and complete their [biblical]
exegesis independently, but in a Maimonidean spirit, as Maimonides
grants them the keys for this activity. Every text requires action on the
part of a reader – the text exists when it is read, when the reader gives it
meaning – but the *Guide* in general, and Maimonides's biblical exegesis in
particular, require especial proactivity. A reader who wants to understand
the biblical commentaries in Maimonides's *Guide*, which are actually,
according to his declaration in the introduction to part one of the book,

---

[1] See my *Maimonides as Biblical Interpreter* (Boston, MA: Academic Studies Press, 2007), pp. 201–204.
[2] See Saadia Gaon, Introduction to *The Book of the Beliefs and Convictions*, in C. Manekin (ed. and tr.), *Medieval Jewish Philosophical Writings* (Cambridge University Press, 2007), p. 4.
[3] Ḥasdai Crescas, *Or ha-Shem*, ed. Shlomo Fischer (Jerusalem: Sifre Ramot, 1990).

its very purpose, is therefore required to partake in a particularly active reading.[4]

As is known, Maimonides begins the *Guide* with a series of chapters that are mainly explanations of polysemic words that appear in Scripture, often in reference to God, and he illustrates their use with different biblical verses. He explains that the reader ought not to relate to the lexicographical chapters as a normal dictionary, which explains the various meanings that these Hebrew terms have, but as a theological-philosophical dictionary, which serves his purposes in the *Guide*: to indicate the concord between philosophy and the biblical text and to facilitate an understanding, as far as possible, of *the Account of the Beginning* and *the Account of the Chariot*.[5] The dictionary that he has fashioned is geared also to the *Guide*'s active reader. It is an aid for the ideal reader of the *Guide*, who is expected to interpret other biblical verses in the light of the scriptural explanations offered by Maimonides. In *Guide* i.8, he explicitly states this:

> Know with regard to every term whose equivocality we shall explain to you in this Treatise that our purpose in such an explanation is not only to draw your attention to what we mention in that particular chapter. Rather do we open a gate and draw your attention to such meanings of that particular term as are useful for our purpose, not for the various purposes of whoever may speak the language of this or that people. As for you, you should consider the books of prophecy and other works composed by men of knowledge, reflect on all the terms used therein, and take every equivocal term in that one from among its various senses that is suitable in that particular passage. These our words are the key to this Treatise and to others.[6]

## Revelation in the Cleft of the Rock

Active reading is required first and foremost of one who reads the chapters of Maimonides's biblical-philosophical lexicon.[7] The most important biblical text whose exposition can be established in this way is the description of God's promising Moses a revelation in the cleft of the rock.

---

[4] *Guide* I introduction, tr. Pines, pp. 5–6. Unless otherwise noted, page references to the *Guide* are to the Pines translation.
[5] *Guide* II 2, p. 254.   [6] *Guide* I 8, p. 34.
[7] L. Strauss describes these chapters as lexicographic. See his introductory essay in the Pines translation, "How to Begin to Study *The Guide of the Perplexed*," p. xxv.

See, there is a place by me where you shall stand on the rock; and while my glory passes by I will put you in a cleft of the rock, and I will cover you with my hand until I have passed by; then I will take away my hand, and you shall see my back; but my face shall not be seen (Ex. 33: 21–23).

Reading the biblical-philosophical lexicon in the first part of the book shows that Maimonides explains eight key terms, in these chapters, pertaining to the revelation to Moses in the cleft of the rock, each in a different chapter: 'place' (chapter 8), 'to stand' (chapter 15), 'rock' (chapter 16), 'to pass' (chapter 21), 'glory' (chapter 64), 'to see' (chapter 4), 'back' (chapter 38), 'face' (chapter 37).[8] Moreover, in most cases he also illustrates these terms' derived meanings by using parts of verses taken from this revelation. Combining these explanations of words and parts of verses allows the active reader to explain independently the promise of this revelation in its entirety. Scattering the explanation of words and verse sections from the revelation in the cleft of the rock is not rooted in Maimonides's esotericism. He does not aspire to hide the meaning of God's promise. On the contrary, he has a clear interest in eradicating the corporeality of God in scripture, and to teach an immaterial interpretation also to the masses. These chapters are aimed, among others, at those among the masses who are capable of understanding the explanation of biblical verses that do not imply divine corporeality. The scattering of these terms stems from the manner in which Maimonides chose to write the *Guide*. The lexicographical chapters in this composition are designed to serve several exegetical goals simultaneously. In most cases, the central and most obvious goal is explaining words that, when they appear in sentences in which God is the subject, object, or predicate, entail divine corporeality. The revelation in the cleft of the rock is one of the secondary topics of exegesis in these same chapters, alongside the more important esoteric topics, *the Account of the Beginning* and *the Account of the Chariot*, which also demand active reading in order to be explained. Nevertheless, it is a secondary topic that is important to Maimonides, and that is attested by the fact that, in each chapter, he employs verses from Exodus 33 to illustrate the use of the polysemic terms. In choosing to do so, perhaps Maimonides directs the reader to combine the meanings in order to arrive at a fuller explanation of Moses's request and God's reply.

---

[8] See H. Kasher, "Maimonides' Interpretation of the Story of the Cleft of the Rock," *Da'at*, 35 (1995), pp. 29–66 (Heb.), and my "Maimonides' Exoteric and Esoteric Biblical Interpretations in the *Guide of the Perplexed*," in *Maimonides as Biblical Interpreter*, pp. 202–206.

A similar proactive approach is demanded of the reader who wishes to understand fully Maimonides's exegesis of the revelation in the cleft of the rock in Exodus 33: 21–23. Alongside his exegesis of words from the description of this revelation in the lexicographical chapters, Maimonides also dedicates a particular chapter of the *Guide* to an explanation of Exodus 33–34. *Guide* i.54 mainly focuses on explaining other parts of this biblical narrative. The explanation is embedded in a different thematic framework from that which governs the evident and central layer of the lexicographical chapters, in chapters that deal with divine attributes. At the beginning of this chapter, through biblical exegesis, Maimonides presents a confirmation and completion of a theoretical discussion, from new perspectives, of the question of divine attributes that appeared in the previous chapters, 51–53, and particularly in the logical discussion in chapter 52. He concentrates here on explaining Moses's first request of God, "Show me your ways," to which God responded, "I will make all of my goodness pass before you," and mainly on the actual revelation that Moses received when he ascended Sinai, and which was expressed in ethical terminology: "Lord, Lord, God, merciful and gracious," etc.[9] At the beginning of the discussion, he indicates the central idea of the revelation in Exodus 33: 21–24, "Behold, there is a place by me, and you shall stand upon the rock . . . and you shall see my back but my face shall not be seen." He does not quote the verses but rather presents an integrated and general explanation of the revelation that does not appear in the lexicographical chapters, but which has its exegetical justification scattered in the interpretation of terms found therein. In the continuation of the discussion, he presents the interpretation of Moses's request, "Show me please your glory," and that of God's reply, "you cannot see my face, for no man can see me and live," without justifying them by way of explaining the words in these chapters. Whoever wishes to understand how Maimonides explains the verses in Exodus 33–34, and how he arrives at the exegetical conclusions that he presents in chapter 54, therefore needs independently to construct an interpretation that accords with the text by combining the explanation of words in the lexicographical chapters, the interpretation of words in Moses's second request, and God's reply. In *Guide* i.54, Maimonides essentially explains Moses's first request, and the actual revelation that he received, which is related in Exodus 34: 36–37.

---

[9] *Guide* I 54, p. 123.

## The Garden of Eden Story

Another prominent explanation that is dispersed through the *Guide* is that of the narrative of the creation of Man and the Garden of Eden.[10] Maimonides explains the Eden story in *Guide* i.2 and ii.30. Each of the explanations is presented in a different thematic framework and in different contexts. Each one deals with a different aspect of the story, and serves a different immediate exegetical purpose, that of the chapters surrounding it. The commentary in part one is presented in the framework of lexicographical chapters that are concerned with human knowledge. The emphasis is on the human condition before and after the sin as two different conditions that can be characterized as different types of knowing. The sin explains the transition from knowing intelligible and intellectual perfection, the human condition before the sin, to knowledge of generally admitted beliefs and a loss of intellectual perfection, the human condition after the sin. The commentary in part two is presented as a continuation of the commentary to the narrative of the world's creation in Genesis 1. In this context, the story is not presented as a historical narrative with Adam, Eve, and the serpent, as protagonists, but as a philosophical allegory that explains Adam's sin on the basis of Aristotelian psychology.[11] In each of these commentaries, Maimonides explains different verses of the biblical story. It can be said to the knowledgeable that, in various respects, the relationship between these two commentaries is that of the fifth cause of contradictions, the pedagogical necessity of assuming something imprecisely because of the level of the student.[12]

Whoever wishes to know how Maimonides interprets the stories about Adam's creation and the Garden of Eden needs to read each of the two commentaries individually, to try to understand them, usually on the basis

[10]  See S. Klein Braslavy, *Perush ha-Rambam la-sippurim 'al Adam be-farashat Be-reishit: Peraqim be-torat ha-Adam shel ha-Rambam* (*Maimonides' Interpretation of the Adam Stories in Genesis – A Study in Maimonides' Anthropology*) (Jerusalem: Rubin Mass, 1986); "On Maimonides' Interpretation of the Story of the Garden of Eden in the *Guide of the Perplexed* I,2," in S. Klein-Braslavy, *Maimonides as Biblical Interpreter*, pp. 21–69; L. V. Berman, "Maimonides on the Fall of Man," *AJS Review*, 5, (1980), 1–15; Z. Harvey, "Maimonides' Interpretation of Gen. 3:22," *Da'at*, 12 (1984), 15–22 (Heb.); Z. Harvey, "Maimonides and Spinoza on the Knowledge of Good and Evil," *Iyyun*, 28 (1979), 167–185; S. Pines, "Truth and Falsehood versus Good and Evil," in I. Twersky (ed.), *Studies in Maimonides* (Cambridge, MA: Harvard University Press, 1990), pp. 95–157; J. Stern, "The Maimonidean Parable, the Arabic Poetics, and the Garden of Eden," Midwest Studies in Philosophy XXXIII (2009), pp. 209–247; H. Kreisel, "The Problem of 'Good' in Maimonides' Thought," Iyyun, 38 (1989), pp. 183–208; Klein-Braslavy, "Bible Commentary," in K. Seeskin (ed.), *The Cambridge Companion to Maimonides* (Cambridge University Press, 2005), pp. 261–268.
[11]  See *Maimonides' Interpretation of the Adam Stories*, pp. 294–324.    [12]  *Guide* I introduction, p. 17.

of additional chapters in the *Guide* in which terms and ideas appearing in the story are explained and, independently, to build a single complete interpretation from both of them.[13]

Alongside the challenge of a "naïve" active reading of Maimonides's biblical exegesis, a reading that depends on building a continuous explanation of biblical texts by combining parts of their explanations, which are scattered around the *Guide*, more sophisticated active readings are also demanded of the reader in order to arrive at Maimonides's interpretations.

One of the *Guide's* central methodological presuppositions is that scripture belongs to an esoteric kind of literature. It is written in figurative language, in metaphor and allegory (lit. 'riddle') so as to make its message suitable to one among the masses, as emerges from Alfarabi's political teaching, which Maimonides adopts in the *Guide*,[14] but also to hide the message from such a person. The central reason for this concealment is that since the masses are unable to understand philosophical teachings, especially divine teachings and those of natural science that overlap with it, disseminating such teachings among them is likely to cause misunderstanding and thereby harm to their faith.

Maimonides presents his book as one that deals with the "secrets" or "mysteries of the Torah." It contains strata of esotericism: The texts that he explains – biblical books and the rabbinic homilies that comment on them – are esoteric texts. But the *Guide* itself is also esoteric.[15] The *Guide's* reader therefore deals simultaneously with reading and deciphering two esoteric texts: the biblical text (and to a lesser degree also the midrashic text) and the text of the *Guide*.

Since Maimonides holds that the bible imparts an esoteric message, and since he considers himself bound to the rabbinic prohibition against publicizing this esoteric message, he writes part of his biblical interpretations with an exegetical method designed to conceal the truth from those who are unfit to receive it while aiming hints at those who are fit.[16] In these

---

[13] I carried out this project in *Maimonides' Interpretation of the Adam Stories*.

[14] See L. Berman, "Maimonides the Disciple of Alfarabi," *Israel Oriental Studies*, 4 (1974), 154–178. Alfarabi says that the prophet produces religion through his imaginative faculty as an imitation of philosophy. See F. Rahman, *Prophecy in Islam: Philosophy and Orthodoxy* (London: George Allen & Unwin 1958). In the present volume, C. Manekin argues that Maimonides understands Mosaic prophecy differently from the Alfarabian conception of prophecy.

[15] See L. Strauss, "The Literary Character of the *Guide of the Perplexed*," in S. W. Baron, *Essays on Maimonides* (New York: Columbia University Press, 1941), reprinted in *Persecution and the Art of Writing* (University of Chicago Press, 1988), pp. 38–94, on p. 55.

[16] In the introduction to the *Guide*, Maimonides says that he will transmit the *Account of the Chariot* in chapter headings and he will scatter them and entangle them with other subjects so that the truths will be glimpsed and then again be concealed. *Guide* i. intro, pp. 5–6.

interpretations, he does not present a clear interpretation or complete explanation of the words, verse, or pericopes, but only "hints" at their meaning. This writing method demands another kind of active reading. The reader must understand Maimonides's hints and independently build the interpretation of scripture on the basis of this understanding. The reader is the one who is expected to give the meaning to the biblical text, and not to combine meanings and parts of interpretation that she finds in the text, as with the attempt to understand Maimonides's explanation of the revelation to Moses in the cleft of the rock. I will show this sort of reading by interpreting one kind of hinting.

Some of these hints are anchored in the explanation of terms, but not in the explanation of polysemic terms, to which Maimonides's scriptural-philosophical dictionary is devoted, and the nature of whose polysemy is portrayed in works of Aristotelian logic, but in the explanation of terms whose meanings are discovered by the reader, with the aid of Maimonides. These are terms whose meanings are anchored in their imagined or real etymologies. The meanings of these terms, in the biblical contexts in which they appear, are not derived from those contexts, but the terms themselves indicate the meanings they have to offer. Such terms include "serpent,"[17] in the Eden story, "Satan," in the framing story of the book of Job,[18] "Sama'el,"[19] in the midrash that Maimonides uses to explain the serpent's tempting Eve, and also the series of terms in Ezekiel's chariot story: ḥashmal, brass, burnished brass, calf's foot.[20] Aside from the claim that these terms ought to be understood by means of their etymology, Maimonides offers extra hints at their meaning in the case of only one, the term "Satan." It is up to the reader to understand the meanings that these terms indicate through the hint that their meanings are concealed in their etymology.

Understanding this hint is complex, and it requires a number of exegetical processes. First of all, the reader must understand the hint on the basis of an understanding of the philosophical meaning of the concealed layer of the text, i.e., from the context of these terms in the concealed layer of the verses. The upshot is that the general meaning, or the realm of meaning of this concealed layer, must be uncovered before the interpretation of those words whose meaning is indicated by their etymology.

The interpretation of the realm of philosophical meaning of the text relies on the reader's knowledge of theoretical matters. As such, further

---

[17]  *Guide* ii.30, pp. 356–357.   [18]  *Guide* iii.22, p. 489.   [19]  *Guide* ii.30, p. 357.
[20]  *Guide* ii.29, p. 348.

activity is required. A reader must connect the theories that Maimonides himself opens up in other chapters or parts of chapters of the *Guide*, which concern topics with which the concealed layer of the biblical text deals, with his biblical exegesis. It falls on the reader to find and to clarify those philosophical-theological theories of Maimonides that serve, in his opinion, an interpretation of scripture in a given set of verses, independently and apply them.

While the exegesis of polysemic terms of the logical sort usually leads to a single interpretation of the biblical text, accepted by all, the exegesis by means of terms that are understood through their etymology, which is exegesis by way of hinting, allows a number of interpretations of the same text, and therefore a number of understandings of Maimonides's interpretation.

The reader undergoes this process, for example, when he attempts to interpret the figure of "Satan" in the framework story of the Book of Job. The reader must build his interpretation out of the hints to the meaning of the term "Satan," on the basis of its etymology, on the basis of further hints that Maimonides gives during his exegesis of the Book of Job in *Guide* iii.22, and on the basis of the chapters in which Maimonides discusses the question of the source of evil in the world.[21] Since hints and the reader's exegetical activity in deciphering them are the subject of discussion, a number of interpretations of the character "Satan" are possible here. In its first appearance in the Book of Job, "Satan" could be privation, matter, or perhaps accident, and in its second appearance it could be the imagination, ignorance, or perhaps particular privation.[22]

But that is insufficient. The reader must not only be familiar with the *Guide* and the theological-philosophical teachings presented in it in order to interpret Maimonides's hints, but also make use of knowledge from outside the text, philosophical theories that, according to Maimonides's interpretation, stand at the base of the biblical text but which Maimonides does not present in the *Guide*. As the ideal addressee of the book, someone who has read and understood the books of the philosophers, the reader is expected to know these philosophical teachings before reading Maimonides's exegesis of these biblical texts. And so, as someone who is also "wise," i.e., philosophically educated, and also "capable of understanding on his own," he is able to understand these hints and complete the interpretation alone.

---

[21] *Guide* iii.11–12, pp. 440–445.
[22] Klein-Braslavy, *Perush ha-Rambam la-sippurim 'al Adam*, 213–226.

For example, in his commentary on the Eden story, Maimonides claims that the word "serpent" should be understood through its etymology. In order to understand the hint, the reader must try to understand the figure of the serpent on the basis of the word's etymology and also Aristotelian psychology that Maimonides adopts, and assumes is familiar to his readers.

I once suggested that the etymological interpretation to which Maimonides alludes in the term "serpent" (*naḥash*) is *ḥash* in the sense of "hasty" or *ḥush* in the sense of "hurry," i.e., one who hurries to perform a task.[23] On the basis of Aristotelian psychology, I identified it with the appetitive faculty of the soul, the faculty that desires an object presented to it by another of the soul's faculties. In the Eden story, that is the imaginative faculty, I identified "Sama'el," which, according to the midrash in *Pirqei R. Eliezer* chapter 13 that Maimonides uses to complete this interpretation, is said to ride on the serpent, i.e., to rule over the serpent, with the imaginative faculty, which, in this case, provides the appetitive or desiderative faculty with its desired object. Efodi and Shem Tov understand the term "serpent" (*naḥash*) to be derived from "to guess" (*niḥesh*). Efodi writes, "the serpent (*naḥash*) is the imaginative faculty, and it is called so because it is particular to soothsayers (*menaḥashim*) and magicians."[24] Shem Tov explains similarly that "the meaning is that the serpent is the imaginative faculty, since through it the soothsayers guess."[25]

I now move to the challenges that the *Guide* presents the reader on the theoretical plane.

## The Methodological Approaches and Assumptions Upon Which the *Guide* Is Founded

A number of assumptions and methodological approaches lie at the base of the *Guide*'s discussions. Attempting to determine when Maimonides uses each one of them, applying each one of them in its own right while reading the book, determining the limits of the application, and attending to the relationships that hold between them, constitute a set of intellectual challenges of the highest rank that makes reading the book a thrilling journey that produces a variety of readings. I will illustrate this set of challenges very briefly by way of a single example.

[23] Ibid., p. 223.
[24] *Moreh Nevukhim be-ha'ataqat ha-Rav Shmuel ibn Tibbon 'im arba'a perushim* (Jerusalem, 1960) on *Guide* ii.30, p. 61a–b.
[25] Ibid., p. 61b.

## Philosophical Esotericism

As mentioned above, the *Guide* is an esoteric book presenting in esoteric fashion both Maimonides's biblical exegesis and his own theological and philosophical teachings. Many of the *Guide*'s commentators, medieval and modern, consider this to be the central methodological assumption on the basis of which one needs to understand the *Guide*.[26] According to his own words, Maimonides offers "chapter headings," which he purposefully scatters throughout the *Guide* in unsystematic fashion, and he also purposefully uses contradictions.[27] The assumption that the *Guide* itself is written in an esoteric fashion that leads the reader to search the book for Maimonides's real, hidden opinion.

The most prominent issue that is discussed in this connection is the creation of the world. In *Guide* i.35, Maimonides says that the issue of creation is "truly one of the mysteries of the Torah," a topic that can be revealed only to the intellectual elite.[28] If the manner of the creation of the world is an esoteric topic, knowledge of the truth of which is liable to harm the wider public, one can conclude that Maimonides's true opinion is the opinion that is furthest from that of the masses. The masses believe in creation after absolute privation[29] so the opinion that Maimonides conceals is the philosophical Aristotelian opinion that the world is everlasting.

## Limiting Human Knowledge – the Critical Spirit

Alongside the assumption of philosophical esotericism, the *Guide* also contains another methodological assumption, which is that human awareness is limited and cannot achieve certainty in all topics that arise for discussion. Maimonides asserts that when it is impossible to prove a particular theory demonstratively one ought to suspend judgment, to stop and not settle on a position at all.[30] This claim entails a critical, some say skeptical, position toward philosophical teachings widespread in his time and toward the very possibility of the human intellect to uncover the whole truth about the world and human beings.[31] It denies the naïve

---

[26] See, for example, my *Perush ha-Rambam le-sippur beri'at ha-'olam* (Jerusalem: Maimonides' Interpretation of the Story of Creation (Heb.) (Jerusalem: ha-Ḥevrah le-ḥeker ha-Miḳra be-Yisra'el, 1978), p. 52, and J. A. Diamond, *Maimonides and the Hermeneutics of Concealment: Deciphering Scripture and Midrash in the Guide of the Perplexed* (Albany: SUNY Press, 2002).

[27] For "chapter headings" see *Guide* i. intro. p. 6. For the use of contradictions see *ibid.*, p. 19.

[28] *Guide* i.35 p. 80.    [29] *Guide* ii.13, p. 281.    [30] *Guide* i.32, p. 70.

[31] For the skeptical reading see J. Stern, *The Matter and Form of Maimonides' Guide* (Cambridge, MA: Harvard University Press, 2013). See also Kenneth Seeskin's contribution to this volume.

conception of philosophy's status, according to which the philosophical teachings accepted at the time are necessarily true, and therefore also the assertion that philosophy is *always* the criterion for expounding the biblical and midrashic texts and interpreting religious beliefs. It also leads to the fact that Maimonides will not always possess philosophical solutions to the questions that he presents.

Maimonides does not clarify which topics the limits of knowledge apply to. The reader needs to determine on the basis of explicit statements in the *Guide*, and interpretation of Maimonides's discussions of the different theological and philosophical discussions, what the boundaries of these limits are, according to Maimonides, and to what he applies them. The reader then needs to deduce the conclusions that are called for from applying the principle of the limitations of knowledge regarding the topics to which Maimonides applies them according to Maimonides's interpretation.

In a previous article written years ago,[32] I raised the possibility that the topic of the world's creation is one of those to which the principle of the limitations of knowledge is to be applied: Maimonides holds that it is impossible to decide the question of the manner of the world's creation on the basis of intellectual investigation, and so he "stops" and does not determine a position. At the time, I relied on his biblical exegesis and claimed that, according to Maimonides's own interpretation, the biblical text of the creation story is opaque, and does not present a clear, unequivocal position that can be accepted on the basis of the plain meaning. He presents a plurality of interpretations to the verb that is key for understanding the way that the world is created in the Bible, the verb "to create," and also explains the creation story as a whole as a description of physics and philosophical anthropology. This interpretation accords both with the opinion that the world is created and also with the opinion that it is eternal.[33]

The claim that Maimonides applied the criterion of limiting human knowledge to the question of the world's creation, and refrained from a decision, sits well with the assumption of his esotericism, with his explicit claim that the issue of the world's creation is one of the "mysteries of the Torah." Maimonides needed to conceal the opinion that there is no unequivocal answer to the question from the wider public; the opinion

---

[32] S. Klein-Braslavy, "Maimonides' Interpretation of the Verb 'Bara' and the Creation of the World," (Heb.) *Da'at*, 16 (1986), p. 44.

[33] Ibid.

that the world is created after absolute privation needs to be taught to them, since it is the foundation of their belief in God's existence.[34]

## The Limitations of Knowledge and the Theological Conception

There is also room to say that the limitations of knowledge should be understood in the framework of the confrontation between philosophy and religion in Maimonides's teaching, as the late Pines claimed.[35] It is possible to see the task of limiting knowledge not only as the action of a critical philosopher who is concerned to find the philosophical truth and is unwilling to accept opinions that are unproved but also, and perhaps mainly, as the action of a theologian who is concerned to limit knowledge in order to limit philosophy and make way for religious beliefs and opinions. Determining the boundaries of intellectual knowledge makes room for positive theological statements. Regarding topics to which philosophy can offer no answer, one should accept the religious truth.

In *Guide* ii.25, Maimonides claims that since there is no demonstrative proof for Aristotle's opinion that the world is eternal, nor for Plato's opinion that the world is created out of pre-existing matter, one should accept the plain meaning of the biblical texts on this question, which is that the world is created after absolute privation.[36] Should one see Maimonides's true opinion in these claims? If so, why does he claim that the topic is esoteric? The opinion that the world is created after absolute privation is the one that is accepted by the masses.

## The Dialectical Method and the Effort to Reach Truth

The above discussion of the question of the world's creation is rooted in the assumption that it is possible to know only that which has been proven through demonstration. Only a demonstrative proof allows knowledge of the truth. Maimonides shows that there is no demonstrative proof regarding the question of the creation of the world. Therefore, it is possible to conclude that human knowledge stops at this point, and leaves room for religion. However, in other chapters of the *Guide*, including the chapters on the limitations of knowledge, Maimonides points at a different method

---

[34] Guide ii.31, p. 360.
[35] S. Pines, "The Limitations of Human Knowledge According to Al-Fārābī, ibn Bājja, and Maimonides," in I. Twersky (ed.), *Studies in Medieval Jewish History and Literature* (Cambridge, MA: Harvard University Press 1979), pp. 82–109.
[36] *Guide* ii.25, p. 329.

to decide a speculative question, a method that he is prepared to accept as scientific, which is the dialectical method, although Maimonides does not explicitly call it thus.[37] When there is no demonstrative proof for a particular opinion, one can accept it on the basis of a weaker scientific method, on the basis of strong claims, i.e., claims that are better than those that support the antithesis, which have fewer difficulties and doubts that those in favor of the opposed opinion. Maimonides claims that Aristotle himself made use of this method in his discussion of the world's eternity and on its basis, not on that of demonstrative proof, he decided that the world is eternal.[38] And indeed, in Guide ii.19, Maimonides presents strong arguments in favor of the thesis that the world is created, and he considers them to be better arguments than those of Aristotle that support the opinion that the world is eternal.[39] The conclusion that can be drawn from his discussion there is that the world is created, but not necessarily after absolute privation. It seems reasonable to suppose that Maimonides accepts Plato's opinion, that the world is created from pre-existent matter.[40] But in *Guide* ii.25, Maimonides says that he does not "favor" Plato's opinion because it is not established by demonstration,[41] So the conclusion could be that the world is created after absolute nothingness or that Maimonides accepts Plato's opinion and wants to hide it. What, then, is Maimonides's true opinion regarding creation? Which of the factors or of his methodological presuppositions should we accept when determining his position in the question? This is one of the intellectual challenges that the *Guide* puts before its readers.[42]

## Conclusion

Why does the *Guide* continue to exert such a vivid and pressing fascination for readers of various kinds even today? I have suggested that the challenge it presents us with is at the root of this interest, and that such a challenge manifests itself through different features of the *Guide* that render it difficult, if not impossible, to decipher completely. In order to illustrate

[37] See J. Kraemer, "Maimonides' Use of (Aristotelian) Dialectic," in Cohen and Levine (eds.), *Maimonides and the Sciences* (Dordrecht: Kluwer Academic, 2000), pp. 111–130.
[38] *Guide* ii.15, p. 290.    [39] *Guide* ii.19, pp. 302–312.
[40] H. Davidson, "Maimonides' Secret Position on Creation" in I. Twersky (ed.), *Studies in Medieval Jewish History and Literature* (Cambridge MA: Harvard University Press, 1979), pp. 16–40.
[41] *Guide* ii.25, p. 329.
[42] Different answers are argued for and critiqued in a symposium that appeared in R. Jospe and D. Schwartz (eds.), *Jewish Philosophy: Perspectives and Retrospectives* (Brighton: Academic Studies Press, 2012), pp. 157–232.

some of those features, I have focused on a variety of literary techniques that Maimonides uses in order to communicate his exegesis of biblical texts, and through them his real beliefs, to those who are capable of solving the *Guide*'s puzzles. These present an ongoing challenge that continues to speak to intelligent readers today, as it has constantly for over eight centuries.

# CHAPTER 7

# *Jewish Ritual as Trial in the* Guide of the Perplexed

## *Yehuda Halper*

According to Maimonides's *Mishneh Torah*, a Jewish worshipper ought to take care to observe the "presence of the sanctuary" when praying.[1] The worshipper observes this by facing the site of the Temple in Jerusalem, especially the Holy of Holies. In *Guide of the Perplexed* iii.45, Maimonides explains this law:

> *Abraham our father* singled out *Mount Moriah* because of its being the highest mountain there, proclaimed upon it the unity (*al-tawḥīd*), and determined and defined the direction toward which one would turn in prayer (*al-qibla*), fixing it exactly in the West. For *the Holy of Holies* is in the West. This is the meaning of the dictum [of the Sages]: *The Indwelling is in the West*. [The sages] made clear in the *Gemara* of the Tractate *Yoma* that *Abraham our Father* fixed the *qibla*, I mean *the Temple of the Holy of Holies* …. In my opinion there is also no doubt that the place singled out by *Abraham* in virtue of prophetic inspiration was known to *Moses our Master* and to many others. *Abraham* had recommended to them that that place should be a house of worship, just as the translator (*Onqelos*) sets forth when he says, "*Abraham worshipped and prayed in that place and said before the Lord: Here will worship the generations, and so on.*"[2]

The peculiarity of this passage has somehow escaped scholars and commentators, who, aside from Salomon Munk, focused almost exclusively on the lack of explicit references to this in BT *Yoma*.[3] Yet, this is far from the only difficulty the passage raises. Some of these difficulties are geographical: First, Mount Moriah is not the highest mountain "there" (*hunāka*); Mount Scopus is, as would have been apparent to Maimonides when he

---

[1] "*Nokhaḥ hamiqdash*," *Code of Law, Prayer* i.3, v.1, 3.

[2] *Guide* iii.45, tr. Pines p. 575 (translation modified), citing Onqelos's paraphrase of Genesis 22:14.

[3] Cf. Pines, p. 575, n. 3. See also Schwarz trans. vol. 2, p. 601, n. 6 and the sources that discuss possible passages in *Yoma* from which Maimonides may have derived this position. Note, however, that Maimonides does not mention the establishment of the *qibla* in his *Commentary on the Mishnah* to *Yoma*. *Qibla*, a characteristically Muslim term, also appears frequently in *Siddur R. Saadja Gaon*, ed. I. Davidson, S. Assaf, and B. I. Joel (Jerusalem: Rubin Mass, 2000), e.g., pp. 20, 30.

visited the Temple Mount in 1165.[4] Second, Mount Moriah is not "exactly in the West" (*li-'ain al-gharb*), a fact that also could not have escaped Maimonides, especially since to face the Temple from Spain, Morocco, or Egypt, he would have had to face East.[5] Other difficulties are interpretive: the mention of Mount Moriah and the quote from Onqelos on Genesis 22 make clear that Maimonides is discussing the *Binding of Isaac*. Yet, here Maimonides focuses on proclaiming the *tawḥīd* and establishing the site of the House of Worship and the *qibla* for future generations. None of these elements feature in Genesis 22 and all require some interpretive work to conjoin them in this way. In what follows, I shall argue that the prayers, in Maimonides's view, also recall Abraham's binding of Isaac at Moriah. In the second part of the chapter, I shall examine Abraham's trial on Moriah and Maimonides's notion of trial (*nissayon*). In the third part, I argue that prayer, like a trial (*nissayon*), accustoms one to the proper beliefs and actions, but without putting lives directly in harm's way.

### Prayer and the Binding of Isaac

Let us begin with the geographical difficulties. Maimonides's claim that Mount Moriah is in the West could appear to be a resolution to a Talmudic debate about the direction of prayer; the Mishnah in Berakhot apparently recommends turning to face the Holy of Holies in Jerusalem while praying,[6] while according to the Gemara in Baba Bathra (25a), Rabbi Aqiba's opposition to building tanneries in the western parts of a city is because the "Indwelling is in the West," i.e., because one prays toward the West. In the *Commentary on the Mishnah*, Maimonides addresses this issue only in his comments to the passage in Baba Bathra ii.9. There, he notes, "the cities of *al-Shām* [i.e., Israel and Syria] and that

---

[4] On Maimonides's visit to Jerusalem, see J. Kraemer, *Maimonides: The Life and World of One of Civilization's Greatest Minds* (New York: Doubleday, 2008), pp. 135–137. The topography of the Temple Mount may have been unknown to many commentators, especially those from Western Europe.

[5] J. Qafih somewhat reluctantly speculates that because Maimonides's illustrations in the *Commentary* are oriented with West on the top, Maimonides may have worked while sitting on a North-South oriented bed (in accordance with *Code of Law, Temple* vii.9), facing West, i.e., away from the *qibla*. See Qafih's introduction to his edition of the *Perush ha-Mishnah*, p. 20. Moreover, throughout the *Commentary on the Mishnah*, Maimonides often refers to Arabic words used "in the West" (*fi al-gharb*), i.e., in Morocco and Spain, implying thereby that he regarded Egypt (and the Land of Israel) as the East.

[6] BT *Berakhot* iv.5: "If one was riding a donkey, he should dismount from it [while he prays]. And if he is unable to dismount, he should turn his face [towards Jerusalem]. And if he is unable to turn his face, he should focus his heart toward the Holy of Holies." From Sefariya.com. See also Mishnah vi and *Tosefta Berakhot* iii.16.

which is behind them are toward the West."[7] Accordingly, Maimonides notes there, "Rabbi Aqiba is only worried about Western winds because the Sanctuary is in the West. This is the meaning of his dictum, 'The Indwelling is in the West.'" Here Maimonides, indeed, seems to be suggesting that Rabbi Aqiba and the Mishnah in Berakhot are in agreement that prayer is in the direction of the Sanctuary, even if reaching such an agreement requires assimilating *al-Shām* and everything "behind" it into "the West." The inclusion of this same statement of Rabbi Aqiba in *Guide* iii.45 might suggest that Maimonides is employing the same understanding of "West" there too.

However, Maimonides dispels any such notions in *Guide* iii.45 when he explains Abraham's choice of the Western direction: "In my opinion, the reason for this is as follows: Inasmuch as at that time the opinion generally accepted in the world was ... that the sun should be worshipped ... all men turned when praying toward the East. Therefore *Abraham our Father* turned, when praying on *Mount Moriah* – I mean in the *Sanctuary* (*miqdash*) – toward the West, so as to turn his back upon the sun."[8] Moreover, Maimonides recalls that when Israel returned to worshipping the sun, as described in Ezekiel 8, they had "their faces toward the East; and they worshiped the sun."[9] Accordingly, for Maimonides and most of his readers, praying toward the *qibla* (at least in the morning[10]) would be praying toward the rising sun, precisely the opposite of Abraham's intention in the prayer.

Some details of the layout of the Temple Mount help explain what Maimonides saw as Abraham's intention in establishing the *qibla*. According to Maimonides in the *Mishneh Torah*, "There was a tradition known to all that the place where David and Solomon built the altar in the threshing floor of Araunah was the same place where Abraham built the altar on which he bound Isaac."[11] Earlier, Maimonides had identified the Holy of Holies as the place toward which Abraham had turned and as therefore the *qibla*. If Abraham was standing at the altar and facing the future site of the Holy of Holies, then he was facing West. This is bolstered by the apparent identification of "the site of the altar" with the "Sanctuary"

[7] "*Allatī hiya bilād al-Shām wa-mā ba'duhā li-jihat al-gharb*" *Commentary on the Mishnah, Seder neziqin*, p. 103 (Heb. pag.).
[8] Pines, p. 575.   [9] Ibid., quoting Ezekiel 8:16.
[10] Abraham, it seems, would have prayed once a day, in the morning, according to Maimonides's *Code of Law, Prayer* i.
[11] Maimonides, *The Code of Maimonides: Book Eight: The Book of Temple Service*, tr. M. Lewittes (New Haven: Yale University Press, 1957), *Temple* ii.2, p. 10.

(*miqdash*) in the *Code of Law*.[12] So, when *"Abraham our Father* turned, when praying on *Mount Moriah* – I mean in the *Sanctuary* (*miqdash*) – toward the West," he turned toward what would become the Holy of Holies.

Consequently, it seems that when Maimonides mentions the *qibla* as the direction of Jewish prayer, he does not mean that Jews face the West wherever they are, but that they face the Holy of Holies. Since they, including Maimonides himself, are not literally facing West, they can only emphasize that they are not praying to the sun in a non-literal fashion. In any case, once the Rabbis ordained two prayer services during the day and one at night[13] there was no way to face West literally and away from the sun at every service. Rather, the direction of prayer in relation to the sun had to become figurative. Indeed, in the *Mishneh Torah,* rather than talk about a *qibla* or the direction of prayer, Maimonides uses the expression "in the presence of the sanctuary."[14] Here it is clear that it is not the literal presence of the sanctuary that is intended, but that one should feel or imagine the presence of the sanctuary. If "sanctuary" here also refers to the altar of the Temple, then one who is at prayer is to imagine himself as if he is at the altar, facing the Holy of Holies, which is to the West of the altar.[15]

If the description of the *qibla* is so that one can imagine himself praying on the Temple Mount, the assertion that it is "the highest mountain there" should also refer to the imagined area of prayer. This area must be quite limited indeed since the immediately adjacent hills, including Mount Zion, are all taller than Mount Moriah. The one at prayer would then have to imagine no more than Mount Moriah in order to conceive of it as the highest mountain "there" (*hunāka*). Alternatively, Salomon Munk suggests that when he calls Mount Moriah "the highest mountain there" he is referring to Ezekiel 20:40, where Ezekiel seems to be using the expression *har marom* to refer to the Temple Mount.[16] Ezekiel's expression

---

[12] Ibid., ii.1: "The site of the Altar was defined very specifically and was never to be changed.... It was on the site of the Sanctuary that Isaac was bound ... " (translation modified).

[13] *Code of Law, Prayer* i.5–6.    [14] See note 1 above.

[15] The process of imaging one's location may also explain Maimonides's uncharacteristic prolixity in *Laws of Prayer* v.3: "How can one be in the presence of the sanctuary? If he is standing outside of Israel, he directs his face to the presence of Israel and prays. If he is standing in Israel, he directs his face toward Jerusalem. If he is standing in Jerusalem, he directs his face toward the Sanctuary. If he is standing in the Sanctuary, he directs his face to the Holy of Holies. One who is blind or unable to determine the direction, or is travelling on a ship, directs his heart toward the Indwelling and prays" (my translation). This passage could have read, "One directs his face toward the Holy of Holies, unless he is blind, etc." The case-by-case scenario suggests that one who is about to pray imagines himself in Israel, in Jerusalem, in the Sanctuary, and then facing the Holy of Holies.

[16] See *Guide*, ed. Munk, vol. 3, p. 348, n. 4

echoes Maimonides's citation of *"harim meromim"* (*"high mountains"*) from Deuteronomy 6:9 and 11:20 referring to the places of prayer of idolaters at the beginning of *Guide* iii.45. If Munk is correct, then Maimonides's terming Mount Moriah "the highest mountain" may not refer to its size, but rather to its "exalted station, nobility, and great worth" – which Maimonides explains is a meaning of words from the root *ram* in *Guide* i.20.[17] The exaltedness of Mount Moriah before the Binding of Isaac would in all likelihood be due to its being, at least according to the *Mishneh Torah*, the site where Adam was created and brought sacrifices, where Cain and Abel brought their sacrifices, and where Noah brought a sacrifice after the flood.[18]

In *Guide* iii.45, Maimonides, then, interweaves the story of Abraham, the Binding of Isaac, the establishment of the *qibla*, and the proclamation of the *tawḥīd* on a mountain. Moreover, by positioning oneself in the same direction, even in one's imagination, as Abraham during the sacrifices and daily prayers, Maimonides implies that the primary Jewish rituals somehow recall Abraham's Binding of Isaac at Mount Moriah.[19] This is despite the feeling, which I think is quite unavoidable, that the association of Abraham with the *qibla* and the *tawḥīd* on Mount Moriah in *Guide* iii.45 is somewhat artificial. Indeed, Maimonides does not explain in iii.45 *why* these events should be associated with the Binding of Isaac.

## The Meaning of Trial (*nissayon*)

Maimonides elucidates the Binding of Isaac in his description of trial in *Guide* iii.24. This chapter is somewhat like the chapters explaining equivocal Biblical terms in Part I of the *Guide* as it purports to be an exposition of the meaning of the Hebrew term for trial, *nissayon*.[20] Accordingly, Maimonides mentions a variety of different meanings of the term, from "what is generally accepted among people" to "the external meaning of the *trials* mentioned in the Torah" to "the aim and meaning of all the *trials*

---

[17] Tr. Pines, p. 46.

[18] See *Code of Law, Temple* ii.2. Cf. *Pirkê de Rabbi Eliezer*, tr. G. Friedlander (London: Kegan Paul, Trench, Trubner and New York: Bloch, 1916), pp. 143, 226–227.

[19] Cf. also *Commentary on the Mishnah, Tamid* iv.1, p. 418, where Maimonides, following the Talmud, derives the laws for binding sacrificial animals in the Temple from the way Isaac was bound by Abraham on Moriah. See also pp. 20–21 of the same volume for a further association of Mount Moriah with the sacrifices.

[20] Unlike the lexicographical chapters, however, iii.24 begins with *amr al-nissayon*. The Arabic term, *amr*, can mean "meaning" (Ibn Tibbon has *'inyan* here) but also "command."

mentioned in the Torah."²¹ Additionally, these meanings of the Hebrew term *nissayon* are distinct from the meanings Maimonides sees in the Arabic terms that are usually used for trial, *miḥna* and *balā'*. By comparing how Maimonides does use these Arabic terms in the *Guide* with the various meanings Maimonides assigns to the term *nissayon* we shall see that Maimonides sees *nissayon* as akin to a parable (*mathal*), if not actually a parable. In the final section of this chapter, we shall see that it is the parable-like character of *nissayon* that allows Maimonides to connect the Binding of Isaac to Abraham's declaration of the *tawḥīd* and to the rituals performed on the Temple Mount.

Throughout iii.24, Maimonides takes care to use the Hebrew term *nissayon* and its Hebrew verb *nissah* in all but two places; that is, he generally avoids giving it an Arabic equivalent. This is in contrast to the *Commentary on the Mishnah* where Maimonides used the Arabic *miḥna* and *'imtaḥana* for *nissayon* and *nissah* respectively.²² The association between these terms must have been common as we find it in both Saadia al-Fayyūmī²³ and Baḥya ibn Paquda.²⁴ Maimonides's first use of this Arabic term in iii.24 is in explanation of "the external meaning (*ẓāhir*) of the *nisyonot* mentioned in the Torah." According to Maimonides, "they took place in order to test (*al-'imtiḥān*) and to receive information so that one could know the degree of faith or the degree of obedience of the individual or nation in question."²⁵ Maimonides calls this "the great difficulty" and suggests that his explanation of *nissayon* will resolve the difficulty.²⁶ The explanation of *nissayon*, however, does not relate to the notion of "test," *al-'imtiḥān*. Maimonides's second use of the term occurs at the end of iii.24, when he says, "It should not be [understood²⁷] that God, may He be exalted, wants to test (*yamtaḥinu*) and try out a thing in order to know that which He did not know before."²⁸ This negative formulation suggests that a test, *miḥna*, is one that tests something the tester did not know before.

²¹ *Guide* iii.45, pp. 497–498.
²² See Maimonides's discussion of the ten trials of Abraham described in Mishnah *Aboth* v.3 in *Commentary on the Mishnah, Avot*, pp. 452–454.
²³ In both *Tafsir* to Genesis 22 and in *Opinion and Beliefs*; see A. van der Heide, *'Now I Know': Five Centuries of Aqedah Exegesis* (Amsterdam: Springer, 2017), pp. 59–70; S. Feldman, "The Binding of Isaac" in T. Rudavsky (ed.), *Divine Omniscience and Omnipotence in Medieval Philosophy* (Dordrecht, Boston, Lancaster, 1985), pp. 106–109. Feldman emphasizes that one meaning of *miḥna* is affliction, a meaning also clearly present in Baḥya ibn Paquda's writing.
²⁴ See, e.g., Baḥya ibn Paquda, *Torat ḥobot helebabot*, ed. and Heb. tr. J. Qafih (Jerusalem: Aqiba Joseph, 1972/3), pp. 230–231.
²⁵ *Guide* iii.45, p. 498.      ²⁶ *Guide* iii.24, p. 498.
²⁷ Pines has "believed" here, though this is not justified by the Arabic.      ²⁸ *Guide* iii.24, p. 502.

This interpretation of *miḥna* is born out in Maimonides's uses of forms of the term *miḥna / 'imtaḥana* in three other places in the *Guide*. In the Epistle Dedicatory, he mentions having received his student's letter and rhymed prose composition, but not yet having put his grasp (*taṣawwur*) to the test (*'imtaḥana*); in this case, it is intellectual capabilities that are put to the test in the form of studying the science, not simply a test of faith or obedience. In ii.40, Maimonides addresses the reader in the second person about how to test (*'imtiḥān*) people who claim to be prophets: through considering the perfection of the individual, studying their actions and way of life.[29] This has a certain parallel in the account of *nissayon* in iii.24, where God tries (*menasseh*) "you." That is, it seems God tries (*menasseh*) the people of Israel by sending a false prophet and Israel responds by testing (*'imtiḥān*) the false prophet. Israel passes God's trial, *nissayon,* by successfully making her own *'imtiḥān.* The test (*'imtiḥān*) Israel is to make appears to include both intellectual capabilities ("the perfection of the individual") and, especially, moral perfection. The third occurrence of the term is in iii.23, where Maimonides appears to translate Job's statement (9:23), *le-massat neqiyyim yil'ag,* by the Arabic, *fa-bi-miḥnat al-abriyā yahza'u,* both of which probably mean, "He [viz. God, according to Job's supposition] will mock the test of the guiltless."[30] The character of this test is described generally in Job 9, with the result being Job's initial position toward the beginning of the Book of Job that God is too great to mind the affairs of men with anything other than mockery. These examples suggest that Maimonides sees *miḥna* and *'imtaḥana* (which he associates with the Hebrew *massah*) as tests that human beings set up regarding moral and conceptual issues. The examples further highlight that the human beings who set up a *miḥna* do not know the outcome; Maimonides does not know whether his student will be able to understand the book, the people testing the self-proclaimed prophet do not know if he is in fact a prophet, and Job has no idea why God is punishing him.

Accordingly, we can surmise why Maimonides says that "the great difficulty" is the notion that *nissayon* is a test (*'imtiḥān*) "so that one could know the degree of faith or the degree of obedience of the individual or nation in question."[31] If the outcome of a *miḥna* is unknown, then if

---

[29] *Guide* iii.24, p. 384.

[30] *Guide* iii.24, p. 491. Pines, following the JPS translation, translates the Hebrew *massah* and the Arabic *miḥna* as "calamity." Cf. *Commentary on the Mishnah, Avot* v. 3 for the discussion of trial in Exodus 17:7, Deuteronomy 6:16 and 33:8, and Psalm 95:8, all of which use the term *massah* probably as "test."

[31] Ibid., p. 498. On this as the "great difficulty" see H. Kasher, "Afflictions without Transgression: Towards the Meaning of 'Trial' in the *Guide of the Perplexed,*" *Daat,* 26 (1991), 35–41 (Heb.).

God made a *miḥna*, he would have to *not know* whether the individual or nation in question was faithful or obedient. Indeed, this seems to be the implication of three verses from the Bible: "Now I know that thou fearest God" (Genesis 22:12, referring to the Binding); "For the Lord your God tries you out to know whether you do love the Lord" (Deuteronomy 13:4, referring to the false prophet); and "To know what was in your heart" (Deuteronomy 8:2, referring to Israel's 40 years in the desert).[32] Yet, Maimonides is adamant that God does not gain knowledge through a *nissayon*. Thus, his statement at the end of iii.24 that one ought not understand God to be making a test (*yamtaḥinu*) "in order to know that which He did not know before." The "great difficulty" is suggested by the verses in the Bible, according to which it would seem that God does in fact want to come to know something about the subject of the tests. Accordingly, Maimonides's interpretations of the meanings of *nissayon* will explain how the Bible does not, despite appearances to the contrary, actually hold this view. That is, Maimonides clarifies that once one understands "the meanings of the *nisyonot*" according to Maimonides's clarification in *Guide* iii.24, he will understand how they are emphatically *not* a *miḥna* for the benefit of God's knowledge.

Another Arabic term Maimonides could have used in association with *nissayon* is *balā'*, which, like *miḥna*, can mean both affliction and trial. It appears in Quran 37:106 where Allah explicitly calls the Binding of Abraham's son "a clear *balā'*."[33] To my mind, Maimonides's use of the plural of this term, *balāya*,[34] is in response to the Quran and meant to be understood in contrast to the Hebrew meanings of *nissayon*. Thus, Maimonides does not use the term in connection with Abraham, but it comes up primarily in connection with Job in *Guide* iii.23.[35] Thus, "Job and his friends" agree that "God had caused these *balāya* to befall him."[36] Moreover, according to Maimonides, the purpose of the story of Job is to

[32] *Guide* iii.24, p. 498.
[33] See also Quran 2:124, which likely refers to the Binding. *balā'* became the standard term for referring to the trials of Abraham.
[34] On the plural form, see Lane, vol. 1, p. 256.
[35] There are three exceptions: 1. In *Guide* iii.12, p. 442, where Maimonides refers to Abū Bakr al-Rāzī's claim that the world is more bad than good, he says that al-Rāzī sought to investigate *balāya*. 2. In iii.17, p. 469, Maimonides says "our opinion, I mean the opinion of our Law" is "all of [the *balāya* that occur] are determined according to the deserts of the men concerned." In both of these cases, it is clear that there is nothing to be gained from studying the afflictions themselves. 3. According to iii.53, p. 632, God is called "judge" because there are good things that happen in the world but also *balāya*, all "necessitated by judgment which is consequent upon wisdom." This seems to agree with the second incidence of *balāya*.
[36] *Guide* iii.23, p. 490.

make known the opinions of each of the interlocutors as to why "the greatest and heaviest *balāya* befall the most perfect individual."[37] The situations of Job and the Quranic Abraham are in some respects quite similar: a perfect human being is given a *balā'* from God and must become reconciled to the *balā'* and accept God.[38] The stories of Job and Abraham differ, however, in that Job undergoes a complete transformation after the *balāya*, whereas Maimonides's Abraham undergoes no such transformation. When he first received the *balāya*, Job "had no true knowledge and knew the deity only because of his acceptance of authority, just as the multitude adhering to the Law know it."[39] It is in this stage that he mentions God's mockery of human tests. However, by the end of the book, after philosophical speculation, "when he knew God with a certain knowledge, he admitted that true happiness, which is the knowledge of the deity, is guaranteed to all who know Him and that a human being cannot be troubled in it by any such *balāya*."[40] This transformation allows Job to aim for true happiness without being troubled by "the things thought to be happiness," including wealth and children. Moreover, by focusing on knowing God, Job ceases to concern himself with thinking about the *balāya*. As a result, Job learns from his *balāya*, becomes a model penitent, leaves behind his thoughts about his children and wealth, and strives to think only of God.

By choosing to avoid the Arabic term *balā'* entirely in iii.24, after using it repeatedly in iii.23, Maimonides is clearly signaling that he does not see *nissayon* as equivalent to *balā'*. This is especially striking since Maimonides's expression, "God had caused these *balāya* to befall [Job]," resonates at the beginning of Maimonides's account of the "generally accepted" (*mashhūr*) view of *nissayon*: "God causes calamities (*'āfāt*) to befall an individual, without their having been preceded by a sin, in order that his reward be increased."[41] In iii.17, in the only mention of the term *nissayon* in the *Guide* outside of iii.24, Maimonides says that it is an error to associate Abraham's *nissayon* at Moriah with the Mu'tazilite notion of providence, according to which everyone receives compensation for the bad things that happen to

---

[37] Ibid., p. 491.
[38] Cf. al-Ghazālī's notion of trial in *Al-Ghazālī on Patience and Thankfulness: Book XXXIII of the Revival of the Religious Sciences*, tr. H. T. Littlejohn (Great Shelford: The Islamic Texts Society, 2011), pp. 189–204.
[39] *Guide* iii.23, 492. Note also that according to Job the *balāya* themselves encourage one to adopt certain opinions at first.
[40] Ibid., pp. 492–3, translation modified.     [41] Ibid., p. 497, translation modified.

them.[42] Maimonides's use of "reward" (*'ujrah*, a term that usually denotes monetary payment[43]) when describing the "generally accepted" view of providence in iii.24 suggests that it is the same as the Mu'tazilite notion of compensation outlined in iii.17. This notion of compensation is erroneous when applied to providence and so would seem to be erroneous when applied to the concept of *nissayon*.

Nevertheless, there is "one passage [in the Torah] whose external meaning suggests such a notion,"[44] *viz.* the Mu'tazilite notion of compensation. It turns out that the passage he has in mind is Deuteronomy 8:16, concerning *manna* in the desert. According to the Biblical passage, the manna was provided "that He might afflict thee, and that He might try thee out [*nasotekha*], to do thee good at thy latter end."[45] To explain this passage, Maimonides says:

> *nasotekha* [try thee out] may mean: to accustom thee.. . . It is as if it said that He, may He be exalted, has first accustomed you to misery in the desert in order to make your well-being greater when once you came into the land.. . . And it is known that but for their misery and weariness in the desert, they would not have been able to conquer the land and fight.. . . For prosperity does away with courage, whereas a hard life and fatigue necessarily produce courage – this being the *good* that, according to the story in question, will come *at their latter end*.[46]

To explain this notion, then, Maimonides introduces a new meaning of *nissayon*: that of accustoming one to something. In this way, a *nissayon* does, indeed, bring about a good (*al-tobah*) in return for affliction. Yet this good is not monetary compensation, but a virtue, in this case courage. Moreover, in this case, the affliction itself is a necessary cause of the good. Monetary compensation (*'ujrah*) is a different kind of return; even though it may be a compensation for affliction, it is not necessarily caused by the affliction itself. The development of courage, however, is. Moreover, it is in keeping with human nature to gain virtues after the proper regimen of accustoming and accordingly the "good . . . at their latter end" is a natural outcome of their activities. The "generally accepted" view of *nissayon* is

---

[42] Ibid., pp. 470–471. Saadia is probably "among the latter-day Gaonim [who] have heard [this notion of Providence] from the Mu'tazila and have approved of it and believed it." See Saadia, *Tafsir* to Genesis 22.

[43] The term *'ujrah* appears six times outside of iii.24, in ii.46 and iii.49. In all of those cases, Pines translates the term "wages" (pp. 406 and 604). Maimonides's use of this term for "reward" or recompense may be influenced by *Mishnah Aboth* v.23: "Ben He He says, the reward (*agra'*) is in accordance with the pain."

[44] *Guide* iii.24, p. 498.     [45] Ibid., p. 499.     [46] Ibid., pp. 499–500.

thus not entirely incorrect. God does "cause calamities to befall an individual, without their having been preceded by a sin," but not in order that
they can receive a monetary reward, but, at least in some cases, so that they
can acquire a virtue through a process of accustoming.

In light of this, we may ask once again why Job is said to have suffered
*balāya*, but not a *nissayon*. The *balāya* Job suffered caused him and his
friends to contemplate God until he learned what he could infer from
natural matters,[47] and came to know God with certain knowledge. This
process, which Maimonides notes involves "prophetic revelation,"[48] is the
result of a long discussion and serious contemplation. That is, in the wake
of the *balāya*, Job goes from having the same opinion about God as the
multitude, through an intense process of study and inquiry, into a scientific
opinion of God, which if not true happiness itself, aims at true happiness
and is close enough to true happiness to be a form of prophecy. The *balāya*,
then, apparently cause Job to become accustomed to a different worldview
and thereby to acquire intellectual virtue. The story of Job would thus seem
to be an example of the "commonly accepted" view of *nissayon*, corrected
by replacing the Muʿtazilite notion of compensation with accustoming for
the purpose of acquiring virtue. Why then does Maimonides describe Job's
ordeal as *balāya* and not *nissayon*?

Comparison with Abraham is illustrative: Like Job, Abraham is faced
with losing children at God's request. Moreover, Abraham is unperturbed
in the face of God's request because of his love and fear of God. Abraham's
prophecy, as well as his love and fear of God are intellectual, based on
knowledge of God. Later in the *Guide*, Maimonides tells us that when
Abraham grew up

> it became clear to him that there is a separate deity that is neither a body nor
> a force in a body and that all the stars and the spheres were made by Him,
> and he understood that the fables upon which he was brought up were
> absurd ... He publicly manifested his disagreement with [the Sabians
> around him] and called *in the name of the Lord, God of the World* – both
> the existence of the deity and the creation of the world in time by that deity
> being comprised in that call.[49]

Like Job, Abraham came to an understanding of God by studying the
natural world. Also like Job, he moves beyond the opinion of those around
him and adopts an opinion based on scientific inference. Yet, this opinion
finds its expression in Genesis 21:33, right in the middle of events that lead

---

[47] Ibid., pp. 496–497.    [48] *waḥy*, p. 496.    [49] Ibid., p. 516.

up to the Binding of Isaac in Genesis 22. That is, Abraham has apparently gained his understanding of God and the world, or at least the chief elements in it, *before* he has the prophecy leading to the binding of Isaac. Consequently, Abraham's *nissayon* does not change him in the way that Job's *balāya* changed him. Indeed, there is no indication in *Guide* iii.24 or elsewhere that Abraham undergoes any change at all through the *nissayon*. If we can apply the message of *Guide* iii.23 to iii.24, we might say that Abraham's focus on knowing God and his pursuit of happiness thereby leave him unfazed by the experience of the Binding. It would seem then that the difference between the *balāya* and the *nissayon* lies in that the subject of the *balāya* is changed by the process or at least can be, while the subject of the *nissayon* need not be changed by it.

In sum, we have seen that in the *Guide* Maimonides uses the Arabic terms *miḥna* and *balā'* to signify tests or misfortunes that are for the sake of different groups. The *miḥna* is for the sake of those who make the test and through the test come to some kind of knowledge. The *balā'* is for the sake of those who suffer the *balāya*, because in questioning the justice of the natural world, they come, or at least *can* come to an understanding of the natural world and to an understanding of God.[50] Now, neither of these terms can apply to Abraham's *nissayon* at Moriah. It is not a *miḥna* from God since the notion that God would construct such a test to know something He did not know before ought not be accepted. It is also not a *balā'*, since Abraham does not undergo a fundamental change in response to it; his main insights into God's oneness were prior to the Binding of Isaac, and we have no indication that they changed in response to the event.

Thus, Maimonides turns to the Hebrew word *nissayon* to describe a different kind of trial made for the sake of a different group. After describing the generally accepted view and the external meaning of *nisyonot*, Maimonides says:

> Know that the aim and meaning of all the *nisyonot* is to let the people know what they ought to do or what they must believe. Accordingly, the notion of a *nissayon* consists as it were in a certain act being done, the purpose being not the act itself, but the latter's being an example to be imitated or followed.[51]

---

[50] Thus, in iii.53, p. 632, Maimonides says that God is called "judge" because He gives people *balāya*, thereby encouraging them to become better. As in the examples in note 35, there is nothing to be gained by studying the *balāya* themselves, only by the study of the justice inherent in the natural order.

[51] *Guide* iii.24, p. 498, translation modified.

The *nissayon*, then, is for the sake of "the people," particularly, it seems from the ensuing discussion, for "the religious communities" (*al-milal*). That is, it is the believers, possibly including Muslims and Christians as well, who are to benefit from the *nissayon*, not the one being tried, nor the one setting up the trial.[52] This allows us to modify the "external meaning" of the *nissayon* as a test (*al-'imtiḥān*) of faith and obedience to a demonstration of faith and obedience to a larger audience of people. One of the problems Maimonides identified with the Binding was that it "was known only to God and the two individuals involved," *viz.* to Abraham and Isaac. How, then, could it be addressed to "the people" or to "the religious communities"? Maimonides does not answer this question, but it is nevertheless clear that the story of the Binding gains its general audience through its inclusion in a public narrative, i.e., in the Bible. Indeed, it is because of its inclusion in the Bible that it becomes "an example to be imitated and followed" and so a *nissayon* for "the people."

That the beneficiaries of the *nisyonot* include the readers of the Bible is suggested in the other examples of *nisyonot* that Maimonides brings in iii.24.[53] Thus, with regard to the *nissayon* of the false prophet, Maimonides notes:

> God wished to make known hereby to the religious communities the extent of your certitude with regard to His Law, may He be exalted, and your apprehension of its true reality; and also to make known that you do not let yourselves be deceived by the deceptions of a deceiver and that your faith in God cannot be disturbed. This will be a support for everyone who seeks the truth, for he will seek out the beliefs that are so firm that when one has them

---

[52] Maimonides, like Saadia before him, relies on interpreting the Hebrew *yada'ti* to mean not "I [God's angel] know" (*'araftu*), but "I have made known" (*'arraftu*). See van de Heide, *'Now I know'*, 64–66 and 192–193. Kasher, "Afflictions," 40, suggests that the reading, "Now I have made known," depends on Maimonides's identification of the angel with the Active Intellect in *Guide* ii.45. Thus, when the angel knows, all humanity knows, or at least has the potential to know; in effect, only the intellectual elite can know this.

[53] At the beginning of iii.24, Maimonides says, "The Torah mentions [the term *nissayon*] in six places, as I shall make clear to you" (my translation). Usually, Maimonides accompanies such claims with clear lists. Here he is somewhat less clear. Maimonides speaks of four events clearly: the Binding of Isaac (Genesis 22); False Prophet (Deuteronomy 13:4); Manna (Exodus 16:4, Deuteronomy 8:2, 16); and Sinai (Exodus 20:20, incorrectly listed by Pines as Exodus 20:17 on p. 500, n. 21). The trial of the Manna could perhaps be separated into three "places": two of them describing the *manna* (Exodus 16:4 and Deuteronomy 8:16) and one describing all of the afflictions during Israel's 40 years in the desert (Deuteronomy 8:2). However, this seems to be in fact two events (manna and desert) or else two passages, Exodus 16 and Deuteronomy 8 (which is continuous here). As a result, there seem to be five, rather than six "places" where the Torah speaks about *nissayon*. It seems possible to me that Maimonides sees the entire Torah as a *nissayon*. This would be parallel to Muslim views that the entire Quran can be understood as a trial. See John Nawas, "Trial," in *Encyclopaedia of the Qur'ān* (Brill Online, consulted 2018).

one pays no attention to the man who tries to compete through working a miracle.[54]

We saw earlier, that when someone who claims to be a prophet arises, the people of the time are to test (*'imtiḥān*) him or her to find out if the claim is true. Here, Maimonides indicates that such a test is a *nissayon* because it addresses "the religious communities" and "everyone who seeks the truth." How does it attain such a wide audience? Perhaps through people hearing about the test, but it is more likely that it is through people reading about the test in the Bible. We noted earlier that both Maimonides's injunction to make a *miḥna* of the claimant to prophecy in *Guide* ii.40 and the statement in Deuteronomy 13:4 that God makes a trial (*menasseh*) are addressed to a second-person object, which in context is the people of Israel. In the first, Israel makes a test to find out whether the claimant is a prophet or not. In the second, Israel is the object of the *nissayon*; that is, Israel is undergoing the *nissayon*. If the benefit of a *nissayon* is not for the subject, nor for the object, but for the audience, then it is clear why the "religious communities" and "everyone who seeks the truth" benefit from it. Again, their access to this *nissayon* is either through hearsay at the time it happens, or else through the Bible. What is learned by the Biblical reader is that impossible things cannot undermine truly firm beliefs. This has a political benefit in Israel, *viz.* not undermining the regime, but also a theoretical benefit, as "everyone who seeks the truth" will then seek out those beliefs.

Similarly Israel's *nisyonot* of the *manna* and the afflictions in the desert were "in order that the religious communities should know ... and that it should be generally accepted throughout the world that those who wholly devote themselves to His service, may He be exalted, are provided by Him with food in an unthought-of way."[55] Again, the Bible speaks of "trying you" (*nassotekha*), i.e., Israel, but the beneficiary of the trial is "the religious communities ... throughout the world." God's accustoming of the Israelites for the sake of acquiring courage is indeed for the benefit of the Israelites, but in Maimonides's presentation this is only secondary. Indeed, if the religious communities are to learn of the benefits of devotion to God, then the gradual inculcation of courage may be a great example to learn from.

What do the readers of the Bible learn from a *nissayon*? In his definition of *nissayon* above, Maimonides says that it is "not the act itself" that is the

[54] *Guide* iii.24, pp. 498–499.    [55] *Guide* iii.24, p. 499.

intention of the *nissayon*. Rather, the act is an example for what is to be imitated or followed. Yet, it is clear that the example he has in mind is not an example of the act itself, but of what should be learned from the act. Thus, the readers of the Bible are not urged to undergo the afflictions of the desert; nor are they expected to follow the example of Abraham by tying their children up on altars. Rather, they are to imitate that of which the *nissayon* is an example. Indeed, Maimonides says here that the act of the *nissayon* is meant to teach people "what they ought to do or what they must believe."

Accordingly, the act of the *nissayon* is a kind of parable, or at least functions like a parable. That is, it is a text in the Bible that, aside from its literal narrative, is intended to teach its readers actions and beliefs. In the introduction to *Guide* i, Maimonides says of prophetic parables, "Their external meaning (*ẓāhir*) contains wisdom that is useful in many respects, among which is the welfare of human societies . . . Their internal meaning (*bāṭin*), on the other hand, contains wisdom that is useful for beliefs concerned with truth."[56] In *nisyonot* and in parables we see the various elements: the narrative text, the benefit for communal welfare, and the "wisdom that is useful for beliefs concerned with truth."

The presence of these elements in the examples brought above is, for the most part, clear. The *nissayon* of the false prophet (and the events on Sinai) protects the integrity of the Law and thereby contributes to the welfare of the community. Moreover, "everyone who seeks the truth," both Jews and non-Jews who hear of this episode, "will seek out the beliefs that are so firm that when one has them one pays no attention to the man who tries to compete through working a miracle."[57] Similarly, concerning the *manna* and the afflictions of Israel in the desert, the reader will learn about the inculcation of courage, which can certainly contribute to the welfare of society, and about the usefulness and benefits of adherence to the Law. Maimonides does not explicitly point to a theoretical benefit gained by the reader with respect to these *nisyonot*, but we may infer one by comparison with the *nissayon* of the false prophet: The reader may be urged to seek out the truth of those theoretical beliefs that led Israel to undergo such afflictions in order to inculcate courage.

---

[56] *Guide* i.int., p. 12. Compare with *Guide* iii.50, p. 613, "All the stories that you find mentioned in the *Torah* occur there for a necessary utility for the Law; either they give a correct notion of an opinion that is a pillar of the Law, or they rectify some action." My understanding of parable here has benefitted greatly from J. Stern, The Matter and Form of Maimonides' *Guide* (Cambridge, MA: Harvard University Press, 2013), pp. 18–63.

[57] *Guide* iii.24, p. 499.

Returning to the case of Abraham's *nissayon*, if the external meaning (properly understood) of a *nissayon* is a demonstration of faith and obedience to a large audience of people, as I argued above, then we can see how the story of the Binding reinforces faith and obedience among those who adhere to the Law. Abraham's *nissayon* shows "the limit of love for God, may He be exalted, and fear of Him,"[58] a formulation that emphasizes the dedication to following the Law to which all believers ought to aspire. Such dedication would undoubtedly contribute to the success of the Law and thereby the welfare of the society that adheres to it. Moreover, Maimonides says, it is an example of the importance of belief in that which prophets receive "from God in a prophetic revelation,"[59] i.e., in the entire Law. Maimonides does not tell us a theoretical inner meaning (*bāṭin*) of this *nissayon*, but again we can infer one by comparison with the false prophet *nissayon*. One reading or hearing of Abraham's dedication and obedience would undoubtedly seek out the beliefs that are so firm that when one has them one is willing to go so far as to sacrifice one's son for their sake.[60]

## Performing the *tawḥīd*

The power of the story of the Binding of Isaac to contribute to the welfare of the community and to encourage readers to seek out true beliefs does not explain its connection to the *tawḥīd*. As we saw, in *Guide* iii.45 Maimonides says that when Abraham chose Mount Moriah, he "proclaimed upon it the unity (*al-tawḥīd*)," a proclamation that does not feature in the Biblical story of the Binding. It could be understood from certain Midrashim[61] or it could be based on a kind of pun between the Hebrew for Binding (*'aqedah*) and the Arabic for creed, or expression of belief, especially belief in the unity of God (*'aqīda*), both of which are spelled the same in Hebrew letters. Maimonides, though, does not explicitly reveal his source for the connection between the Binding and the declaration of the unity (*tawḥīd*). Indeed, the only connection

---

[58] *Guide* iii.24, p. 500.    [59] *Guide* iii.24, p. 501.

[60] James Diamond, through examining Maimonides's Bible hermeneutics, also argues that contemplating Abraham and the Binding leads to contemplating God. See "'Trial' as Esoteric Preface in Maimonides' *Guide of the Perplexed*: A Case Study in the Interplay of Text and Prooftext," *The Journal of Jewish Thought and Philosophy* 7 (1997): 1–30.

[61] E.g., *Midrash Tanḥuma*, Genesis 22 (Warsaw: Unterhendler, 1877): "Abraham turned his eyes toward heaven and said, 'Master of the World, You have chosen me, You have set me apart, and You have revealed Yourself to me. You said to me, "I am one (*yaḥid*) and you are one (*yaḥid*); by your hand shall My name be known in My world; now, offer your son Isaac as a sacrifice to me"'" (my translation). A similar version of the story can be found in BT *Sanhedrin* 89b.

Maimonides identifies between the *tawḥīd* and the Binding is stated at the
end of *Guide* iii.24:

> In truth it was fitting that ... the *binding* should come to pass through the
> hand of *Abraham* ... For *Abraham our Father* was the first to make known
> the *tawḥīd*, to establish prophecy, and to perpetuate this opinion and draw
> people to it .... Thus just as they followed his correct and useful opinions,
> namely, those that were heard from him, so ought one to follow the
> opinions deriving from his actions.[62]

This passage does not say that Abraham made known the *tawḥīd* at the
time of the Binding, but that because he had already made known the
*tawḥīd*, he was suited for the trial of the Binding. Yet, the passage also
suggests that the followers of Abraham are to follow his opinions and "the
opinions deriving from his actions." In context here, the opinions in
question seem to be God's oneness (expressed in the *tawḥīd*) and the
establishment of prophecy. Earlier, in iii.24, Maimonides argues that the
reliability of prophecy is one of the notions made known by the Binding.
The statement in iii.45 seems to suggest that the oneness of God is also such
a notion. That is, when Maimonides says in iii.45 that Abraham proclaimed the *tawḥīd*, he apparently means that God's oneness is an opinion
deriving from Abraham's actions.

Maimonides's mentions of the *tawḥīd* in the *Guide* generally treat the
notion as one that is sought through demonstration, embedded in
religious opinions, and also reflected in ritual. Most of the mentions of
the *tawḥīd* in the *Guide* occur in connection with attempts to provide
reliable demonstrations (*burhānāt*) that God is one. *Guide* i.75 is concerned with showing the problems with the various proofs of the
Mutakallimūn of the *tawḥīd*, and *Guide* ii.1 contains acceptable
Aristotelian proofs of the *tawḥīd*. It is clear that the most proper way to
perform the *tawḥīd* is not merely to proclaim it, but to know it through
demonstrative proofs. Presumably, this is what Abraham did when he
"made known" (*taʿarīf*) God's oneness. That is, Abraham presumably
taught people, or at least informed them of the proofs of God's oneness.
Merely being informed of the *tawḥīd* and accepting it without having
a proper demonstration is, according to Maimonides, less good, but still
advantageous to the many,[63] since adopting these beliefs can be for the
sake of attaining "ultimate perfection."[64] Thus, the acceptance of the
*tawḥīd* is, according to Maimonides, the first basis of the Law of Moses.[65]

---

[62] *Guide* iii.24, p. 502, translation modified.    [63] See *Guide* i.31, p. 81.    [64] *Guide* iii.28, p. 512.
[65] *Guide* ii.13, Pines, p. 282.

Accordingly, there are rituals adopted to support this view, including the Abrahamic ritual of circumcision, which Maimonides says is "a covenant made by *Abraham our Father* with a view to the belief in the *unity of God* (Hebrew: *yiḥud hashem*) . . . This covenant imposes the obligation to believe in the *tawḥīd*."[66] Additionally, there is the obligation not to worship other gods, which Maimonides calls "the affirmation of the *tawḥīd*."[67] Moreover, Maimonides also says, "Those laws concerning sacrifices and repairing to the temple were given only for the sake of the realization of this fundamental principle . . . the fundamental principle of My *tawḥīd*."[68] The temple ritual thus joins circumcision in being a support or a guide to the *tawḥīd*. Accordingly, the temple ritual has a similar function to the Binding of Isaac: They are both external acts that indicate the *tawḥīd*. Both suggest the importance of adopting the belief that there is one God and encourage the intellectually curious to seek out demonstrative proofs of God's oneness, thereby completing the *tawḥīd* in the most perfect way.

In his very short chapter on ritual prayer, *Guide* iii.44,[69] Maimonides says:

> The end of these actions pertaining to divine service is the constant commemoration of God, the love of Him and the Fear of Him, the obligatory observance of the *commandments* in general, and the bringing-about of such belief concerning Him, may He be exalted, as is necessary for everyone professing the Law.[70]

Clearly, the *tawḥīd* is among such beliefs. Maimonides refers his readers to his explanations in the *Code of Law*. There, he emphasizes the connection between the *Shemaʿ* prayer (Deuteronomy 6:4: "Hear O Israel, the Lord is our God; the Lord is one") and the affirmation of His oneness (Hebrew: *yiḥud*).[71] In the *Book of Commandments*, Maimonides explicitly says that the second commandment[72] is "that which we have been commanded concerning believing in the *tawḥīd* . . . and it is His statement, may He be exalted, 'Hear O Israel, the Lord is our God; the Lord is one'."[73]

---

[66] *Guide* iii.49, p. 610.    [67] *Taqrīr al-tawḥīd, Guide* ii.31, p. 359.
[68] *Guide* iii.32, p. 530, translation modified.    [69] I.e., not the intellectual worship of *Guide* iii.51.
[70] *Guide* iii.44, p. 574.    [71] *Code of Law, Qeriʾat Shemaʿ*, i.2.
[72] Note that he uses the Arabic word for commandment, *amr*, the same word he uses at the opening of *Guide* iii.24. See note 20 above.
[73] *The Book of Commandments*, positive commandment 2 (my translation). Moreover, Maimonides goes on to connect the continuation of the *Shemaʿ* to the Love of God in positive commandment 3. Fear of God, which he discusses in positive commandment 4, does not refer to the *Shemaʿ*.

The *Shema'*, of course, does not have a direct connection to Abraham, but it is connected to love and fear of God.[74]

Now the Binding of Isaac was said by Maimonides to exemplify "the limit" of love and fear of God. Accordingly, by connecting the Binding with the *tawḥīd* in *Guide* iii.45, Maimonides suggests that the constant commemoration of God, the recitation of the *Shema'*, and even the sacrifices and Temple rituals are to aim for, but not exceed, the love and fear of God expressed by Abraham in the Binding. It seems likely that Maimonides associates the Binding of Isaac with the *tawḥīd* in order both to encourage the intellectually curious believer to seek out demonstrative proofs for God's oneness and to remind all believers how much love, fear, and dedication to God they should strive to attain. In so striving, they all may be led to seek out the principal belief that guides their actions, *viz.* the oneness of God.

---

[74] Fear of God in the *Shema'* is particularly related to God's threats of withholding rain. See *Guide* iii.30.

CHAPTER 8

# Maimonides on the Divine Authorship of the Law[*]

## Charles H. Manekin

In his *Commentary on the Mishnah*, Maimonides maintains that God revealed the text of the Torah in its entirety, together with its explanation, to Moses. This revelation occurred in an act metaphorically called 'speech' and in a manner known only to Moses, who wrote down all the commandments, narratives, and chronicles, from the first verse of Genesis to the last verse of Deuteronomy, like someone at the rank of a scribe (*nāsikh*), without composing even a single verse on his own. God's authorship of the Torah is taught in the verse, "By this you will know that God has sent me . . . and not from my mind [have I composed them]" (Deut. 16:28), and Moses's role as scribe is learnt from the Biblical description of him as *meḥoqeq*, 'inscriber' (Deut. 33:21). According to Maimonides, belief in the divine origin of the Torah "as found in our hands today" is a foundation and principle of "our Law."[1]

Despite Maimonides's statement in the *Commentary on the Mishnah*, and similar statements in various books and letters,[2] and despite his never having written anything to the contrary, several scholars in the last half century have maintained that the divine authorship of the text of the Torah is incompatible with Maimonides's philosophical principles, that Maimonides maintained this traditional stance for the sake of the multitude, and that he considered Moses to be the real author of the Torah.[3] In this chapter

[*] I would like to thank Daniel Davies, David Shatz, Kenneth R. Seeskin, and an anonymous reader for their helpful comments.

[1] Moses Maimonides, *Commentary on the Mishnah, Introduction to Chapter Ḥeleq* (Seventh Principle), ed. I. Shailat, pp. 372–373 (Ar.), p. 144 (Heb.). The translation of 'lawgiver' or 'legislator' for *meḥoqeq* in this context is an error.

[2] In addition to the ones discussed below, see the *Letter to Yemen* in *Iggerot ha-Rambam*, ed. I. Shailat, p. 90 (Ar.) and p. 127 (Heb.).

[3] See A. Reines, "Maimonides' Concept of Mosaic Prophecy," *Hebrew Union College Annual*, 40/41 (1969–1970), 325–361, esp. 348; K. Bland, "Moses and the Law According to Maimonides," in Jehuda Reinharz and Daniel Swetschinski, with . . . Kalman P. Bland (eds.), *Mystics, Philosophers and Politicians: Essays in Jewish Intellectual History in Honor of Alexander Altmann* (Durham, NC: Duke University Press, 1982), pp. 49–66, esp. p. 63; L. Kaplan, "I Sleep but My Heart

I consider some of the arguments advanced by those scholars and conclude that there is no incompatibility between Maimonides's oft-stated claim of the divine authorship of Torah and his philosophical principles. The Mosaic authorship interpretation relies on assuming this incompatibility, and assuming further that Maimonides was aware of it and deliberately concealed it. If divine authorship is shown to be compatible with Maimonides's philosophical principles, the Mosaic authorship interpretation loses whatever persuasiveness it may *prima facie* possess.[4]

Some preliminary points are worth mentioning: First, the view that God was the author of the entire text of the Torah, though rooted in some rabbinic sources, was not universally held in rabbinic literature, as has been amply demonstrated.[5] To take one example: Maimonides's older contemporary, Abraham Ibn Ezra, accepted a rabbinic opinion that the last eight verses of Deuteronomy were written by Joshua after the death of Moses.[6] The degree of Maimonides's familiarity with Ibn Ezra's work is a matter of scholarly dispute,[7] but he certainly was familiar with the teachings of his father's teacher, Rabbi Joseph Ibn Migash, whose learning he highly esteemed. Ibn Migash ruled that the last eight verses of the Torah can be publicly read without a quorum based on the rabbinic tradition that Joshua wrote them.[8] Maimonides also permitted the public recitation of these verses without a quorum, even though these verses are "all [of them] Torah, and Moses said them from the mouth of the Almighty."[9] Maimonides,

Waketh: Maimonides' Conception of Human Perfection," in I. Robinson, L. Kaplan, and J. Bauer (eds.), *The Thought of Moses Maimonides: Philosophical and Legal Studies* (Lewiston, NY: E. Mellen Press, 1990), pp. 130–166, esp. 139; A. Ivry, *Maimonides' Guide of the Perplexed: A Philosophical Guide* (Chicago/London: University of Chicago Press, 2016), p. 232; H. Kreisel, *Prophecy: The History of an Idea in Medieval Jewish Philosophy* (Dordrecht: Kluwer Academic Press, 2001), p. 261. For popular presentations of this interpretation of Maimonides, see B. Sommer, *Revelation and Authority: Sinai in Jewish Scripture and Tradition* (New Haven: Yale University Press, 2015), pp. 99–147 and M. Goodman, *Maimonides and the Book That Changed Judaism: Secrets of the Guide for the Perplexed* (Philadelphia: Jewish Publication Society, 2015), pp. 98–102.

4   Of course, Maimonides claims that God is the author of the entire text, as opposed to merely some of it. The scholars under consideration read him as denying God's authorship of any part of the text.
5   See A. Heschel, *Heavenly Torah as Refracted Through the Generations*, ed. and tr. G. Tucker with L. Levin (New York/London: Continuum 2005), pp. 341ff. and passim, especially the distinction between the maximalist and minimalist approaches in chapters 31 and 32.
6   See Ibn Ezra's commentary on Deut. 34:1.
7   For an overview of the problem see M. Cohen, *Opening the Gates of Interpretation: Maimonides' Biblical Hermeneutics in Light of His Geonic-Andalusian Heritage and Muslim Milieu* (Leiden: Brill, 2011), pp. 25–26 and references.
8   Cited in *Shitah Mequbezet* on *Baba Bathra* 15a (in Bezalel Ashkenazi, *Sefer Shitah Mequbezet*, 2nd ed. [Tel Aviv: Tsiyoni, 1961], 8: 72–73). The reference is cited in Heschel, *Torah min ha-shamayim be-aspaklaria shel ha-Dorot* (London: Soncino, 1962) 2: 387, n. 45.
9   *Code of Law*, Prayer xiii.6.

more than many of his predecessors, emphasized the divine origin of every word of the written text of the Torah. Although he may have been motivated in part by interreligious polemic, this does not fully explain his emphasis on the doctrine.

Second, one should not infer from the fact that Maimonides's statement in the *Commentary on the Mishnah* occurs within the context of his thirteen principles of the Law that he intended the principles to be adopted only by the multitude. On the contrary, his use of terms like 'existent', 'agent intellect', 'species', and 'genus' in the formulation of the principles, and more significantly, his demand that the principles become "secured" and "verified" by each individual, imply that Maimonides did not intend them as a catechism for the multitude, but as principles to be understood, albeit according to the level of the believer. He writes in the *Treatise on Resurrection* that because he saw that even legal scholars were ignorant of some of these principles, he decided to mention them without proofs in his juridical works. When he writes, "We chose to have the truths accepted by the community and nothing less,"[10] he means that he wished that people assent to the principles based, at least, on traditional authority with a rudimentary understanding that preserved their truth. More educated readers would be expected to accept them based on their proofs. However, the principles should be taught to all Jews because he held that that they were binding upon all Jews.

Third, while Maimonides does not expound upon the divine origin of the Torah in his later writings, he does include in his law code *Mishneh Torah*, under the category of the 'deniers of Torah', i.e., those who do not merit the world to come, "the one who says that the Torah is not from God, even one verse, even one word, if he says that Moses said it from himself."[11] And if one reads carefully *Guide of the Perplexed* iii.35–49, the chapters devoted to uncovering the rationale behind the Law, one never finds the attribution of a law, or a detail of a law, to Moses – whereas God is mentioned frequently as author. *Guide* iii.50 is devoted to refuting the claim that Moses filled in parts of the Biblical narrative on his own initiative. Indeed, in these chapters the divine authorship of the Law takes center stage.

[10] *Treatise on the Resurrection of the Dead* in *Letters*, ed. I. Shailat, p. 320 (Ar.), p. 342 (Heb.) The Arabic term translated here as "community" (following Joshua Blau's Judeo-Arabic dictionary) is *al-kāffa*, which Ibn Tibbon misleadingly translates as *he-hamon*, 'the multitude', the Arabic word for which is generally *al-jumhūr*. His translation may be the cause of subsequent misunderstandings.
[11] *Code of Law, Repentance* iii.5.

## The Mosaic Authorship Interpretation

Given that Maimonides states explicitly that Moses did not compose even a single word of the Torah, what arguments can be put forth to defend the Mosaic authorship interpretation? We may divide them into two categories: (i) arguments from the alleged incompatibility of God's authorship with divine activity; and (ii) arguments from the alleged incompatibility of the Law with the nature of Mosaic prophecy. If God cannot be the author, and Moses cannot receive the Law in a prophetic act, we are supposed to conclude that Moses is the author.

### Arguments from the Alleged Incompatibility of God's Authorship of the law with Divine Activity

Maimonides holds that although humans are unable to apprehend God in His true reality, they can demonstrate that He is incorporeal, hence intellect. God is described as intellect, intellecter, and intelligible in a simple unity.[12] According to the Mosaic authorship interpretation, this constitutes a problem for the position that God transmits the literal words of Scripture to Moses for several reasons: First, as incorporeal, God has no organs of speech and hence cannot speak the very words of scripture to Moses.[13] Second, according to Maimonides, languages, including Hebrew, are conventional, but God's actions are not.[14] Third, the Torah includes commandments, narratives, and chronicles, almost none of which can be called "intelligibles," i.e., eternally true objects of knowledge, which are cognized, in some manner, by the divine intellect. According to Maimonides, only two of the ten commandments revealed at Sinai, the affirmative commandment to believe in God and the negative commandment not to confer divinity on anything besides God, have the status of intelligibles, since they can be cognized through reason alone. The remaining eight commandments belong to the classes of generally accepted and traditional opinions.[15] Similarly, the vast majority of the

[12] In *Guide* i.68 Maimonides explains this "well-known saying of the philosophers," and he refers his reader to the discussion of divine unity in the Mishneh Torah, where he employs the saying explicitly. See *Code of Law, Foundations of the Torah* 2:10.
[13] This point is made in Ivry, *Maimonides' Guide of the Perplexed*, p. 232.
[14] *Guide* ii.30, tr. Pines, p. 358 and 3:32, p. 525. Unless otherwise noted, page references to the *Guide* are to the Pines translation. On the conventionality of Hebrew see also J. Schacht and M. Meyerhof, "Maimonides against Galen, on Philosophy and Cosmogony," *Bulletin of the Faculty of Arts of the University of Egypt*, 5 (1937), 53–88 (Arabic text and English translation of part of the twenty-fifth chapter of the *Fusūl Mūsa*). A new translation by G. Bos is forthcoming.
[15] Cf. *Guide* I.2, p. 24.

Torah's commandments, though eminently reasonable and useful, cannot be derived through reason alone. The historical narratives and chronicles, needless to say, cannot be considered intelligibles.

How, then, does an incorporeal God take the universal truths and particularize them into the nitty gritty of particular laws and narratives, rooted in the concrete historical experience of the Israelites?[16] How does God bridge the gap between His actions, which, Maimonides glosses as the "natural actions,"[17] and His Law, which Maimonides describes as conventional?[18] In short, how can God, described as an incorporeal intellect, compose a work, so little of which belongs to the class of intelligibles?

The assumption underlying these questions is that because pure intellects lack corporeal faculties, they cannot communicate matters that humans generally know through their corporeal faculties. But this assumption is not shared by Maimonides. Consider, for example, a historical fact recorded in Genesis 33:22, "And the sister of Lotan was Timna." As we shall see below, Maimonides holds that Moses did not compose the narratives of earlier periods by copying the work of earlier prophets but rather wrote them down as spoken to him by God.[19] Leaving aside the manner of divine communication for the moment, can God have communicated a sentence like "And the sister of Lotan was Timna," which is clearly a matter of historical fact and not a universal law of nature? If He cannot, then this is presumably because a Supreme Intellect cannot *know* anything that is not an eternal truth of physics and metaphysics. But this directly contradicts Maimonides's view that God apprehends things produced in time, i.e., concrete temporal particulars, albeit in ways that are beyond human comprehension.[20] So God knows *in some unknown manner* that Timna was the sister of Lotan, and that knowledge, which is acquired by humans through the senses, must be described in God's case as intellectual, since, as we noted earlier, it can be demonstrated of God that He is incorporeal, hence, He can be described as intellect.

Maimonides addresses this erroneous assumption in the *Guide*, when he writes that King David, in Psalm 94: 6–9, refuted the claim of "some [or: one] of the philosophers" who had thought that because God lacks senses, He cannot apprehend matters that humans apprehend through the senses. His answer is that He knows these matters with an intellectual apprehension.[21]

[16] Cf. Kaplan, "I Sleep but My Heart Waketh," p. 62.    [17] *Guide* iii.32, p. 525.
[18] *Guide*, ii.40, p. 382.
[19] "Letter to Mar Joseph Ibn Jābir" in *Letters*, ed. Shailat, p. 405 (Ar.), pp. 410–11 (Heb.).
[20] *Guide* iii.20, p. 483.
[21] This can be generalized as follows: Whatever humans perceive through a non-intellectual faculty, God knows through intellect.

Can someone endowed with intelligence conceive that the humors, mem-
branes, and nerves of an eye – which, as is known, are so well arranged and of
which have as their purpose the final end of this act of seeing – have come
about fortuitously? . . . Rather, does this craftsmanlike governance proceed,
according to the opinion of the philosophers, from an intellectual principle,
*and according to us it is the act of an intelligent being who impressed all the
faculties in question into all the things in which a natural faculty exists.*[22]

The key distinction here is not between sense/imagination and intellect,
but between that which comes about through purpose, and that which
comes about either from an intellectual principle, hence, necessarily, or by
accident. Any phenomenon that comes about through divine purpose is
known and willed by God, in accordance with His wisdom. In order to
claim that God could not have been the author of Biblical narratives and
parables, it is not sufficient, or even relevant, to argue that God lacks an
imaginative faculty to conceive them. One has to show that such passages
are without purpose or end, which would indeed rule out God as their
author. According to Maimonides, this is what the heretic Menasseh
claimed when he said that Moses did not have to write, "And the sister
of Lotan was Timna."[23] But Maimonides spends twenty-five chapters in
the *Guide* finding reasons for particular law after particular law, and even
reasons for recording facts like "And the sister of Lotan was Timna," thus
demonstrating the wisdom of a Law that that has been created, i.e.,
particularized by a purposeful Deity. Even particulars of commandments
for which no reason can be found do not constitute counterexamples to
divine authorship since "wisdom required – or, if you will, say that
necessity called for – there being particulars for which no cause can be
found."[24] If necessity called for there being particulars, for which no cause
is found, then God's wisdom required the existence of these "reasonless"
particulars.[25] Likewise, if many of the commandments rest on generally
admitted propositions, or propositions based on traditional authority, with
a given content, then God's wisdom requires that there be commandments
of this sort *with that content.*

One may respond to this argument by granting that God in some
manner knows historical facts like Timna's being the sister of Lotan,
inasmuch as they follow from determinate causes. But what of the

---

[22] *Guide* iii.19, p. 478–9. In citations from the sources, italics added for emphasis are my own.
[23] Ibid. iii.50, p. 613.     [24] Ibid. iii.26, p. 509, with modifications.
[25] For Maimonides's views on this issue, see J. Stern, *Problems and Parables of Law: Maimonides and
Nahmanides on Reasons for the Commandments (Ta'amei Ha-Mitzvot)* (Albany: State University of
New York Press, 1998), pp. 15–66.

commandments, which are promulgated with the ends of providing for "generally . . . the welfare of the body and the welfare of the soul"?[26] How can God, who, by hypothesis is said to know eternal truths of nature, be the author of laws that provide the means to the end of attaining correct opinions and a well-ordered society? Wouldn't that suggest that the Supreme Intellect possesses something akin to what we would call, in the case of humans, a practical intellect? This is indeed how God appears to us, according to Maimonides. Explaining why some people incorrectly believe that divine laws should not have a useful purpose, he writes:

> For they think that if those laws were useful in this existence and had been given to us for this or that reason, it would be as if they derived from the reflection (*fikra*) and understanding (*rawīya*) of some being possessing intelligence (*dhī ʿaql*). If, however, there is a thing for which the intellect could not find any meaning at all, and that does not lead to something useful, it indubitably derives from God; for the reflection of man would not lead to such a thing. It is as if, according to these people of weak intellects man were more perfect than his maker.[27]

The commandments of the Law are indeed "useful in this existence" and "given to us for this or that reason." They should accordingly appear to us as if they were the product of an intelligent being possessing "reflection" and "understanding," terms used by Maimonides for the power of deliberation.[28] Indeed, Maimonides would say the same of the world created by God, that it displays purpose and design. To be sure, Maimonides does not say that God actually *has* a practical intellect any more than he says that God *has* a theoretical intellect – only that we can demonstrate of God that He is intellect, and that He can be described as intellect, intellecter, and intellected, and that His creation and Law, which itself is created, displays His wisdom.[29] The Mosaic authorship interpretation assumes that God cannot know that murder should be forbidden or honoring one's parents mandated, or that animal sacrifices should be commanded to recently liberated Hebrew slaves, on the grounds that these laws are conventions, and God can only know

---

[26] *Guide* iii.27, p. 510.     [27] Ibid., iii.331, p. 524.

[28] See H. Kreisel's chapter on the practical intellect in his *Maimonides' Political Thought: Studies in Ethics, Law, and the Human Ideal* (Albany: State University of New York Press, 1999), pp. 63–92, especially p. 75.

[29] For the question of "practical intellect" in Maimonides, see Kreisel, *Maimonides' Political Thought*, pp. 63–92. Summing up, Kreisel writes on p. 90: "In his various enumerations of the activities belonging to the rational faculty [in the *Eight Chapters*], [Maimonides] includes types of practical knowledge as well as theoretical knowledge."

intelligibles. But this not only confuses human and divine modes of knowledge, it also treats the divine law as mere convention, whereas Maimonides explicitly claims that the divine law, "although it is not natural, enters into what is natural"[30] and that the divine law "assimilates itself to nature, perfecting the natural matters in a certain respect."[31]

These two claims suggest a "naturalization of the Mosaic law,"[32] in which both the Law and the natures of things revealed to Moses are viewed by Maimonides as the product of divine activity, just as the Law's commandments and natural actions are viewed as God's actions. To suggest that Moses receives in a prophetic act the "natures of things," and then "translates" or "frames" this natural governance as commandments and narratives by means of his practical intellect or imaginative faculty, is to fail to appreciate Maimonides's statements that "[Moses] apprehended 'all His goodness' – I mean to say all His actions" and that "[God's] commandments, may He be exalted . . . undoubtedly are comprised in His actions";[33] from which it follows that Moses apprehended the divine commandments *together with* the natures of things. According to *Guide* i.54, Moses was taught to assimilate his actions in governing Israel to those of God in governing humans. This he achieved, in part, by transmitting, teaching, interpreting, and administering the divine law revealed to him.

Maimonides treats nature and Law as twin aspects of divine activity elsewhere, e.g., when he explains that the Law's inability to perfect individuals in all cases is like that of nature, "for not everything that derives necessarily from the natural specific forms is actualized in every individual." Unlike medicine, whose treatment is particularized for every individual in accordance with that individual's condition and temperament, "the governance of the Law ought to be absolute and universal . . . for if it

---

[30]  *Guide* ii.40, p. 382.
[31]  *Guide* iii.43, p. 571. Although the Law is the product of divine wisdom, Maimonides does not believe that knowledge of the particulars of the Law in itself enables the knower to be with God, or to inherit the world to come. See *Guide* iii.51, pp. 619–629. However, thoughtful observance of the Law, and believing the true opinions that it teaches, does give the knower a measure of immortality. On this see C. Manekin, "Maimonides on Joseph Ibn Jābir's Ultimate Happiness," in a forthcoming festschrift honoring Steven Harvey.
[32]  The phrase is borrowed from M. Lorberbaum's *Politics and the Limits of Law: Secularizing the Political in Medieval Jewish Thought* (Stanford, CA: Stanford University Press, 2001), pp. 30–34, but used differently here. See Stern, *Problems and Parables of Law*, pp. 19–20.
[33]  In *Guide* i.54, p. 127. I have not seen where the proponents of the Mosaic authorship interpretation deal with the claim that the commandments of the Torah are undoubtedly comprised within God's actions.

were made to fit individuals, the whole would be corrupted, and 'you would make out of it something that varies.'"[34]

While the *governance* of the Law ought to be absolute and universal, the Law itself is revealed to a particular people at a particular time and place, and thus must take into account the nature and development of the people to whom it is first addressed, i.e., the recently liberated Hebrew slaves. Maimonides's well-known doctrine of Divine accommodation considers God to have devised laws that were geared to the spiritual level of the people as a whole, although this meant retaining modes of worship associated with idolatrous practices. Failure to accommodate the people's spiritual level would make a law that could not achieve its primary end.[35]

As for why God simply didn't alter the nature of the Hebrews to receive laws that were less associated with idolatrous practices, Maimonides writes:

> Though all miracles change the nature of some individual being, God does not change at all the nature of human individuals by means of miracles . . . We do not say this because we believe that the changing of the nature of any human individual is difficult for Him, may He be exalted. Rather is it possible and fully within capacity. But according to the foundations of the Law, of the Torah, He has never willed to do it, nor shall He ever will to do it.[36]

Just as God will not change the Law, though He could do so, He will not change nature permanently, though He could do so:

> we believe that what exists is eternal *a parte post* and will last forever with that nature which He, may He be exalted, has willed; that nothing in it will be changed in any respect unless it be in some particular of it miraculously – although He, may He be exalted, has the power to change the whole of it, or to annihilate any nature in it that He wills.[37]

The parallel that Maimonides draws between the non-abrogability of the Law and the eternity of the world *a parte post* makes sense if he

---

[34] *Guide* iii.34, pp. 534–535. Cf. *Guide* iii.26, p. 509.

[35] Ibid. iii.32, p. 528: "For just as it is not in the nature of man that, after having been brought up in his slavish service, one should all of a sudden proceed to fight against the children of Anak, so it is also not in his nature that, after having been brought up upon very many modes of worship and customary practices . . . he should abandon them all of a sudden. And just as the deity used a gracious ruse in causing them to wander perplexedly in the desert . . . all this having been brought about by Moses our Master by means of divine commandments . . . so did this group of laws derive from a divine grace, so that they be left with the kinds of practices to which they were accustomed and so that consequently the belief, which constitutes the first intention, should be validated in them."

[36] Ibid, p. 529.  [37] *Guide* ii.29, p. 346.

considers God to be the author/creator of the Law and the creator of the world.

Perhaps the most striking feature of Maimonides's naturalization of the law of Moses is its *universal binding quality*: the "call" or "mission" to others to obey the Law followed only from Moses's apprehension of the Divine. Although commandments were previously revealed to individuals and their descendants, including the patriarchs and Noah, only the law of Moses has this feature.[38] This dovetails with a "great principle" that Maimonides adopts elsewhere, i.e., that only the commandments revealed by God to Moses in the Torah obligate Jews.[39] Maimonides's deviation from scriptural and rabbinic tradition, which speaks of commandments binding upon Jews because they were observed by Abraham and Jacob,[40] was used against him by his opponents in Bagdad, who claimed that he did not consider the verses describing the covenant of circumcision with Abraham to be the source for the Jewish obligation to circumcise males. His reply to one of his supporters is worth citing at length:

> Whoever does not believe that these verses were said together with the entire Torah to Moses directly from God is included with one who says there is no Torah from Heaven. How would we know [about these covenants] had not Moses known what was said to Abraham at the time he was commanded about circumcision? Since we learned of this from Moses at Sinai, it follows that the root of this commandment and its obligation is from Moses, peace be upon him, and we were commanded the thirteen covenants by virtue of what he told us ... What is prior to [the revelation at Sinai], like the seven commandments to Noah and [the commandment] of circumcision to Abraham, is not believed by us because it is prior but because of the posterior command peculiar to us, the congregation of Jacob. Elaborating further is a waste of time.[41]

Just as the commandment of circumcision and the prohibition of eating the sciatic nerve are no longer binding because of the original divine directives, but because they were contained in the Torah revealed by God to Moses, so, too, the Noahide laws are no longer binding because of the original commands to Noah but because they form part of the law of Moses. In a well-known passage of the *Mishneh Torah*, Maimonides writes

---

[38] *Guide* ii.39.    [39] *Commentary on the Mishnah, Hullin* vii.6

[40] See D. Henshke, "The Commandments of the Forefathers and the Commandments of Sinai: The Case of the Sciatic Nerve as a chapter in Maimonides' Halakhic Conception," in N. Rabinovich, Zvi Heber, and Karmi'el Kohen (eds.), *Mi-Birkat Moshe: Qovez maamarim be-mishnat ha-Rambam li-khevodo shel ha-Rav Nahum Eliezer Rabinovich . . . .* 2 vols. (Maaleh Adumim: Maaliyot, 2011), pp. 619–646.

[41] Letter to Mar Joseph Ibn Jābir in *Iggerot ha-Rambam*, ed. Shailat, pp. 405 (Ar.), pp. 410–11 (Heb.).

that those who accept and observe the Noahide laws are not considered the "pious of the gentile nations" unless they accept and observe them "because God commanded them in the Torah and made known by means of Moses his servant, that the sons of Noah were previously commanded [to observe them]" and not because their opinion determines them to do it. Nor does this apply only to the Noahide laws. When queried whether a Jew can circumcise a gentile, Maimonides replied:

> An Israelite may circumcise a gentile, if the gentile intends to cut off the foreskin and remove it, because a gentile receives reward for every commandment he performs (although not like [the reward of] one who is commanded and performs it) – *provided that he performs it because he accepts Moses' prophecy, which commands [circumcision] in the name of the Lord, may He be exalted,* and not for another, nor according to an opinion that he sees [fit] for himself, as was explained in the Baraita of R. Eliezer ben Jacob, and as we explained at the end of our great compilation. [Kings 8:10].[42]

The Baraita of R. Eliezer, also known as *Mishnat R. Eliezer,* is considered by scholars to be the probable source of Maimonides's ruling concerning the conditions under which Noahides are considered pious gentiles.[43] But whereas the ruling in the *Mishnah Torah* bases the obligation on God's command to Noah as articulated in Mosaic revelation, the *Mishnat R. Eliezer* bases it simply on God's command to Noah:

> Since pious gentiles observe the seven commandments that the sons of Noah were commanded, with all their details, they are called "pious." This applies when they observe them saying *"By virtue of the fact that our father Noah commanded us from the mouth of the Almighty, we do so."* And if they do so, they inherit the world to come, like an Israelite ... But if they observe the seven commandments, saying "We heard this from so-and-so" or by virtue of their own opinion because their opinion indeed determines this, or they associated it with idolatry, then if they observed the entire Torah they only get their reward in this world.[44]

By insisting that the law of Moses is the only ground of obligation for both Israelites and Noahides, Maimonides, in effect, *universalizes the law of Moses to apply to all humanity.* Just as all creation is subject to the governance of nature, so too all human beliefs and actions are subject to the

[42] Letter to the Students of R. Ephraim in *Letters,* ed. Shailat, pp. 207 (Ar.), 214 (Heb.).

[43] See I. Twersky, *Introduction to the Code of Maimonides (Mishneh Torah)* (New Haven: Yale University Press, 1980), p. 455 and n. 239.

[44] *Mishnat Rabi Eliezer o midrash sheloshim u-shetayim middot,* ed. H. G. Enelow (New York, 1933), p. 121.

unique "true Law,"[45] the law of Moses. The absolute and universal applic-
ability of the Law, uniquely emphasized by Maimonides, fits well with his
naturalization of the Law.

### Arguments from the Alleged Incompatibility of the Law with the Nature of Mosaic Prophecy

Advocates of the Mosaic authorship interpretation find a difficulty with
Moses's role as receiver of the Law similar to the one they find with God's
role as author: Given Maimonides's position that Moses received his
prophecy without the mediation of non-intellectual psychic faculties,
how can a purely intellectual revelation, which should consist of universal
truths of natural and divine science, contain a Law that contains few such
truths? How can a purely intellectual prophecy contain the particulars of
Mosaic law that cannot be derived through reason, but belong to the class
of the generally accepted opinions? How can the Torah contain parables, if
Moses did not prophesy by means of parables?

One possible answer is that notwithstanding Maimonides's explicit
statements to the contrary, Moses's prophecy did indeed involve his
imaginative faculty, which "particularized" the general intellectual emanation by casting it into the form of particular laws, narratives, and chron-
ologies. One could perhaps explain this in the way that Averroes explains
the phenomenon of veridical dreams concerning the future. In the case of
veridical dreams, the intellect receives from the active intellect the universal
determinate causes of a future event, which are in turn transformed by the
imaginative faculty into particulars "by virtue of the fact that it is in
matter," and contextualized by the dreamer's concrete circumstances.[46]
If one replaces "future event" by "past event" and "law," the revelation of
the Law could be explained in this manner on the Mosaic authorship
interpretation, i.e., the intellectual principles that underlie the Law are
converted, by an internal, natural process, into the particular laws of the
Law. In that case, "authorship" would be metaphorical since the internal
process would not involve deliberation.

But the advocates of the Mosaic authorship interpretation generally
accept Maimonides's claim that Mosaic prophecy was purely intellectual.
So they hold that Moses's composition of the Torah is *external* and *posterior*

---

[45] *Guide* iii.27, p. 511.
[46] Averroes, *Talkhīṣ kitāb al-ḥiss wal-maḥsūs*, ed. H. Blumberg (Cambridge, MA: Medieval Academy of America, 1961), p. 79; idem, *Epitome of Parva Naturalia*, tr. H. Blumberg (Cambridge, MA: Medieval Academy of America, 1961), pp. 46–47.

to the prophetic experience. In other words, after Moses received the intelligibles through prophetic revelation, he deliberately composed, with the aid of the practical intellect and the imaginative faculty, a law that 'imitates' or 'translates' those intelligibles into a particular law for a particular people in a particular historical context.[47]

Our answer to this interpretation is as before: If God, who is described as intellect, can know particulars, including particular events, then there is no reason why He cannot communicate via an intellectual emanation to Moses the particulars of a Law, each of which has causes, and whose words contain wisdom. Even in the case of non-Mosaic prophecy, the active intellect communicates information first to the intellectual faculty, which then emanates to the imaginative faculty, which in turn displays that information consisting of images as if derived from the senses.[48] The intellectual element – the element of wisdom – is already present in the intellectual faculty. The imaginative faculty is required for translating the intelligibles to the prophet into visions, riddles, and dreams. That step is unnecessary in Mosaic prophecy.

It has been suggested that that when Maimonides states in the Eighth Principle that Moses played no role in authoring the Torah, the emphasis is less on the origin of the text than on its wisdom; Moses authored a wise text, and he was not responsible for composing any unnecessary filler. It is then argued that provided that the Torah is "replete with wisdom in all its parts" it can be *considered* divine, even if it was formulated as law by Moses in imitation of nature.[49] But this suggestion won't do, because if the Torah is *entirely* wise, it can only be "Mosaic" in so far as Moses conjoins with intellect and becomes the intermediary through which the Torah is revealed. No word in the Torah can be considered to be Moses's original contribution. That makes the Law as much the product of Moses as a printed page is the product of an inkjet printer. Neither can be considered the author of the output.

If we assume that Moses achieved intellectual perfection there seems to be no real bar to his receiving the divine law that not only contains correct opinions and actions, but provides a regimen that will allow its adherents

---

[47] See the references to Reines, Bland, Kaplan, and Ivry, in n. 1 above. Some of these authors refer to Alfarabi's treatment of the prophet-lawgiver, and wish to assimilate Maimonides to Alfarabi, as they interpret him. For Alfarabi, religion is an imaginative imitation of philosophy designed for the welfare of non-philosophers. Maimonides gives us no indication that he views the Law in this manner. He does refer approvingly to the "philosophers" in his discussion of prophecy in *Guide* ii.37, p. 374, but in another context altogether.

[48] *Guide* ii.36, p. 369.   [49] See Bland, "Moses and the Law," pp. 65–66.

to achieve their ultimate happiness, according to their varying levels. The latter is as much a result of divine wisdom as is the former. When Maimonides states that Moses did not prophesy through parables, he means that Moses's prophecy did not come to him in parabolic form.[50] He does not mean that the texts of the divine law, which "speaks according to the language of the men," cannot contain parables. A teacher may be instructed to employ particular parables to convey a point, without having learned that point by means of parables.

## The Revelation of the Law of Moses – Miraculous or Natural?

If Maimonides considered the revelation of the law of Moses to be miraculous, that would relieve his readers of making philosophical sense of it. But Maimonides never calls the revelation of the Law itself miraculous,[51] and it is hard to see this as an oversight on his part, given his general disinclination to consider something miraculous unless it has been clearly marked by Scripture as a miracle, and the scriptural text cannot be explained otherwise.[52] If a naturalistic interpretation of Moses's receiving the Law can be offered that is compatible both with Maimonides's claim of divine authorship and with his conception of Moses as scribe, then that will remove the last support from the Mosaic authorship interpretation.

The task is complicated by the fact that in *Guide* ii.36 Maimonides declares his intention to write "not a word" about Moses's prophecy. Everything he writes about prophecy in the chapters devoted to prophecy refers only to the "form" of prophecy of other prophets, e.g., his definition of the "true reality and quiddity" of prophecy as "an emanation emanating from God, may He be cherished and honored, through the intermediation of the active intellect, toward the rational faculty in the first place, and thereafter toward the imaginative faculty";[53] The term "prophecy" is an ambiguous term in reference to Moses and other prophets.[54] But although

[50] Ibid., i.26, p. 56.
[51] Reines, "Maimonides' Concept of Mosaic Prophecy," pp. 333–338, which considers Mosaic prophecy to be natural; J. Levinger, *Ha-Rambam ke-filosof u-ke-foseq* (Jerusalem: Mossad Bialik, 1989), p. 32. Cf. Bland, "Moses and the Law according to Maimonides," p. 56 and Kreisel, *Prophecy*, p. 194. If Moses received the Law through hearing a voice or sound created by God then revelation would be miraculous. But as we will see below, Maimonides entertains the possibility of purely intellectual revelation.
[52] *Guide* ii.25. Cf. *Treatise on Resurrection* in *Letters*, ed. Shailat, p. 330 (Ar.), p. 361 (Heb.).
[53] *Guide* ii.36, p. 369.
[54] Abrabanel notes Hebrew manuscripts of the *Guide* where "ambiguous" is replaced by "equivocal," and he argues that the latter is correct; this is not confirmed by the Arabic editions. See A. Reines, *Maimonides and Abrabanel on Prophecy* (Cincinnati: Hebrew Union College Press, 1970), p. 66.

he mentions some characteristics and features of Mosaic prophecy, he does not indeed say anything about the *form* of Mosaic prophecy, i.e., he does not *explain* Mosaic prophecy. Instead, he refers readers to the *Commentary on the Mishnah* and the *Mishneh Torah*, where he distinguishes Mosaic prophecy from non-Mosaic prophecy in four ways: only Moses prophesied (i) in a waking state and not in a vision; (ii) without an intermediary or an angel, i.e., without receiving prophecy in the form of riddles and parables; (iii) without fear or a weakening of his constitution; (iv) whenever he wished.[55] These differences do not speak to the essential nature of Mosaic prophecy.

Maimonides says a bit more about Mosaic prophecy in the *Commentary on the Mishnah*, but then defers discussion to a subsequent work or works, which he ultimately did not write.[56] Since this comment immediately precedes the discussion of the divine authorship of the Torah, it is worth examining in some detail:

> The seventh principle – the prophecy of our teacher Moses, i.e., to believe that he is the father of all prophets before and after him, all of whom are beneath him in rank, and that He is God's chosen of the entire human species, who apprehends of Him, may He be exalted, more than what every man who lived and will live, apprehended and will apprehend. [One should believe] that he, peace be upon him, attained such an exceedingly lofty level above humanity that he reached the angelic rank[57] and [thus] became of the rank of the angels. No veil remained that he did not rend; no corporeal impediment hindered him; no defect marred him, neither minor nor major. His imaginative and sensory faculties were nullified in his apprehension, as was his appetitive faculty stunned, so that he remained only an intellect. On account of this it was said of him allusively (*kanā 'anhi*) that he would speak with the Lord without the mediation of the angels.[58]

Scholars have puzzled over what Maimonides means when he says that Moses received his prophecy "without the mediation of the angels." Some have interpreted him to be saying that Moses received the divine emanation directly from God, without the mediation of the incorporeal

---

[55] *Code of Law*, Foundations of the Torah 7:6.
[56] Some of the material was presumably incorporated into the *Guide*.
[57] The translation is based on J. Blau, *Dictionary of Medieval Judaeo-Arabic Texts* (Jerusalem: Academy of Hebrew Language, Israel Academy of Science and Humanities, 2006), s.v. *malakūtī*. H. Davidson has drawn my attention to the possibility of its being translated "supernal rank," based on the Muslim religious notion of *'ālam al-malakūtī*, the supernal region of dominion. Otherwise, Maimonides appears to be redundant. (Personal communication).
[58] *Commentary on the Mishnah*, Introduction to Chapter Ḥeleq, ed. Shailat pp. 371 (Ar.), p. 142–43 (Heb.)

intelligences such as the active intellect.[59] While there is textual support for this interpretation, Maimonides writes that it is "on account of this," i.e., on account of Moses receiving prophecy without the mediation of his non-intellectual faculties, that it was said of him that he would speak with the Lord without the mediation of the angels. And with one exception that we shall consider below, "without the mediation of the angels" means without the mediation of the non-intellectual faculties, especially the imaginative faculty, which is also called "angel":

> How can this be [i.e., that Isaiah and Micaiah heard speech coming from God] in view of the fact that our principle states that all prophets hear speech only through the intermediary of an angel, the sole exception being Moses our Master, of whom it is said: "With him do I speak mouth to mouth" (Exod. 33:11). Know then that this is in fact so and that in these cases the intermediary is the imaginative faculty. For a prophet can hear only in a dream of prophecy that God has spoken to him. Moses our Master, on the other hand, heard Him "from above the ark-cover from between the two cherubim," without action on the part of the imaginative faculty.[60]

Maimonides refers the reader to his interpretation of "mouth to mouth" in the *Mishneh Torah*, where the meaning is that Moses did not receive prophecy by means of an angel, but rather "he sees as it truly is without riddle and parable," i.e., without the imaginative faculty.

The exception is *Guide* ii.34, where Maimonides probably understands the angel referred to in Exodus 20:20–23 as the separate intellect who will communicate with the prophets. He then contrasts this kind of prophecy with that of Moses, who did not receive prophecy through an angel.[61] But even if we allow that the angelic intermediary may be interpreted in some cases as the imaginative or non-rational faculties and in other cases as the active or separate intellects, there is no reason to suggest that this ambiguity reflects an esoteric/exoteric distinction. Maimonides says in the seventh principle that Moses achieved the angelic rank and that he experienced no

[59] See H. Wolfson, "Hallevy and Maimonides on Prophecy," *Jewish Quarterly Review*, n.s. 32.4 (1942), 345–370, rept. in H. Wolfson, *Studies in the History of Philosophy and Religion*, eds. Isadore Twersky and George H. Williams (Cambridge, MA: Harvard University Press, 1973), pp. 60–119, especially p. 108. For a dissenting view, see A. Altmann, "Maimonides and Thomas Aquinas: Natural of Divine Prophecy?" *AJS Review* 3 (1978), 1–9, esp. 16.
[60] *Guide* ii.46, p. 403.
[61] See Abrabanel, *Commentary to the Guide of the Perplexed*, ad loc. Abrabanel notes that Maimonides uses Exodus 23:21 in the context of his discussion of separate intellects and spheres in *Guide* ii.7. Even the earlier commentators who suggest that "angel" in Exodus 23:20–23 refers to a prophet (e.g., Efodi, Shem Tov) say that Scripture calls the prophet an angel because he receives prophecy from the angel, i.e., the separate intellect.

fear when prophesying "on account of the strength of his attachment (*ittiṣāl*) with the intellect." Unlike other prophets, Moses doesn't receive an emanation to his human intellect from the active intellect. Rather he transcends his humanity and achieves the rank of an incorporeal intellect through the strength of his attachment with the intellect. Though still embodied, his corporeal faculties have no effect upon his reception of the divine emanation. There is no need to claim that this emanation bypasses the natural order of intelligences, i.e., that Moses miraculously attaches himself to God. Any talk of attachment to God can be understood in terms of a transcendent attachment to the (active?) intellect in which Moses receives prophecy unaffected by corporeal faculties. All other prophets, who have a lesser attachment to the active intellect, receive an emanation from it. Part of Moses's prophecy contains the divine law and the divine command to write down all the written Law in all its particulars.

How that command is received by Moses is unclear, although Maimonides considers it to be obvious that God does not literally speak to Moses, and he has no compunction about saying so openly.[62] Based on his explanation of the terms saying (*amirah*) and speaking (*dibbur*) with reference to God, he writes that God's speech refers to "a notion that has been grasped by the understanding having come from God," in which case it makes no difference whether the notion was grasped by means of sounds miraculously created by God, or through one of the ways of prophecy.[63] There is evidence that Maimonides adopted the position that Moses heard a created voice and wrote it down; he mentions that the "general consensus of the community" is that the Torah was created, which is "meant to signify that His speech that is ascribed to Him is created,"[64] and in his letter to R. Hasdai ha-Levi, he argues on the basis of the verse "And [Moses] heard the voice of the Lord speaking to him" (Num. 7:89) that Moses heard the created voice in the Tent of Meeting between the cherubim rather than receive a purely intellectual emanation.[65] But for our purposes nothing rides on the distinction; the divine authorship of the Law is preserved under either interpretation. This is true even for the specific language of the Law; one doesn't have to assume that God or separate intellects think in Hebrew in order for the revelation to be

---

[62] *Guide* i.65, pp. 158–169.  [63] Ibid., p. 158.  [64] Ibid., p. 158.

[65] Letter to Hasdai ha-Levy in *Iggerot*. Cf. *Guide* i.21 and i.37, p. 86. (The authenticity of this letter was challenged by I. Shailat.) My view is that Maimonides never resolved the issue. For a recent radical esotericist reading of his views on the created light and the created voice, see Esti Eisenmann, "The Term 'Created Light' in Maimonides' Philosophy," *Daat*, 55 (2005), 41–57.

understood as Hebrew. One has to assume that there is divine wisdom and purpose in its being in Hebrew.

A more interesting question is the relation of Mosaic prophecy to the law of Moses. We saw above that only the law of Moses contains the "mission" or "call" to obedience. Maimonides makes this claim on the basis of scriptural prooftexts. One can speculate that it is the rational nature of Mosaic prophecy that is responsible for the universal nature of Mosaic law, and that only Moses the perfect human can be the intermediary by means of which the perfect law is revealed. In that case, Moses's role as God's scribe would be an exalted one for which only he was worthy. The form of the revealed Law would be tied to the particular role of Moses as the messenger or intermediary without requiring that Moses consciously and deliberately formulate scientific truths into law by means of his practical intellect and/or his imagination. We could describe this process as 'translation', as when we speak of the cartridge head of an inkjet printer "translating" electrical impulses into drops of ink on a page, or of a scribe "translating" into written words the sounds that he hears. Neither the printer nor the scribe are considered the authors of their output.

However attractive this speculation may be, it should be noted that Maimonides does not tie the revelation of the Law to the uniqueness of Mosaic prophecy. When arguing that the Law will never be changed or superseded, he appeals instead to scriptural evidence, as well as to the general consideration that something that is as perfect as possible in its species will not be replaced by something that is less perfect. He does not appeal to the fact that there will never be a prophet as great as Moses as justification for the view that the Torah will never be superseded or abrogated. He does not suggest that in transcending humanity, Moses shed his personality, became pure intellect, and hence the perfect vessel for the unadulterated reception of God's Torah. These are moves that he could have made, but since he did not, we are left to fill in the gaps with speculation.

To sum up: Maimonides throughout his writings maintains that God gave the Law to the Israelites through Moses as intermediary. He refers to that Law both as "the law of the Lord" and "the law of Moses," claiming that God, the author, dictated the Law to Moses, who wrote it down word for word. Following some, though not all, rabbinic opinion, Maimonides interprets this to mean that every verse of the Torah was authored by God and transmitted to Moses in the form that we have it today. Some recent readers of Maimonides have considered this to be Maimonides's "exoteric" view that he intended for the vulgar. His secret view was that Moses authored the Torah by translating the purely intellectual prophecy he received into laws and narratives relevant to the circumstances. Since Maimonides never even hints at this view, their arguments rest on the assumption that the divine authorship view is incompatible with Maimonides's philosophical principles, notably his naturalizing tendencies. I have argued that the divine authorship view is compatible with Maimonides's views on divine knowledge of particulars and his tendency to naturalize and universalize the Law. For Maimonides, there is no more impediment to God's particularizing a universal law for the welfare of mankind than there this for God's particularizing the natures of things; both the commandments and natural actions are considered by Maimonides to be included among God's actions. Although Maimonides does not elaborate on the nature of Mosaic prophecy, his view that Moses achieves conjunction with intellect to such an extent that he transcends his humanity and becomes angelic suggests that Moses functions as lawgiver in the manner that the active intellect functions as the giver of forms: Both have reason and choice,[66] and both are intermediaries by which God accomplishes His purpose. The Law instantiated at a given historical moment through the mediation of Moses as prophet can be viewed no differently than any instantiation of divine wisdom and purpose in the creation of the world; Moses is the "platform" by which the divine purpose transmits the verses of scripture.

If one believes that Maimonides secretly adopted the positions of the Aristotelian philosophers, then little of the above will carry weight. All counterevidence from Maimonides will be dismissed as a smokescreen or as a "noble lie." But if Maimonides viewed what he considered to be the foundations of the Law as compatible with what he understood were the demands of reason, then dismissing some of those foundations as intended for the vulgar reads him against the grain. Maimonides was a proud Andalusian Jew who maintained that all the Andalusian Jews "cling to the affirmations of the philosophers and incline to their opinions, in so far as these do not ruin the foundations of the Law."[67] He also maintains that the secrets of the Law were not concealed "because they undermine the foundations of Law, as is thought by ignorant people who deem that they have attained a rank suitable for speculation."[68] If anything is to be dismissed, it is interpretations of Maimonides that question his philosophical allegiance to his foundations of the Law.

[66] This should not be confused with the rational power of deliberating between alternatives.
[67] *Guide* i.71, p. 177.   [68] *Guide* i.33, p. 71.

CHAPTER 9

# *Divine Knowledge and Providence in the* Guide of the Perplexed

## Daniel Davies

Divine knowledge and providence are two central doctrines that Maimonides addresses in part three of the *Guide*. He declares his belief that God "has known all the things that are produced anew before they have come about and has known them perpetually,"[1] and that the source of all existent beings "apprehends all that is other than itself; that in all the things that exist, nothing whatever is hidden from it."[2] His stated view is that God knows all things, including changing things and particulars. On the other hand, he argues that God's providence extends to all created species but not to their individuals. In the case of humans, providence can extend to some individuals, in accordance with the perfection of their intellects.

In today's scholarship, the question of how these two doctrines are related to one another constitutes a major difficulty.[3] It is claimed that Maimonides's account of God's providence has consequences for his teaching about God's knowledge, and that the two are inconsistent. With this supposed inconsistency, it is sometimes thought that he deliberately contradicts himself by presenting two different models of God's knowledge. Moreover, in line with the popular view that Maimonides includes at least two different theological positions in the *Guide*, and that they are directed at different kinds of people, it has been argued that when he presents a view that God knows all things he is speaking to the masses, and that when he presents his doctrine of God's providence, he is qualifying his teaching about God's knowledge in a way that would be detected only by the elite.

---

[1] *Guide* iii.20, tr. Pines, p. 480.  [2] *Guide* iii.20, p. 482.
[3] See, for example, T. Rudavsky, *Maimonides* (Chichester: Wiley-Blackwell, 2010), p. 149; A. Even-Chen, "Of the Divine Knowledge and the Rational – Emotional Experience of the Known Single, Under Providence, and the Beloved in *The Guide of the Perplexed* [sic]," [Heb.] *Daat* 74–75 (2013), 105–134; and K. Seeskin's contribution to this volume.

Accordingly, Maimonides's real opinion is that God's knowledge is limited.[4]

The claim that Maimonides's presentation of God's knowledge is incompatible with his account of divine providence has a distinguished history. For example, Gersonides criticized Maimonides for his presentation of divine omniscience while adopting central aspects of his theory of providence, which seems closer to his own.[5] Furthermore, he states that "on Maimonides' theory of providence, divine knowledge does not extend to particulars as particulars."[6] However, while such criticisms express a disagreement, Gersonides did not seem to think that Maimonides deliberately contradicted himself in order to hide his opinion, or even that any apparent contradiction was at all deliberate. Nevertheless, in an assessment that reflects the prevailing current attitudes, Maimonides's view of providence has recently been described as "one of the most impenetrable areas of his thought" and as a matter on which he is "unusually evasive."[7] The main purpose of this chapter is to question the view that Maimonides's presentations are incoherent. It will distinguish Maimonides's account of God's knowledge from that of God's providence, in line with an observation made by Samuel Ibn Tibbon, thereby arguing that there is no conflict of the kind that should lead one to conclude that he hid his belief about either of these two theological doctrines.[8] God's knowledge precedes creatures and is therefore not dependent on them, on this reading of Maimonides's

---

[4] See, for example, A. Ivry, "Providence, Divine Omniscience and Possibility: The Case of Maimonides," in T. Rudavsky (ed.), *Divine Omniscience and Omnipotence in Medieval Philosophy: Islamic, Jewish and Christian Perspectives* (Dordrecht: Reidel, 1985).

[5] See S. Feldman, *Gersonides: Judaism within the Limits of Reason* (Oxford: The Littman Library of Jewish Civilization, 2010), pp. 120–121. In his commentary on *Guide* iii.19, Falaquera seems to slide between talk of God's knowledge and providence and seems to hint that he disagrees with Maimonides, *Moreh ha-Moreh*, ed. Y. Shiffman (Jerusalem: World Union of Jewish Studies, 2001) p. 317.

[6] Gersonides, *The Wars of the Lord*, vol. 2, tr. S. Feldman (Philadelphia, New York, Jerusalem: Jewish Publication Society, 1987), p. 208.

[7] R. Eisen, *The Book of Job in Medieval Jewish Philosophy* (New York: Oxford University Press, 2004), p. 44. D. Schwartz outlines three competing early interpretations of Maimonides's teaching on providence in "The Debate over the Maimonidean Theory of Providence in Thirteenth-Century Jewish Philosophy," *Jewish Studies Quarterly*, 2 (1995), 185–196.

[8] I characterize the issues I will discuss as theological, thereby disagreeing with L. Strauss's claim that everything after *Guide* iii.7 is purely political. "The Place of the Doctrine of Providence According to Maimonides," *Review of Metaphysics*, 57 (2004), 538. Strauss bases his argument on the fact that at the end of iii.7, p. 430, Maimonides tells his readers that he will have nothing more to say about *ma'ase merkava*. As is well known, Maimonides takes *ma'ase merkava* to mean "divine science," or metaphysics, which Strauss identifies with theology. Therefore, Strauss argues, there is no theology in the remainder of the *Guide*, which contains the sections about God's knowledge and providence. My opinion is that the referent in iii.7 is Ezekiel's vision of the chariot, also known as *ma'ase merkava*, because nothing needed to decode that vision appears thereafter.

account, whereas providence depends on the natures of created beings. If the argument in this chapter is correct, there is no need to view Maimonides's arguments about providence as evasive since they can be accepted at face value.[9]

## Maimonides's Account of God's Knowledge

Maimonides states that God knows all things. There is no individual, material particular of which God is ignorant.[10] In Gersonides's terms, Maimonides's presentation involves the very strong claim that God "knows particular, contingent things insofar as they are particular."[11] One of the difficulties such a claim gives rise to is that it seems to be nonsense. It ought to be impossible for God to know material particulars because they are by nature unknowable.[12] Maimonides writes that "matter is a great veil preventing apprehension of the separate things as they truly are."[13] Particulars in the sublunar world are material, and therefore cannot be apprehended "as they truly are." Knowledge is of essences abstracted from matter by the intellect, which means that it is of universals rather than particulars. On the question of the nature of universals, Maimonides seems to align himself with Avicenna when he states that "there is no existent species outside the mind, but the species and the other universals are mental notions, as you know, and that every existent outside the mind is only an individual or individuals."[14] Objects that exist outside the mind, to which knowledge is related, differ from the knowledge itself, which is intellectual and involves abstractions from the particular matter.[15] Avicenna discusses universals in relation to essences of things. The essence of a thing described is neither particular nor universal in its

---

[9] There is a vast literature interpreting Maimonides's view of providence in ways that do not accord with the reading I offer here, which adopts a straightforward approach to Maimonides's philosophical views. I justify my methodology in *Method and Metaphysics in Maimonides' Guide for the Perplexed* (New York: Oxford, 2011).

[10] *Guide* iii.21, p. 485.     [11] Gersonides, *Wars*, Vol. 2, p. 91.

[12] This of course does not mean that it is impossible to make true judgments about particulars. Philosophical issues such as those pertaining to singular thoughts are beyond the scope of the present chapter.

[13] *Guide* iii.9, p. 436. For the background of Maimonides's understanding of matter and form, see Ivry, "Providence, Divine Omniscience and Possibility," pp. 144–147.

[14] *Guide* iii.18, p. 474. For further discussion on the Avicennian background of Maimonides's epistemology see B. Kogan, ""What Can We Know and When Can We Know It?" Maimonides on the Active Intelligence and Human Cognition," in E. Ormsby (ed.) *Moses Maimonides and His Time* (Washington, DC: CUA Press, 1989), pp. 121–137.

[15] Matter as understood is not included in this discussion. For the distinction, see Ghazālī's *Intentions of the Philosophers*, ed. M. Bejou (Damascus: Maṭbaʿa al-Ḍabbāḥ, 2000) p. 63.

own right. An essence exists either as a particular, in which case it is instantiated in matter, or as a universal, in which case it is instantiated in an intellect. The essence can therefore only become a universal as a result of the mind's abstraction, which is possible because of the fact that the essence is predicable of multiple individual things.[16]

These difficulties lead to the following argument. Because knowledge of particulars is impossible, and because God cannot do what is impossible, God does not know particulars.[17] In the *Guide*, Maimonides presents this opinion as that of the philosophers. His response is to emphasize the equivocal meanings that the two uses of the word "knowledge" have. Whereas it might be true to say that human knowledge is impeded by an object's materiality, the same might not be true of God's knowledge. Maimonides argues that the philosophers confuse God's knowledge with human knowledge, which Maimonides distinguishes in accord with his general explanation of divine predication, and charges them with inconsistency. The philosophers know that God is unlike any created thing because there is no multiplicity in God's essence, so they should realize that God's knowledge is unlike human knowledge. However, in order for their arguments to hold, there needs to be a certain similarity between divine and human knowledge. When they argue that God cannot know because knowledge derives from senses, or that God's knowledge must change when the objects of God's knowledge change, they argue on the basis of a position that they themselves ought to reject. By saying that God can know only universals they try to fit divine knowledge into some form of category that likens it to human

---

[16] For further on Avicenna's view see M. Marmura, "Quiddity and Universality in Avicenna," *Neoplatonism and Islamic Philosophy* (1992), 77–88. By accepting the view that universals have only mental existence, Maimonides distances himself from the opinion that they are separate, independent forms, existing outside of both intellect and of any instantiation in a particular. Such a view was adopted by al-Kindī and his followers. See P. Adamson, *Al-Kindi* (New York: Oxford University Press, 2007), p. 109. On this view, Adamson has argued, not only strict, scientific knowledge of particulars would be denied to humans, but any knowledge whatsoever of particulars. Adamson writes that "Avicenna held that there is no such thing as knowledge of particulars." This form of knowledge is also applicable to God, says Avicenna, so that God knows particulars only inasmuch as they are subsumed under universals. See P. Adamson, "On Knowledge of Particulars," *Proceedings of the Aristotelian Society*, 105 (2005), 274. Maimonides might also have been indicating his disagreement with Alfarabi and the Aristotelian school that followed him, who held that universals do have an extra-mental existence. See P. Adamson, "Knowledge of Universals and Particulars in the Baghdad School," *Documenti e Studi sulla Tradizione Filosofica Medievale*, 18 (2007), 141–164.

[17] *Guide* iii.15, p. 459. That God cannot do what is logically impossible is explained further by Ivry, "Maimonides on Possibility," in Reinharr and Schwetschinski (eds.), *Mystics, Philosophers, and Politicians: Essays in Jewish Intellectual History in Honor of Alexander Altmann* (Durham: Duke University Press, 1982), pp. 67–84.

knowledge.[18] But if God does not possess knowledge in the same sense as humans do, their objections do not hold and, conversely, if their objections do not hold, the two instances of "knowledge" have nothing in common. So in order to argue that it is plausible to posit knowledge of all things in God, Maimonides states that the word "knowledge" when applied to God's knowledge of creatures has a totally different meaning than when it is applied to human knowledge of creatures. The two terms are absolutely equivocal.[19]

To express the absolute difference between them, Maimonides outlines five characteristics that pertain to God's knowledge but not to human knowledge: God knows multiple species of things without that knowledge leading to plurality in the divine; God knows non-existent things; God knows infinites; God's knowledge does not change when the things known change; God's knowing a contingent thing does not make that thing necessary.[20] None of these can apply to human knowledge. Were they to do so, the person they are ascribed to would not possess something that is called knowledge. Take for example God's knowledge of infinites, which are material particulars. Material things cannot be known because matter is unknowable in principle, so if knowledge of material things is posited, the word "knowledge" must have something other than its usual sense. These characteristics of God's knowledge can therefore only be ascribed if the word "knowledge" is used by way of equivocation.

The equivocation is further emphasized when Maimonides says that, unlike humans, God knows existing things as their cause. In making this statement he is not necessarily characterizing God's knowledge entirely as creative. A distinction can be drawn between how God knows those things that exist, as their cause, and God's knowledge per se. One consequence of this distinction is that God's knowledge need not be limited to those things that exist at some time. The view that God's knowledge can extend to possible things that never exist makes sense of some of his comments about God's ability to act. For example, he insists that God is able to "lengthen a fly's wing or to shorten a worm's foot,"[21] a statement that can only be true if God's "creative" knowledge is not restricted only to what God actually creates. If it is acceptable to extend God's knowledge to unactualized possibilities, God would be able to create a world different from that

---

[18] *Guide* iii.20, p. 482.    [19] *Guide* iii.20, p. 483.

[20] These five differences are explained in iii.20. For a medieval defense of Maimonides's view, see C. Manekin, "Maimonides on Divine Knowledge – Moses of Narbonne's Averroist Reading," *American Catholic Philosophical Quarterly*, 76 (2002), 51–74.

[21] *Guide* ii.22, p. 319.

which is actually created and, similarly, if God's knowledge is not inherently creative, it follows that God might be able not to create a world at all.[22] These statements warrant the view that Maimonides does not consider God's knowledge to be limited by existing particulars when he says that God knows existents as their cause. God's knowledge encompasses everything that is within God's power to create, but not everything that God wills into existence.[23] If everything that is willed is created, some might prefer to think of God's will as an attribute of action, when used in this sense, indicating that everything that God creates has a purpose, therefore preserving final causality and the truth of Aristotelian science.[24]

In summary, material things are distinguished from one another and made individual instantiations of a form by virtue of their bodies. Matter is the principle of individuation, while form is the principle of intelligibility. In the case of human knowledge, matter is a barrier to understanding. God is not prevented from knowing by the unknowability of matter, however, because God's knowledge is the cause of matter. Again, this solution requires Maimonides to insist that the word knowledge must be absolutely equivocal when used of both human knowledge of material objects and God's knowledge of material objects.[25]

One might well ask, in that case, whether Maimonides is justified in using the word knowledge at all. In what way could God's knowledge be considered knowledge? It seems that what Maimonides attributes to God is not knowledge, because knowledge, in the strong sense, cannot be of

---

[22] See Manekin's observation that will follows wisdom in every instance in which Maimonides mentions them together. "Divine Will in Maimonides' Later Writings," *Maimonidean Studies*, 5 (2008), 216. Everything that is willed by God must be known by God, but it does not follow that everything that is known by God is also willed by God. Therefore, when Maimonides says that everything that exists can be attributed to God's will or to God's wisdom, it does not follow that he is equating them or negating one or the other.

[23] Maimonides also states that things that never exist are "not an object of God's knowledge." *Guide* iii.20, p. 481. However, this is no counter evidence if, as I have suggested, he is there considering kinds of things. When this is combined with a principle of plenitude, the conclusion follows that such things are not possible, and connects with his claim that God creates everything that can be created. See *Method and Metaphysics in Maimonides*, p. 184, n. 28.

[24] I discuss an example of an interpretation that interprets Maimonides's different statements about God's willed actions in various ways. See "Reason, Will, and Purpose: What's at Stake for Maimonides and His Followers in the Doctrine of Creation," in *Creation ex Nihilo: Origins, Development, Contemporary Challenges* (Notre Dame: University of Notre Dame Press, 2017), pp. 213–231.

[25] Maimonides does not explicitly go as far as Averroes, who argues that God's knowledge, while all-encompassing, is neither particular nor universal, since both are modes of human perception rather than of God's causative, and therefore equivocal, knowledge. See C. Belo, "Averroes on God's Knowledge of Particulars," *Journal of Islamic Studies*, 17 (2006), 177–199. Nevertheless, this statement is not obviously incompatible with Maimonides's view.

material particulars, matter being unknowable. Gersonides criticizes
Maimonides for this reason, and claims that God's knowledge encompasses particulars only inasmuch as they are knowable. As members of an
ordered, and therefore intelligible, whole, particulars can be known, and
God knows them in such a way. But to deny that God knows them in the
respect in which they are not part of an ordered, intelligible whole is not to
say that God is ignorant of anything, since there is nothing aside from the
order to be known.[26] Perhaps Maimonides could have responded by
arguing that Gersonides does not appreciate how deeply the equivocation
is rooted in the idea that God's apprehension of existing things is connected to God's creative ability. God's knowledge is not an instance of
knowledge, but neither is it ignorance. To which Gersonides could have
reasserted his response that Maimonides is not entitled to use the word in
such a way. God's knowledge must be a perfect instance of knowledge,
which only God is able to possess. He may also have added that such an
absolute creation of matter is not possible since matter itself must in some
sense be uncreated. If so, there must be some sense in which matter is
unknown even to God, as creator. As prime matter, and therefore possessing some form, it is knowable inasmuch as it is informed, but as the
formless matter out of which the world was created, it is not.[27]
In Gersonides's view, matter is therefore inaccessible to God's knowledge,
even though God is the creator, as it is to human knowledge.

In Gersonides's view, Maimonides attempts to say that what for humans
is confusion, error, or opinion is, in God's case, knowledge.[28] Gersonides
suggests that Maimonides was motivated by his need to defend principles
of the Torah, and argued only with that in view, so he sufficed himself with
refuting the philosophers without making sure that his view was philosophically acceptable.[29] That God's knowledge is not an instance of knowledge is, as Gersonides recognizes, exactly Maimonides's point. It is
sufficient to refute the philosophers, if it is true; God's knowledge is said
to be totally different from any kind of knowledge with which humans are
familiar and can therefore be complete, as the law teaches. His position can
be summed up when he states that one ought "to believe that everything is

[26] There are competing interpretations of Gersonides's views. See T. Rudavsky, "Divine Omniscience
and Future Contingents in Gersonides," *Journal of the History of Philosophy*, 21 (1983), 513–536. And
see also C. Manekin, "Conservative Tendencies in Gersonides' Religious Philosophy," in D. Frank
and O. Leaman (Eds.), *The Cambridge Companion to Medieval Jewish Philosophy* (Cambridge:
Cambridge University Press, 2003), pp. 304–342.
[27] For an account of Gersonides on formless matter, see Feldman, *Gersonides*, pp. 53–55.
[28] Gersonides, *Wars*, vol. 2, p. 107.    [29] Gersonides, *Wars*, vol. 2, p. 98.

revealed to his knowledge, which is his essence, and that this kind of apprehension is impossible for us to know at all."[30]

On this reading, when Maimonides says that God knows all things he is making a theological statement that accords with his claims about religious language. He argues that people can know nothing of God's essence and that all words must therefore be used of God, on the one hand, and of creatures, on the other, by way of absolute equivocation: A word must have one meaning when used of creatures and an entirely different meaning, one that humans cannot understand, when used of God.[31] Ultimately, because words gain their meanings from the way people use them, they should not be used of God at all. In the case of knowledge, to say that God in a strict sense knows particulars secures this difference, since when humans know they do so through universals. The human intellect does not deal with individuals, but with abstract forms and judgments. It knows particulars only inasmuch as they are subsumed under the universal concept. Strictly speaking, humans do not know particulars: God does. We apprehend them by sensing them; God apprehends them as their creator.

Since our question regards the concord or otherwise between what Maimonides says about knowledge and providence, there is no need to examine further Gersonides's own view. Nevertheless, one might ask why Maimonides would argue that God has knowledge of particulars, if to do so is in effect to predicate something of God that is not knowledge at all, as it includes that which is essentially unknowable. I contend that he considers this position to be implied by other of the law's doctrines that are opposed to the philosophers and of which he is uncertain.[32] Maimonides notes that neither his opinions on "these great and sublime notions" nor those of the philosophers are demonstrable. Although his view can only be asserted as the law's opinion rather than as certainly true, it accords with the wider beliefs that the law entails.[33] "With regard to all problems with reference to which there is no demonstration, the method used by us with regard to this question – I mean the question of the deity's knowledge of

[30] *Guide* iii.21, p. 485.
[31] For further on Maimonides's negative theology see C. Manekin, "Belief, Certainty and Divine Attributes in the *Guide of the Perplexed*," *Maimonidean Studies*, 1 (1990), 117–141.
[32] This paragraph sums up an argument made in greater detail in *Method and Metaphysics*.
[33] *Guide* iii.21, p. 485. On the differences between doctrines affirmed with certainty, as a result of demonstration, and those affirmed to be true without certainty, on the basis of dialectical arguments, see A. Hyman, "Demonstrative, Dialectical and Sophistic Arguments," in Ormsby (ed.), *Moses Maimonides and His Time* (Washington: Catholic University of America Press, 1989), pp. 35–51, and J. Kraemer, "Maimonides' Use of (Aristotelian) Dialectic," in Cohen and Levine (eds.), *Maimonides and the Sciences* (Dordrecht: Kluwer Academic, 2000), pp. 111–130.

what is other than He – ought to be followed."[34] Of course, another such problem is creation ex nihilo and de novo, which Maimonides argues cannot be demonstrated but, rather, is a doctrine that can only be asserted on the basis of the law's authority, with the support of rational arguments, and not as certainly true. God's knowledge is inherently connected to the law's view of creation, which posits an absolute beginning and, he argues, allows for the possibility of miracles. Maimonides states that miracles are created but not through a regular natural cause.[35] He argues that miracles occur when something happens to a particular thing that is apparently unnatural for that thing, but they do not permanently change its nature. If God causes all things through God's knowledge, and God knows particulars, miracles are possible because God is able to cause each individual particular to be otherwise than it is. The Aristotelian view renders them impossible because it denies God knowledge of particulars.[36] So Maimonides presents the issues of God's knowledge and the world's creation as bound up with one another, and both can be asserted only on the basis of dialectical arguments, not as demonstrable truths.

## Relationship between Knowledge and Providence

Notwithstanding Gersonides's critique, he is clear that his own position differs from that of Maimonides. To say that Maimonides ought not to have made a particular claim is not to say that he did not in fact believe it to be true. However, that is the view taken by scholars today who have dealt with what Maimonides says about God's providence. It is claimed that Maimonides indicated that he did not hold that God knows particulars by introducing an inconsistency into his account of God's knowledge. While he extends God's knowledge to particulars, he limits God's providence in a way that seems to make it incompatible with God's knowledge of particulars. Gersonides also seemed to find Maimonides's view of providence more acceptable, although it is not exactly the same as his own, so the assumption that knowledge and providence are coextensive appears to be justified on philosophical grounds.[37] Recently, this difficulty has been forcefully stated by Alfred Ivry, who writes as follows: "God is not ignorant of anything, Maimonides says in a number of places, asserting that divine omniscience extends to all individual existents. . . . Maimonides explicitly

[34] Guide iii.2, p. 485.    [35] Guide ii.29, p. 345.
[36] The connection between miracles and the law is made in Guide ii.25, p. 329.
[37] See Feldman, Gersonides, p. 107.

qualifies this position, however, as soon as he develops his theory of providence."[38]

The assumption behind this position must be that all that is known by God is also subject to God's providence, and Maimonides does indeed write that "everything that is governed is also known."[39] However, it is not obvious that this statement can be converted so that the claim that everything that is known is also governed, or provided for, would therefore hold true. It would be possible for Maimonides to deny that claim, as Ibn Tibbon does when he asserts that God's knowledge is wider in scope than God's providence.[40] Ibn Tibbon saw no inconsistency between Maimonides's presentations of these doctrines. Separating them in this way allowed him to preserve Maimonides's explicit positions alongside his previous claim that the discussions about them are connected. In an exposition of Psalm 73, Ibn Tibbon distinguishes "empirical proofs" for God's lack of knowledge from "speculative" or "intellectual" proofs. He then follows Maimonides in claiming that the initial motivation for denying God's knowledge of particulars was the lack of order in human affairs, specifically, the problem of apparent injustice when the righteous suffer and the wicked prosper.[41] Maimonides explains that since "everyone who knows a certain matter must necessarily either exercise care in the governance of what he knows, or neglect it,"[42] the philosophers argue that God cannot be ordering the lives of those who do not receive their just rewards. Nevertheless, God is good and therefore cannot be said to neglect what God knows. Now if God does not provide for all things but, being good, provides for all things God knows, God does not know all things.[43]

Maimonides denies that these arguments have any bearing at all on the question of God's knowledge. The "intellectual proofs" are those that

---

[38] Ivry, "Providence, Divine Omniscience and Possibility," p. 149. Ivry's explanations of Maimonides on God's knowledge seem to me to be closer to Gersonides than to anything found in Maimonides. The same is true of his accounts of Maimonides on creation, and his assertion that the existence of matter is somehow independent of God's creative activity. See, for example, *Maimonides' Guide for the Perplexed: A Philosophical Guide* (Chicago: University of Chicago Press, 2016), pp. 181–183. Ivry states that "Gersonides makes explicit that which I have given as Maimonides' esoteric view." It seems to me that these ideas are connected. If one argues that Maimonides thought that there was an uncreated, formless matter, it makes sense to say that God knows only the order that God can impose upon that matter. As Gersonides argues, God's knowledge can then be said to be of the same kind as human knowledge. Since Maimonides does not make such claims about either matter or God's knowledge, they can only be presented as esoteric views.

[39] *Guide* iii.17, p. 466.

[40] Samuel Ibn Tibbon, *Ma'amar Yiqqavu ha-Mayim* (Pressburg: Anton Edlen v. Schmidt, 1837), p. 82.

[41] *Guide* iii.16, p. 461, and *Yiqqavu ha-Mayim*, p. 86.    [42] *Guide* iii.16, p. 462.

[43] This can be stated similar to what is now known as the classical formulation of the problem of evil. Rudavsky, *Maimonides*, p. 143.

Maimonides responds to by explaining that God knows existents as their
cause, and include the arguments mentioned above. He states that these
arguments were driven by the need to justify the claim that God is ignorant
of human affairs, in light of the disorder they detect.[44] At the end of the
chapter, in which Maimonides summarizes the philosophers' opinion, he
states that "the discourses about knowledge and about providence are
connected with one another."[45] In the subsequent two chapters, he
explains providence in a way that responds to the "empirical proofs,"
effectively claiming that the philosophers' confusion is in the way that
they connect knowledge with providence. They would have been justified
in drawing the conclusion that God's providence does not extend to
particulars but err when they make that claim about God's knowledge as
well: Those who deny God's knowledge of particulars ought to deny God's
providence over particulars.

## The Account of Providence

In light of this connection between the two issues, Maimonides next
discusses the different ways in which providence is usually understood.
He divides the opinions into five, and adds his own interpretation.[46] His
own view, he states, is similar to Aristotle's, but with some qualifications
that bring it into line with "what has clearly appeared as the intention of
the book of God and of the books of our prophets," although not into line
with many of those who have previously expounded the law's view, namely
"the multitude of our scholars" and "some of our latter-day scholars."[47]
Aristotle's opinion, he writes, "is the opinion of those who hold that
providence watches over some things and that these are [as they are]
through the governance of one who governs and the ordering of one
who orders, whereas other things are left to chance."[48] Aristotle's position
can be divided into two parts. One concerns providence over superlunar
affairs; the other is his view of providence in the sublunar world. In the
superlunar world, providence extends to all individuals, while in the
sublunar world it extends only to the species and to individuals inasmuch
as they contribute to the permanence of the species. Since Maimonides
agrees entirely with Aristotle's position regarding the superlunar realm, and
with the general outlines of Aristotle's view about the sublunar realm, it is

[44] *Guide* iii.16, p. 463.   [45] *Guide* iii.16, p. 464.
[46] The various positions have been well summarized in previous studies, so there is no need to rehearse
them here. See, for example, Rudavsky, *Maimonides*, p. 144.
[47] *Guide* iii.17, p. 469.   [48] *Guide* iii.17, p. 464.

worth outlining how he explains Aristotle. Ultimately, I will suggest, there
is no difference between providence in the two realms. Both superlunar
and sublunar creatures are governed by providence inasmuch as they are
unchanging and fulfilling a constant goal.

Maimonides describes Aristotle's view of providence over the spheres as
follows. "He holds that God, exalted, takes care of the spheres and of what is
in them and that for this reason their individuals remain permanently as they
are. Alexander has formulated this, saying that in Aristotle's opinion God's
providence ends at the sphere of the moon."[49] Because God's providence
extends to the spheres, everything in the superlunar realm is unchanging.
This quotation implies that whatever is covered by God's providence does
not change. And regarding the spheres, "whose individuals are permanent,
and what is in them, providence regarding them means that they remain
permanent in a changeless state."[50] In the sublunar world, where particulars
are generated and corrupted, the situation is different. Only the species as
a whole is said to be watched over by providence, while the individuals are
not permanent. "To sum up, the basis of his opinion is as follows:
Everything that, according to what he saw, subsisted continuously without
any corruption or change of proceeding at all – as, for instance, the states of
the spheres – or that observed a certain orderly course, only deviating from it
in anomalous cases – as, for instance, the natural things – was said by him to
subsist through governance; I mean to say that divine providence accompanied it."[51] The particulars of the superlunar realm are ordered to
a particular end, and they are always fulfilling that end. Therefore, providence extends to them permanently. However, Maimonides goes on to
explain that, in Aristotle's view, providence also watches over the species of
the sublunar realm because they too are unchanging. When stating that
providence watches only over generalities, Maimonides's Aristotle expresses
a belief that God's providence involves the perpetuation of each species but
not of the concrete individuals belonging to the species. Although
Maimonides adopts the Avicennian view that species exist only in the
mind, as stated above, species nevertheless have a basis in external reality.
In the mind the species exists as a universal, which can be predicated of
multiple things, and in external reality, the species can be predicated of
many. As Avicenna explains, "the universal, inasmuch as it is universal, is not
specifically in this [particular instance] but not in that."[52] Rather, permanent

---

[49]  *Guide* iii.17, p. 465.   [50]  *Guide* iii.17, p. 465.   [51]  *Guide* iii.17, p. 466.
[52]  *Avicenna's De Anima: Being the Psychological Part of Kitāb al-Shifā'*, Fazlur Rahman, ed. (London:
    Oxford University Press, 1959), p. 207: 2.

providence over the species is satisfied because there are always individuals of which the species is predicable.

One of the reasons it is prima facie tempting to say that providence and knowledge are equivalent is that the way that he explains Aristotle sounds close to Maimonides's explanation of some of the philosophers' opinions about God's knowledge: "some said that he knows only the species and not the individuals whereas others said that he knows nothing at all outside himself."[53] And one of the motivations for these opinions is the belief that that since God does not change, what God knows cannot change. If providence can only be attached to that which does not change, and therefore, in the sublunar world, only to species, it seems to be equivalent to knowledge. If providence and knowledge are equivalent to one another, in both the superlunar and sublunar spheres, the kind of providence exercised is the same, in that it is providence over the species of things. The difference between the two realms is simply that sublunar species contain more than a single individual. But in the sublunar sphere, God's providence, like God's knowledge, is unchanging and concerns only that which is ordered and unchanging. Furthermore, in the case of the spheres, God can be said to know all the particulars of the superlunar realm without introducing plurality into God's knowledge, because each one of those individuals constitutes an entire species, being the lone instantiation of the species. And if God is said to know particulars in the sublunar realm in a universal way, the philosophers' claim that God's knowledge cannot extend to particulars since that would entail multiplicity in God's knowledge can also be answered.[54] So when Maimonides states his broad agreement with Aristotle's view of providence, he could be indicating his agreement with the philosophers' account of God's knowledge.

However, it is still possible to distinguish the account of providence from the philosophers' position on God's knowledge. In theory, more than one member of a species could be watched over by providence if there are multiple individuals that are unchanging, but that might not be true of God's knowledge. God's knowledge was said by the philosophers to extend only to those individuals that are singular in their species. In the case of providence, what is important is not whether there is a single member of a species, so that God's providence could not be prevented from covering distinct individuals because of their plurality, but the relationship between

[53] *Guide* iii.16, p. 463.
[54] See M. Marmura, "Some Aspects of Avicenna's Theory of God's Knowledge of Particulars," *Journal of the American Oriental Society*, 82 (1962), 299–312.

the purpose of the individuals and the permanence of the species. This follows from Maimonides's explanation that providence, in Aristotle's view, watches over what is permanent. So even according to the philosophers' theory, in which God's providence and knowledge seem to be equal in extent, the two doctrines seem to have a different meaning. Knowledge concerns the order that is bestowed on created beings; providence concerns the degree to which an individual thing is constantly fulfilling its function.

In the positions that Maimonides espouses, the two doctrines are even further apart. If God's knowledge of created beings is connected with God's creative ability, as I have argued, and providence is connected with permanent aspects of a species, viz. the fulfillment of the formal and final causes, which do not change as the material particulars change, the two doctrines should not be equated. That providence follows the fulfillment of the final cause, not God's creativity, can be seen in the way in which Maimonides accounts for providence over human beings.

### Providence over the Human Species

Maimonides brings Aristotle's account of providence into line with what he considers to be the requirements of the Law by distinguishing providence over the human species from providence over all other sublunar things.[55] There are two fundamental ideas that Maimonides wishes to preserve. The first is that humans have free choice; the second is that people receive providence to the extent that they deserve. Whereas the first is not necessarily opposed by the philosophers' account of God's providence, the second seems to be. In order to uphold the belief that reward is just, Maimonides qualifies Aristotle's view by stating that individual humans can receive divine providence in accordance with the perfection of their intellects.

For the most part scholars have concentrated on the limits Maimonides draws to God's providence over humans, but it is important to ask about what it means for other creatures as well. God's providence extends to them also, if only in a general way. What is it about the difference between humans and, for example, dogs, that means that individual dogs are not provided for but individual humans can be? The same question can be asked of oak trees and applies to all other natural species. When individuals of such natural kinds achieve their good by fulfilling their goal they do not become permanent. They can, however, reproduce and perpetuate the

---

[55] *Guide* iii.17, p. 469.

species. Through their reproduction, they fulfill their function and the species is perpetually ordered.

The providential distinction follows from the specific difference of humans and, therefore, the nature of the human goal.[56] If the human goal is to know the final causes of all natural kinds, it differs essentially from that of all other sublunar creatures. Maimonides distinguishes other natural kinds from humans who have achieved a level of particularly human perfection. The examples that he uses when he rejects Aristotle's view are telling. He explains that Aristotle's opinion requires believing that there is no difference between the death of an ant and the death of a prophet, or the death of perfect people worshipping.[57] With regard to providence, it is relevant that Maimonides distinguishes ants from perfect people, not from all people. Humans do not endure by perpetuating the species in the same way as other animals, but by perfecting their intellect. So Maimonides distinguishes between non-human sublunar species and people who have reached a degree of perfection. Both worshippers and prophets have perfected themselves in a way that renders them mean-ingfully different from ants, and from the multitude. God's providence watches over those who have attained a degree of perfection because they have actualized their intellects to some extent. By contrast, someone who has not reached such perfection is like "a beast having the shape and configuration of a human being,"[58] and can only engender the continua-tion of the animal part of her nature. If such a person reproduces, what endures is animal, not specifically human. The specifically human form, the intellect, does not survive through reproduction of the animal part of human nature. Moreover, when a person actualizes the specifically human aspect of her nature, that aspect can be said to be permanent. Theoretical, contemplative knowledge, which is the goal of the human intellect, involves apprehending the nature of existing beings in an abstract way.

At the end of the *Guide*, Maimonides returns to clarify providence. He introduces the subject with the remark that "a most amazing insight has now occurred to me through which doubts are dissolved and divine secrets uncovered."[59] He then proceeds to say that that a person would be protected from all evil as long as she is engaged in the intellectual activity that activates

---

[56] *Guide* iii.17, p. 474.   [57] *Guide* iii.17, p. 466.   [58] *Guide* iii.8, p. 433 and iii.51, p. 618.

[59] *Guide* iii.51, p. 624. I use "insight" to translate *wajh naẓar*, literally "aspect of an insight." *Naẓar* can also be "speculation." Pines translates the construct as "speculation," which could give the impres-sion of linguistic support to the notion that Maimonides is presenting an entirely different account of divine providence to that which appears earlier. Such a difference is not warranted by the Arabic, although it cannot be definitively ruled out solely on a linguistic basis.

divine providence: "if someone's thought is free from distraction, and he apprehends God, exalted, in the right way and rejoices in what he apprehends, that individual can never be afflicted with evil of any kind, for he is with God and God is with him."[60] Ibn Tibbon asked whether there were two different accounts of providence in the *Guide*, and wondered whether that which appears at the *Guide's* end is miraculous.[61] Maimonides seems to argue that there is some sort of special providence that protects the virtuous from suffering any evil whatsoever. Such providence involves "the safeguard and the protection from all bodily ills, both the general ones and those that concern one individual rather than another, so that neither those that are consequences upon the nature of being nor those that are due to the plotting of man would occur."[62] Scholars continue to argue that Ibn Tibbon successfully identified a different version of providence opposed to that explained in the *Guide's* earlier chapters, but Ibn Tibbon himself appears to have thought that there is no miraculous form of providence, although he continued to ponder the passage.[63] He points out that had Maimonides been introducing a new, miraculous form of providence, he should not have stated that "the secret with regard to this has been explained even according to the requirements of their [the philosophers'] opinions."[64] Maimonides's entire account fits with Aristotle's view of the way the world works, indicating that there is nothing supernatural in what Maimonides says about providence. Intellect works the way that Aristotle says, but humans who do not fulfill their potential do not lead to the permanence of the human species qua human. The statement appearing at the end of the *Guide* is therefore merely a refinement of his previous position. He is simply expanding on the consequences of the theory he set out earlier on, in which he stated that providence is graded according to the perfection of the individual provided for.[65]

The substance of the insight is as follows: "An individual of perfect apprehension whose thought sometimes, for a certain time, is emptied of

---

[60] *Guide* iii.51, p. 625.

[61] Z. Diesendruck published the letter in which Ibn Tibbon asks this question. "Samuel and Moses Ibn Tibbon on Maimonides' Theory of Providence," *Hebrew Union College Annual*, 11 (1936), 341–366.

[62] *Guide* iii.51, p. 626.

[63] See, for example, C. Touati, "Les Deux Théories de Maïmonide sur la Providence," in *Studies in Religious and Intellectual History* (Alabama: University of Alabama Press, 1979), p. 340. For Ibn Tibbon's comment, see *Yiqqavu ha-Mayim*, p. 98.

[64] *Guide* iii.51, p. 625. For a statement by Avicenna that the divine emanation is cut off from the human intellect when the soul turns away from seeking forms, see *Avicenna's De Anima*, p. 245. For Ibn Tibbon's comment, see Diesendruck, "Providence," pp. 358–359.

[65] The proof texts Maimonides uses in iii.51 would imply a miraculous form of providence if they were taken literally, but he does not indicate that they should be so understood.

God, is watched over by providence only during the time when he thinks of God; providence withdraws from him during the time when he is occupied [with something else]."[66] Maimonides then says that this is similar to the case of a skilled scribe who is not engaged in writing. The image evokes Aristotle's explanation of first and second entelechy, or perfection.[67] Aristotle says that there are two levels of perfections in this context, the first of which is like possessing knowledge, and the second of which is like using that knowledge. The scribe who possesses a skill but is not using it, possesses a first level of perfection. One who is employing that skill possesses a second level, which is an actuality, or use, of the skill. So Maimonides seems to be saying that individual providence is a perfectly natural occurrence that pertains when someone who already possesses the knowledge necessary for speculation on truth is exercising that knowledge. She is thereby fulfilling the final cause of humans by actualizing that aspect of herself in virtue of which she is a human rather than a non-rational animal. However, providence does not watch over someone who possesses the knowledge to engage in speculative worship of God but is not exercising it. Maimonides then explains that evils occur to someone who is perfect only when they are not using their potential to be watched over by providence or, in other words, are not actualizing their capacity for speculative thought: "the greatness of the calamity being proportionate to the duration of the distraction or to the vileness of the matter with which he is engaged."[68]

Maimonides's new insight explains the connection between evil and the withdrawal of providence. He argues that providence over individual humans ceases when they stop actively engaging in reason, that faculty which makes them properly human. Evil does not have the same effect on a perfect person who is actively engaged in contemplation as it would on another animal. Providence is not affected by, for example, a sheep step-ping on a broken bottle and injuring its foot. Providence has nothing to do with any harm or evil that occurs to a particular sheep, but is concerning the permanence of the species as a whole; pain does not prevent it from

---

[66] *Guide* iii.51, p. 625.

[67] *De Anima* 412a. On the Arabic reception of the word as "perfection" in this passage (*tamām* or *kamāl*) see R. Wisnovsky, *Avicenna's Metaphysics in Context* (London: Duckworth, 2003), pp. 21–24.

[68] *Guide* iii.51, p. 625. The metaphor used to describe the person enjoying the ultimate in God's providence, one whom the sun shines on, is similar to that which Maimonides uses in his introduction to the *Guide* when he describes prophetic knowledge, which is likened to lightning flashes on a dark night. *Guide* i.int, p. 7. Prophecy is also natural, in Maimonides's view, and the result of human perfection. See A. Altmann, "Maimonides and Thomas Aquinas: Natural or Divine Prophecy?" *AJS Review*, 3 (1978), 1–19.

being a sheep. However, a person who steps on a broken bottle and is forced to divert her attention from thinking about truth towards treating the injury will no longer be watched over by providence. The difference between them is that if the person had been engaged in speculative thought, thereby to some degree fulfilling the purpose of her rational faculty, she is affected by a withdrawal of the kind of providence that depends on her intellect. Since she is no longer engaged in the specifically human activity of reasoning, but in dealing with something that depends on her animal nature, i.e. pain, providence does not attach to what is permanent about her nature. Now, however, Maimonides is still able to differentiate between her and the sheep on the basis that the specifically human aspect of providence remains available to her, even if it is not fully engaged at that moment. To an extent, what is important is not the pain itself but the distraction. Should somebody not be distracted, the damage would not be an evil in itself from the point of view of the effect it has on the human species. However, inasmuch as a bodily evil is distracting, it is an evil to the human nature of the individual. Should evil happen to an individual who is cut off from individual providence, that person would be "left to chance," as Aristotle stated.[69] A plausible way to understand being subject to chance is that it indicates that such things are not properly ordered. God's purposive agency is connected to science and, therefore, final causes. Everything that is created has a purpose. Individuals that are not equivalent to the purpose can be said to be left to chance, as they do not exist in the way that they are "intended" by completing their final causes. Their goal is to know God as far as possible and to know God's governing of creatures. That is, humans are perfect inasmuch as they know the order of existing things and their final causes and inasmuch as their own souls are ruled by their intellects.[70] This is the perfection of humans because things are perfected when they realize their goal, and the human goal is to know.

## Conclusion

If the argument in this chapter is correct, Maimonides's professed belief about both God's knowledge and God's providence can be accepted together. There is no conflict between them since they are different doctrines. God's knowledge of created beings is not limited by matter because it causes them, and so it is of a different sort to human knowledge.

---

[69] See above (note 48).     [70] *Avicenna's De Anima*, p. 50.

God's providence is said to attach only to the ultimate goods of creatures, which are in themselves unchanging. The way Maimonides explains providence connects it with the nature of created beings. "Providence also extends over the earth in the way that corresponds to what the latter is, just as providence extends over the heavens in the way that corresponds to what they are."[71] In the case of human nature, the ultimate goal involves perfecting theoretical reason. The perfection of the individual is what makes the animal a human animal, and it is this that endows the species "human" with permanence. This is also of a different sort of providence to that which humans might exercise over other creatures, which does not involve purely contemplation of natural kinds. Additionally, Maimonides's views about providence itself, as it appears in the middle and end of part three of the *Guide*, can be accepted as a coherent whole rather than two distinct doctrines. If such conclusions are acceptable, there is no need to claim that Maimonides contradicts himself in order to hide his real opinion about either God's knowledge or God's providence.

[71] *Guide* iii.54, p. 637.

# The World and the Eye: Perplexity about Ends in the Guide of the Perplexed *iii.13 and iii.25*

## David Wirmer

Maimonides begins *Guide* iii.13 as follows:

> Often the minds of perfect men have grown perplexed over the question of what is the end of this being. Now I will explain that in all schools this question is abolished.[1]

The "schools" mentioned are identified as "our opinion who assert that the world has been originated" and "the opinion of Aristotle who holds that the world is eternal."[2] In the course of the chapter Maimonides proposes to show how first Aristotelian philosophy, then the Law abolishes the quest for the *telos* of "this being" (i.e., the world). And at least in some places in the chapter the denial of "ends" is extended also to each "part of the world." The abolishment of the question supposedly lifts the perplexity that attaches to it. But what was the perplexity about in the first place? Maimonides never says.

One might think that the sense of the question becomes clear enough from the reasons Maimonides gives for renouncing it. This has obviously been the attitude of virtually all commentators who pay small, if any, attention to the problem or problems that motivated the composition of *Guide* iii.13. But the resulting interpretations differ widely: Some come to the conclusion that Maimonides completely rejects Aristotelian final

---

[1] *Guide* iii.13, p. 323, lines 22–23 (Ar.), p. 448 (Eng.). The first reference is to the page and line number of the Munk-Joel Judeo-Arabic edition; the second is to the Pines English translation. See Introductory Note, above. Multiple changes have been introduced on the basis of the Arabic without special notice; only changes of particular conceptual interest are commented on in the notes. *Ghāya* is always rendered by the single term "end" instead of "final end." For the translation "this being" and similar formulations see below, pp. 12–13.

[2] *Guide* iii.13, p. 324, lines 5–6 (Ar.), p. 449 (Eng.). Pines translates *ḥudūth, muḥdath*, etc. as "produced in time." However, Maimonides in *Guide* ii.13 interprets *ḥudūth* as being "after having been purely and absolutely nonexistent" but explicitly not as a "temporal beginning" (*mabda' zamānī*), for time as an accident of motion is itself created. Pines's translation thus obscures the possible nuances with which Maimonides's "language regime" invests the term and has here been replaced by "originated."

causes,[3] some that he adopts a moderate criticism denying solely external finality,[4] some that he accepts final causes in nature and only rejects the conception of God as a necessary rather than a freely and designedly acting cause.[5] It has been claimed, on the one side, that Maimonides in *Guide* iii.13 wishes to exhibit a far-reaching congruence between Aristotelian philosophy and Judaism in both accepting and limiting final causes,[6] and, on the other side, that he believes in a sweeping external finality and polemically wants to show to "'perplexed' philosophers" the incoherence of Aristotle on this issue.[7]

A full discussion of the perplexity to which Maimonides alludes in the opening statement, and the way it is resolved, would require an analysis of the entire challenging chapter. Instead, I would like to discuss how a passage in *Guide* iii.25 that mentions "perplexity in the quest for the end of the existence of the world as a whole or the end of every part of it" contributes to the understanding of iii.13, both with respect to the perplexity that the latter addresses and with respect to the distinction that Maimonides appears to draw between the "local" search for particular ends and the "global" search for the end of all being. While a proper interpretation of the perplexity in *Guide* iii.25 sheds light on the nature of the perplexity of the "perfect men" in the earlier chapter, it also conflicts with some of its apparently fixed premises and, in particular, contradicts its assumptions about the relationship between particular ends and the global end.

## What Is the Perplexity of the Perfect Men in *Guide* iii.13?

Before we start our examination of the perplexity concerning ends in *Guide* iii.25, a few general remarks on the two key terms "perplexed" and "perfect

---

[3] S. Pines, "Translator's Introduction: The Philosophic Sources of the *Guide of the Perplexed*" in Maimonides, *The Guide of the Perplexed* (Chicago: Chicago University Press, 1963), pp. lxx–lxxi with notes 27 and 29; W. Z. Harvey, "Spinoza and Maimonides on Teleology and Anthropomorphism," in Y. Melamed (ed.), *Spinoza's Ethics. A Critical Guide* (Cambridge: Cambridge University Press, 2017), pp. 43–55.

[4] J. Parens, *Maimonides and Spinoza. Their Conflicting Views of Human Nature* (Chicago: University of Chicago Press, 2012), pp. 13–14, 153–161.

[5] H. Wolfson, *The Philosophy of Spinoza* (Cambridge, MA: Harvard University Press 1934), vol. 1, pp. 400–440, especially pp. 409, 424; H. Wolfson, "Hallevi and Maimonides on Design, Chance and Necessity," *Proceedings of the American Academy for Jewish Research*, 11 (1941), 105–163, especially 151–159, 163; A. Hyman, "Maimonides on Causality," in S. Pines and Y. Yovel (eds.), *Maimonides and Philosophy* (Dordrecht: Martinus Nijhoff, 1986), pp. 157–172. Both authors ignore the negative statements of iii.13.

[6] E. Goldman, "On the End of Existence in the *Moreh Nevukhim*," in A. Kasher and Y. Lewinger (eds.), *Sefer Yeša'yahu Leibowicz* (Tel-Aviv: Agudat ha-studentim, 1977), pp. 164–191, especially p. 191 (Heb.).

[7] D. Schwartz, *Central Problems of Medieval Jewish Philosophy* (Leiden: Brill, 2005), pp. 35–38, 44–45.

men" occurring in the opening statement of iii.13 are in order. Some interpreters have understood this opening as a criticism of the people who are confused about ends,[8] but such a reading goes against the grain of the *Guide* where "perplexity" (*ḥayra*) has always to do with being caught between two contradictory claims or arguments that seem to possess equal force.[9] The "perplexed" are those to whom Maimonides wants to afford guidance, not because they are wrong but because they see the problems and are hence undecided and confused.

This is here underlined by their designation as "perfect men" (*al-kāmilūn*), a term that in the *Guide* means those to whom the book is primarily addressed.[10] The ideal reader of the *Guide*, "a perfect man . . ., devoted to the Law and . . . perplexed,"[11] is an intellectually perfect (i.e., philosophically educated) individual who is perplexed because "the externals of the Law" contradict the results of scientific reasoning. The perplexity consists in the impossibility to uphold both claims to truth, the claim of philosophy and the claim of the Law, as long as the latter is understood according to its external sense. The perplexity dissipates when one realizes that the objectionable terms are equivocal, and the problematic passages are parabolic.[12] The perfect man "who is already informed" (*qad ʿalima*) then understands Scripture according to his previous scientific knowledge.[13]

However, Maimonides also indicates that the "secrets" of the tradition, i.e., physics and metaphysics insofar as they are treated in the religious sources, cannot be completely clarified even by perfect men like himself.[14] The main reason for this – or so I would argue – is the fact that parabolic speech, not being literally true, will, when used to convey certain truths of theological concern, always contradict other, no less important truths.[15] The perplexity bred by parabolic speech thus remains ineffaceable to a certain degree because it resists by its very character every attempt at complete clarification.

---

[8] Schwartz, *Central Problems*, p. 38; Harvey, "Spinoza and Maimonides," p. 54.

[9] Cf. W. Z. Harvey, "Maimonides on the Meaning of Perplexity (*ḥayra=aporía*)," *CISMOR Proceedings*, 7 (2013), 68–76.

[10] Cf. *Guide* Epistle Dedicatory, p. 1, lines 14–15 (Ar.), 3 (Eng.).

[11] *Guide* i. Introduction, p. 10, lines 17–18 (Ar.), 16 (Eng.).

[12] *Guide* i. Introduction, p. 2, lines 14–29 (Ar.), 5–6 (Eng.); cf. p. 6, lines 10–19 (Ar.), 10 (Eng.).

[13] *Guide* i. Introduction, p. 5, lines 8–18 (Ar.), 9 (Eng.).

[14] Cf. *Guide* i. Introduction, p. 3, lines 5–23 (Ar.), 6–7 (Eng.); p. 4, lines 12–17 (Ar.) and p. 4, line 26–p. 5, line 1 (Ar.), 8 (Eng.).

[15] This is the situation Maimonides describes with respect to divine attributes in *Guide* i.20, p. 32, lines 4–7 (Ar.) and i.59, p. 95, line 12 (Ar.); in both cases the *kāmilūn* are mentioned.

Coming back to *Guide* iii.13 we may then say that there is every reason to suppose that Maimonides, by employing the terms "perfect men" and "perplexed," introduces the question about "the end of this being" precisely as one of those questions which leads philosophizing adherents of the Law into an impasse between the results of rational speculation and the "traditional" understanding with its potentially incompatible implications. Our analysis will bear that out.

Now, what is the perplexity about? W. Z. Harvey has recently pointed out the relevance of the "perplexity" mentioned in *Guide* iii.25 for the theme of iii.13. He argues that in both cases the perplexity is caused by an anthropocentric assumption that is false. Here is the passage from *Guide* iii.25:

> Know that the majority of the false imaginings that call forth perplexity in the quest for the end of the existence of the world as a whole or the end of every part of it have as their root an error of man about himself and his imagining that all that exists exists because of himself alone, as well as ignorance of the nature of inferior matter and ignorance of what is primarily intended – namely, the bringing into being of everything whose existence is possible, existence being indubitably a good. It is because of this error and of the ignorance of these two notions that the doubts and the perplexity arise, so that some of God's actions are imagined to be frivolous, others futile, and others vain.[16]

According to Harvey's reading of this passage (which he quotes only in part) it demonstrates "that the 'perplexity' attendant upon the futile search for final causes in nature is mostly due to the error of anthropocentrism."[17] In this perspective then, if I correctly understand Harvey's condensed presentation, human conceit pushes man to undertake the search for final causes in nature only in order to confirm his presumption that he himself is the end of nature. However, inasmuch as there are no final causes, the search remains futile and, as a result, instead of flattering his vanity man falls into perplexity. Anthropocentrism would thus be the principal cause of perplexity and its rejection the main aim of *Guide* iii.13.

This interpretation accords well with the larger context of the chapter. As E. Goldman points out, it belongs to a part of book iii, namely chapters 8–24, that can be described as dealing with theodicy. The evil that man experiences nourishes the impression that the world is not well-ordered.

---

[16] *Guide* iii.25, pp. 367, line 14–368, line 3 (Ar.), 505–506 (Eng.). Cf. Harvey, "Spinoza and Maimonides," pp. 46–47; he quotes until "because of himself alone."
[17] Harvey, "Spinoza and Maimonides," p. 46, my italics.

An element of Maimonides's attempt to dispel this impression is his rejection of the misguided expectations human beings have about the course of nature: The world is made neither for our individual benefit nor for our benefit as a species, and the harm we suffer is therefore not indicative of a lack of order in the world. Rather this assumption reveals a lack of understanding and humility on our part. In this context *Guide* iii.13 has the function, so Goldman suggests, of explaining Maimonides's reasons behind his non-anthropocentric vision of the world. He mentions two important elements of this vision: First, being is hierarchically organized, and man, although he has the highest rank among sublunar beings, is not the highest being absolutely. Second, being is only grounded in divine will, and this implies a rejection of final causes of being. *Guide* iii.13 explains and underlines this rejection.[18]

Although the rejection of an unalloyed anthropocentrism is undoubtedly an important motive in *Guide* iii.13,[19] the above interpretation fails to account for the perplexity of which Maimonides there speaks. The partial reading of the passage quoted from *Guide* iii.25 that Harvey proposes leaves out important elements. Thus, the full passage does not single out man's exaggerated self-esteem as the one cause of perplexity. Instead the "root" of "false imaginings" that then produce perplexity is described as threefold: (1) anthropocentrism combined with (2) ignorance about the nature of matter and with (3) ignorance about the value of all possible being.

The role of matter is treated in *Guide* iii.8 and 10, where Maimonides explains that matter is a necessary condition for certain types of being, namely generated being, and that because privation is a necessary concomitant of matter, everything generated is also corruptible. All evils are privations of some goods, they are relative non-being, while "all being is a good." Therefore, while "evil" necessarily attaches to the generable and corruptible beings brought into existence by God, he does not bring evil into existence in an "essential act" (*yafʿalu . . . bi-l-dhāt*) and by "primary intention" (*qaṣdan awwaliyyan*), rather: "the true reality of the act of God in its entirety is good, for it is being."[20] This means that evil is, so to speak, condoned by God insamuch as it is a necessary concomitant of the material

---

[18] Goldman, "On the End of Existence," pp. 171–172.

[19] Cf. *Guide* iii.13, pp. 325, line 25–326, line 16 (Ar.) (refutation of anthropocentrism); pp. 326, line 16–327, line 9 (Ar.) (every being is willed for its own sake); pp. 327, line 20–328, line 13 (Ar.) (interpretation of anthropocentric language in the Bible); pp. 328, line 13–329, line 10 (Ar.) (the low rank of humans compared to heavens and angels).

[20] Quotes from *Guide* iii.10, p. 317, lines 2–10 (Ar). Pines writes: " . . . is the good, for the good is being," 440 (Eng.); according to my reading both *khairan* and *huwa* in line 317, 10 relate to *fiʿl*.

being that he brings into existence because imperfect being is still better than non-being.[21] There is an intimate connection then between ignorance about matter and ignorance about being. But what do they have to do with the search for final causes?

The denial of primary "intention" expressed both in the discussion of matter in *Guide* iii.10 and in our quotation from *Guide* iii.25 gives us a hint. When reality is considered as intended by God, one may, being ignorant of matter and being, become confused about the way God's actions relate to their respective ends. As Maimonides explains at the beginning of *Guide* iii.25, actions can be grouped into four classes with respect to their ends. An action is "good" (*khair*) when it fulfills three conditions: It is (1) for the sake of an end, (2) which is noble, and (3) it actually attains this end. The action will be "frivolous" (*la 'b*) when an end is intended and attained but not noble but rather "unnecessary and not very useful." The action is "vain" (*bāṭil*) when the intended end is not attained, and "futile" (*'abaṯ*) when no end is intended.[22]

What the passage quoted from *Guide* iii.25 aims to show is thus that the divine actions do have noble ends and attain them and that the failings that matter necessarily implies must not lead one to suppose that the divine actions either do not have ends (i.e., are futile) or do not attain those ends (i.e., are vain). Concerning the apparently futile: Privation and what follows from it, for instance death, is not an intended being and thus need not and cannot be accounted for by specific ends, but only understood as a necessary concomitant of matter, which in its turn is only a necessary condition for the general end of being. Concerning the apparently vain: The less-than-perfect constitution of individual beings, for instance stupid or cruel or lewd human beings, likewise does not admit of a direct final account; it is simply an effect of material conditions.[23]

Our reconstruction of the background of the passage quoted from *Guide* iii.25 shows two things: First, that in this context Maimonides is not criticizing the search for final causes but rather defends the finality of the world by reminding his reader that with respect to certain phenomena no immediate end must be sought because they relate to ends in an indirect

---

[21] Cf. Aristotle, *De generatione et corruptione* II.10, 336b27–34.

[22] *Guide* iii.25, p. 365, lines 5–30 (Ar.), 502–503 (Eng.).

[23] Cf. *Guide* i.34, p. 52, lines 6–17 (Ar.), 76–77 (Eng.); ii.40, p. 270, lines 7–17 (Ar.), 381–382 (Eng.); and iii.34, p. 391, lines 7–9 (Ar.), 534 (Eng.), where Maimonides explains the fact that the divine Law is not adapted to individual cases with a reference to nature: "it is your business to reflect on the natural things in which the general utility, which is included in them, nonetheless necessarily produces [*lāzim*] damages to individuals, as is clear from our discourse and the discourse of others."

(but not less necessary) manner. The passage then, contrary to what Harvey suggests, is not based on the assumption that there are no ends. The opposite is true; as we will see in the next section, the present passage comes as a conclusion to an argument that insists on the existence of final causes in nature. Second, the ignorance about matter and being, diagnosed by Maimonides, explains two of the "false imaginings" about "God's actions," namely the suspicion they might be futile or vain. There is good reason then to assume that the third root of error, anthropocentrism, is responsible for the idea that God's actions might be "frivolous" (i.e., aimed at "something unnecessary and not very useful"). It is easy enough to see why anthropocentrism would have this effect: If man considers himself the sole end of creation, the creation of everything not useful for man must appear as frivolous. As will be seen in the next section, this is exactly the argument that Maimonides employs against anthropocentrism in *Guide* iii.13.

In sum, Maimonides in *Guide* iii.25 presents anthropocentrism together with other misconceptions as a source for perplexity "*in* the quest for the end [*fī ṭalab ghāya*] of the existence of the world as a whole or the end of every part of it," where this quest itself is portrayed as a meaningful enterprise. The problem with anthropocentrism is that it can prevent us from identifying the *correct* end. But the more fundamental problem treated in *Guide* iii.13 is whether there are *any* ends in God's actions – *alias* nature[24] – whether this quest is meaningful in the first place. It is important to notice that in iii.13 Maimonides begins his discussion of the position of the Law by formulating two views that he will subsequently argue against. The first opinion he mentions is that the belief in the origination of the world imposes the search for the end of all existence. The second opinion – a position defended by Saadia – is that "the end of all existence is solely the existence of the human species so that it should worship God, and that all that has been made has been made for it alone."[25] It is quite evident here that the second opinion, anthropocentrism, is different from the first opinion. The first opinion says *that* the creation of the world, considered as an intentional act of God, must be directed at an end; the second opinion says *what* this end is. Obviously, if anthropocentrism suggests the wrong end, this does not necessarily imply that there is no end at all.

[24] Cf. *Guide* iii.32, p. 383, line 20 (Ar.), 525 (Eng.).
[25] *Guide* iii.13, p. 325, lines 18–20 (Ar.), 451 (Eng.). On the implicit criticism of Saadia see N. Lamm, "Man's Position in the Universe. A Comparative Study of the Views of Saadia Gaon and Maimonides," *Jewish Quarterly Review*, 55 (1965), 208–234.

What is more, we have just seen that Maimonides in *Guide* iii.25 very much insists on the end-directedness of God's acts. The chapter functions as a kind of watergate connecting the preceding discussion of providence with the following discussion of the commandments that starts in *Guide* iii.26. In the opening statement Maimonides establishes a parallel between the two questions:

> Just as there is disagreement among the men of speculation among the adherents of Law whether His works, may He be exalted, are consequent upon wisdom or upon the will alone without being intended toward any end at all, there is also the same disagreement among them regarding our Laws, which He has given to us.[26]

As Maimonides continues to explain, in the case of the Law the correct position held by "all of us – both of the multitude and of the elite" is that all commandments have a "cause," that is to say, they all have an "end" (*ghāya*) that is "intended" (*maqsūd*) by them or, expressed differently, they are given "in view of" (*min ajl*) some "utility."[27] Does the parallelism of the two questions concerning ends – in nature and in Law – extend to the respective answers? If so, Maimonides would indicate here – without, however, saying so explicitly – that the question whether there are ends in nature has to be answered affirmatively in the same way as the existence of reasons for all the commandments has to be affirmed.

Now, what have we learned from *Guide* iii.25 concerning the perplexity of iii.13? On the one hand, there is the negative result that anthropocentrism obviously is not the main problem. On the other hand, it has become clear that the apparently total rejection of ends in iii.13 is in open conflict with Maimonides's defense of divine providence. It is hence necessary to examine more carefully the scope of Maimonides's denial of final causes. A full treatment of this question would require an analysis of his use, in *Guide* iii.13, of Aristotelian concepts such as the distinction between "primary" and "ultimate" ends as well as between internal and external (inter-species) finality.[28] While this cannot be accomplished here, the comparison with iii.25 can bring to light the importance Maimonides attaches to the distinction between finality *in* the world and finality *of* the world.

---

[26] *Guide* iii.26, p. 368, lines 19–21 (Ar.), 506 (Eng.). For the parallelism cf. also note 23 and 24.
[27] *Guide* iii.26, p. 368, lines 21–26 (Ar.), 506–507 (Eng.).
[28] Cf. *Guide* iii.13, p. 324, lines 10–18 and p. 324, line 24–325, line 16 (Ar.), 449–450 (Eng.).

## Global and Local Finality: Which (Dis-)Proves Which?

The opening sentence of *Guide* iii.13, quoted above, denies that there is an "end of this existence" (*hādha l-wujūd*). Pines's translation introduces an ambiguity by rendering the abstract noun *wujūd* (being, existence) by verbal circumscriptions like "that which exists." This could give the impression that Maimonides talks about the absence of ends for each and every being, when in fact the Arabic evidently speaks not about particular beings but about being in a global manner. As the demonstrative pronoun *hādha* indicates, this global being is not a metaphysical abstraction, the fact of existing, but the concrete reality taken collectively. This is confirmed by some further formulations, quite obviously synonymous with those mentioned until now: "the end of the totality of being" (*jumlat al-wujūd*), "the end of being in its entirety" (*al-wujūd bi-asrihī*), and "the end of all being" (*al-wujūd kullihī*).[29]

Thus, the starting point of the reflections offered in *Guide* iii.13 is certainly the claim that "the world [*al-ʿālam*] in its entirety" has no end.[30] However, the ambiguity between whole and part is not a feature of Pines's translation only, but an inbuilt feature of Maimonides's discussion. Many of the arguments propounded in the core of the text deal not with the world as a whole but with the end "of any of the parts of the world."[31] Most importantly, the conclusion of the chapter seems to favour this – let us call it – "distributive" reading of the denial of ends, inasmuch as Maimonides explicitly envisages every single being and suggests two different lessons – (a) and (b) – to be drawn from the preceding reflections:

> For when man knows his own soul, makes no mistake with regard to it, and understands *every being according to what it is* [*kull maujūd bi-ḥasabihī*], he becomes calm and his thoughts are not troubled [a] by seeking an end for what has not *that end* [*tilka l-ghāya*]; or [b] by seeking any end for what has no end except its existence [. . .].[32]

Only for cases of type (b) is the existence of ends denied, or rather, things of the (b) type have no end other than their existence. Things of the (a) type, on the contrary, are said to have an end, although they may not have the

---

[29] *Guide* iii.13, p. 324, lines 4–5 (Ar.), 449 (Eng.); p. 325, line 2 (Ar.), 450 (Eng.); p. 325, line 19 (Ar.), 451 (Eng.).

[30] Cf. *Guide* iii.25, p. 366, lines 22–25 (Ar.), 504 (Eng.), where "the world" is employed as a synonym of *jumlat al-wujūd*.

[31] *Guide* iii.13, p. 324, lines 6–7 (Ar.), 449 (Eng.); cf. also p. 326, lines 20–21 and p. 327, line 13 (Ar.), 452–453 (Eng.).

[32] *Guide* iii.13, p. 329, lines 11–13 (Ar.), 456 (Eng.).

end that one expects to find. Nothing is stated in this conclusion about being as a whole (the world), whether it can be assigned to one of those two cases. Rather Maimonides says that one should understand "every being," and he seems to assume that "every being" belongs either in group (a) or (b). While it would be a category mistake to call "being" (*wujūd*) in the sense of the metaphysical abstraction "a being" (*maujūd*), it is not evident that the totality of real being cannot be considered as a being. In fact, that is precisely what Maimonides does in Guide i.72, where he argues – against the theories of the Mutakallimūn, which result in a complete denial of nature[33] – that "this whole being is one individual."[34] Be that as it may, however, the conclusion of *Guide* iii.13 manifestly talks about a plurality of beings and is hence not focused, or at least not exclusively, on a putative end of being in the global sense.

Furthermore, the conclusion does not any longer outright deny finality but, quite to the contrary, confirms the existence of ends for type (a) beings and, for type (b) beings, still allows the use of teleological terminology by saying that these have no end "except" their own being. This latter description is perfectly compatible with a finalistic account of the beings in question, inasmuch as their being as they are can legitimately be called their end. They are hence ends in themselves.

To come back to the part–whole distinction, we have to ask what causes Maimonides to waver between these two undoubtedly related but nevertheless distinct questions: whether the world as a whole has an end and whether "every being" in the world has an end. The answer, for which the following analysis will provide evidence, is simply this: Maimonides has reasons both for assuming and denying that the two questions must receive the same response.

In *Guide* iii.13 Maimonides discusses in brief the part-whole relationship when presenting the reasons for which Aristotelian philosophy, allegedly, abolishes the quest for an end of the world. Maimonides's account can be broken down into the following main steps:[35]

(1)   According to Aristotle's opinion concerning the eternity of the world "it makes no sense to search an end for the totality of being."

---

[33] Cf. *Guide* i.71, pp. 126, line 1–127, line 2 (Ar.), 182–183 (Eng.).

[34] *Guide* i.72, p. 129, line 25 (Ar.), 187 (Eng.); cf. p. 127, line 10 (Ar.), 184 (Eng.), etc. Cf. also ii.1, p. 174, lines 3–5 (Ar.), 250 (Eng.); ii.10, p. 188, lines 7–11 (Ar.), 270 (Eng.).

[35] *Guide* iii.13, p. 324, lines 4–10 (Ar.). Pines (449) uses language of command and interdiction ("it is not permitted to ask," etc.), but Maimonides's expressions do not indicate an interdiction but rather an inappropriateness because of intrinsic reasons.

(2)  The reason for this (*dhālika anna*) is that in accordance with the eternity thesis one does not search for "the ultimate end of any part of the world."

(3)  The preceding statements are explained (*idh*) by the fact that "everything . . . takes place according to an eternal necessary nexus" (*al-kull . . . 'alā jihat al-luzūm al-abadī*).

The denial of a final cause for the world as a whole (1) is here accounted for by the absence of final causes for parts of the world (2). The latter is explained by two key features of Aristotelian natural philosophy: eternity and necessity (3). However, Maimonides makes no attempt to show that eternity indeed precludes finality; he pretends evidence.

While an independent examination of this portrayal of the Aristotelian position is beyond the scope of the present study, we may briefly turn to Moses Narboni's commentary to show the doubts that attach to it. Narboni reckons Maimonides cannot have ignored Aristotle's real position on the necessity of final causes for scientific knowledge and points to *Guide* i.69 where Maimonides agrees to the notion of God as final cause of the world. Thus, according to Narboni, Maimonides does not mean to deny in *Guide* iii.13 that there is no ultimate end for the world, but only "that according to the belief in eternity there is no ultimate end except God, may he be exalted, and that there is no end which originates through an intention for the sake of which the maker has made it." Maimonides, so Narboni surmises, only hints at this position because it implies "the eternity of the beings."[36]

We will come back to this point in the conclusion and concentrate now entirely on the part-whole relationship. To resume, in *Guide* iii.13 Maimonides ascribes to Aristotelian cosmology the following *a fortiori* argument: Inasmuch as in an eternal and necessary world no part of the world can have an (ultimate) end, the world as a whole cannot have an end either. Maimonides's discussion of the position of the Law in *Guide* iii.13 makes no explicit use of the part-whole relationship, but in *Guide* iii.25 we find a critical assessment of the inferences that certain creationists draw on the basis of this relationship:

> As for those who say that no end is intended in any of the acts of God, they were led to this by necessity, namely, by considering the totality of being in accordance with their opinion. For they say: What is the end of the existence of the world in its entirety? Hence they assert of necessity what everyone

---

[36]  Moses Narboni, *Be'ur Narboni*, ed. J. Goldenthal (Vienna, 1852) p. 52r12–19, long quote 52r17–18.

asserts who maintains the origination of the world: He willed it so not for another cause.[37] Thereupon they proceed to apply this assertion to all the particular things in the world. They go so far as not to concede that the hole in the uvea and the transparency of the cornea exist for the sake of letting the visual spirit pass so that it might apprehend, and do not even regard this at all as a cause of sight.[38]

The argument may be reconstructed as follows: The first part of the paragraph describes the starting point of reflection that Maimonides appears to share, namely that on the basis of a belief in creation the question "What is the end of the world?" has to be rebutted. God does not create the world because of something else – one may only say that he willed it to be. In other words, all creationists necessarily deny that the world exists in view of an end. The second part of the paragraph depicts an untoward use that some creationist thinkers – the Mutakallimūn[39] – have made of this basic principle by applying it to each and every part of the world; that is, by considering everything as admitting of no other explanation than that "He willed it so," completely ignoring the finality that natural things – for example, the eye – so clearly exhibit. Maimonides's criticism then attempts to draw a dividing line between whole and part: The parts do have ends, the whole does not. The error of some creationists is that they illegitimately transfer the property of the whole to the parts.

Now if we confront Maimonides's criticism of the Kalām's denial of ends in nature with his affirmative report, in *Guide* iii.13, of the supposed denial of ends by Aristotelian philosophy, it becomes evident that both cannot be true at the same time. The two arguments are negative images of each other:[40] While the first reasons from part to whole, the second reasons from whole to part. The "Aristotelian" proof starts with the premise that no part of the world has an end and concludes that the world as a whole has no end either; premise and result are supposed to be true. The Kalām proof starts with the premise that the world as a whole has no end and concludes that no part of the world has an end; the premise is supposed to be true and

---

[37] Pines translates "there being no other cause." However, the expression *lā li-ʿilla ukhrā* does not exclude a cause alternative to God's will but specifies that God did not will *because of something* – his willing is not determined by any ulterior consideration; cf. Moses Maimonides, *The Guide of the Perplexed: Hebrew Translation from the Arabic with annotations, appendices, and indices by Michael Schwarz* (Tel Aviv: University Press, 2002), p. 510 (*shehu' ḥafeṣ bekhakh beli ṭaʿam aḥer*).

[38] *Guide* iii.25, p. 366, lines 22–28 (Ar.), 504 (Eng.).

[39] That the argument is directed against the Kalām view is aptly stated by Munk, cf. *Le Guide des égares*, vol. 3, tr. and ed. S. Munk (Paris: 1866), p. 198, note 3.

[40] This has already been pointed out by Z. Diesendruck, "Die Teleologie bei Maimonides," *Hebrew Union College Annual*, 5 (1928): 415–534, esp. 419–424.

the conclusion false. Both proofs agree in holding that the world as a whole has no end, but in the "Aristotelian" proof this is what the proof is supposed to demonstrate while the Kalām proof assumes it on other grounds, not specified. Both proofs strongly disagree with respect to the finality of the parts of the world: The "Aristotelian" proof takes its denial as a premise, true according to Maimonides's presentation in *Guide* iii.13; the Kalām proof derives the same denial as a conclusion that, however, is false according to Maimonides's presentation in *Guide* iii.25. The comparison thus shows that in spite of the apparent evidence of the reasoning shown in *Guide* iii.13, this has absolutely no secure basis. It is neither clear whether inferences between parts of the world and the whole are permitted, nor whether the premise of the proof is correct or not.

What is more, the premise of the Kalām proof from *Guide* iii.25 involves Maimonides in another set of contradictions internal to creationism. For, as we have briefly seen in the previous section, in *Guide* iii.13 Maimonides attempts to show, against some of his coreligionists, that according to the position of the Law the world has no end. That is, he proves that which, in *Guide* iii.25, is taken as a "necessary" premise affirmed by all believers in creation. However, the proof in *Guide* iii.13 implies too much. If it is accepted, it shows not only that the world as a whole has no end but also that no part of the world has an end – that is to say, it demonstrates both the premise of the Kalām proof, which Maimonides apparently accepts, and the conclusion, which he explicitly rejects. Let us now reconstruct his claims and their incongruent implications.

Maimonides's proof in *Guide* iii.13 argues indirectly against that which we have above called the first opinion, namely that the belief in creation forces us to search for a final end of the world. On the face of it, the proof is primarily directed against the second belief, namely, "that the end of all existence is solely the existence of the human species so that it should worship God, and that all that has been made has been made for it alone."[41] Maimonides never really makes explicit how the refutation of this second opinion can at the same time serve as a refutation of the first opinion. However, the position that he attacks proposes a model according to which one part of the world—man—would be the end of all other parts of the world and hence the "end of all existence" absolutely. The refutation of anthropocentrism thus functions only as an example demonstrating that no part can be the end of the whole.[42]

---

[41] *Guide* iii.13, p. 325, lines 19–20 (Ar.), 451 (Eng.).
[42] Cf. Diesendruck "Teleologie," pp. 428–429.

Maimonides's first argument, expressed in form of a rhetorical question, consists in asking whether God would have been able (*qādir*) to bring man into existence without any "preliminaries" (*tauṭi'āt*) or whether this was possible (*yumkin*) only after the existence of these preliminaries.[43] In what follows Maimonides considers only the positive answer, ostensibly because a negative answer to this question would constitute an outright denial of God's power. Thus, his opponents assume that God could indeed have created man without the other parts of the world.[44] Maimonides objects that this theory is self-contradictory: If all other parts of the world are not ends but "exist for the sake of a thing," namely man, that is to say, if all other parts of the world are means for the existence of man, and man could have existed without these means, this has the absurd consequence that these things have no end at all.[45] Thus, according to Maimonides's analysis, the believers who assume that man is the end of the world must hold both that all other beings are means for the existence of man and that they are not necessary for and hence not means for the existence of man. Or, expressed differently, they hold that man is the end for the existence of the rest of the world and, at the same time, that this end does not account for the existence of the world.

Maimonides's second argument consists in pointing out that the assumption of man's worship as end of the world cannot constitute a definitive answer to the question for the end because this question may always be repeated with respect to any answer given.[46] He specifically mentions two scenarios: Either the worship is considered as something that happens for the sake of God, but then one may ask "what for," inasmuch as God in his perfection obtains nothing through man's worship. Or the worship is for the sake of man's perfection, but then again one may ask what makes man's perfection an end.[47] Therefore, Maimonides argues, only one answer to all these questions is possible: "God has wished it so," "there does not exist an end except the Will alone."[48] In other words, no final cause can explain the existence of the world and the manner in which it exists but only a divine efficient cause, which is not bound by any ends beyond the exercise of its voluntary causality.

[43] *Guide* iii.13, p. 325, lines 25–28 (Ar.), 451 (Eng.).
[44] *Guide* iii.13, p. 325, lines 28–29 (Ar.), 451 (Eng.).
[45] *Guide* iii.13, pp. 325, line 29–326, line 1 and p. 326, lines 14–16 (Ar.), 451–452 (Eng.).
[46] Goldman, "On the End of Existence," p. 181, splits this second argument into two, but my summary shows why the two scenarios mentioned together form one argument.
[47] *Guide* iii.13, p. 326, lines 2–7 (Ar.), 451 (Eng.).
[48] *Guide* iii.13, p. 326, lines 7–12 (Ar.), 451–452 (Eng.). The ambiguity between divine will and wisdom as it appears in this passage, though important, cannot be treated here.

The result of the second argument is thus precisely what the Kalām proof in *Guide* iii.25 assumes as a premise: The existence of the world can only be explained by referring it to divine will. However, while Maimonides there denies that this implies the negation of ends for parts of the world – with the stark consequence that the complex structure of an eye could not be said to be for the sake of sight – this implication cannot be avoided here. For the first argument shows that no *part* of the world can be the end of the world as long as one assumes, as the creationists are wont to do, that each part could have existed independently of all the others. Maimonides is not shy to spell this out:

> the belief in origination making it indispensable for us to say that it is possible that something different from this being, its causes and effects could exist.[49]

Now, if no part requires any other, then none can be or have an end. Or, put more generally, there cannot be sufficient causes in nature. The second argument agrees with the first in assuming that everything is in God's power without any external constraints: No end we could postulate has the explanatory force to break the infinite regress of ends, and thus divine will is the only possible explanation. If this is the case, then it concerns the parts of the world to the same degree that it concerns the world as a whole. By consequence, Maimonides's creationist arguments from *Guide* iii.13 succeed to refute global finality only by arguing at the same time against local finality – and, in the last analysis, against all causality – whereas Maimonides's criticism of Kalām in *Guide* iii.25 tries to dissociate both claims.

To which point the two positions are contradictory can be learned by asking which effect the affirmation of ends for parts of the world would have on the arguments presented in *Guide* iii.13. The answer is straightforward: The Maimonides of *Guide* iii.25 who accepts final causality in nature would have to respond "no" to the question whether God could have created man without any "preliminaries"; he thus holds the position that is rejected out of hand in the argumentation of *Guide* iii.13.

Nor is this contradiction – internal to the Maimonidean interpretation of the Law's position – limited to a tension between the two chapters. For in his remarks immediately following the exposition of the two arguments from *Guide* iii.13 that we have analysed, Maimonides now gives a very different turn to his statements about will as ultimate cause.

---

[49] *Guide* iii.13, p. 326, lines 13–14 (Ar.), 452 (Eng.), considerably adapted.

Allegedly drawing a conclusion from the preceding discussion, Maimonides now presents in a summary fashion what, according to his own opinion ('*indi*), is the right understanding of "the beliefs of the Law" and in accordance with "the speculative views."[50] In this statement he makes two moves by which he noticeably departs from the results reached before. First, Maimonides restates the result that the other beings do not exist for the sake of man and depend only upon the divine will, by saying that "the other beings too have been intended for their own sakes not for the sake of something else." He thus silently transforms the complete negation of finality into an affirmation of ends in themselves and identifies this auto-finality as the purpose of divine creation. By an ingenious double interpretation of the verse from Proverbs 16:4 "the Lord hath made everything *lama'anehu*" as meaning both "for its own sake" and "for the sake of His will,"[51] Maimonides tries to make the reader forget that the autonomy of a freely willing divine agent and the autonomy of natural beings are, in fact, not identical but opposites.

The second move consists in taking back even the limitation of finality to auto-finality. Maimonides drops the Kalām premise on which, as documented above, his argument relied, and according to which there are no necessary and sufficient causes, whether final or other. He now passes surreptitiously to the opposite assumption:

> For we say that in virtue of His will He has brought into existence all the parts of the world, some of which have been intended for their own sakes, whereas others have been intended for some other thing that is intended for its own sake.[52]

And:

> In respect to every being He intended that being itself; and whenever the existence of some thing was impossible unless it was preceded by some other thing, He first brought that thing into existence—as in the case of the senses, which precede reason.[53]

It should be noted that this division of beings into ends in themselves and things having an end corresponds exactly to the concluding statement of the chapter, analyzed before. Even in *Guide* iii.13 then Maimonides affirms

---

[50] For this and the following see *Guide* iii.13, p. 326, lines 16–26 (Ar.), 452 (Eng.).

[51] *Guide* iii.13, pp. 326, line 26–327, line 1 (Ar.), 452–453 (Eng.).

[52] *Guide* iii.13, p. 326, lines 21–23 (Ar.), 452 (Eng.).

[53] *Guide* iii.13, p. 326, lines 25–26 (Ar.), 452 (Eng.); cf. p. 327, lines 4–9 (Ar.), 453 (Eng.). Goldman, "On the End of Existence," p. 183, aptly remarks that this statement shows that the preceding arguments are based on the opponents' assumptions, not Maimonides's own.

the existence of teleological relationships between different parts of the world, and he even disguises these affirmations as conclusions drawn from an absolute denial of ends.

## The World and the Eye: Science and Creation

With respect to our guiding question in the last section, we can now formulate the following results: In *Guide* iii.25 Maimonides explicitly attempts to sever the ties between the local finality of parts of the world and the global finality of the world as a whole. The avowed but, as of yet, insufficiently explained reason was that the belief in creation requires one to deny that the world has a final end, whereas both scientific evidence and the defense of divine providence indicate that beings in the world do have ends, as witnessed, for instance, by the physiology of the eye. The reason for linking creationism to the denial of an end of the world has started to become clear from *Guide* iii.13. For creationism an autonomous divine will, unconditioned by any ends and requirements intrinsic to the created beings, must be posited. Once posited, however, this divine will not only supersedes a hypothetical global end but simply all ends, and hence necessarily leads into the Kalām denial of finality, causality, and nature, which Maimonides wishes to avoid. This is why, in *Guide* iii.13, he both categorically denies ends and then tries to rescue finality in most respects, with the exception only of an end for the whole of being.

This equilibrium, however, is untenable. As J. Guttmann already pointed out, it has the absurd consequence that the world is supposed to be purposefully organized by God, but as a whole has no purpose at all and is hence, according to the requirements of *Guide* iii.25, "futile."[54] What this shows more fundamentally is that on behalf of the Law Maimonides has to employ two contradictory conceptions of divine will. Providence requires a will that is led by purposes and is in this sense end-directed. Creation, on the contrary, requires an autonomous will that is not conditioned by any purpose or end.

Natural philosophy agrees, up to a certain point, with the requirements of providence, but it must interpret "ends" not as purposes but as final causes. Maimonides allies himself with Aristotelian natural philosophy, in order to avoid the counterintuitive and anti-rational consequences of the

---

[54] J. Guttmann, *Die Philosophie des Judentums* (München: Ernst Reinhardt, 1933), pp. 197–198. Goldman, "On the End of Existence," 187–190, tries to refute this by arguing, correctly, that Maimonides does not accept unlimited divine will but binds it to "the laws of nature." He fails to see, however, that this implies the abolishment of creation.

Kalām position. By doing so, however, Maimonides risks all the necessi-
tarian and eternalist implications of philosophy's definition of ends as
causes. That could be the reason why in *Guide* iii.13 Maimonides claims –
against the overwhelming evidence of Aristotle's writings and, as Narboni
emphasized, against his own account elsewhere in the *Guide* – that eternity
and necessity preclude ends. Eternity and necessity indeed contradict
divine purpose, but they go hand in hand with final causality and, in
particular, with the notion, exposed in *Guide* i.69, that God is the final
cause of the world.[55] Maimonides was well aware of this contradiction and
in *Guide* ii.21 criticized some "latter-day philosophers" – obviously thinking of Avicenna – for trying to call God a "maker" (*fāʿil*) and someone who
acts with purpose (*qāṣid*) while affirming at the same time that he acts
"always" and with "necessity." Maimonides insists: "But this is not the
meaning of purpose [*qaṣd*], as we propose to conceive it."[56]

According to Aristotle, Maimonides explains in *Guide* ii.20, the world
follows from God with necessity, albeit not in a corporeal manner as
a shadow is caused by a body, but in the manner in which an intelligible
is caused by an intellect. For Aristotle's first cause is an intellect, but not
one that purposes and can will anything different.[57] There is then
a fundamental difference between an intellect functioning as a necessary
principle and an intelligent agent acting with purpose. Characteristically,
in *Guide* iii.13 Maimonides twice equates both notions: "the purpose of an
intelligent being [*dhī ʿaql*], I mean to say … that which has an intellectual
principle [*mabdaʾ ʿaqlī*]." And: "the one that Aristotle calls the intellectual
or divine principle, that being the one that makes one thing for the sake of
another."[58] As sketched above, in *Guide* iii.13 and iii.25 antagonistic tendencies within the position of the Law come to the fore, some of these
requiring the coupling of final cause and purpose, some their dissociation.
A passage that perfectly illustrates this uneasy situation occurs in *Guide*
iii.19:

> Can someone endowed with intelligence conceive that the humors, mem-
> branes, and nerves of the eye – which, as is known, are so well arranged and

---

[55] *Guide* i.69, p. 117, lines 2–22 (Ar.), 169–170 (Eng.). Even there Maimonides proposes a mixed
account, speaking both about causes and about will, but explains that God's will is identical with
God's essence. Now, what follows from God's essence must follow with necessity. Significantly
Maimonides there refers forward to iii.13, pp. 326, line 26–327, line 1 (Ar.), 452–453 (Eng.) as
explaining that the "imitation" of God as end of the world is the meaning behind the identity of will
and essence – that is, the identity of divine will and natural necessity/final causality.

[56] *Guide* ii.21, pp. 219, line 20–220, line 13 (Ar.), 314–315 (Eng.), quote 220, line 8–9 (Ar.).

[57] *Guide* ii.20, pp. 218, line 19–219, line 8 (Ar.), 313–314 (Eng.).

[58] *Guide* iii.13, p. 324, lines 2 and 20–21 (Ar.), 448–449 (Eng.).

all of which have as their purpose the end of this act [of seeing] – have come about fortuitously? Certainly not. But as every physician and every philosopher has set forth, this is brought about of necessity through a purpose of nature. Now according to the general consensus of philosophers, nature is not endowed with intellect and the capacity for governance. Rather does this craftsmanlike governance proceed, according to the opinion of the philosophers, from an intellectual principle [*mabda' 'aqlī*]; and, according to us, it is the act of an intelligent being [*dhī 'aql*] who impressed all the faculties in question into all the things in which a natural faculty exists.[59]

With respect to the eye, with respect to organs and faculties of natural beings, it seems easy enough to align the creationist story and the account of natural philosophy and to coin amalgams like "purpose of nature" while, at the same time, insisting on the different assumptions, here and there, about the character of the ultimate principle of nature. However, when turning from the eye to the world as a whole this symbiosis necessarily breaks down and, in collapsing, reveals irreconcilable assumptions within the Law itself. This, I would suggest, is the real "perplexity" of "perfect men" in *Guide* iii.13.

---

[59] *Guide* iii.19, p. 346, lines 18–24 (Ar.), 479 (Eng.).

# Early Quotations from Maimonides's Guide of the Perplexed in the Latin Middle Ages

## Diana Di Segni

## Introduction

Moses Maimonides's *Guide of the Perplexed* counts among the most influential Jewish philosophical and theological texts, not only within the Jewish tradition. Indeed, the *Guide* had a remarkable impact especially on the Latin-speaking world from the thirteenth century onwards. Shortly after its two Hebrew translations, three different Latin versions of the *Guide* started to circulate. The first is the *Liber de parabola* (1223–1224), often attributed to Michael Scot.[1] The recipient of this text is Romanus (maybe cardinal Romanus, who went to Paris as a papal legate),[2] and the *Liber* was probably composed in Rome. The *occasio scribendi* is a question asked by Romanus concerning the use of salt instead of honey for offerings at the Jerusalem Temple.[3] The question leads the author to treat the subject of biblical metaphors. Then the *Liber* approaches the question of biblical precepts by dividing them into positive and negative ones. From *folio* 4r on, the content of the text corresponds to Maimonides's *Guide* iii.29–30; 32–49 on the allegorical interpretation of the biblical law. The *Liber de parabola* can be considered a compendium rather than a translation, most probably composed on the basis of Ibn Tibbon's version. While its author seems to be a Jew, the *Liber de parabola* is intended for a Christian public; in fact, no references to the *Talmud* are found, a sign that the text has been adapted for Christian readers.

---

[1] Cf. W. Kluxen, "Literargeschichtliches zum lateinischen Moses Maimonides," *Recherches de théologie ancienne et médiévale,* 21 (1954), 23–50, 41–46. See also G. Hasselhoff, "The Reception of Maimonides in the Latin World: The Evidence of the Latin Translations in the 13th–15th century," *Materia giudaica,* 6/2 (2001), 258–280, p. 261. The *Liber de parabola* is transmitted by Paris, Bibliothèque de la Sorbonne, Ms. 601, foll. 1ra–16vb [E], cf. *Catalogue général des manuscrits des Bibliothèques publiques de France: Université de Paris et Universités des Départements* (Paris: Plon, 1918), p. 150. The catalogue attributes it to Michael Scot, since the same manuscript transmits his translation of the *De celo et mundo.*

[2] Cf. Kluxen, "Literargeschichtliches," p. 44.     [3] Cf. ms. E, fol. 1ra.

The second writing originating from Maimonides's *Guide* is the *Liber de uno Deo benedicto* (around 1240), which is a translation of the twenty-five philosophical premises to *Guide* ii, and of ii.1.[4] The introduction summarizes Aristotelian principles, while the first chapter deals primarily with the proof of God's existence and God's incorporeality. This text seems to be completely independent of the other two Latin versions.

The complete translation of the *Guide of the Perplexed* appeared in Latin under the title *Dux neutrorum*. The translation was mainly based on Al-Ḥarizi's Hebrew text.[5] However, recent research has revealed that another source was involved; whether the second source was Ibn Tibbon's translation or the Arabic original is still not clear.[6] We have information neither on the identity of the translator nor on the time and place of the composition. Different hypotheses have been formulated by scholars: Steinschneider,[7] Perles,[8] Sermoneta,[9] Thorndike,[10] and Freudenthal[11] support the hypothesis that it derives from the court of Frederick II; Kluxen[12] suggested a composition in Southern France; Hasselhoff[13] supports a Parisian origin.

---

[4] Rabbi Moyses, "Liber de uno Deo benedicto," edited by W. Kluxen, in P. Wilpert, *Judentum im Mittelalter: Beiträge zum christlich-jüdischen Gespräch* (Berlin: De Gruyter, 1966), pp. 167–182.

[5] Cf. J. Perles, "Die in einer Münchener Handschrift aufgefundene erste lateinische Übersetzung des Maimonidischen 'Führers'," *Monatsschrift für Geschichte und Wissenschaft des Judentums*, 24 (1875), 9–24; 67–86; 99–110; 149–159; 209–218; 261–268.

[6] Some incongruities with al-Ḥarizi's text have been pointed out by M. Rubio, *Aquinas and Maimonides on the Possibility of the Knowledge of God* (Dordrecht: Springer, 2006), pp. 275–276. Moreover, a collation of *loci critici* between al-Ḥarizi's, Ibn Tibbon's, the Arabic and the Latin texts is provided in D. Di Segni, *Moses Maimonides and the Latin Middle Ages. Critical Edition of Dux neutrorum I, 1–59*, Inauguraldissertation zur Erlangung des Doktorgrades der Philosophischen Fakultät der Universität zu Köln im Fach Philosophie, Digitalpublikation KUPS, 2016, pp. XCII–CXI.

[7] M. Steinschneider, "Kaiser Friedrich II. über Maimonides," *Hebräische Bibliographie* VII (1864), 62–66, p. 65. For the Jewish sources on Frederick II, see C. Sirat, "Les traducteurs juifs à la cour des rois de Sicile et de Naples," in G. Contamine (éd.), *Traduction et traducteurs au Moyen Age* (Paris: CNRS, 1989), pp. 169–191.

[8] Cf. Perles, "Die in einer Münchener Handschrift," pp. 80–81.

[9] Cf. G. Sermoneta, *Un glossario filosofico ebraico-italiano del XIII secolo* (Roma: Edizioni dell'Ateneo, 1969), pp. 40–42.

[10] Cf. L. Thorndike, *Michael Scot* (London: Nelson, 1965), pp. 28–29.

[11] Cf. G. Freudenthal, "Pour le dossier de la traduction latine médiévale du Guide des égarés," *Revue des études juives*, 147 (1988), 167–172, 171.

[12] Kluxen, "Literargeschichtliches," pp. 32–34.

[13] G. Hasselhoff, *Dicit Rabbi Moyses: Studien zum Bild von Moses Maimonides im Lateinischen Westen vom 13. bis zum 15. Jahrhundert* (Würzburg: Königshausen & Neumann, 2004), pp. 123–124. Y. Schwartz, "Authority, Control, and Conflicts in 13th Century Paris: The Talmud Trial in Context," in E. Baumgarten, J. Galinsky (eds.), *Jews and Christians in 13th Century France* (New York: Palgrave MacMillan, 2015), pp. 93–110, p. 103, evokes the hypothesis that the Talmud trial in Paris around 1240–1244 could have been connected to the Maimonidean controversy.

Recently, I showed that the manuscript tradition bears some traces of a vernacular language that was used in the translation process.[14] The geographical origin of these linguistic traces is difficult to identify indubitably, but some elements seem to be connected to Spanish. This would only be the mark of the language spoken by the translator, which does not necessarily correspond to the place where the translation was actually made.

Today, the *Dux neutrorum* is transmitted in thirteen manuscripts and the printing made by Agostino Giustiniani in 1520.[15]

While the *Liber de parabola* and the *Liber de uno Deo benedicto* had limited circulation[16], the reception of the *Dux neutrorum* was more widespread. In the first part of this contribution, a general overview of its fortune will be given; the second part will focus on the earliest quotations. It is generally assumed that William of Auvergne was the first author to cite Maimonides, although no explicit quotation from the *Dux neutrorum* has yet been found. Furthermore, no proper attention has been given to the question whether William quoted from the *Dux neutrorum* or from another source. Inquiry into the question contributes to defining the window in which the *Dux neutrorum* started to circulate in Paris, and as a consequence establishes a time limit for its composition. Secondly, Maimonides's thought was received at an early stage by Moneta of Cremona in his *Summa adversus Catharos et Valdenses*. Little research into this text has been done, which is a crucial proof for the diffusion of the Latin Maimonides outside Paris. Until now, the earliest attestations of the *Dux neutrorum* have been found in the Parisian area, this being one

---

[14]  Cf. D. Di Segni, "Traces of a Vernacular Language in the Latin Translation of Maimonides' *Guide of the Perplexed*," *Recherches de Théologie et Philosophie Médiévales*, 83(1) (2016), 21–48.

[15]  For the manuscript tradition, see: [A] Città del Vaticano, Bibliotheca Apostolica Vaticana (BAV), Ottoboniano Latino Ms. 644; [B] Paris, Bibliothèque Nationale de France, Ms. fonds latin 15973 (Sorbonne 173); [E] Paris, Bibliothèque de la Sorbonne, Ms. 601, foll. 21ra-103vb; [C] Saint-Omer, Bibliothèque de l'agglomération, Ms. 608; [D] München, Bayerische Staatsbibliothek, Clm 7936b; [F] Cambridge, University Library, Ms. Ii. I.19 (1711), foll. 1r–183r; [G] Graz, Universitätsbibliothek, Ms. II.482, foll. 16va–98rb; [H] Todi, Biblioteca comunale "Lorenzo Leonj," Ms. 32; [I] Oxford, Bodleian Library, Ms. Bodl. 437; [K] Città del Vaticano, BAV, Cod. Vaticano Latino, Ms. 1124; [L] Città del Vaticano, BAV, Cod. Vaticano Latino, Ms. 4274; [N] Kassel, Landes- und Murhardsche Bibliothek, 2 Ms. theol. 67; [M] Cambridge, Trinity College, Ms. O.8.37, foll. 1r–229v. For the printed edition, see Rabi Moyses Aegyptius, *Dux seu director dubitantium aut perplexorum*, ed. Augustinus Iustinianus (Parisiis, 1520). The critical edition of *Dux neutrorum* I, 1–59, is provided in my doctoral dissertation: Di Segni, *Moses Maimonides and the Latin Middle Ages*.

[16]  The *Liber de parabola* was known to William of Auvergne (see *infra*), while the *Liber de uno Deo benedicto* was quoted by Albert the Great, cf. C. Rigo, "Zur Rezeption des Moses Maimonides im Werk des Albertus Magnus," in W. Senner (ed.), *Albertus Magnus. Zum Gedenken nach 800 Jahren: Neue Zugänge, Aspekte und Perspektiven* [Berlin: Akademie Verlag, 2001], pp. 29–66.

of the main arguments in favor of a French composition. Pointing out a
reception independent from that in Paris will contribute to a more precise
image of the diffusion of Maimonides's Latin *oeuvre*.

## The *Dux neutrorum*'s Fortune in the Latin Middle Ages

The most common name with which Latin authors mention Maimonides
is "Rabbi Moyses," an epithet that clearly refers to his religious affiliation.
The authority of Maimonides is both philosophical, since he inherits the
knowledge transmitted only in Arabic, inaccessible to Latin readers,[17] and
religious, as a source for information on Judaism and for interpreting the
Bible. The fortune of the Latin Maimonides can be explained precisely
through this double perspective: The Jewish philosopher opened the way
to a non-radical Aristotelianism that could be reconciled with biblical
teachings.

The *Dux neutrorum* was known and quoted mainly by Dominican
authors, such as Albert the Great,[18] Thomas Aquinas,[19] and Meister
Eckhart.[20] But it was diffused also among Franciscans, especially

---

[17] Albert the Great clearly defines Maimonides as a "philosopher," cf. for instance Albertus Magnus, *II Sent.*, d. 3, a. 16, ed. Paris., t. 27, p. 94b.

[18] Albert mentions Maimonides about 120 times (according to Rigo, "Zur Rezeption," p. 36). On the reception of Maimonides in Albert, cf. M. Joel, *Verhältniss Albert des Grossen zu Moses Maimonides: Ein Beitrag zur Geschichte der mittelalterlichen Philosophie* (Breslau: Schletter'schen Buchhandlung, 1863); Rigo, "Zur Rezeption," pp. 29–66.

[19] Thomas explicitly mentions Maimonides 80 times, cf. C. Vansteenkiste, "Autori arabi e giudei nell'opera di San Tommaso," *Angelicum*, 37 (1960), 336–401, 372–393; this has been reviewed by R. Imbach, "Alcune precisazioni sulla presenza di Maimonide in Tommaso," in D. Lorenz and S. Serafini (eds.), *Istituto san Tommaso: Studi 1995* (Roma: Pontificia Università S. Tommaso d'Aquino, 1995), pp. 48–64. However, in numerous passages Maimonides's name is not explicitly mentioned. On the reception of Maimonides in Aquinas, see J. I. Dienstag (ed.), *Studies in Maimonides and St. Thomas Aquinas* (New York: Ktav, 1975); A. Wohlman, *Thomas d'Aquin et Maïmonide: un dialogue exemplaire* (Paris: Editions Du Cerf, 1988); R. Imbach, "Ut ait Rabbi Moyses. Maimonidische Philosopheme bei Thomas von Aquin und Meister Eckhart," *Collectanea Franciscana*, 60 (1990), 99–116; A. Wohlman, *Maïmonide et Thomas d'Aquin. Un dialogue impossible* (Fribourg: Editions Universitaires, 1995); Imbach, "Alcune precisazioni"; G. K. Hasselhoff, "Anmerkungen zur Rezeption des Maimonides in den Schriften des Thomas von Aquino," in W. Kinzig and C. Kück (eds.), *Zwischen Konfrontation und Faszination: Ansätze zu einer neuen Beschreibung jüdisch-christlicher Beziehungen* (Stuttgart: Kohlhammer, 2002), pp. 55–73.

[20] Eckhart mentions Maimonides 117 times (cf. D. Di Segni, "'verba sunt Rabbi Moysis': Eckhart e Maimonide," in L. Sturlese (ed.), *Studi sulle fonti di Meister Eckhart*, vol. II [Fribourg: Dokimion, 2013], pp. 99–135). For the reception of Maimonides in Eckhart, see J. Koch, "Meister Eckhart und die jüdische Religionsphilosophie des Mittelalters," *Jahresbericht der Schlesischen Gesellschaft für Vaterländische Kultur*, 101 (1928), 134–148 (rep. in: J. Koch, *Kleine Schriften*, vol. I [Roma: Edizioni di Storia e Letteratura, 19/3], pp. 349–365); H. Liebeschütz, "Meister Eckhart und Moses Maimonides," *Archiv für Kulturgeschichte*, 54 (1972), 64–96; Y. Schwartz, "Zwischen Einheitsmetaphysik und Einheitshermeneutik: Eckharts Maimonides-Lektüre und das Datierungsproblem des 'Opus tripartitum'," in A. Speer, L. Wegener (eds.), *Meister Eckhart in*

Thomas of York.²¹ Some of *Dux neutrorum*'s arguments entered into the condemnation of 1277 and in Giles of Rome's *Errores philosophorum*.²² In what follows, an overview of the main topics connected to Maimonides's authority in the philosophical and theological fields will be given. Since it is impossible here to give a complete and detailed account, the presentation will be limited to some major topics and authors; for a more detailed treatment, see the bibliography provided in the notes.²³

One of the most famous arguments is related to the question of the world's eternity.²⁴ Latin authors saw in Maimonides an authority both reporting Aristotle's opinion and responding to him. Maimonides's answer to the problem received much attention: According to him, Aristotle considered the world's eternity a hypothesis that still must be proven by cogent demonstrations.²⁵ Maimonides thereby rendered the notion of the world's creation compatible with a scientific Aristotelian approach. It is interesting to note that Latin authors seem not to notice that Maimonides's

*Erfurt, Miscellanea Mediaevalia*, 32 (Berlin-New York: De Gruyter, 2005), 259–279; Y. Schwartz, "Meister Eckhart and Moses Maimonides: From Judaeo-Arabic Rationalism to Christian Mysticism," in J. M. Hackett (ed.), *A Companion to Meister Eckhart* (Leiden: Brill, 2012), pp. 389–414; P. Heidrich, *Im Gespräch mit Meister Eckhart und Maimonides*, ed. H. M. Niemann (Berlin: Lit Verlag, 2010); Di Segni, "verba sunt Rabbi Moysis."
²¹ On the English reception of Maimonides, see J. I. Dienstag, "Maimonides in English Christian Thought and Scholarship: An Alphabetical Survey," *Hebrew Studies*, 26 (1985), 249–299. I am thankful to Fiorella Retucci and Marco Maniglio, who are preparing the critical edition of Thomas of York's *Sapientiale*, for letting me read their transcription of the passages in which Maimonides is quoted.
²² According to R. Hissette, *Enquête sur les 219 articles condamnés à Paris le 7 Mars 1277* (Louvain, Vander-Oyez, Paris: Publications Universitaires, 1977), the articles n° 185; 186; 205 might originate from Maimonides. Cf. also K. Flasch, *Aufklärung im Mittelalter?: Die Verurteilung von 1277* (Mainz: Dieterich, 1989), article no 215. Chapters 12 and 13 of the *Errores philosophorum* deal with Maimonides, cf. Giles of Rome, *Errores philosophorum*, ed. J. Koch, trans. J. O. Riedl (Milwaukee: Marquette University Press, 1944), pp. XLVII–LI. On the *Errores*, cf. also W. Kluxen, "Maimonides and Latin Scholasticism," in S. Pines, Y. Yovel (eds.), *Maimonides and Philosophy* (Dordrecht: Martinus Nijhoff Publishers, 1986), pp. 224–232, 226–229.
²³ For a general overview of Maimonides's Latin reception, see Kluxen, "Literargeschichtliches"; W. Kluxen, "Maimonides und die Hochscholastik," *Philosophisches Jahrbuch der Görresgesellschaft*, 63 (1955), 151–165; W. Kluxen, "Die Geschichte des Maimonides im lateinischen Abendland als Beispiel einer christlich-jüdischen Begegnung," in Wilpert (ed.), *Judentum im Mittelalter*, pp. 146–66; Kluxen, "Maimonides and Latin Scholasticism"; S. Pines, "Maïmonide et la philosophie latine," in S. Pines, *The Collected Works of Shlomo Pines*, vol. V (Jerusalem: The Magnes Press, 1997), pp. 393–403; Hasselhoff, "The Reception of Maimonides in the Latin World"; Hasselhoff, *Dicit Rabbi Moyses*; W. Kluxen, "Maïmonide et l'orientation philosophique de ses lecteurs latins," in T. Levy, R. Rashed (éd.), *Maïmonide philosophe et savant (1138–1204)* (Louvain-Paris: Peeters, 2004), pp. 395–409.
²⁴ See especially *Guide* i.73; ii.13–18; 26; 28. Cf. K. Seeskin, *Maimonides on the Origin of the World* (Cambridge University Press, 2005).
²⁵ According to C. Dales, "Maimonides and Boethius of Dacia on the Eternity of the World," *The New Scholasticism*, 56 (1982), 306–319, this idea was introduced in the Latin world by Maimonides. On the contrary, L. Bianchi, *L'errore di Aristotele. La polemica contro l'eternità del mondo nel XIII secolo* (Firenze: La Nuova Italia, 1984), p. 130, n. 62, is more cautious on the role played by Maimonides in diffusing this argument.

position on the topic is not clear and that some of the *Guide*'s chapters seem to contradict each other.[26] Furthermore, the terms used in the *Dux neutrorum* for creation and eternity, *antiquitas* and *novitas mundi* (which translate the Hebrew *kadmut* and *ḥiddush*), are also transmitted to Latin authors: For instance, they are present in Thomas Aquinas[27] and Thomas of York.[28]

Albert the Great mentions the seven arguments in favor of the world's eternity that Maimonides ascribed to Aristotle and the Peripatetics (*Guide* ii.14); moreover, Albert argues that these are not demonstrative proofs. In general, the entire presentation of the question follows Maimonides's method, arguments, and examples.[29] The structure of the argumentation in Thomas Aquinas also closely follows the *Dux neutrorum* but, surprisingly, the name of Maimonides does not appear, while in other passages the Jewish philosopher is explicitly mentioned.[30] Thomas's solution to the question, namely that it is not possible to demonstrate the world's eternity *demonstrative simpliciter*, clearly depends on Maimonides. Furthermore, Thomas used Maimonides's metaphor of an orphan to describe the human condition when dealing with the problem of the world's eternity (*Guide* ii.17), and in this context Maimonides's name explicitly appears.[31] The

---

[26] Cf. *Guide* i.71 in which God's existence is demonstrated on the basis of the world's eternity. On Maimonides's "exoteric" position on creation, see for instance H. Davidson, "Maimonides' Secret Position on Creation," in I. Twersky (ed.), *Studies in Medieval Jewish History and Literature* (Cambridge, MA: Harvard University Press, 1979), pp. 16–40. According to Albert the Great, Maimonides clearly stood for the creation of the world, cf. Albertus Magnus, *II Sent.*, d. 1, a. 10, ed. Paris, t. 27, p. 29a; ibid., d. 12, a. 1, p. 232a.

[27] Cf. for instance Thomas Aquinas, *ST*, I, q. 46, a. 2 c.

[28] Cf. for instance Thomas of York, *Sapientiale*, II, c. 6.

[29] Cf. A. Rohner, *Das Schöpfungsproblem bei Moses Maimonides, Albertus Magnus und Thomas von Aquin: ein Beitrag zur Geschichte des Schöpfungsproblems im Mittelalter* (Münster: Aschendorff, 1913). For the list of the passages in which Albert refers, explicitly or implicitly, to Maimonides's doctrine of creation, see Rigo, "Zur Rezeption," p. 53, n. 141.

[30] See Thomas Aquinas, *ST*, I, q. 46, a. 1. According to Imbach, "Alcune osservazioni," pp. 60–61, the fact that Thomas 'concealed' his source is a proof that the relationship between Thomas and Maimonides cannot be considered as an 'exemplar dialogue' (cf. Wohlman, *Thomas d'Aquin et Maïmonide: un dialogue exemplaire*). Moreover, Thomas's source might have been Raymond Martini, who presents the same arguments but explicitly ascribing them to Maimonides (*Raymundi Marti Ordinis Praedicatorum Pugio Fidei adversus Mauros et Judaeos cum observationibus Josephi de Voisin, et introductione Jo. Benedicti Carpzovi* [Leipzig: Friederich Lanckis, 1687], I, c. 14, 3). The relationship between Aquinas and Martini has long been discussed by secondary literature, on the topic of world's eternity cf. J. I. Saranyana, "La creacion 'Ab aeterno': Controversia de santo Tomas y Raimundo Marti con San Buenaventura," *Scripta Theologica*, 5 (1973), 127–174. Cf. also W. Dunphy, "Maimonides and Aquinas on Creation. A Critique of their Historians," in L. P. Gerson (ed.), *Graceful Reason, Essays in Ancient and Medieval Philosophy Presented to Joseph Owens* (Toronto: Pontifical Institute of Mediaeval Studies, 1983), pp. 361–379; K. Seeskin, "Maimonides and Aquinas on Creation," *Medioevo*, 23 (1997), 453–472.

[31] Thomas Aquinas, *II Sent.*, d. 1, q. 1, a. 5 resp.; *In symbolum Apostolorum*, n. 880.

same metaphor is recalled by Eckhart,[32] who also mentioned Maimonides's opinion on the difference between Aristotle's teaching regarding the sublunary sphere and the heavens.[33] Moreover, Maimonides's authority on the topic is invoked at length in the second book of Thomas of York's *Sapientiale*.[34]

Secondly, Maimonides's most famous elaboration of divine attributes and the resulting doctrine of negative theology received much attention among Latin thinkers.[35] In numerous chapters of the *Guide* (i.56; 58–61), Maimonides explains the impossibility of attributing anything positive to God, human language being inadequate to describe God. As a consequence, any analogical discourse is excluded, since any positive formulation about humans cannot be predicated of God. This doctrine is problematic for Christianity, since it presupposes equivocity of language and derogates the principle of the *analogia entis*, fundamental for Christian theology. Thomas Aquinas indeed criticized it for preventing any knowledge of God.[36] On the contrary, according to him, it is possible to know the cause through the effects, and since creatures are effects of God, they can then reach a certain knowledge of their Creator.

In Eckhart, the theory of negative theology is treated at length, being instrumental to the demonstration of God's pre-eminence.[37] Eckhart shares with Maimonides a theocentric view: The impossibility of positive statements on God leads to the subordination of human beings to the divine, and as a consequence to the leaning towards God. However, Eckhart does not exclude any positive attribution. Furthermore, Maimonides's theory on God's names, such as the Tetragrammaton, was treated by Eckhart.[38]

[32] Index, n. 55 in Di Segni, "verba sunt Rabbi Moysis," p. 126.   [33] Index, n. 57, ibid.
[34] Cf. especially Thomas of York, *Sapientiale* II, 6.
[35] Cf. S. Feldman, "A Scholastic Misinterpretation of Maimonides' Doctrine of Divine Attributes," *Journal of Jewish Studies*, 19 (1968), 23–39. For Albert, see Albertus Magnus, *I Sent.*, d. 2, 3, 28. On God's names, cf. also *Super Dion. De div. nom.*, c. 1, ed. Colon., t. 37, 1, p. 39, 17–19; ibid., c. 13, p. 448, 63–64.
[36] Cf. Thomas Aquinas, *ST*, I, q. 13, a. 2 resp.; *I Sent.*, d. 2, q. 1, a. 3 resp.; *De potentia*, q. 7, a. 2 c. 2; ibid., q. 7, a. 5 resp.; ibid., q. 7, a. 7 resp.; ibid., q. 7, a. 10 resp.; ibid., q. 9, a. 7 resp.; *De veritate*, q. 10, a. 12 resp. Cf. C. L. Miller, "Maimonides and Aquinas on Naming God," *Journal of Jewish Studies*, 28 (1977), 65–71; D. B. Burrell, *Knowing the Unknowable God: Ibn-Sina, Maimonides, Aquinas* (University of Notre Dame Press, 1986); A. Broadie, "Maimonides and Aquinas on the Names of God," *Religious Studies*, 23 (1987), 157–170; J. A. Buijs, "The Negative Theology of Maimonides and Aquinas," *Review of Metaphysics*, 41 (1988), 723–738; N. Stubbens, "Naming God: Moses Maimonides and Thomas Aquinas," *Thomist*, 54 (1990), 229–267; Rubio, *Aquinas and Maimonides*.
[37] For the list of Maimonides's quotations on the topic, cf. Index, n. 13; 14; 16; 17; 19; 21–27; 29; 31–39; 106 in Di Segni, "verba sunt Rabbi Moysis," pp. 115–135.
[38] Index, n. 36; 40–44, ibid. For God's name in Thomas, cf. Thomas Aquinas, *I Sent.*, d. 8, q. 1, a. 1s.c.

Thirdly, Maimonides's prophetology (*Guide* ii.32–48), involving questions such as the natural disposition to prophecy, its definition, and the position of prophets with respect to the human species, had a reception in the Latin world. According to Maimonides, only a person with a balanced disposition, a perfect imagination and a full intellectual capacity can attain prophecy. Furthermore, Maimonides underlines the uniqueness of Moses's prophecy with respect to the other prophets. Albert receives Maimonides's definition of prophecy, for instance his distinction between dream and prophecy, and the different stages of perfections in imagination and intellectual faculties.[39] Maimonides's relationship between intellect and imagination is received by Thomas too; however, he disagrees that prophecy is the result only of natural disposition: Natural perfections are required for natural prophecy, but prophecy is ultimately a divine gift.[40]

One Maimonidean argument received Aquinas's special attention: The five reasons that prevent people from beginning their studies with metaphysics (*Guide* i.34) were taken by Thomas as an argument proving the necessity of believing in God[41]. The same argument was received by Meister Eckhart, but with its original meaning[42].

Other Maimonidean philosophical themes received by scholastic authors are: divine providence;[43] cosmological questions,[44] such as the

---

[39] Cf. Rigo, "Zur Rezeption," pp. 56–62. Cf. for instance Albertus Magnus, *De somno et vig.*, l. 3, tr. 1, c. 1, Ed. Paris., t. 9, p. 178a; ibid., c. 3, p. 180b–181b; ibid., c. 5, p. 183a–184a; ibid., c. 10, p. 190b–193a; ibid., c. 12, p. 195a–195b; *III Sent.*, d. 37, a. 2, ed. Paris., t. 28, p. 682a, 684a; *IV Sent.*, d. 1, a. 8, ed. Paris., t. 29, p. 21a, p. 22b; *Super Dion. Epist.*, 7, ed. Colon., t. 37, 2, p. 507, 4–9.24–28.

[40] Cf. Thomas Aquinas, *De veritate*, q. 12, a. 2, arg. 6; q. 12, a. 2, ad 6; q. 12, a. 5 resp.; ibid., q. 12, a. 12, arg. 6; q. 12, a. 12, ad 6; *IV Sent.*, d. 49, q. 2, a. 7, ad 2. On the requirement of natural perfections, see *De veritate*, q. 12, a. 4 resp. Cf. L. J. Elders, "Les rapports entre la doctrine de la prophétie selon Saint Thomas et le Guide des égarés de Maïmonide," *Divus Thomas*, 78 (1975), 449–456; A. Altmann, "Maimonides and Thomas Aquinas: Natural or Divine Prophecy?," *Association for Jewish Studies Review*, 3 (1978), 1–19; A. Wohlman, "La Prophétie: Maïmonide et Thomas d'Aquin," in *Ibn Rochd, Maïmonide, Saint Thomas ou "la filiation entre foi et raison": Colloque de Cordoue, 8, 9, 10 mai 1992* (Paris: Castelnau-le-Fez, 1994), pp. 341–349.

[41] Cf. Thomas Aquinas, *III Sent.*, d. 24, q. 1, a. 3, qc. 1 resp.; *De veritate* q. 14, a. 10 resp.; *In Boethium de Trinitate*, q. 3, a. 1 resp.

[42] Index, n. 12, in Di Segni, "verba sunt Rabbi Moysis," p. 118.

[43] Cf. for instance Albertus Magnus, *Summa I*, tr. 1, q. 5, c. 4, ed. Colon., t. 34, 1, p. 21, 34–37; *Super Iob* 3, 1, ed. Weiss, 1904, Sp. 50, 39–43. Thomas Aquinas, *I Sent.*, d. 39, q. 2, a. 2 resp.; *ST*, I, q. 22, a. 2 resp.; ibid., I, q. 22, a. 2 ad 5; *De potentia*, q. 3, a. 17 resp.; *De veritate*, q. 2, a. 3 resp.; ibid., q. 5, a. 9 ad 4; *In threnos Hieremiae*, c. 3, l. 13.

[44] Cf. Thomas Aquinas, *De potentia*, q. 4, a. 1 ad 2; ibid., q. 4, a. 1 ad 5; ibid., q. 4, a. 1 ad 15. For creation, cf. Thomas Aquinas, *ST*, I, q. 69, a. 1 ad 5; ibid., I, q. 74, a. 3 ad 3; ibid., I, q. 74, a. 3 ad 4.

motion of the heavens,[45] celestial spheres,[46] astronomy;[47] matter and
form;[48] motion;[49] angelology;[50] intellect.[51] Moreover, Maimonides is
sometimes considered an authority in reporting other philosophical
doctrines.[52]

In the biblical field, Maimonides's authority was mainly invoked for
hermeneutics.[53] Meister Eckhart devoted special treatment to his metaphorical interpretation of the Bible.[54] Finally, Maimonides is considered a
source for biblical commandments and for the difference between *moralia*,
*caerimonialia* and *iudicialia*.[55]

---

[45] Cf. Albertus Magnus, *II Sent.*, d. 14, a. 6, ed. Paris., t. 27, p. 265b–266a; *Phys.*, l. 8, tr. 2, c. 8, ed. Colon., t. 4, 2, p. 607, 15–48; *Metaph.*, l. 11, tr. 2, c. 10, ed. Colon., t. 16, 2, p. 495, 52–73; *De causis et proc. univ.*, l. 1, tr. 4, c. 7, Ed. Colon., t. 17, 2, p. 53, 68; p. 54, 87. Cf. also Thomas Aquinas, *II Sent.*, d. 14, q. 1, a. 1–2; ibid., d. 14, q. 1, a. 5; *ST*, I, q. 66, a. 1 ad 5.

[46] Cf. Albertus Magnus, *De IV coaeq.* (II red.), tr. 3, q. 16, a. 2, ed. Paris., t. 34, p. 440b; *De caelo et mundo*, l. 1, tr. 3, c. 10, ed. Colon., t. 5, 1, p. 76, 10–18. Thomas Aquinas, *ST*, I, q. 68, a. 1, ad 1; *SCG*, II, 92. For Eckhart, cf. Index n. 88; 89 in Di Segni, "verba sunt Rabbi Moysis," p. 132.

[47] Cf. Albertus Magnus, *De causis et proc. univ.*, l. 1, tr. 4, c. 8, ed. Colon., t. 17, 2, p. 56, 84–90; *Summa II*, tr. 2, q. 10, ed. Paris., t. 32, p. 143a; *De caelo et mundo*, l. 2, tr. 2, c. 5, ed. Colon., t. 5, 1, p. 135, 62–66; ibid., tr. 3, c. 3, p. 147, 39–44; c. 4, p. 150, 13–20; c. 11, p. 169, 3–17.

[48] Cf. Albertus Magnus, *De IV coequevis*, t. 1, q. 2, ed. Paris., t. 34, p. 327a. Cf. Thomas Aquinas, *II Sent.*, d. 3, q. 1, a. 1 resp. Cf. also Meister Eckhart, Index, n. 71–72, in Di Segni, "verba sunt Rabbi Moysis," p. 129, for the metaphor of the matter as the adulterous woman (*Guide* iii.9).

[49] Cf. Thomas Aquinas, *II Sent.*, d. 2, q. 2, a. 3 resp.

[50] Cf. Albertus Magnus, *I Sent.*, d. 37, a. 24, ed. Paris., t. 26, p. 265b–266a; *De IV coaeq.* (II red.), tr. 4, q. 59, a. 1, ed. Paris., t. 34, p. 625b–626a; *Super Dion. De cael. hier.*, c. 13, ed. Colon., t. 36, 1, p. 212, 17–26; *II Sent.*, d. 8, a. 2, ed. Paris., t. 27, p. 170a–170b; *De causis et proc. univ.*, l. 1, tr. 4, c. 8, ed. Colon., t. 17, 2, p. 58, 19–29. On the identification of angels and spheres, cf. Albertus Magnus, *II Sent.*, d. 3, a. 3, ed. Paris., t. 27, p. 64b–66a. Cf. Thomas Aquinas, *II Sent.*, d. 3, q. 1, a. 3 resp.; *ST*, I, q. 50, a. 3 resp.; *Questio disputata de spiritualibus creaturis*, a. 8, arg. 16; *De potentia*, q. 6, a. 7 resp.

[51] Thomas Aquinas, *De anima*, a. 3, arg. 6.

[52] For Arabic thinkers, cf. Thomas Aquinas, *De veritate*, q. 5, a. 9 ad 4; *SCG* III, 97; *De potentia* q. 3, a. 7 resp. For Aristotle, *III Sent.*, d. 12, q. 2, a. 1, ad 4.

[53] Cf. Thomas Aquinas, *I Sent.*, d. 35, q. 1, a. 2 resp.; *De veritate*, 2, a. 3 resp.; *In Psalmos*, ps. 18. Cf. A. Funkenstein, "Gesetz und Geschichte: Zur historisierenden Hermeneutik bei Moses Maimonides und Thomas von Aquin," *Viator*, 1 (1970), 147–178; W. Z. Harvey, "Maimonides and Aquinas on Interpreting the Bible," *Proceedings of the American Academy for Jewish Research*, 55 (1988), 59–77; I. Dobbs-Weinstein, "Medieval Biblical Commentary and Philosophical Inquiry as Exemplified in the thought of Moses Maimonides and St. Thomas Aquinas," in E. Ormsby (ed.), *Moses Maimonides and His Time* (Washington: The Catholic University of America Press, 1989), pp. 101–120.

[54] See in particular Index n. 1; 3–6; 11; 71; 72; 51–54, in Di Segni, "verba sunt Rabbi Moysis." Y. Schwartz, "Meister Eckharts Schriftauslegung als Maimonidisches Projekt," in G. Hasselhoff, O. Fraisse (eds.), *Moses Maimonides (1138–1204). His Religious, Scientific, and Philosophical Wirkungsgeschichte in Different Cultural Contexts* (Würzburg: Egon, 2004), pp. 173–208. The topic is also present in Thomas Aquinas, cf. for instance *IV Sent.*, d. 48, q. 2, a. 3, ad 6.

[55] Cf. Thomas Aquinas, *II Sent.*, d. 15, q. 3, a. 3, arg. 3; *III Sent.* d. 37, q. 1, a. 5, qc. 1 c. 2; ibid. d. 37, q. 1, a. 5, qc. 1 resp.; *IV Sent.*, d. 1, q. 2, a. 3, qc. 1 resp.; ibid., d. 1, q. 2, a. 5, qc. 2 resp.; ibid., d. 33, q. 1, a. 3, qc. 3 resp.; ibid., d. 40 q. 1, a. 4 resp.; ibid., d. 42, q. 2, a. 2 resp.; *ST*, I–II, q. 101, a. 3 ad 3; ibid., q. 102, a. 3 ad 4; ibid., q. 102, a. 3 ad 6; ibid., q. 102, a. 3 ad 11; ibid., q. 102, a. 4 ad 2; ibid., q. 102, a. 5 ad 4; ibid., q. 102, a. 6 ad 1; ibid., q. 102, a. 6 ad 8; ibid., q. 105, a. 2 ad 12. On *caerimonialia*, *ST*, I–II, q. 101,

## The Earliest Quotations from the *Dux neutrorum*

As already mentioned, the earliest appearance of the Latin Maimonides is found in William of Auvergne. However, there is no scholarly consensus over whether William was quoting from the *Dux neutrorum* or from the *Liber de parabola*.[56] A close inquiry of textual correspondences between William's work and the *Dux neutrorum* will help to date the first appearance of the complete Latin translation in Paris. More generally, even when verbatim correspondence is lacking, William's references to Maimonides's doctrines testify to the interest raised by the Jewish philosopher, also in the years before the *Dux neutrorum*'s composition. Secondly, inquiry into Moneta da Cremona's *Summa adversus Catharos et Valdenses* testifies to the reception of the Latin Maimonides at an early time outside Paris. This adds a further dimension to Maimonides's reception, since scholarly attention has so far been focused mainly on the Parisian reception.

In William of Auvergne's *De legibus* (probably composed around 1230), some arguments closely correspond to *Guide* iii, even though Maimonides's name is never mentioned. At the beginning of the *De legibus*, William of Auvergne approaches the question of the rational explanation of commandments and sacrifices.[57] In accordance with Maimonides, William maintains that biblical laws have multiple meanings besides the literal one.[58] Moreover, he states that the function of commandments is to prevent paganism;[59] in particular, the Bible intends to fight the Sabians.[60] He also reports an opinion, shared by Maimonides, about the building of the altar and circumcision.[61] On the other hand, William disagrees with Maimonides on sacrifices, since he does not believe that they are a concession to paganism: "Non solum propter consuetudinem idolatriae, ut quidam opinati sunt."[62] The "quidam" might refer to Maimonides, since this doctrine corresponds to *Guide* iii.32; 46.

---

a. 1, arg. 4. Cf. A. Schenker, "Die Rolle der Religion bei Maimonides und Thomas von Aquin," in A. Schenker, *Recht und Kult im Alten Testament* (Éditions universitaires de Fribourg, 2000), pp. 178–202. For Meister Eckhart, cf. Index n. 69; 100; 101; 120, in Di Segni, "verba sunt Rabbi Moysis."

[56] Cf. J. Guttmann, "Guillaume d'Auvergne et la littérature juive," *Revue des études juives*, 18 (1889), 243–255, considered that William was quoting from the *Dux neutrorum* and therefore hypothesized an earlier date of composition for the *Dux neutrorum*. Kluxen, "Literargeschichtliches," pp. 45–46, criticized Guttmann's arguments. Gilbert Dahan generally referred to a knowledge of the Latin Maimonides, cf. G. Dahan, "L'exégèse de la Bible chez Guillaume d'Auvergne," in F. Morenzoni, J.-Y. Tilliette, *Autour de Guillaume d'Auvergne* (Turnhout: Brepols, 2015), pp. 237–270, p. 258.

[57] William of Auvergne, *De legibus*, Paris, 1674, I, c. 2, p. 29 ff.    [58] Ibid., c. 16, p. 47, col. 1.

[59] Ibid., c. 1, p. 24, col. 1.    [60] Ibid., c. 6, p. 36, col. 2.

[61] Ibid., c. 2, p. 31, col. 1; ibid., c. 3, p. 33, col. 1.    [62] *Ibid.*, c. 2, p. 29, col. 2.

The references found in *De legibus* correspond to *Guide* iii, which is also the section of the text that was summarized in the *Liber de parabola*. Moreover, the fact that Maimonides is never named, while other authorities are explicitly mentioned,[63] is a clue that he used the *Liber de parabola* rather than the *Dux neutrorum*. The *Liber de parabola* did not contain any information about its authorship, while in the *Dux neutrorum* the author is explicitly called "Rabbi Moyses." Notwithstanding, the content of the *Liber de parabola* clearly shows its Jewish background. Considering these elements, and the fact that the *De legibus* was probably composed around 1230, it is plausible that at that time William of Auvergne knew the *Liber de parabola* but not the *Dux neutrorum*.

The case of the *De universo* (1231–1236) is more complicated, since William discusses opinions that are not present in the *Liber de parabola*. In one passage, William reports an opinion taken from the *Chapters of Rabbi Eliezer*, and the response of a "quidam ex aliis eorum philosophus."[64] The discussion follows exactly *Guide* ii.26, and the opinion mentioned in the answer is that of Maimonides:

Table 11.1. *References to the* Chapters of Rabbi Eliezer

| William of Auvergne, *De universo*, I, pars 1, c. 36, p. 631, col. 2 | *Dux neutrorum* ii.27 (ms. A, fol. 134rb; ms. B, fol. 108ra; ms. C, fol. 60rb) |
|---|---|
| Et fuit quidam, quem Hebraei reputant philosophum, qui dixit, quod Deus splendore pallii sui fecit coelum, terram vero de nive, quae erat sub throno eius. Et quia sapiens apud Hebraeos reputatus est, cum iuxta planum suum sermo iste manifeste erroneus sit, quidam ex aliis eorum philosophus non aliud eum intellexisse in sermone isto exposuit, nisi quod per eum aliam fuisse materiam coeli, aliam vero terre insinuare voluit per sermonem illum. | Dixit enim, quod celi creati sunt de luce vestimenti eius. Accepit Creator et extendit sicut pannum, et protrahebantur et expandebantur sicut dixit David: 'Amictus lumine sicut vestimentum, et extendens celum sicut pellem'. Dixit etiam: unde creata fuerit terra? Scilicet de nive, que est sub throno glorie sue ... Appone igitur cor tuum et vide quomodo revelavit tibi sapiens iste, quod materia eorum, que sunt in terra, scilicet omnium eorum que sunt sub sphera lune, est una communis eis. Et dixit, quod materia celorum et omnium, que sunt in eis, est alia materia, que non est sicut illa. |

---

[63] For instance, Avicebron is explicitly mentioned, cf. William of Auvergne, *De universo*, Paris, 1674, I, pars 1, c. 25, p. 621, c. 2.

[64] William of Auvergne, *De universo*, I, pars 1, c. 36, p. 631, col. 2.

The content of the passage in William of Auvergne is the same as the corresponding text in the *Dux neutrorum*; however, no literal correspondence is found. For instance, William speaks of the "splendor pallii," while in the *Dux neutrorum* the expression "lux vestimenti" is found. It must be noted that this interpretation might have been already famous; it is said to have been discussed by Frederick II.[65]

Secondly, William refers to an argument according to which Aristotle's opinions are only true for the sublunary world; the same position is maintained by Maimonides in *Guide* ii.22:[66]

Table 11.2.  *Validity of Aristotle's opinions*

| William of Auvergne, *De universo*, II, pars 2, c. 150, p. 998, c. 2 | *Dux neutrorum* ii.23 (ms. A, fol. 129ra-b; ms. B, fol. 104ra; ms. C, fol. 58rb) |
|---|---|
| Tu autem audivisti nonnullos ex nobilioribus philosophis dixisse Aristoteli credendum esse de his que sunt sub circulo lunae; de altioribus sive superioribus nequaquam, quoniam in eis non profundavit usque ad perfectum. | Quicquid dixit Aristoteles in omnibus entibus, que sunt a sphera lune usque ad centrum terre, verum est sine dubio . . . Quicquid vero locutus est Aristoteles de hiis, que sunt a sphera lune superius, est verisimile . . . et sunt in eis deceptiones multe et dampnum manifestum cunctis gentibus, et multiplicantur contraria, nec est inducta demonstratio super illis. |

It is difficult to establish whether this argument results from a direct knowledge of the *Dux neutrorum*, since no explicit quotation has been found. Kluxen leaned towards explaining these passages through an oral account.[67] The fact that William of Auvergne, when treating the eternity of the world, did not make any reference to Maimonides is for Kluxen evidence that he had no direct knowledge of the *Dux neutrorum*. Precisely this question is absent in the *Liber de parabola*, while it is prominent in the *Dux neutrorum* and received in general great attention by Christian authors. However, two elements must be taken into consideration: First of all, the eternity of the world was treated by William in the *De trinitate*, which was composed in 1223, and there is no textual evidence that the *Dux neutrorum* had already been translated at that early date.

[65] Cf. Sirat, "Les traducteurs juifs," pp. 172–173.
[66] William of Auvergne, *De universo*, II, pars 2, c. 150, p. 998, c. 2.
[67] Cf. Kluxen, "Literargeschichtliches," pp. 44–45.

Secondly, it has just been shown that, in *De universo*, the Maimonidean argument according to which Aristotle did not intend to demonstrate anything about the celestial world is evoked. Precisely this argument is characteristic of Maimonides's treatment of the problem of the world's eternity.

Certainly, William of Auvergne had sources other than the *Liber de parabola* (and possibly the *Dux neutrorum*) for information on Judaism. In *De universo*, he criticizes the "fables of the Jews," meaning the *midrashim*. Some of the *midrashim* he reported are also found in the *Dux neutrorum*[68]:

Table 11.3. *References to* midrashim.

| William of Auvergne, *De Universo*, I, pars I, cap. 59, p. 676, col. 1. | *Dux neutrorum* ii.31 (ms. A, fol. 148ra; ms. B, fol. 118va; ms. C, fol. 66rb) |
|---|---|
| Unum est autem ex deliramentis eorum, quod arbor, sive lignum vitae in altitudine habeat iter quingentorum annorum, quapropter grossities eius, hoc est trunci vel stipitis eius, maior erat grossitie totius terrae. | Arbor vite iter quingentorum annorum et omnes species prime distinguuntur sub ipsa, et ostenderunt in hoc, quod mensura ista est profunditas stature sue, non capitis sui, neque latitudinis ramorum. |

Both passages refer to the same *midrash* (*Bereshit Rabbah*, 15), but no literal correspondence is found, especially for terms such as "arbor," "statura," "caput" and "latitudo," while in William other terms are found, such as "arbor sive lignum," "altitudo," "truncus vel stipes."

Moreover, in William's work other *midrashim* not present in Maimonides are quoted.[69] It is known that William took part in the controversy surrounding the Talmud in Paris in the 1240s;[70] on that occasion he gained access to other sources about Judaism, and possibly about Maimonides too. It is therefore not necessary to presuppose a direct knowledge of the *Dux neutrorum* for the arguments not present in the *Liber de parabola*. The lack of literal correspondence and the

---

[68] Cf. William of Auvergne, *De universo*, I, pars I, cap. 59, p. 676, col. 1.

[69] Cf. for instance William of Auvergne, *De legibus*, cap. 26, p. 81, col. 2: "Et idolatria quidem ignis in Caldaea vigebat tempore Abrahae patriarchae, quem iuxta traditiones Hebraeorum Babilonii vivum exurere volentes in ignem miserunt pro eo, quod ignem colere detestabatur, unde illaesum eum omnipotens Deus servavit et de igne liberavit, utpote cultorem sanctissimum suum, et hoc est quod aiunt quod iam crebro legitur in sacra scriptura, quod Abraham liberavit Deus de Hur Caldaeorum. Hur enim interpretatur ignis, expresse autem dicit Esdras in nono et Neemias in oratione sua ad Deum: Tu ipse, domine Deus, qui eligisti Abraham et eduxisti eum de igne Caldaeorum" (Cf. *Bereshit Rabbah*, 39).

[70] Cf. L. Smith, "William of Auvergne and the Jews," *Studies in Church History*, 29 (1992), 107–117.

absence of Maimonides's name seem to exclude a direct involvement of the *Dux neutrorum.*

In these same years, Maimonides's reception is also attested in Northern Italy, since Roland and Moneta of Cremona mention his text. In his *Summa theologica* (around 1230), Roland of Cremona refers to Maimonides as "philosophus hebreorum"[71] and to a book "against the eternity of the world."[72] It is not clear whether this title refers to the *Dux neutrorum*; on the one hand, it is true that in *Dux neutrorum* II, 13–27 Maimonides treats the problem of the world's eternity, and that on this question he was widely referenced; on the other, the quotation does not correspond to the *Dux neutrorum*:

> diximus enim in superioribus, quod trecenta et XLVIII precepta sunt in lege secundum numerum ossium, que sunt in homine ... et hoc tradidit rabi mose in libro suo quem fecit contra antiquitatem mundi[73].

Besides the mistaken enumeration of the precepts – due certainly to the paleographic resemblance between the two digits – in the *Dux neutrorum* the number of commandments is compared to "numerum membrorum" and not to "numerum ossium." The expression "numerum ossium" is found in the *Liber de parabola*.[74] The discrepancy between the information about the book "against the eternity of the world" and the quotation corresponding to the *Liber de parabola* (which did not include the chapters from *Guide* ii) might be evidence of an indirect source or for an oral account of Maimonides's text.

Both the cases of William of Auvergne and Roland of Cremona show that there was an interest in Maimonides before the complete Latin translation appeared and that some information must have been circulated before the completion of the *Dux neutrorum*.

The first unquestionable dependence upon the *Dux neutrorum* is found in the *Summa adversus Catharos et Valdenses* (1241–1244) by Moneta of Cremona.[75] Here the authority of Maimonides is introduced through the

---

[71] Cf. Roland of Cremona, *Summa Theologica*, Ms. Paris, Bibliothèque Mazarine, Cod. lat. 795, fol. 31b, quoted according to E. Filthaut, *Roland von Cremona O.P. und die Anfänge der Scholastik im Predigerorden: ein Beitrag zur Geistesgeschichte der älteren Dominikaner* (Vechta i. O.: Albertus-Magnus-Verlag, 1936), p. 72.

[72] Ibid., fol. 73b.      [73] Ibid.

[74] "Et aliter processerunt dicta et sermones in mandatis Dei, sicut dicam in capitulis mandatorum, et circa mandata sexcenta et XIII: ducenta et XLVIII preceptoria et affirmatoria, et tot sunt ossa in homine, et trecenta sexaginta V prohibitoria, iuxta numerum dierum in anno," ms. E, fol. 1ra.

[75] Moneta of Cremona, *Adversus Catharos et Valdenses libri quinque*, ed. T. A. Ricchinius, Roma, 1743.

expression "quidam iudeus dictus Rabbi Moyses."[76] As Kluxen noted, such
a general formulation suggests that Maimonides was, at that moment,
unknown.[77] Besides this explicit mention, the *Dux neutrorum* is often
implicitly quoted, for instance when Moneta treats the question of the
world's eternity. An example of this literal correspondence is given in the
following table (literal quotations appear in bold; paraphrases appear in
italic):

Table 11.4. *Correspondence of arguments on eternity vs. creation of the world*

| Moneta of Cremona, *Adversus Catharos et Valdenses*, pp. 477–478 | *Dux neutrorum* ii.14 (ms. A, fol. 111ra-112ra; ms. B, fol. 88va-89va; ms. C, fol. 50rb-51ra) |
|---|---|
| **Opiniones hominum** de *eternitate* **vel novitate mundi apud** homines **qui credunt, quod Deus est, sunt tres.** | **Opiniones hominum** in *antiquitate* **vel novitate mundi apud** omnes **qui credunt, quod Deus est, sunt tres.** |
| **Prima est** catholicorum virorum et recte credentium, **et est, quod** *totus orbis et* **omnia**, *que in ipso sunt* per **Creatorem**, habuerunt esse *post non esse absolutum*, idest non ens simpliciter, idest tam actu quam potentia materiali sive passiva. **Et quod** *solus Deus* **sit ens eternum** sine causa et sine initio et sine inchoatione essendi; sed omnia alia duplicem habuerunt originem, scilicet causalem et initialem ... | **Prima est** sententia omnium, qui tenent legem Moysi, **et est, quod** *universum mundum, scilicet* **omnia** *entia* preter **Creatorem**, fecit ipse esse *post privationem veram et absolutam*, **et quod** *Creator ipse* **fuit ens eternus** solummodo, et non fuit preter ipsum nec angelus, nec celum nec aliquid quod est infra celum ... |
| **Secunda opinio est sententia philosophorum, qui dicunt,** *quoniam vanum est* credere, **quod Creator faciat aliquid ex nihilo.** Secundum quos **non potest aliquid corrumpi in nihilum;** hoc est dicere, **quod** nihil sit **ex privatione** *simpliciter* **et absoluta ipsius materiei,** nec **convertitur** *ad privationem* **simplicem et absolutam eiusdem materiei.** Privationem absolutam dicunt privationem esse actualis, et possibilis possibilitate materiali. *Dicunt enim*, quod hoc idem esset, ac si **crearet quadratum, cuius diameter esset equalis lateri.** Et dicunt, | Similiter non est abbreviatio potentie Creatoris, **si non potest facere aliquid de nichilo. Istud enim est de universitate impossibilium ...** **Secunda opinio est sententiam philosophorum,** quorum sensum et verba vidimus, **qui dicunt,** *quia vanitas est*, **quod Creator faciat aliquid ex nichilo.** Sic etiam **secundum eos non potest aliquid corrumpi in nichilum. Hoc est dicere, quod** non convenit, ut fiat aliquod ens constans ex materia et forma **ex privatione** *simplici* **et absoluta illius materie,** neque corrumpetur, ut **convertatur** *in privatione* **illius materie** |

Table 11.4. (*cont.*)

| Moneta of Cremona, *Adversus Catharos et Valdenses*, pp. 477–478 | *Dux neutrorum* ii.14 (ms. A, fol. 111ra-112ra; ms. B, fol. 88va-89va; ms. C, fol. 50rb-51ra) |
| --- | --- |
| *quod sicut non est ex impotentia Creatoris, si id non facit, ita non est ex impotentia eiusdem,* **si non potest facere aliquid de nihilo. Istud enim est de universitate impossibilium.** | **simplicem et absolutam.** *Dixerunt etiam,* quod potentia Creatoris in hoc est, sicut eius potentia super coniunctione duorum contrariorum in eadem hora, vel quod creet similem sibi, vel quod faciat se corpus, vel quod **creet quadratum, cuius diameter sit equalis lateri,** et impossibilia similia istis. Quod autem intelligit ex verbis ipsorum est, quod dicunt, *quia non est diminutio potentie Creatoris, si non facit impossibilia esse . . .* |
| Ista autem opinio duplex est: una Platonis et sequacium eius. Ipse enim posuit **materiam antiquam** *sive coeternam Deo,* unde posuit, quod caret principio inchoationis, sed non principio causalitatis. *Ipse enim Deus est causa eius,* ut sol radii, nec praecessit materiam per moram aliquam temporis vel eternitatis, sed tantum per modum cause, et ipsa est ei **sicut argilla figulo, et Creator quandoque creavit de illa celos et terram, quandoque alia.** Ipse etiam posuit, **quod celi sunt generabiles et corruptibiles, sed non sunt generati de nihilo** absolute, imo de materia praeiacente. | Omnes autem isti credunt, quod **materia est antiqua,** *sicut et Creator,* nec ipse est sine ea, nec ipse sine eo, neque credunt, quod est sicut gradus eius in sua essentia. *Sed ipse est causa essentie sue,* et ipsa est ei per viam similitudinis, **sicut argilla figulo** et ferrum fabro, de quo facit, quod sibi placet, **sic et Creator quandoque creat de materia illa celos et terram et quandoque creat alia.** Homines vero huius sentencie credunt, **quod celi sunt generabiles et corruptibiles, sed non sunt generati de nichilo,** neque corrumpentur in nichilum, sed sicut singularia animalium generatur ex materia ente, et corrumpuntur in materia ente, sic et celi generantur et corrumpuntur et generatio et corruptio illorum est sicut generatio et corruptio ceterarum rerum . . . |
| *Contra hanc opinionem disputavit Aristoteles, ut patet in libris naturalibus. Invenitur autem illa* **Platonis sententia in libro, qui dicitur Timeus.** | Platonis etiam ista est sententia et invenies, *quod Aristoteles locutus est contra eum in libro de Auditu.* Et dixit quod Plato credidit quod celi sunt generabiles et corruptibiles. *Invenies etiam* **sententia Platonis in libro qui dicitur Tymeus** . . . |
| Alia *fuit opinio* **Aristotelis et sequacium eius et eorum, qui exposuerunt libros** | Tertia **opinio** *est sententia* **Aristotelis et sequacium eius et eorum, qui** |

Table 11.4. (*cont.*)

| Moneta of Cremona, *Adversus Catharos et Valdenses*, pp. 477–478 | Dux neutrorum ii.14 (ms. A, fol. 111ra-112ra; ms. B, fol. 88va-89va; ms. C, fol. 50rb-51ra) |
| --- | --- |
| eius. **Ipse namque dixit** *materiam coeternam Deo*, non sine forma, sed sicut nunc distincta est per varias rerum species. *Et posuit, quod celi non cadunt sub generatione et corruptione.* Hoc autem satis potest concedi, scilicet quod non fuerunt generabiles et corruptibiles proprie, sumpto nomine generationis et corruptionis, ut sumitur in Philosophicis. Dicit ergo, quod *mundus sicut modo est fuit coeternus Deo*, et **quod motus celi et tempus sunt eterni esse**. | exposuerunt libros ipsius. **Ipse namque dixit**, sicut dixerunt illi, quorum premisimus mentionem, quod *non erit constans ex materia de non materia omnino*. Adiecit etiam super hoc, *quod celi non communicant cum generatione et corruptione ullo modo*. Depuratio vero huius sententie est quod, dixit, quia *universum esse secundum quod est, non desiit nec desinet esse, sicut est*, et quia illud firmum, quod non cadit sub generatione et corruptione, quod est celum, non desinet esse sicut est, et **quod tempus et motus sunt sempiterni esse**, nec sunt generabilia, nec corruptibilia. |

Moneta's use of Maimonides demonstrates that the *Dux neutrorum* was known very early in Northern Italy. It is difficult to say whether this diffusion is independent from the knowledge circulating in Paris. Moneta of Cremona could have known Maimonides through Roland of Cremona but, as mentioned above, in Roland there is no trace of a direct knowledge of the *Dux neutrorum*. Moneta studied at the Dominican *studium* of Bologna, and there is no evidence that he ever went to Paris, but the *studium* in Bologna was in contact with the Parisian *studium*.[78] However, had Maimonides's text been brought by Parisian Dominican masters to Bologna as an authority to study, one would expect a more deferential formulation rather than "quidam iudeus dictus Rabbi Moyses." Therefore, it seems plausible that Moneta would have read the *Dux neutrorum* independently of the Parisian authors;[79] in any case, Moneta's quotations surely demonstrate that manuscripts of the *Dux*

[78] Cf. G. B. Melloni, *Atti o memorie degli uomini illustri in Santità nati o morti in Bologna raccolte e illustrate da Giambattista Melloni (1713–1781)*, ed. A. Benati and M. Fanti (Roma: Multigrafica, 1971), p. 61.

[79] It must be noted that Moneta could have had contacts with Southern France, since his *Summa* is directed against French heretical movements.

*neutrorum* were circulating as early as between 1241 and 1244, not only in Paris but also in Northern Italy.

In Paris, the first explicit quotations from the *Dux neutrorum* date back to the 1240s and appear in Albert the Great's work. Caterina Rigo discovered an early version of *De IV coaequaevis* (1241), in which Albert displays no knowledge of the *Dux neutrorum*, while in a later version (1246) of the same writing he does quotes it.[80] Furthermore, Albert certainly knew the *Dux neutrorum* in 1244, since it is cited in his commentary to *Sentences* I.

In conclusion, it has been demonstrated that the earliest clearly identifiable quotations from the *Dux neutrorum* date back to the years 1241–1244 for Moneta of Cremona and between 1241 and 1246 for Albert the Great. The circulation in Northern Italy might have depended upon Paris, but no chronological argument can be formulated in favor of this hypothesis, since quotations are attested in the two places at the same time. Considering Albert's prominent position in his contemporary cultural context, it is highly probable that he learned of such a significant book as soon as it became available. There is no reason therefore to suppose that the work circulated in Paris any earlier than in Northern Italy.

[80]  Cf. Rigo, "Zur Rezeption," pp. 31–35.

CHAPTER 12

# The Agendas of Shlomo Pines for Reading the Guide of the Perplexed from 1963 to 1979 *

## Josef Stern

Apart from the transformative effect of his English translation of the *Guide of the Perplexed*, and his rich analyses of Maimonides's place within the world of Arabic philosophy, Shlomo Pines set two research agendas that have guided students of the *Guide* for the last sixty-plus years. By 'setting an agenda' I mean a species of influence, not by expressing a position, doctrine, or interpretation, but by raising a set of questions or research goals that determine the direction of inquiry. Impact by agenda-setting can lead as much to claims that challenge those of the agenda-setter as to ones that confirm his initial assumptions; what count are the problems that the scholars address. Pines's two agendas – which are usually identified with 1963, the year when his translation was published, and 1979, the year in which he published his classic paper, "The Limitations of Human Knowledge According to Al-Farabi, ibn Bajja, and Maimonides," which was followed by four more papers developing the same theme[1] – are often

---

* The first version of this paper was delivered as the Shlomo Pines Lecture in May 2014 and a second expanded version was given at the conference "Pines' Maimonides: The History of the Translation and Interpretation of *The Guide of the Perplexed*," held at the University of Chicago in January 2014 to mark the fiftieth anniversary of the publication of Shlomo Pines's English translation of the *Guide* by the University of Chicago Press. I am indebted to Zev Harvey, Charles Manekin, and Daniel Davies for comments on an earlier draft of this paper.

[1] S. Pines, "The Limitations of Human Knowledge According to Al-Farabi, ibn Bajja, and Maimonides," in I. Twersky (ed.), *Studies in Medieval Jewish History and Literature* (Cambridge, MA: Harvard University Press 1979), pp. 82–109, rep. in S. Pines, *Studies in the History of Jewish Thought, The Collected Works of Shlomo Pines*, vol. V, eds. W. Z. Harvey and M. Idel (Jerusalem: Magnes Press, 1997), pp. 404–431; "Les limites de la métaphysique selon al-Farabi, ibn Bajja, et Maimonide: sources et antithèses de ces doctrines chez Alexandre d'Aphrodise et chez Themistius," *Miscellanea Mediaevalia* 13 (1981), 211–225, rep. in S. Pines, *Studies in the History of Jewish Thought, The Collected Works of Shlomo Pines*, vol. V, eds. W. Z. Harvey and M. Idel (Jerusalem: Magnes Press, 1997), pp. 432–446; "Dieu et l'être selon Maimonide: Exégèse d'Exode 3, 14 et doctrine connexe," in A. de Libera and É. Zum Brunn (eds.), *Celui qui est: Interprétations juives et chrétiennes d'Exode 3, 14*, (Paris: Les Editions du Cerf [Collection "Patrimoines"], 1986), pp. 15–24, rep. in S. Pines, *Studies in the History of Jewish Thought, The Collected Works of Shlomo Pines*, vol. V, eds. W. Z. Harvey and M. Idel (Jerusalem: Magnes Press, 1997), pp. 447–456; "Le discours théologico-philosophique dans les oeuvres halachiques de Maimonide comparé avec celui du *Guide des Égarés*," in *Délivrance et*

linked together but in fact they stand in opposition and, to make matters even more perplexing, they are both present in his introduction to his translation.[2]

The first, and more prominent, agenda is that the *Guide* is to be read as a politically attuned work with multiple levels of meaning, one exoteric, the other esoteric: a revealed meaning in conformity with the Law, or religious tradition, addressed to the community at large (or the multitude) and a concealed meaning whose content is philosophical truth, generally, Aristotle, addressed to a philosophical elite. Its main topic is what I shall call a '*meta*-philosophical' question about the relation between Philosophy and Religion or Law: Are the two compatible, identical, or in contradiction? And, depending on how we answer this question, what did Maimonides himself believe?[3]

The second agenda became explicit, and came to dominate Pines's own writings, only in the 1979 paper. This agenda is based on the hypothesis that Maimonides believed that there exist severe limitations on the human intellect that prevent knowledge of metaphysics and that he accepted its consequences for human happiness and perfection. Pines's claim has elicited some support and much criticism and resistance from scholars over the last thirty-five years, and it would be fair to say that it has become *the* liveliest question in contemporary Maimonides literature. But Pines's own position aside, by proposing this reading of the *Guide*, he set a new agenda according to which the primary issue that the *Guide* raises is a classic *philosophical* (as opposed to *meta*-philosophical) question: What does a human know and what are the consequences of the scope of her

---

*fidelité: Maimonide [Textes du Colloque tenu à l'Unesco en decembre 1985 à l'occasion du 850 anniversaire du philosophe]* (Paris, 1986), pp. 119–124; "The Philosophical Purport of Maimonides' Halachic Works and the Purport of *The Guide of the Perplexed*," in Y. Yovel and S. Pines (eds.), *Maimonides and Philosophy [Sixth Jerusalem Philosophical Encounter, 1985]*, (Dordrecht: Martinus Nijhoff, 1986), pp. 1–14, rep. in S. Pines, *Studies in the History of Jewish Thought, The Collected Works of Shlomo Pines*, vol. V, eds. W. Z. Harvey and M. Idel (Jerusalem: Magnes Press, 1997), pp. 463–476.

[2] S. Pines, "Translator's Introduction: The Philosophic Sources of the *Guide of the Perplexed*," in Maimonides 1963, pp. lvii–cxxxiv.

[3] For similar sentiments during roughly the same period, see S. Pines, "Jewish Philosophy," *Encyclopedia of Philosophy*, vol. IV (New York: Macmillan, 1967), pp. 261–277; rep. in S. Pines, *Studies in the History of Jewish Thought, The Collected Works of Shlomo Pines*, vol. V, eds. W. Z. Harvey and M. Idel (Jerusalem: Magnes Press, 1997), pp. 1–51, 5, 21; S. Pines, "Maimonides," *Encyclopedia of Philosophy*, vol. V (New York: Macmillan, 1967), pp. 129–134; rep. in S. Pines, *Studies in the History of Jewish Thought, The Collected Works of Shlomo Pines*, vol. V, eds. W. Z. Harvey and M. Idel (Jerusalem: Magnes Press, 1997), 335–349, 337, 341; S. Pines, "*Harza'ah al Moreh Ha-Nevukhim le-Rambam* [A Lecture on Maimonides's *Guide of the Perplexed*]," *Iyyun* 47 (1998), 115–128, 117, 125. This lecture was delivered at a symposium in Jerusalem in 1955 and found and published only after Pines's death.

knowledge for the best human life? According to Maimonides's Aristotelian framework, human perfection consists in intellectual perfection. Given Pines's constraints on the intellect, can we retain that conception of human perfection and, if not, what might an alternative be?

My concern in this chapter is not with the correctness of Pines's own positions in either of these two agendas. Rather I am concerned with the relation between the two agendas themselves. As I said, Pines '63 is often contrasted with Pines '79, but it is striking that all the main ingredients for the later position are already cited and present in the Introduction. These include a brief outline of Alfarabi's controversial remarks in his lost *Commentary on the Nichomachean Ethics* that the only happiness is this-worldly, that it is political happiness, that the only "existence" is that known to the senses, and that the immaterial immortality of the soul is nothing but an old wives' tale. Pines also mentions ibn Tufayl's report of Alfarabi, ibn Bājja's defense of him, ibn Bājja's own two theories of human knowledge of immaterial beings, Averroes's critique of Alfarabi's conception of the hylic intellect, and his critique of Alfarabi's implication that it is impossible for a human intellect to achieve conjunction with the active intellect.[4] Pines writes: "It can be argued that these views of Al-Farabi, set forth in a work known to Maimonides, may legitimately be taken into account in an interpretation of [Maimonides's] philosophy."[5] It "*can* be argued" and "*may* legitimately be taken into account," Pines writes, yet he does not advocate this interpretation. The question is, Why not? Why did Pines not draw the conclusion in 1963 that he later drew in 1979? Instead, Pines '63 takes Maimonides's presentation of negative theology to be part of "his didactic method,"[6] inserting contradictory theses, and he rejects the ethical or political interpretation of the last paragraph of the *Guide*[7] – according to which an integral part of true human perfection is practical, the very reading he later adopts in 1979. Pines '63 and Pines '79 are not merely different doctrines or claims but different agendas. Why the change in agenda?

We can sum up two reasons in two words: Averroes and Spinoza. I begin with Averroes. Like many of Maimonides's thirteenth- and fourteenth-century commentators, Pines '63 read the *Guide* through the lens of

---

[4] Pines, "Translator's Introduction," pp. lxxx–lxxxii, civ–cvi. Pines, "Philosophical Purport," adds that, in addition to the influence of Alfarabi's lost *Commentary*, Maimonides's critical epistemology "may have been brought about through his increased attention to passages in Aristotle and Alexander of Aphrodisias ... which put forward the view that certain Aristotelian theories are no more than probable," p. 11, repr. in *Studies*, 473.

[5] Pines, "Translator's Introduction," p. lxxxi.     [6] Pines, "Translator's Introduction," p. cviii.

[7] Pines, "Translator's Introduction," pp. cxxi–cxxii.

Averroes – and this, despite the fact that Pines writes that "there is no conclusive proof that at the time of the writing of the *Guide* Maimonides was in any way influenced by Averroes's doctrines."[8] Nonetheless Pines goes on to say that a comparison between Maimonides and Averroes would be "instructive" in "view of their common culture," by which he means not just their Andalusian origins but their "similar naturalistic hardheadedness" as members of the Spanish Aristotelian school; hence, "the problems" with which the two were concerned "were identical."[9] By that, I take Pines to mean that, notwithstanding their different solutions, Maimonides and Averroes shared agendas. This agenda included grappling with the twelfth-century crisis in astronomy in Spain. But its primary agenda-setting problem is what I have called the '*meta*-philosophical' question about the relation of Philosophy to Religion. This question *was* a primary concern of Averroes, as we can see in his *Decisive Treatise*; it also deeply engaged Maimonides's thirteenth- and fourteenth-century commentators; and, still more recently, it is perhaps *the* main concern of Leo Strauss.[10] All these readers, medieval and modern, share an agenda shaped by this issue, but they give opposed answers. Among the medievals, one can detect a continuum of views, but all tend to see Philosophy and the Torah as at least compatible (with exceptional points of disagreement, say, on creation vs. eternity) and some even hold that the true, inner meaning of the Torah simply *is* Philosophy (i.e., some brand of Aristotle). Strauss – and Pines '63 – draw the opposite conclusion: Religion and Philosophy stand in unsurmountable opposition. It is significant, however, that the central figure in this agenda for Pines is not Al-Farabi, as it is for Strauss, but Averroes. It is in the section of the "Introduction" devoted to Averroes that Pines says that for both Maimonides and Averroes "mankind is essentially divided into philosophers," the "few ... capable of grasping philosophical doctrines," and the multitude "of the ... religious community."[11] Of course, there are also differences between the two philosopher-jurists of Cordova. Averroes takes the intermediate class of mutakallimun to be even more dangerous than the multitude, and Maimonides envisions an educational program for the multitude that

---

[8]  Pines, "Translator's Introduction," p. cviii.
[9]  Pines, "Translator's Introduction," p. cix. Cf. Pines, "*Harza'ah*," p. 124, where he takes Averroes to be a stronger influence on Maimonides than Avicenna.
[10]  Pines, "Philosophical Purport," argues that fourteenth-century commentators like Moses of Narbonne failed to appreciate the significance of the epistemological debate stimulated by Al-Farabi and instead "explained the work with the help of Averroes and thus befogged some issues," p. 11, repr. in *Studies*, 473.
[11]  Pines, "Translator's Introduction," p. cxix.

will enable them to move upward in class to the rank of philosophers.[12] On the other hand, it is by comparison to Averroes that Pines most emphasizes "the danger of philosophy for religious belief ... a danger [that] was not minimized by either Maimonides or Averroes" and that sometimes obligates the philosopher to "dissemble or at least to refrain from giving a public expression to his true opinions."[13] Likewise, Pines emphasizes that both Maimonides and Averroes also attempt to "normalize the philosopher's position in society" by issuing legal "pronouncements on the religious duty of philosophizing."[14]

As part of the same agenda, Pines '63 adopts the Averroistic conception of the deity as an intellect to underwrite the absolute superiority of the theoretical life and of the intellectual virtues – which is incompatible with Pines '79's view of strong limitations on the human intellect that exclude the possibility of theoretical perfection. The same view of the absolute superiority and human attainability of intellectual perfection leads Pines '63 to reject the idea that at the end of the *Guide* "Maimonides ... adopted the quasi-Kantian idea that the ordinary moral virtues and moral notions are of greater importance and value than the intellectual virtues and the theoretical way of life" – the very interpretation of the closing paragraph of the *Guide* that he will draw in 1979.[15] Thus, one factor that orients Pines '63's reading of Maimonides is an Averroistic agenda shaped by the meta-philosophical question of the relation between Philosophy and Religion *and* a deep belief in the superiority and human attainability of intellectual perfection. With blinders imposed by presuppositions of this agenda, Pines '63 simply seems not to see the conclusions he will later draw in '79 from the very Alfarabian sources he cites.

In contrast to this *meta*-philosophical concern with the relation between Philosophy and Religion, Pines '79 is concerned with a classical *philosophical* question: In what does "man's ultimate goal and man's felicity" consist? And as a corollary of this question, if one takes that goal and felicity to be intellectual perfection, the full actualization of

---

[12] Averroes's view in the "Decisive Treatise, Determining the Nature of the Connection between Religion and Philosophy," in G. F. Hourani, trans. and ed. *Averroes: On the Harmony of Religion and Philosophy* (London: Lousac/E. J. W. Gibb Memorial Trust, 1961) should be contrasted to that of *Guide* i.35, pp. 79–81. On the difference between Averroes's view that the multitude must be taught to take scriptural corporeal descriptions of God literally and Maimonides's view that they must be taught to take them non-literally, see Pines, "*Harẓa'ah*," p. 118.

[13] Pines, "Translator's Introduction," p. cxviii.

[14] Pines, "Translator's Introduction," pp. cxvii–cxviii. On the Almohad influence on Maimonides, see now S. Stroumsa, *Maimonides in His World* (Princeton University Press, 2009).

[15] Pines, "Translator's Introduction," p. cxxii.

the human intellectual potential, thus all knowledge of physics and metaphysics, is it in fact humanly achievable? Can material, bodily humans have knowledge of immaterial beings, like God and the separate intellects? Pines calls this philosophical question "one of the most perplexing problems posed by the *Guide*" because a knowledge that excludes metaphysics – knowledge of God and immaterial beings – can hardly be "man's final end" (i.e., ultimate perfection).[16] Based on the same texts of ibn Bājja, Alfarabi, and Averroes that he mentions in the '63 Introduction, Pines '79 then concludes, in a complete turnabout, that "man cannot possibly have knowledge of God" and that Maimonides, anticipating Kant, was a *critical* (though not a *skeptical*) philosopher who sees "no point in setting oneself the aim to intellect or to achieve a conjunction with a separate intellect" and instead gives primacy to the life of political or practical action over that of intellectual perfection.[17] Thus, in the concluding paragraph of the *Guide*, the "highest perfection of man" is the "practical way of life, the *bios praktikos*," which is "superior to the theoretical."[18] Pines's later philosophically oriented agenda has diametrically opposed consequences to those of his earlier *meta*philosophically oriented agenda.[19]

The second figure who dominates Pines's Introduction is Spinoza, whose name surfaces in a number of places, some surprising, and toward whom the first agenda points as the telos of the *Guide*. Consider, for example, Maimonides's fourth cause of disagreement added to Alexander's three causes: "In our times there is a fourth cause that ... did not exist among" the Greeks of Alexander's time, namely, "habit and upbringing" which in turn led the multitude to believe in God's corporeality because they were "habituated to and brought up on [highly regarded] texts ... whose external meaning is indicative of the corporeality of God and other imaginings with no truth in them."[20]

Pines comments:

---

[16] Pines, "Limitations," p. 82, repr. in *Studies*, 404.

[17] Pines, "Limitations," pp. 93–94, repr. in *Studies*, 415–416.

[18] Pines, "Limitations," p. 100, repr. in *Studies*, 422.

[19] For reasons of space I cannot elaborate, but a good example of a topic that is virtually missing from Pines '63 to which Pines '79 gives considerable attention is the question of the immortality of the soul. Pines, "Translator's Introduction," p. ciii, writes: Maimonides "apparently did not regard this as a crucial problem for the relations between philosophy and religion. It is remarkable how little space – even if one counts the indirect references – he devotes to it in the *Guide*." In contrast, see the extended discussion in Pines, "Limitations," pp. 95–96, repr. in *Studies*, 417–418 and "Philosophical Purport," pp. 8–9, repr. in *Studies*, 470–471.

[20] *Guide* i.31, p. 67.

In other words, Maimonides contrasts his own times, which he seems to
have held to be dominated by superstition, to use Spinoza's term and that of
the philosophers of the Enlightenment, with Greek antiquity, in which the
philosophers who aspired to know the true nature of things did not have to
struggle against the dead hand of traditional belief.[21]

Moreover, Pines adds, Maimonides says this notwithstanding the fact
that he well knew that the Greeks were pagans with their own religious
beliefs and observances but which he "apparently chose not to mention."[22]
Here Pines portrays Maimonides as an Enlightenment philosopher in the
image of Spinoza combatting superstition, the paradigm of which is the
"traditional beliefs" inculcated by the literal meaning of the Torah.

Contrast this depiction with Pines's non-Spinozistic analysis of
Maimonides's fourth cause in the appendix to the 1979 paper. There
Pines singles out a "new" problem posed by the fact that Maimonides in
*Guide* i.31 seems to hold that "our times," when people are brought up to
venerate scripture and religious texts, are "less propitious" for the acquisition of true knowledge and avoidance of errors than Alexander's pagan
times. This, he writes, is "difficult to reconcile with Maimonides's well-
known position" according to which the "hints" given in scriptural parables and riddles "help those who have the capacity to become philosophers
to achieve true knowledge."[23] To address this tension, Pines now changes
the very problem Maimonides is addressing in i.31. Adducing a text of
Aristotle (*Metaphysics* II, 3, 995a, 2–6) and its Arabic translation, Pines is
"certain" – based on similar terminology – that it is the source of
Maimonides's idea that habituation to and reverence for religious texts is
a source of corruption, although he finds no textual support for the
complementary claim that in antiquity the Greeks were less "apt" to
"adopt" false beliefs given *their* religious traditions.[24] Likewise, he finds
in Averroes's commentary on the *Metaphysics* no "explicit affirmation" of
the superiority of paganism over monotheism. Rather, following up
Averroes's *Prooemium to the Long Commentary on the Physics*, Pines suggests
a rather different explanation according to which it is *not* religious doctrines or law inculcated through uncritical acceptance of revered, familiar
texts that is an obstacle to the acquisition of philosophical truth. Rather the
problem is two-fold. On the one hand, philosophers have become corrupted by "*people* who corrupt the law" (my emphasis) and no longer hold

[21] Pines, "Translator's Introduction," p. lxviii.     [22] Ibid.
[23] Pines, "Limitations," p. 101, repr. in *Studies*, 423.
[24] Pines, "Limitations," p. 102, repr. in *Studies*, 424.

in "esteem" the ideal of intellectual perfection. On the other, people in general do not consider philosophers "worthy of playing a part in the life of the city"; that is, following Averroes, Maimonides thinks that "in [his] times most of the philosophers are swayed by worldly desires and do not in fact deserve to be regarded as part of the city."[25] Following a suggestion of Steven Harvey, Pines suggests that Averroes and Maimonides may be reacting critically to ibn Bājja's recommendation that philosophers make themselves strangers to the city; instead they want "to integrate philosophy into the life of the community."[26] The issue for Pines '79 is not, as it was in '63, the obstacle posed by religious truth, aka superstition, to the spread of philosophical truth – Maimonides's Spinozistic call for enlightenment – but rather the harm caused by the prejudices of Islamic and Jewish society to the moral character of individuals and especially philosophers. In '79, in short, Pines is not concerned with the meta-philosophical question of the relation between Religion and Philosophy, but rather with the tense relations between two classes of people, followers and especially leaders of religious communities and philosophers.

However, the most prominent Spinozistic influence on Pines '63 is undoubtedly his analysis of *Guide* i.68, according to which God is "generally admitted" by the philosophers to be an intellect in act identical to both the intellectually cognizing subject and the intellectually cognized object. Pines '63 privileges this chapter with its positive characterization of God over the chapters on negative attributes according to which no affirmative description of the deity is allowable. His reason, Pines states, is to "follow Maimonides's *hints* to their logical conclusion – that God may be identical with the system of sciences, including physical science," which is a "higher valuation of natural science than any that may be found in Averroes."[27] The "hints" Pines has in mind are a series of independent theses he sews together. The first is the Aristotelian source for the dictum of i.68, the well-known text of *Metaphysics* XII, 9 which became a stock-formula for Aristotelians but means in its original context that God cognizes only Himself; no other candidate as an object of God's knowledge, hence, its final cause, would meet the excellence demanded for a divine intellect. Prima facie, this excludes God's knowledge of universals or forms and especially those of the natural world. However, as Pines argues elsewhere, insofar as God is the cause of the formal and final structure of the universe, in knowing Himself as such a cause He ipso

---

[25] Pines, "Limitations," p. 103, repr. in *Studies*, 425.  [26] Ibid.
[27] Pines, "Translator's Introduction," p. cxv, my emphasis.

facto knows all His effects including the formal structure of the natural world.[28] Thus God's *self*-knowledge itself includes knowledge of "the workings of the natural order," namely, the subject matter of physics, or what Maimonides also calls the "attributes of action," the scientific understanding of the natural world to which Maimonides refers as "divine, i.e., natural actions," a formula that Pines notes "forcibly calls to mind Spinoza."[29] Given the identity of the knower, intellect in act, and object of intellection, it then follows that God not only knows but is also *identical* with the formal structure of the natural world. From these premises Pines concludes that "the knowledge of the system of nature may represent the essence of God," which he then says "might" explain "the rather enigmatic text in III: 52 according to which God apprehends us by the same light by which we apprehend Him"[30] by which he may mean that not only is "the study of nature and [its] order ... the only way open to man to know something of God"[31] but, more strongly, that if "God is identical with system of the natural sciences," then "man too may to some degree achieve this identity."[32] This, Pines concludes, makes God "out to be something coming perilously close to Spinoza's attribute of thought" and underscores the human attainability of intellectual perfection, indeed a kind of *imitatio Dei*.[33]

Warren Zev Harvey and Carlos Fraenkel have convincingly argued (perhaps carrying out Pines's hints to their conclusion) that i.68 was almost certainly a source for Spinoza.[34] Our question, however, is not whether Spinoza should be read in light of Maimonides but whether Maimonides's own text should be read in light of Spinoza – as Pines '63 in fact reads him. The most serious difficulty is that Spinoza's God also possesses the attribute of extension. Therefore, if one takes Maimonides's God to be identical not only with the formal structure of the natural world but also with its extension, or matter, then we cannot avoid attributing an attribute of extension, or corporeality, to God, a consequence that one would think is

[28] "Some Distinctive Metaphysical Conceptions in Themistius' Commentary on Book Lambda and Their Place in the History of Philosophy" in *Aristoteles Werk und Wirkung Paul Moraux Gewidmet*, Zweiter Band, herausgegeben von Jurgen Wiesner (Berlin/New York: Walter De Gruyter, 1987), pp. 177–204; rep. in S. Pines, *Studies in the History of Arabic Philosophy, The Collected Works of Shlomo Pines*, vol. III, ed. S. Stroumsa (Jerusalem: Magnes Press, 1996), pp. 267–294.

[29] *Guide* iii.32 cited in Pines, "Translator's Introduction," p. xcvi.

[30] Pines, "Translator's Introduction," p. cxv.     [31] Pines, "Translator's Introduction," p. xcvi.

[32] Pines, "Translator's Introduction," p. cxv.     [33] Pines, "Translator's Introduction," p. xcviii.

[34] W. Z. Harvey, "A Portrait of Spinoza as a Maimonidean," *Journal of the History of Philosophy* 19 (1981), 151–172; C. Fraenkel, "Maimonides' God and Spinoza's *Deus sive Natura*," *Journal of the History of Philosophy* 44 (2006), 169–215. Fraenkel mentions the objection raised next in the text but does not seem to view it as a problem for the Spinozistic reading of Maimonides.

absolutely excluded by Maimonides's unqualified opposition to idolatry, which is first and foremost conceiving of God corporeally. Furthermore, in i.68 Maimonides goes out of his way – and, as Pines emphasizes, for the first time in the Aristotelian tradition – to compare the conception of the divine intellect in the *Metaphysics* with the conception of the human intellect of *De Anima*. Both intellects, divine and human, are identical in act to their subject and object, the only difference between them being those times when the human intellect is not in act but in potentia; that is, there exists the possibility for the human intellect to be an intellect in potentia but not for the divine intellect. But if we then couple that thesis with Maimonides's further claim that the divine attributes of action, the scientific understanding of natural phenomena, are the only positive knowledge of God possible to man, it then follows that when the human intellect cognizes this knowledge of nature, the human subject, intellect in act, and the natural order that is intellectually apprehended are *themselves* one and identical. In other words, given the theory of the intellect of i.68 and the unity of the subject, act, and object of intellection, there exist times at which *both* God in act *and* the man who knows in act the entire system of the natural sciences turn out to be identical with that body of knowledge and – if the previous conclusion were not disturbing enough, although Pines does not explicitly draw it – *with themselves*. Moreover, their identity is simply in virtue of their knowing natural science and without knowing metaphysics. No less than the conclusion that God has an attribute of extension, or is corporeal, this conclusion is incompatible with Maimonides's insistence that God is incomparable, unique, and unrelated to anything else and it makes intellectual perfection – what could that be if not identity with the divine intellect? – all too easy. Or is Pines's point really that Maimonides's *philosophical* view is in fact that God *is* corporeal and that it is the view *only* of the Torah, or of the Torah on its exoteric understanding, that God is *not* a body?[35] And that indeed knowledge of metaphysics is not necessary for intellectual perfection? These consequences turn the meta-philosophical question on its head.

In the Introduction Pines concludes his discussion of i.68 by emphasizing that *either* the negative theology spelled out in chapters. i.50–63, according to which no positive statement about God is true, *or* the positive characterization of God in i.68 is "prima facie . . . admissible." Recalling Maimonides's statement that he deliberately inserted contradictions in the

[35] See Pines, "*Harza'ah*," p. 123, where he seems to read Maimonides as endorsing Spinoza's conclusion that God is the extension of the world.

work, Pines asks whether this is "an instance of this didactic method and, if
so, which of the two doctrines represents Maimonides's real opinion?"[36]
However, having said that, he then goes on to infer from Maimonides's
example of the human intellect's abstraction of a form from a material
object, a piece of wood, and from the analogy between the human and
divine intellects, that Maimonides's divine intellect inclines toward the
positive characterization of i.68 and the Spinozistic reading that the divine
intellect apprehends the scientific system of the natural world. And to
critics who might reply that Maimonides might have inconsistently or
inadvertently not realized these consequences of his own reasoning, Pines
famously replies that this would "amount to a grave ... and very implau-
sible accusation of muddle-headedness."[37]

Pines '79 does not elaborate the problematic consequences that follow
from privileging i.68 and its Spinozistic reading. Spinoza is no longer on
stage, and Spinozism only makes a brief cameo appearance. Pines's agenda
has shifted: It is now directed toward a philosophical problem that turns on
his critical epistemology, which presupposes the absolutely unknowable
God of the chapters on negative theology.

> It is obvious that if Maimonides' epistemology is accepted, man cannot possibly
> have the knowledge of God that is presupposed in the "dictum of the philoso-
> phers" [of i. 68]. In this respect, the analogy drawn ... between God's and man's
> intellection does not and probably is not intended to prove anything.[38]

He emphasizes that Maimonides qualifies the dictum as "*shuhra*" –
"generally admitted" – which he compares to the Arabic term *mashhūr*
from the same root, the term Maimonides uses throughout the *Guide* for
conventional moral notions (that are objects of the imagination rather than
intellect), which Pines now describes as "notions that are generally
admitted without either being self-evident indubitable truths or having
been proven by rigorous reasoning."[39] He does not, however, explain why
Maimonides engages the dictum of the philosophers in i.68 if it is not
meant to prove anything.[40] In any case, its significance is now to motivate
a distinction between "two strata" in "Aristotelian philosophical doctrine":

---

[36] Pines, "Translator's Introduction," p. xcviii.    [37] Ibid.
[38] Pines, "Limitations," p. 93, repr. in *Studies*, 415.
[39] Pines, "Limitations," p. 94, repr. in *Studies*, 416.
[40] J. Stern, *The Matter and Form of Maimonides' Guide* (Cambridge, MA: Harvard University Press,
     2013), pp. 232–240, argues that, not only is the dictum only "generally admitted" but also that, by
     ascribing it to the philosophers, Maimonides is disavowing it as his *own* view. Rather the point of
     the chapter is a *critique* of the philosophers' representation of God as an intellect on the grounds that
     it fails to represent His unity in a form that is representationally true to His unity.

one stratum of "intellectually cognized notions whose truth is absolute" that "form a coherent system" and one stratum that is "more comprehensive and ambitious" but comprised of propositions "that cannot be cognized by the human intellect" and at "best" are "merely probable." The first stratum Pines identifies with terrestrial physics, a well-defined and understood science; the second with celestial physics and metaphysics, which he calls "a system of beliefs, somewhat analogous, as far as the truth function is concerned, to the religious beliefs of lesser mortals."[41] However, note that *this* distinction is *within* Aristotelian doctrine, not *between* Philosophy and Religion. Furthermore, inasmuch as "metaphysics" falls in the second stratum because its conceptions "do not conform to" Maimonides' empiricist epistemology, Pines adds that he is using "metaphysics" or "metaphysical" not in its medieval sense but "as in many modern writings, in a somewhat pejorative sense"; indeed "another possible designation" of these conceptions that "transcend the limits of human knowledge would be to describe them as forming a part of a philosophical theology."[42] Here the term "theology," understood epistemologically, is only related indirectly to religion and, not at all, to *kalām*, as Pines '63 describes it.[43] It would have been good had Pines explained what it is for a philosopher to "believe" – the kind of epistemic commitment that is involved – these notions that "transcend the limits of human knowledge" but it is clear that the term "theology" for Pines '79 is closer to its sense in the title "The Theology of Aristotle" than in "The Theology of Judaism."

As for the Spinozistic implication of i.68 that "the God of Maimonides has an intimate connection with the cosmos, that in fact he may be conceived, if we use Spinozistic terms, as an idea whose ideatum is the world," Pines '79 now says that it is "invalidated by other passages," presumably those on negative theology, and that "it is of course difficult or impossible to reconcile a conception of this sort with Maimonides's epistemology, *but it could form part of his philosophical theology.*"[44] Now, far

---

[41] Pines, "Limitations," p. 94, repr. in *Studies*, 416.
[42] Pines, "Limitations," p. 93, repr. in *Studies*, 415.    [43] Pines, "Translator's Introduction," p. xxx.
[44] Pines, "Limitations," p. 107, repr. in *Studies*, 429, n. 68, my emphasis. See also Pines, "Philosophical Purport," p. 13, repr. in *Studies*, 475, n. 12, where he adds that in addition to the two conceptions of God discussed in the "Translator's Introduction," there are two more, one taken from Avicenna "that equates God with pure Being" and a second, taken from Themistius, "which regards God as the formal, the efficient, and the final cause of the universe." Because these different conceptions are mutually incompatible, Pines suggests that Maimonides's reason for putting them all forward may be "calculated to make his readers aware of the impossibility of metaphysical knowledge." Although Pines does not put his point in these words, I would suggest that here Maimonides is following a classical skeptic trope, opposing equipollent hypotheses in order to induce suspension of judgment.

from being Maimonides's esoteric intention, the Spinozistic reading of i.68 is theology!

To see how far Pines '79 has moved from the meta-philosophical agenda of '63, consider his view of the *Mishneh Torah* (*MT*) in the later papers. Not only does Pines find it "significant," as Maimonides remarks, that the unity of the divine intellect of i.68 is also set forth in *MT,* which supports the idea that "in both works the thesis forms a part of a theological system which may be believed but cannot be proved to be true"; Pines also proposes as a "tenable hypothesis" that whenever Maimonides refers in the *Guide* to *MT,* either by name or as "our compilations (*tawālīfunā*)," "these references are at least sometimes used by Maimonides to indicate that the passages in the *Guide* in which they occur pertain to theology or a theological philosophy which is not wary of putting forward assertions that the limited human intellect is unable to verify."[45] Pines no longer distinguishes *MT* as Law or Religion as opposed to Philosophy or in terms of its intended audience, that is, as a "text addressed to the general run of men" as opposed to a text "addressed to the small number of people who are able to understand by themselves."[46] Rather he uses Maimonides's cross-reference to *MT* as the author's directive to his reader how to evaluate and interpret the thesis in question in the *Guide*: Know that it is of a less than truth-ascertainable epistemological kind – call it "theological" – that distinguishes it from properly philosophical and scientific claims. The philosophical is that which can be known with certainty, the theological is at best probable. This new agenda is philosophical and in particular epistemological.

In a similar vein, Pines's hermeneutics shifts from '63 to '79. Pines opens the "Translator's Introduction" with a citation from Leo Strauss that contrasts the "methods of exposition" of the *MT* and *Guide*: The one produces order out of the "chaotic disorder of talmudic literature," in the other "order is turned into disorder."[47] Although he does not mention the terms "exoteric" and "esoteric," Pines tells us that Maimonides's contemporaries were "better prepared than modern readers to grasp intentions hinted at in veiled language and doctrines deliberately obscured by an extremely unsystematic method of exposition"; this is because "philosophic science may be dangerous; that the study of philosophy . . . may bring about that state of perplexity – due to an unresolved conflict between

---

[45] Pines, "Limitations," pp. 95–96, repr. in *Studies*, 417–418.
[46] L. Strauss, "The Literary Character of the *Guide of the Perplexed*," in *Persecution and the Art of Writing* (Glencoe, IL: Free Press, 1952), pp. 38–94.
[47] Pines, "Translator's Introduction," p. lvii.

religious tradition and nonreligious knowledge; that strict precautions must be taken … to keep the average reader, who is also an average man, in the dark concerning the philosophic solution propounded by Maimonides."[48]

In contrast, in the '79 agenda and, specifically, in "Philosophical Purport" of 1986, Pines argues that the "somewhat facile assumption … that Maimonides' halachic works are less 'philosophical' or 'Aristotelian' than the *Guide* is by no means true."[49] Instead of a binary exoteric/esoteric hermeneutics, Pines now proposes four "discourses" that can be "discerned" in the *Guide*: (1) a traditional religious discourse, which includes allegorical interpretations of anthropomorphic expressions in the Bible; (2) an Aristotelian discourse; (3) a "critical" discourse that challenges the possibility of a science of metaphysics and claims to certainty regarding incorporeal beings and extraterrestrial physics; and (4) a sufi or mystical discourse, which emerges in iii.51. The philosophical/theological distinction – between the certain and the probable – is now at a right angle to the exoteric/esoteric distinction. Maimonides's halakhic, or legal, compositions like the *MT* are exoteric but, compared to the esoteric *Guide*, more philosophical, or Aristotelian. This change reflects nothing less than a shift in agenda: from the meta-philosophical problem to a philosophical one focused on an epistemological problem.

For another illuminating contrast between the two agendas of '63 and '79, consider Pines's respective analyses of the imagery of a dark night illuminated by lightning flashes and polished bodies in Maimonides's "Introduction" to Part One of the *Guide* in light of Avicenna and ibn Bājja. Maimonides prima facie intends this image to throw light on the fact that, while the secrets of the Torah – physics and metaphysics – are not "fully and completely known by anyone among us," there are differences of degree of partial or incomplete understanding. In particular, Maimonides distinguishes four degrees in terms of four groups: (1) those who remain in the dark without any light; (2) those who are illumined by the reflection of light off polished stones; (3) those that see lightning flashes with different frequencies and for shorter or longer intervals; and (4) the one – identified by prooftext with Moses – who is illumined by lightning flashes as if he were in "unceasing light."[50] Although Pines acknowledges that the image of lightning flashes is found in many different sources with different significances, in '63 he suggests that the "most obvious" interpretation

---

[48]  Pines, "Translator's Introduction," pp. lvii–lviii.
[49]  Pines, "Philosophical Purport," p. 2, repr. in *Studies*, 464.     [50]  *Guide*, i. Introduction, pp. 7–8.

would be to identify those who see the lightning with prophets who "in Avicennean fashion" possess a faculty of intuitive intellection (divination, *ḥads*) that enables them to grasp, with different degrees of ability, true and certain conclusions by just "seeing" them, without reasoning them out syllogistically from premises.[51] Among these prophets, Moses alone sees the flashes continuously, as in a strobe show. Those who remain in the dark are the vulgar multitude, and those who see only by the reflected light of polished bodies, by an indirect form of inference, are the philosophers. In sum, the major contrast is between the competing levels of knowledge achieved in Philosophy and in Prophecy or Religion – the *meta*-philosophical issue – and the obvious lesson is the superiority of the latter over the former.

Pines next, however, compares Maimonides's description to a passage from ibn Bājja's "Epistle on Conjunction"[52] that also distinguishes three categories of people, the second described in terms similar to Maimonides's second group that sees light reflected from polished bodies, such as a mirror. This latter passage "lends color to a different interpretation (which, however, may not be wholly incompatible with the first)." Ibn Bājja's first, and lowest, category see (or *are*) only unpolished bodies that give off little, and distorted, light. His second category are "men of science," or natural philosophers, who reason discursively from empirical data; hence, their theoretical knowledge (*dianoia*) is indirect or reflected (but more or less accurate), and, significantly, it always starts from what can be perceived by the senses. The highest category are "the happy ones," like Aristotle, who directly see the sun itself, "who have achieved union with the Active Intellect and have immediate, intuitive, and certain knowledge of all the systems of science" (i.e., what the Greeks called *nous*).[53] Using this schema to interpret Maimonides's imagery in his "Introduction," those who see lightning flashes, who have intuitive theoretical knowledge (now *nous*, not *ḥads*), ibn Bājja's "happy ones," are now all prophets, chief among whom (apparently by degree) would be Moses. The philosophers are those who see only by the reflected light of polished bodies, what ibn Bājja called "men of science," those who achieve *dianoia* at best. The vulgar multitude are those who are, or see, only unpolished bodies.

---

[51] I ignore differences between Avicenna for whom, among other things, those who have intuitive intellection are *'ārifūn*, "those who know," including sufi mystics, and Maimonides for whom they are the prophets (of different ranks).

[52] *Risālat al-ittisāl*, ed. A. F. al-Ahwani, in Averroes, *Kitāb al-nafs* (Cairo, 1950), pp. 115f, cited in Pines, "Translator's Introduction," p. ciii, n. 76.

[53] Pines, "Translator's Introduction," p. cv.

Pines is now caught in a bind. Is Maimonides proposing not only the superiority of Prophecy/Religion over Philosophy but also that no philosopher, including Aristotle, ever achieved *nous* – and that the supreme knower is Moses, not Aristotle? Or assuming that his readers would know that the highest philosophical knowledge is *nous*, not *dianoia*, is Maimonides simply using scriptural proof texts to legitimate the superiority of philosophy over prophecy and to claim that Moses's superiority is not in virtue of his being the greatest prophet rather than philosopher, but rather *because* he is the greatest philosopher? This is to play out, once again, the *meta*-philosophical question. Pines's answer: "It would seem that in this case as in many others Maimonides deliberately aimed at ambiguity."[54]

Pines '79's approach is different. He interprets ibn Bājja's "Epistle on Conjunction" in light of another text by ibn Bājja,[55] which emphasizes that even though the human intellect has a faculty of insight (*baṣīra*) that enables it to transform imaginative into intelligible forms, which, when actualized, are grasped by the intellect without the senses and body, there are no intelligible forms that are humanly apprehended that did not *originate* in imaginative forms, which themselves were percepts of the senses. As support, Pines adds that the "noblest objects of intellection" for ibn Bājja are the motions of the celestial spheres. Of course, notwithstanding his critique of Alfarabi's view in the *Lost Commentary*, this position of ibn Bājja's is nothing but Alfarabi's.[56] And to make the implications even worse, Pines introduces Averroes's view that, given the identity of the intellect in act and the object of intellection, if what an intellect can know is something subject to corruption – namely, something material or sensible in the sublunar sphere – then the intellect itself must be subject to corruption. Turning then to the text from the "Epistle on Conjunction," Pines now focuses on the second category of natural philosophers – who are compared to polished surfaces, closer to the light of the sun, but not that light itself – who reason from empirical evidence, using their intellects but also their senses. What is now significant for Pines is not only that the intellects in this second category begin (as in Alfarabi's epistemology) from sensible or imaginative forms that are known empirically. In contrast to the third category, the highest "happy ones," who directly see the light of the incorruptible, eternal sun, the intellects in

---

[54] Pines, "Translator's Introduction," p. cvi.
[55] Collected in MS Pococke 20 of the Bodleian Library (cited in Pines, "Limitations," p. 82, repr. in *Studies*, 404), the same manuscript in which he reports and evaluates Alfarabi's position in the lost *Commentary on the Ethics*.
[56] Pines, "Limitations," p. 86, repr. in *Studies*, 408.

the second category – the intellects of natural philosophers – are, given Averroes's theory, corruptible.

Finally, Pines employs ibn Bājja to interpret Maimonides's imagery of lightning flashes in a dark night, but now the focus is not on Moses versus Aristotle, or Prophecy versus Philosophy, but on Maimonides's second category, who are illumined by "a polished body," the language for which recalls ibn Bājja's second group of natural philosophers who reason from, and require, sensible evidence based on the perception of corporeal (and corruptible) bodies. From this, Pines now concludes that Maimonides's point is that only prophets, those who see the lightning flashes directly, can apprehend abstract forms that did not originate in sense perception or from imaginative forms. All philosophers fall in the second group illumined by "a polished body." Hence, because Maimonides did not consider himself a prophet, his own knowledge – and the knowledge of all philosophers like him – is limited to intelligibles abstracted from material or sensible objects. If Aristotle is one of the "happy ones," then, like prophets, the greatest of whom is Moses, his knowledge is not something that a human can achieve. The point of the passage is philosophical rather than *meta*-philosophical: to show what kind of knowledge a human philosopher who is not a prophet is capable of achieving. The line Pines is concerned to draw is no longer between Philosophy and the Law but between what a human intellect can and cannot apprehend through its native intellectual powers. As for Maimonides's position on prophets and their cognition, Pines simply dismisses it: "the possibility that [it] may have been determined by theologico-political reasons need not concern us for the moment."[57] Pines's agenda has changed.

To sum up the argument thus far: Pines's meta-philosophical reading of the *Guide* in 1963 through the lens of Averroes with his long-range sights on Spinoza set an agenda, a group of philosophical problems and scholarly questions, that blocked the "critical epistemological" implications he later drew in 1979, which arose out of a completely different philosophical agenda, directed toward answering questions about human happiness that in turn depend on questions about the perfection of the human intellect and the possibility of human knowledge of metaphysics. Changes of agenda can have major consequences in determining which problems are addressed (and ignored or dismissed). Another excellent example revolves around Maimonides's "ostensible reaction"[58] to the crisis in twelfth-century Andalusia over Ptolemaic astronomy versus Aristotelian

---

[57] Pines, "Limitations," p. 90, repr. in *Studies*, 412.     [58] Pines, "Translator's Introduction," p. cx.

cosmology or celestial physics in *Guide* ii.24, a "skandalon of science," as Pines '63 calls it, according to which Maimonides "apparently" was "incurably skeptical" about the possibility of arriving at a super-lunar "physical theory" of celestial phenomena, an explanation that would be "methodologically as valid as [a theory] of sublunary phenomena."[59] According to Pines's '63 interpretation, Maimonides is focused on the question of the eternity versus creation of the universe – perhaps the central issue in the meta-philosophical debate over Philosophy versus Religion – and *appears* to use the crisis over astronomy to buttress his claim that eternity cannot be demonstrated, opening the possibility for creation and its conception of a Creator deity.[60] However, Pines thinks that this is only the appearance:

> Yet it seems to me that such agnosticism [or a "thoroughly skeptical position," though "the only consistent and logical one"] would stultify all that Maimonides set out to accomplish in the *Guide* and would also be irreconcilable with his general views, expressed in quite different contexts, on man's highest destination and man's knowledge.[61]

Notwithstanding *all* the available evidence for the exoteric "appearance," Pines gestures toward an esoteric interpretation according to which Maimonides nonetheless holds to the Philosophers' position on eternity.

By 1979, as you would expect by now, the story is entirely different. From the perspective of his "critical epistemological" agenda, the controversy over "the eternity of the world or its creation in time" is a "moot question" about which "Maimonides endeavors to prove in the *Guide* at great length, that human reason is incapable of discovering the truth of the matter. It very clearly serves his purpose to drive this fact home."[62] And with respect to the crisis between

> astronomy and celestial physics . . . no theory intended to explain the nature of the heavenly bodies and to account for their motions can, because of the human limitations, be regarded as certain. Moses is the only human being that may be assumed to have had this knowledge.[63]

---

[59] Pines, "Translator's Introduction," pp. cx–cxi.

[60] Pines, "*Harza'ah*," p. 126, calls Eternity versus Creation "the basic question in the debate between Philosophy and Religion."

[61] Pines, "Translator's Introduction," p. cxi.     [62] Pines, "Limitations," p. 97, repr. in *Studies*, 419.

[63] Pines, "Limitations," p. 93, repr. in *Studies*, 415. Pines goes on to contrast Maimonides, who excludes all human scientific knowledge beyond the sublunar world, with ibn Bājja who, as we mentioned earlier in the text, takes "the most sublime object that can be intellected by man" to be "the motions of the heavenly bodies" (ibid.). Cf. Pines, "Philosophical Purport," pp. 7–8, repr. in *Studies*, 469–470.

Here Pines is alluding to a passage at the end of ii.24 where Maimonides
writes:

> And even the general conclusion that may be drawn from them, namely,
> that they prove the existence of their Mover, is a matter the knowledge of
> which cannot be reached by human intellects ... Let us then stop at a point
> that is within our capacity, and let us give over the things that cannot be
> grasped by reasoning to him who was reached by the mighty divine overflow
> so that it could be fittingly said of him: With him do I speak mouth to
> mouth. (Num. 12:8)[64]

The significance Pines sees in this passage is not its denial that the
motions of the heavenly spheres furnish human intellects with knowledge
of the existence of God but the role it assigns to Moses, which, Pines
thinks, "in all probability is connected with Maimonides' interpretation of
Exod. 33, 23," which privileges Moses "for theological reasons, a doctrine
emphasizing the uniqueness of Moses being needed for a defense of
religion."[65] That is, if the claim in question cannot be known with
certainty and, hence, count as philosophy, Pines is suggesting that it
might be known with (at most) probability and, hence, count as theology –
the realm in which one accepts propositions for reasons other than their
certainty. Again, not just the interpretations but the very problems and
questions one addresses (or doesn't) change with a change of agenda.

There remains one unanswered question, the one with which we began:
What motivated Pines to change agendas (if he did)? Here is a stab at an
explanation.

It is a remarkable fact that Shlomo Pines's *first* sustained publication on
Maimonides is his "Translator's Introduction" to the *Guide* in 1963. Prior to
then his only other publication on Maimonides, three pages long, was the
"Excursus on free will and determinism" in an appendix to "Abu'l-Barakat's
Poetics and Metaphysics," published in 1960. And before that, in 1955 Pines
gave the lecture "*Harza'ah al Moreh Ha-Nevukhim le-Rambam*" [A Lecture
on Maimonides's *'Guide of the Perplexed'*] (apart from his lectures at Hebrew
University), which remained unpublished until 1998. That published lecture
is the final entry in the official bibliography of Pines's writings. Echoing
a famous phrase in the *Guide*, it is indeed the First and the Last.

---

[64] *Guide* ii.24, p. 327.
[65] Pines, "Limitations," p. 92–93, repr. in *Studies*, 414–415. The first sentence in the quoted passage
from ii.24 has been the subject of much recent debate, both textual and interpretive. In the
quotation I follow the received Arabic text and Pines's translation. However, it is remarkable that
neither Pines '63 nor Pines '79 even mentions the problematic sentence.

Reading the "Translator's Introduction," one would think that it is the fruit of years and years of research and thought about the *Guide*. And there is no reason to question that. Moreover, all that research and thought contains deep ruminations on Alfarabi, Avicenna, Averroes, and ibn Bājja and their influence on Maimonides, and especially on Maimonides's "critical epistemology." This is evident to any reader of the "Introduction." In light of this history, I would hypothesize that Pines's own position, or at least inclination – both from the start of his career prior to 1963, and again from the beginning of the end in 1979 until his death in 1990 – was the critical Alfarabian view of deep limitations on the human intellect with respect to knowledge of metaphysics. However, for much of that long period, it subsisted in his head and not on paper.

Why then the manifest veer toward Averroes and Spinoza in 1963? In 1954–55 Leo Strauss spent a year as a visiting professor at the Hebrew University in Jerusalem. That year was a milestone for the study of Maimonides in the second half of the twentieth century, especially in Israel.[66] Although Pines and Strauss had been friends since their university days in Berlin, in that one year Strauss made a decisive impact on Pines, making him a Maimonidean of the Averroistic-Spinozistic stripe. On the occasion of Strauss's visit, Pines was stimulated to give the 1955 lecture, which is an anticipation of the '63 Introduction, Strauss and Pines likely began to plan the translation project, and Pines's own thoughts for his "Introduction" may have begun to take shape. However, if my analyses have been on the right track, I have tried to show how Pines, even while writing the "Introduction," was still deeply engaged in his own prior, and original, critical epistemological reading of the *Guide* and, as a result of the tension between the two agendas, found himself making contorted motions to accommodate the Averroistic-Spinozistic agenda with the actual texts of the *Guide* and with his own prior thoughts. As the shadow of Strauss's presence faded with the end of his visit to Jerusalem, with the publication of the translation with Pines's "Introduction," and with undoubtedly Pines's own developing thoughts over the following years – as that process continued, his own critical reading re-emerged in the light of day. But the critical reading was Pines's own first and last reading of Maimonides's *Guide*, momentarily eclipsed by the sudden, blinding appearance of a comet in the sky that appeared not out of nowhere but out of Hyde Park, Chicago.

---

[66] Here I am indebted to an unpublished paper by Warren Zev Harvey delivered at the World Congress of Jewish Studies in 2013, which he was kind enough to share with me. Harvey also discusses the impact of Strauss's visit on Isaiah Leibowitz.

CHAPTER 13

# How to Begin to Study Strauss's "How to Begin to Study the Guide of the Perplexed"[*]

Warren Zev Harvey

Leo Strauss (1899–1973) was without doubt the most controversial interpreter of Maimonides's *Guide of the Perplexed* in the twentieth century. In his *Philosophie und Gesetz*,[1] "The Literary Character of *The Guide for the Perplexed*,"[2] "How to Begin to Study *The Guide of the Perplexed*,"[3] and other works, he painted a portrait of a bold, radical, and subversive Maimonides, who was very different from the pious, tame, harmonizing theologian often portrayed by historians of medieval philosophy.

In 1999, at a conference at the University of Haifa commemorating Strauss's 100th birthday, I gave a talk on "How Leo Strauss Paralyzed the Study of the *Guide of the Perplexed* in the Twentieth Century."[4] I admitted that Strauss "contributed more than any other individual to the advancement of research on the *Guide of the Perplexed* in the twentieth century." He taught us to read the *Guide* as the medievals did. He taught us to attend to its puzzles, and to distinguish between its exoteric and esoteric teachings. He taught us to read it as a book of political philosophy in the tradition of

[*] I thank Charles Manekin, Daniel Davies, Josef Stern, and Steven Harvey for their helpful comments.
[1] L. Strauss, *Philosophie und Gesetz* (Berlin: Schocken, 1935). English translation: *Philosophy and Law*, tr. E. Adler (Albany: SUNY Press, 1995).
[2] Strauss, "The Literary Character of *The Guide for the Perplexed*," in S. W. Baron (ed.), *Essays on Maimonides* (New York: Columbia University Press, 1941), pp. 37–91. Reprinted in Strauss, *Persecution and the Art of Writing* (Glencoe: The Free Press, 1952), pp. 38–94. Page references will be to *Persecution*.
[3] Strauss, "How to Begin to Study *The Guide of the Perplexed*," in Maimonides, *The Guide of the Perplexed*, tr. Pines, pp. xi–lvi. Reprinted in Strauss, *Liberalism: Ancient and Modern* (New York: Basic Books, 1968), pp. 140–184. Abridged in S. Lieberman, S. Spiegel, L. Strauss, and A. Hyman (eds.), *Harry Austryn Wolfson Jubilee Volume* (Jerusalem: American Academy for Jewish Research, 1965), English section, pp. 775–791. Page references will be to the University of Chicago *Guide*. Page references to Maimonides's *Guide* will also be to the University of Chicago edition. Cf. *Dalālat al-Ḥā'irīn*, ed. S. Munk and I. Joël (Jerusalem: Junovitch, 1929).
[4] "How Leo Strauss Paralyzed the Study of the *Guide of the Perplexed* in the Twentieth Century" (Heb.), *Iyyun* 50 (2001), 387–396; English abstract, 51 (2002), 107–108. See also my "Les nœuds du *Guide des égarés*: une critique de la lecture politique de Leo Strauss," in Géraldine Roux (ed.), *Lumières médiévales* (Paris: Van Dieren, 2009), pp. 163–176.

Plato and Alfarabi. In short, "he gave us the means to understand the secrets of the *Guide*."[5] However, I continued, he also *paralyzed* scholarship on the book.

This paralysis, I contended, was caused by Strauss's famous Jerusalem–Athens dichotomy. He interpreted all the *Guide*'s puzzles in the same way. It was always Jerusalem versus Athens, religion versus philosophy, Revelation versus Reason. All the secrets of the *Guide* were reduced to one big secret: The *Guide* is exoterically a Jewish book and esoterically a philosophic book. The truth, however, is that there are many different kinds of secrets in the *Guide*.

I explained that the Jerusalem–Athens dichotomy had been presented by Strauss in such a convincing way that it was widely accepted by both Straussian and anti-Straussian interpreters of the *Guide*, and both groups were paralyzed by it: the former because they could see nothing in the *Guide* except Revelation versus Reason; the latter because they were so scandalized by Strauss's theory that they refused to see any secrets at all in the *Guide*. Thus, Strauss's Jerusalem–Athens dichotomy prevented many interpreters of the *Guide* from discerning its multifaceted mysteries.

I noted that Shlomo Pines, in studies written after Strauss's death, argued that there are not two but *four* levels of meaning in the *Guide*, which may be listed in ascending order of their esotericism: dialectical theology (which corresponds to Strauss's "Jerusalem"), Aristotelian philosophy (which corresponds to Strauss's "Athens"), critical epistemology, and intellectual mysticism.[6] While Pines's fourfold division is more accurate than Strauss's twofold one, it is an underestimate. I prefer Sylvie-Anne Goldberg's metaphor: The *Guide* is a *millefeuille*.[7]

I then added that "Strauss himself, in his later writings," in particular in his "How to Begin to Study the *Guide*," recognized "to a certain degree" that there are different kinds of secrets in the *Guide*, and I cited examples to illustrate this.[8] I am now, however, convinced that Strauss, in his later writings, understood *fully* that there are different kinds of secrets in the *Guide*. Put differently, Strauss paralyzed others but was not himself paralyzed. In what follows, I shall discuss some main themes in Strauss's essay,

---

[5] "How Strauss Paralyzed," 387.
[6] S. Pines, "Le discours théologico-philosophique dans les œuvres halachiques de Maïmonide," in *Délivrance et Fidélité: Maïmonide* (Paris: Érès, 1986), pp. 119–124; " The Philosophic Purport of Maimonides' Halachic Works," in Y. Yovel and S. Pines (eds.), *Maimonides and Philosophy* (Dordrecht: Nijhoff, 1986), pp. 1–14.
[7] She made this remark in response to a talk I gave in 2004 at the École des Hautes Études en Sciences Sociales, Paris. See my "Les nœuds du *Guide*," p. 170, n. 18.
[8] "How Strauss Paralyzed," 389.

"How to Begin to Study the *Guide*." It will become clear that Strauss did not confine himself in this essay to his old Jerusalem–Athens dichotomy, but resourcefully uncovered in it diverse and unexpected kinds of mysteries. The Strauss of "How to Begin to Study the *Guide*" was able to understand secrets in the *Guide* that the early Strauss could not have imagined.

Strauss was a recondite and idiosyncratic author, and "How to Begin to Study the *Guide*" is one of his most intractable works. It is certainly his most abstruse work on Maimonides. As one scholar wrote, in "How to Begin to Study the *Guide*" Strauss "takes his form of esoteric interpretation to extremes not present in his other works on Maimonides."[9] It is not surprising, therefore, that most studies of Strauss's interpretation of Maimonides have focused on *Philosophie und Gesetz* and "The Literary Character of *The Guide*," and have ignored "How to Begin to Study the *Guide*." Two significant exceptions are Steven Lenzner's "A Literary Exercise in Self-Knowledge"[10] and Aryeh Tepper's *Progressive Minds, Conservative Politics*.[11] Notwithstanding the difficulties, it is well worth the effort to study Strauss's "How to Begin to Study the *Guide*." My aim is not to try to clarify everything in this remarkable essay, but only to help the reader to begin to study it.

## Twofold Explanation of Biblical Terms

In the following passage from "How to Begin to Study the *Guide*," Strauss speaks of the "twofold character" of Maimonides's explanation of biblical terms, and his "secret teaching" concerning "idolatrous relics" in the Bible:

> The first chapter of the *Guide* is devoted to "image and likeness." The selection of these terms was necessitated by a single biblical passage: "And God said, Let us make man in our image, after our likeness ... So God created man in his image, in the image of God ... " [Genesis 1:26–27] ...

[9] A. Verskin, "Reading Strauss on Maimonides: A New Approach," *The Journal of Textual Reasoning* 3 (2004), 1. Cf. K. H. Green, *Leo Strauss and the Rediscovery of Maimonides* (University of Chicago Press, 2013), p. 140: "Indeed ... 'How to Begin to Study the *Guide*' ... reached a point of complexity of thought, and subtlety in construction, which parallels, and perhaps deliberately reproduces or even surpasses, the difficulties which most readers meet with in studying the *Guide* itself."
[10] S. Lenzner, "A Literary Exercise in Self-Knowledge: Strauss' Twofold Interpretation of Maimonides," *Perspectives on Political Science* 31 (2002), 225–234.
[11] A. Tepper, *Progressive Minds, Conservative Politics: Leo Strauss' Later Writings on Maimonides* (Albany: SUNY Press, 2013). In his introduction, pp. 11–20, Tepper discusses the general scholarly neglect of Strauss's later writings on Maimonides and mentions authors who were exceptions to the rule.

[This] passage suggests to the vulgar mind more strongly than any other biblical passage that God is corporeal in the crudest sense ... Maimonides tells his addressee that *selem* (the Hebrew term that is rendered by "image") does not mean ... a visible shape; it means the natural form, the specific form, the essence of a being: "God created man in his image" means that God created man as a being endowed with intellect ... The Hebrew term designating form in the sense of visible shape is *to'ar*, which is never applied to God ... Maimonides [then] says: "We have explained to thee the difference between *selem* and *to'ar* and we have explained the meaning of *selem*." He thus alludes to the twofold character of his explanation here as well as elsewhere: one explanation is given to "thee," i.e., to the typical addressee and another is given to indeterminate readers; the latter explanation comes to light only when one considers ... the context of all biblical passages quoted ... It looks as if Maimonides wished to draw our attention to the fact that the Bible contains idolatrous, pagan, or "Sabian" relics. If this suspicion should prove to be justified, we would have to assume that his fight against "forbidden worship" and hence against corporealism is more radical than one would be inclined to believe or that the recovery of Sabian relics in the Bible with the help of Sabian literature is one of the tasks of his secret teaching.[12]

Strauss explains here why Maimonides opens *Guide* i.1, with a discussion of the Hebrew word *selem* ("image" or "form").[13] According to "the vulgar mind," Strauss tells us, the biblical phrase "image of God" (Genesis 1:26–27) indicates that God is corporeal "in the crudest sense." Maimonides, however, forestalls this idolatrous inference by teaching that *selem* in Hebrew does not mean "form" in the sense of visible shape, but rather "the natural form, the specific form, the essence of being," that is, "form" in the Aristotelian sense.[14] Accordingly, the divine image of a human being is the human being's Aristotelian form, namely, the intellect. As for "form" in the sense of visible shape, it is designated by the word *to'ar*. Maimonides sums it up: "We have explained to thee the difference between *selem* and *to'ar* and we have explained the meaning of *selem*." Strauss observes that Maimonides hints here at two different sorts of "explanation" ("We have explained to thee ... and we have explained"), one exoteric and one esoteric. The exoteric explanation is intended for the uncritical reader who accepts Maimonides's words at face value, and the esoteric one is intended for the critical reader who considers the biblical contexts. Now,

---

[12] "How to Begin to Study the *Guide*," pp. xxvi–xxvii. This passage is discussed in my "How to Begin to Study the *Guide of the Perplexed* i.1" (Heb.), *Daat* 21 (1988), 5–23; English abstract, xxiii. On the "Sabians," see Pines, "Translator's Introduction to the *Guide*," in *Guide*, pp. cxxiii–cxxiv; and S. Stroumsa, *Maimonides in His World* (Princeton University Press, 2009), pp. 84–105.

[13] *Guide* i.1, pp. 21–23.     [14] Cf. *Code of Law, Yesode ha-Torah* 4:8.

the biblical passages cited by Maimonides with regard to *ṣelem* include (in addition to Genesis 1:26–27) Psalms 73:20 and I Samuel 6:5 and 11.[15] In those texts, as well as in many other biblical passages, *ṣelem* seems clearly to designate form in the sense of visible shape. Thus, the uncritical reader concludes that in Hebrew the "image of God" refers to intellect, while the critical reader concludes that it refers to visible shape. In other words, the uncritical reader interprets the biblical expression "image of God" in the Aristotelian way, while the critical reader interprets it in the idolatrous way. The exoteric level is Aristotelian, the esoteric idolatrous.

What has happened here? Strauss has shown in effect that Maimonides distinguishes between a *religious and philosophical* interpretation, according to which the "divine image" refers to the intellect, and a *historical and philological* interpretation, according to which it refers to visible shape. The uncritical reader learns that Maimonides's religious and philosophic teaching about the divine image is based on the Hebrew language. The critical reader learns that it is despite the Hebrew. The uncritical reader is served Maimonides's religious and philosophical interpretation as if it were the literal reading of the text, while the critical reader infers that it is not. The uncritical reader learns that the Bible teaches religious and philosophic truth, while the critical reader learns the urgency of reinterpreting miscreant biblical texts in accordance with religious and philosophic truth.

Strauss's discovery of the secret of the "twofold character" of Maimonides's explanation of biblical terms is an extremely important contribution to our understanding of the *Guide*. He has shown that the attempt to understand the Bible against the background of the ancient world is an important part of the "secret teaching" of the *Guide*. Maimonides held that the "idolatrous relics" in the Bible must be reinterpreted, but he also held that they must first be understood.

It will be noticed that the contradiction between the two explanations of the word *ṣelem* is not easily reduced to the Jerusalem–Athens dichotomy. For example, Aristotelian philosophy according to the dichotomy is supposed to be the esoteric doctrine, but the Aristotelian definition of *ṣelem* is the exoteric explanation. In his exposition of the secret of the twofold character of Maimonides's explanation of biblical terms, Strauss freed himself from the chains of the Jerusalem–Athens dichotomy.

There is one side-point in Strauss's analysis that does not seem to me compelling. He identifies the uncritical reader with the "typical addressee," namely, the addressee of the book, Maimonides's pupil, Joseph ben Judah

---

[15] "How to Begin to Study the *Guide*," p. 22.

ibn Simeon, and those like him; and he identifies the critical readers with "indeterminate readers." Joseph is indeed described by Maimonides as a beginning student who is a bit impetuous, but it seems to me that on the whole he was considered by him to be a competent reader.[16] Strauss's comments throughout the essay about the "typical addressee" and the "atypical addressees" require careful evaluation. However, they do not affect the validity of his exposition of the twofold character of Maimonides's explanation of biblical terms.

## Lexicographic Chapters

One of Strauss's notable discoveries in "How to Begin to Study the *Guide*" concerns the "lexicographic chapters." Readers of the *Guide* have of course always known that many chapters of the book, especially in Part I, treat of lexicography. Maimonides defines in them words that appear in the Bible, in particular words used to describe God. Strauss is the first author to examine Maimonides's lexicography systematically. He defines a "lexicographic chapter" as one that opens with the Hebrew *definiendum* or *definienda*. He considers the distinction between lexicographic chapters and nonlexicographic chapters to be a valuable key to understanding Maimonides's esoteric teachings.[17]

In *Guide* i.1–49, the chapters treating of God's corporeality, 30 chapters are lexicographic and 19 nonlexicographic. *Guide* i.1, 6–9, 11–13, 15–16, and 18–25, 28–30, 37–45, are lexicographic, but i.2–5, 10, 14, 17, 26–27, 31–36, 46–49 are not.[18] Sometimes Strauss's lexicographic expositions involve numerology or alphabetology. Thus, he writes:

> Maimonides interrupts his discussion of [words] that refer to place and turns to the explanation of "man" (i.14). A similar interruption occurs shortly afterwards when he turns from "standing" and "rock" (i.15 and 16) to an explanation of the prohibition against the public teaching of natural science (i.17) . . . By this irregularity our attention is drawn to a certain numerical symbolism . . . : 14 stands for man or the human things and 17 stands for nature . . . The connection between "14" and [other chapters] cannot become clear before we have reached a better understanding of . . .

---

[16] See the description of Joseph ben Judah in the Epistle Dedicatory, *Guide*, pp. 3–4. Cf. my "Maimonides' *Guide of the Perplexed*: An Enchanted Book of Puzzles," in Stuart W. Halpern (ed.), *Books of the People* (New Milford: Maggid, 2017), pp. 44–48.

[17] "How to Begin to Study the *Guide*," pp. xxiv–xxv. See S. Efrati, "The Lexicographic Chapters of the First Part of the *Guide of the Perplexed*" (Heb.), doctoral dissertation, Bar-Ilan University, 2016.

[18] "How to Begin to Study the *Guide*," p. xxv. The only other chapter in the book that is clearly lexicographic is I, 70.

nature and convention . . . Incidentally, it may be remarked that 14 is the numerical equivalent of the Hebrew word for "hand" . . . [N]o chapter in the *Guide* is devoted to "hand," the characteristically human organ.[19]

Strauss distinguishes here between the "human" or "conventional" (e.g., "ascending," "descending") and the "natural" (e.g., "standing erect," "rock"). *Guide* i.14, whose subject is the Hebrew word *adam* (= Adam, the human being, the human species), treats of the human or conventional, while i.17, whose subject is *ma'aseh bereshit* (= the Account of the Beginning, natural science, physics) treats of the natural.[20] The distinction between i.14 and i.17 is thus analogous to the Aristotelian distinction between practical and theoretical philosophy, or to the pre-Socratic distinction between *nomos* and *physis*. Strauss now raises an apt question. Why is there no chapter in the *Guide* devoted to the Hebrew word *yad* ("hand")?[21] Is not "the hand of the Lord" (Exodus 9:3 et al) the paradigm case of biblical anthropomorphisms?[22] After all, Maimonides devotes lexicographic chapters to "foot" (i.28 [= 14 × 2]), "face" (i.37), "back" (i.38), "heart" (i.39), "wing" (i.43), and "eye" (i.44). Why not "hand"? Strauss's solution seems to be that the human being (*adam*) is the hand of God, and thus the chapter on *adam* is numbered 14, the numerical equivalent of *yad* or "hand." i.14, the only chapter in the *Guide* beginning with the word "equivocality" (Arabic: *ishtirāk*), is thus the supposedly missing chapter on God's hand. As for the notion that "17 stands for nature," Strauss hints here at Maimonides's interpretation of two biblical verses: "And God saw that it was *good*" (Genesis 1:10 et al.) and "I will make all My *goodness* pass before thee" (Exodus 33:19).[23] According to Maimonides, the word "good" or "goodness" (Hebrew: *tov*) refers in these verses to nature, and the numerical value of *tov* is 17. When multiplied by the Tetragrammaton, 17 gives 68. In *Guide* i.68, Maimonides discusses God as the *intellectus-intelligens-intelligibile*, or, in Shlomo Pines's paraphrase, "the scientific system of the universe."[24]

---

[19] Ibid., pp. xxix–xxx.
[20] Cf. already "The Literary Character of the *Guide*," p. 61: "Maimonides interrupts his explanation of Biblical expressions attributing to God place . . . by an exposition of the meaning of *man* and by a discussion of the necessity of teaching *ma'aseh bereshit* esoterically . . . just as the Bible itself interrupts the story of Joseph by inserting into it the story of Judah and Tamar."
[21] Cf. "How to Begin to Study the *Guide*," p. xxiv: "Why is there a chapter devoted to 'foot' and another to 'wing' but none to 'hand'?" Strauss's repetition of this question (on pp. xxiv and xxx) indicates its importance for him.
[22] See *Code of Law, Yesode ha-Torah* 1:9. See also *Guide* i.46, pp. 100–101; ii.41, p. 387. Cf. Joseph Albo, *Book of Principles*, ed. and tr. I. Husik (Philadelphia: Jewish Publication Society, 1946), iii.10, pp. 92–93.
[23] See *Guide* i.54, p. 124; iii.13, p. 453.
[24] "Translator's Introduction to the *Guide*," p. xcviii. Interpretations based on chapter numbers in the *Guide* (e.g., 14, 17, 68) presume that the numbers were assigned by Maimonides and that we know them. While these are reasonable assumptions, they are open to doubt. The Arabic manuscripts lack

Like those of Rabbi Abraham Abulafia, Strauss's numerological and alphabetological interpretations of the *Guide* are sometimes truly insightful and sometimes just fanciful.[25]

## Disjunctive Proof of the Existence of God

Interpreters of the *Guide* have often been nonplussed by the disjunctive proof of God in *Guide* ii.2 that Maimonides proudly calls "my method."[26] It goes roughly as follows. Either the world is created in time (= generated after nonexistence), as the Kalām theologians hold, or eternal (= not generated or corrupted), as Aristotle holds. The opinions of both the Kalām theologians and Aristotle have not been proved. The opinion of the Kalām theologians is not proved because their arguments are merely "dialectical" or "sophistical."[27] Aristotle's opinion is not proved because his premise regarding the eternal motion of the celestial sphere cannot be verified empirically.[28] However, the two opinions constitute an exclusive disjunction and give rise to a simple constructive dilemma. If the world is created in time, we can argue, following the Kalām theologians, that it is a first intelligible that whatever is created has a creator, and this is God. If the world is eternal, we can argue, following Aristotle, that the sempiternal motion of the celestial sphere requires an incorporeal mover, and this is God. Thus, concludes Maimonides, whether the Kalām theologians or Aristotle are right, we have a valid proof of the existence of God.[29] The curious nature of Maimonides's disjunctive proof derives from the fact that the supernatural God of the Kalām theologians and the natural God of Aristotle are not the same. Does it really make no difference to Maimonides whether the Kalām theologians are right or Aristotle is right? Could it be that he has no preference? In "How to Begin to Study the *Guide*," Strauss illustrates this problem with a fascinating parable:

> [B]oth ways [that of the Kalām theologians and that of Aristotle] are defective. Maimonides' way consists in a combination of these two defective ways . . . Yet the results from opposed premises cannot be simply identical.

chapter numbers; the two medieval Hebrew translations (Ibn Tibbon and Alharizi) have slightly different numberings; and the medieval Latin translation has a numbering that differs slightly from both.

[25] See I. Twersky's reservations about Strauss's "geometric (kabbalistic) approach" in his review of the Pines-Strauss edition of the *Guide* in *Speculum* 41 (1966), 555–558; but see also S. Harvey's defense of Strauss in his "Maimonides in the Sultan's Palace," in J. L. Kraemer (ed.), *Perspectives on Maimonides* (Oxford University Press, 1991), pp. 50–64.

[26] *Guide*, p. 252; cf. i.71, p. 181; i.76, p. 231; ii.1, p. 252.

[27] "How to Begin to Study the *Guide*," p. lii.    [28] Ibid. Cf. pp. liii–lv.    [29] Ibid., p. lii.

For instance, someone might have said prior to the Second World War that Germany would be prosperous regardless of whether she won or lost the war; if she won, her prosperity would follow immediately; if she lost, her prosperity would be assured by the United States of America who would need her as an ally against Soviet Russia; but the predictor would have abstracted from the difference between Germany as the greatest power which ruled tyrannically and was ruled tyrannically, and Germany as a second-rank power ruled democratically. The God whose being is proved on the assumption of eternity is the unmoved mover, thought that thinks only itself and that as such is the form or the life of the world. The God whose being is proved on the assumption of creation is the biblical God who is characterized by Will ... If we consider the situation as outlined by Maimonides, we see that what is demonstrated by his way is only what is common to the two different notions of God or what is neutral to the difference between God as pure Intellect and God as Will or what is beyond that difference or what has only the name in common with either Intellect or Will.[30]

Strauss's parable illustrates how the Gods of the Kalām theologians and of Aristotle are different: One is a God of Will, the other a God of Intellect. His parable is felicitous because it makes clear that the question of which God is preferable is a subjective one. Let us imagine three different Germans responding to the predictor: a chauvinist, a liberal, and a banker. The first would be satisfied only with a German victory, the second would be satisfied only with a German defeat, and the third would be satisfied either way. Similarly, some individuals would prefer the God of Will, others the God of Intellect, and still others would be content with either. Strauss, however, seems to criticize Maimonides's disjunctive proof for reducing the Gods of the Kalām theologians and Aristotle to their lowest common denominator.

In the continuation of his discussion of the disjunctive proof of the existence of God, Strauss gives a more informed and more penetrating analysis of the choice between the God of the Kalām theologians and the Aristotelian God. He writes thus:

If the world or more precisely the [celestial] sphere is created, it is indeed self-evident that it was created by some agent but it does not necessarily follow that the creator is one, let alone absolutely simple, and that he is incorporeal. On the other hand, if the sphere is eternal, it follows, as Aristotle has shown, that God is and is incorporeal; but on this assumption the angels or separate intellects ... are as eternal as God ... It is therefore a

[30] Ibid., pp. lii–liii.

question whether monotheism strictly understood is demonstrable. Maimonides does say that Unity and also Incorporeality follow from certain philosophic proofs that do not presume either the eternity of the world or its creation, but it is, to say the least, not quite clear whether the proofs in question do not in fact presuppose the eternity of the world (cf. ii.2 with ii.1).[31]

In his prior discussion of Maimonides's disjunctive proof of God's existence, Strauss presumed that both disjuncts were possible. In this discussion, he inclines toward the view that both are inadequate. Either-or has turned into neither-nor.[32] The proof of the Kalām theologians is insufficient since, even if it is granted as valid, it can demonstrate only the existence of a creator, but not His unity or incorporeality. The Aristotelian proof is insufficient since, even if it is granted as valid, it can demonstrate only the existence of an incorporeal mover, but not His uniqueness or incomparability. Monotheism seems indemonstrable. This awareness of Maimonides's skepticism was not characteristic of Strauss's earlier writings on the *Guide*, but is very much present in "How to Begin to Study the *Guide*."

Apropos of Maimonides's skepticism, Strauss's comment about "certain philosophic proofs that do not presume either the eternity of the world or its creation" is especially telling. He has in mind a puzzle noted by several medieval authors and described by Rabbi Samuel Ibn Tibbon as "the strongest difficulty found in [the] book."[33] It concerns Maimonides's intentionally contradictory positions regarding the "third philosophic demonstration," as set down in *Guide* ii.1.[34] The demonstration, which involves the argument from contingent existence to necessary existence and which is sometimes called the "Avicennian" demonstration, is explicitly said not to presume the eternity of the world, but it does not work unless

---

[31] Ibid., pp. liii–liv.

[32] For instance, someone might have said prior to the Second World War that Germany would be unsuccessful regardless of whether she won or lost the war; if she won, she would be doomed to live under tyranny; if she lost, she would be a second-rank power dependent on others.

[33] Ibn Tibbon's comment is found in Maimonides, *Iggerot*, ed. I. Shailat, pp. 548–549; cf. C. Frankel, *Min Ha-Rambam le-Shemu'el ibn Tibbon* (Jerusalem: Magnes, 2007, pp. 165–172). See Joseph Kaspi, Two Commentaries on *Moreh Nevukhim*, ed. S. Z. Werbluner (Frankfurt am Main: J. F. Bach, 1848), ii.1, p. 89; 2, p. 90; Hasdai Crescas, *Or Adonai*, ed. S. Fisher (Jerusalem: Ramot, 1990), i.1.29, pp. 57–58; and Profiat Duran (Ephodi), in *Moreh Nevukhim*, tr. Samuel Ibn Tibbon, with Commentaries (Warsaw: Goldman, 1872), pp. 14b–15a, *het*. Cf. S. Munk's note in his French translation: *Le Guide des égarés* (Paris: A. Franck, 1856–1866), ii.1, pp. 39–40, n. 2. See also my *Physics and Metaphysics in Hasdai Crescas* (Amsterdam: Gieben, 1998), pp. 77–82, 92; and my "Maimonides' Critical Epistemology and *Guide* ii.24," *Aleph* 8 (2008), 228–230.

[34] *Guide*, pp. 247–249.

the eternity of the world is presumed.[35] In *Guide* ii.2, Maimonides in effect
suggests to the Kalām theologians that since their own proof fails to
establish monotheism they can complement it with the third philosophic
demonstration, which proves God's "Unity and also Incorporeality" without presuming the eternity of the world.[36] However, since the third
philosophic demonstration does in fact presume the eternity of the world
(in Strauss's wry understatement, "it is, to say the least, not quite clear"),
Kalāmic readers who try to save their own proof by availing themselves of
that demonstration are leaping out of the frying pan into the fire.

The contradiction noted here by Strauss between the opinion that the
third philosophic demonstration does not presume the eternity of the
world and the opinion that it does presume it is a contradiction between
two philosophic opinions (i.e., it is a contradiction inside Athens and
not one between Jerusalem and Athens). In my "How Strauss Paralyzed
the Study of the *Guide*," I cited this contradiction as an example of an
important intentional contradiction in the *Guide* that had been recognized by the medievals but was neglected by recent scholars because it
did not fit Strauss's stultifying Jerusalem–Athens dichotomy.[37] I must
admit that when I prepared "How Strauss Paralyzed the Study of the
*Guide*" in 1999, I overlooked Strauss's astute comments about this
contradiction in his "How to Begin to Study the *Guide*," and thus did
not mention them.[38] I still consider this contradiction to be a good
example of how Strauss paralyzed interpreters of the *Guide*, but I now
know that it is also a good example of how he paralyzed others but was
not himself paralyzed.

Strauss, in "How to Begin to Study the *Guide*," was fully aware that
according to Maimonides's esoteric doctrine both disjuncts in the disjunctive proof of the existence of God are based ultimately on the unproved
premise of the eternity of the world, and even if that premise is granted as
true, neither disjunct is able to prove the One God. In sum, the later
Strauss profoundly understood the secrets of Maimonides's critical epistemology and sought to decipher them in his "How to Begin to Study the
*Guide*."

---

[35] At *Guide* ii.2, p. 252, the demonstration is claimed not to presume the eternity of the world.
However, at ii.1, p. 247, it is argued: if all existents were corruptible, they would all have passed away
[after an elapse of infinite time], but they have not. The argument requires the phrase added in
brackets.

[36] *Guide*, p. 247.      [37] "How Strauss Paralyzed," 391–395; "Les nœuds du *Guide*," pp. 170–176.

[38] This oversight is corrected in my "Maimonides' Critical Epistemology," p. 239, n. 34.

## Divine Unity: Incomparability versus Incorporeality

In the course of our discussion of Strauss's analysis of Maimonides's disjunctive proof of the existence of God, it emerged that Maimonides presupposes two different concepts of Unity: incomparability and incorporeality. The proof of the Kalām theologians can perhaps establish the former but not the latter; that of Aristotle can establish the latter but not the former. Strauss admits his own unease about what he calls "the perplexing and upsetting character of Maimonides' teaching regarding Unity."[39] He writes thus about Maimonides's teaching:

> Maimonides ... makes clear [in *Guide* i.49] that Incorporeality and not Unity is still the theme ... [*Guide* i.50] opens the discussion of Unity. Incorporeality had presented itself as a consequence of Unity; Unity had been ... an unquestioned presupposition. Unity now becomes the theme. ... The most important biblical text [concerning Unity] is "Hear, O Israel, the Lord is our God, the Lord is one" (Deuteronomy 6:4; cf. *Mishneh Torah*, Hilkhot Yesode ha-Torah 1:7). To our very great amazement, Maimonides ... quotes [this verse only] a single time in the *Guide*, imitating the Torah, which, as he says [in his *Treatise on Resurrection*] mentions the principle of Unity, namely this verse, only once ... He quotes the verse in iii.45, i.e., the 169th chapter [= 13 × 13], thus perhaps alluding to the thirteen divine attributes ...

As Maimonides indicates, the meaning of "the Lord is one" is primarily that there is no one or nothing similar or equal to Him and only derivatively that He is absolutely simple ... He develops the notion of God's incomparability ... on the basis of quotations from Isaiah and Jeremiah as distinguished from the Torah (cf. i.55 with i.54). He is silent here on Deuteronomy 4:35 ("the Lord he is God; there is none else beside him").[40]

In Maimonides's discussions of Unity in the *Guide*, incomparability and incorporeality are sometimes inextricably intertwined. Strauss is justified to be perplexed and upset. Moreover, he is also justified to express not only amazement or great amazement but *very great amazement* at the fact that Deuteronomy 6:4, Judaism's traditional proclamation of Unity, appears only once in the *Guide* – and not in the philosophical discussions of Unity

---

[39] "How to Begin to Study the *Guide*," p. l.

[40] Ibid., pp. xlvii–xlviii. Cf. p. xxxiv: the thirteen divine attributes are "the Mosaic theology par excellence." As for the reference to 169, it is a droll example of Straussian self-parody. In the cited passage from his *Treatise on Resurrection*, Maimonides remarks that "the truth of things is not added to by repeated expression" and the principle of Unity is no less true because it appears only once in the Torah. See *Treatise on Resurrection*, tr. H. Fradkin, in R. Lerner, *Maimonides' Empire of Light* (University of Chicago Press, 2000), p. 165.

in Parts i and ii, but in a peripheral text in iii.45, dealing with Sabian errors. In that odd text, Maimonides explains that since the angels, like God, are incorporeal, it was necessary to state "God is one" in order that people not confuse God with them.[41]

Given Strauss's analysis of Maimonides's disjunctive proof of the existence of God, it is reasonable to say that the concept of Unity as incomparability belongs to Jerusalem, while that of Unity as incorporeality belongs to Athens.[42] Nonetheless, Maimonides makes clear in *Guide* iii.45 that the Mosaic proclamation of Unity presupposes incorporeality. Strauss apparently understands Maimonides as teaching that the notion of incomparability, which is the true notion of Unity, is not properly due to Moses (despite Deuteronomy 6:4 and 4:35) but to Isaiah and Jeremiah. The exemplary verses are Isaiah 40:18, 25: "To whom then will ye liken God, or what likeness will ye compare unto Him? . . . To whom then will ye liken Me that I should be equal?"; and Jeremiah 10:6: "There is none like unto Thee, O Lord."[43] Strauss concludes: "Isaiah reached a higher degree in the knowledge of God than did Moses or . . . Isaiah's vision [Isaiah 6:1–5] marks a progress beyond Moses' [Exodus 33:20–25]."[44] The Mosaic theophany concerns the Account of the Beginning (= physics), while the Isaian theophany concerns the more advanced Account of the Chariot (= metaphysics).[45] However, as Strauss also indicates, it follows from *Guide* ii.33 that "unity" as understood in Exodus 20:3 is an intelligible, although "unity" as understood in Deuteronomy 6:4 is not.[46]

Strauss's perspicacious and enigmatic discussion of Maimonides's doctrine of Unity confounds all attempts to distinguish between Jerusalem and Athens. At one point in his discussion, he speaks of "a philosophic exoteric teaching,"[47] a phrase that once would have seemed to him oxymoronic.

---

[41] *Guide* iii.45, pp. 576–577.

[42] See my "Maimonides' Monotheism: Between the Bible and Aristotle," *CISMOR Proceedings* 7 (2013), 56–67.

[43] *Guide* i.55, p. 128.

[44] "How to Begin to Study the *Guide*," p. xxxiii. Cf. *Guide* i.54, pp. 123–128; iii.6, p. 427.

[45] "How to Begin to Study the *Guide*," p. xxxix.

[46] Ibid., p. xxii. Cf. Strauss, "Notes on Maimonides' *Book of Knowledge*," in E. E. Urbach, R. J. Z. Werblowsky, and Ch. Wirszubski (eds.), *Studies in Mysticism and Religion Presented to Gershom G. Scholem* (Jerusalem: Magnes, 1967), pp. 271–272, 279. Reprinted in Strauss, *Studies in Platonic Political Philosophy* (University of Chicago Press, 1983), pp. 194, 201. According to *Guide* ii.33, p. 364, "I" (Exodus 20:2) and "Thou shalt not have" (ibid. 20:3), understood as injunctions to know the existence and unity of God, are the only two *intelligibilia* among the 613 biblical commandments; and thus Deuteronomy 6:4 cannot be counted among the *intelligibilia*. Cf. BT *Makkot* 24a.

[47] "How to Begin to Study the *Guide*," p. xlviii.

## Progress

According to Strauss, as we have seen, Maimonides held that "Isaiah's vision marks a progress beyond Moses'." What kind of ideas about *progress* did he attribute to Maimonides?[48]

In order to explain Maimonides's theory of progress, Strauss cites a passage from his *Treatise on Resurrection,* which was written after the *Guide* and often refers to it. Maimonides observes there that there is no unequivocal affirmation of the doctrine of the resurrection in the Bible until Daniel 12:2, 12. This, he says, is because the earlier biblical books date from the time of the Sabians, when people had no true concept of God and did not believe in miracles. After centuries of education, in the time of Daniel, the people were able to accept the miracle of the resurrection. This shows that in Maimonides's view the atavistic influence of Sabianism on Hebrew religion persisted throughout most of biblical history.[49] "Progress" means "progress in overcoming Sabianism."[50] "[T]he Torah has only one purpose: to destroy Sabianism," but since it was so deeply ingrained among the early Hebrews, it "could be overcome only gradually."[51]

Maimonides, according to Strauss, held that Onqelos and the Talmud represented an intellectual and moral progress beyond the Bible.[52] There has, moreover, been "progress beyond Onqelos and the Talmud."[53] Strauss writes:

> [T]he introduction of philosophy into Judaism [must] be regarded as a great progress, if it is introduced in due subordination to the Law ... as Maimonides introduced it. .... Maimonides regarded the step that he took in the *Guide* as the ultimate step ... in the overcoming of Sabianism. .... He is the man who finally eradicates Sabianism, i.e., corporealism as the hidden premise of idolatry, through the knowledge of Sabianism recovered by him. He recovered that knowledge also through his study of Aristotle, who after all belonged to a Sabian society ... *[T]he Torah for the Perplexed* thus marks a progress beyond the Torah for the Unperplexed.[54]

---

[48] See Tepper, *Progressive Minds, Conservative Politics,* p. 245, s.v. progress. See also his "'Progress' as a Leading Term and Theme in Leo Strauss' 'How to Begin to Study the *Guide*'," in Sh. Wygoda, A. Ackerman, E. Eisenmann, and A. Ravitsky (eds.), *Adam le-Adam* (Jerusalem: Magnes, 2016), pp. 127–151.

[49] "How to Begin to Study the *Guide*," p. xxxiii. Cf. Maimonides, *Treatise on Resurrection* (cited above, n. 40), pp. 169–174.

[50] Ibid., p. xlii.    [51] Ibid., p. xxxv.    [52] Ibid., pp. xxxix–xli.    [53] Ibid., p. xli.

[54] Ibid., pp. xli–xliii. Cf. *Guide* ii.23, p. 322: Aristotle refers to "the ravings of the Sabians" as we refer to "the words of Moses and Abraham." By provocatively translating the title of Maimonides's book as "The Torah for the Perplexed," Strauss suggests that Maimonides's intent in writing it was to revise or perfect Moses's Torah. The transformation of the Mosaic Torah into a Torah *for the Perplexed* was, in Strauss's view, "a great progress." See Maimonides's reference to the word "*torah*" at *Guide* iii.13, p. 453. Cf. Tepper, *Progressive Minds, Conservative Politics,* p. 245, s.v. great progress.

Following Strauss's analysis of Maimonides's views, one can chart the "progress in overcoming Sabianism" from Moses, through Isaiah, through Onqelos and the Talmud, until Maimonides himself. As for Aristotle, it is not at all easy to determine to what extent Maimonides saw him as part of the solution, and to what extent he saw him as part of the problem. Needless to say, much insight into the "progress in the overcoming of Sabianism" may be achieved by examining Maimonides's twofold explanations of biblical terms. Strauss's sagacious reconstruction of Maimonides's theory of progress throws new light on his concept of history and on his notion of the development of the monotheistic religions.

## Limitations of Human Knowledge

The common wisdom among Maimonidean scholars today is that Shlomo Pines, in his later studies, broke with Strauss over the question of the limitations of human knowledge. Pines maintained that according to Maimonides it is impossible for human beings to achieve knowledge of metaphysics or celestial physics, and only knowledge of terrestrial physics is possible.[55] It was generally presumed that Pines's critical interpretation of Maimonides was contrary to Strauss's approach. However, such a presumption cannot be made by anyone who reads Strauss's "How to Begin to Study the *Guide*." Toward the end of the essay, he writes:

> Maimonides is compelled to question the adequacy of Aristotle's account of heaven. That question culminates in the assertions that Aristotle had indeed perfect knowledge of the sublunar things but hardly any knowledge of the things of heaven and ultimately that man as man has no such knowledge: man has knowledge only of the ... earthly things. ... Even the proof of the First Mover ..., i.e., the philosophic proof of God's being, unity, and incorporeality ... becomes a subject of perplexity (ii.22, 24; cf. ii.3, 19; iii.23) ... Maimonides had said ... that very little demonstration is possible regarding divine matters ... Now he seems to suggest that the only genuine science of beings is natural science or a part of it [i.e., terrestrial physics].
>
> It is obvious that one cannot leave it at this apparent suggestion ... [T]he strange remarks ... occur within the context in which Maimonides questions Aristotle's account of heaven in the name of astronomy or, more precisely, in which he sets forth [in *Guide* ii.24] the conflict between

[55] Pines, "The Limitations of Human Knowledge according to Al-Fārābī, Ibn Bājja, and Maimonides," in I. Twersky (ed.), *Studies in Medieval Jewish History and Literature* (Cambridge, MA: Harvard University Press, 1979), pp. 82–109; " Le limites de la métaphysique selon Al-Fārābī, Ibn Bājja, et Maïmonide," *Miscellanea Mediaevalia* 13/1 (1981), pp. 211–225.

philosophic cosmology and mathematical astronomy – that conflict which he calls "the true perplexity": the hypotheses on which astronomy rests cannot be true and yet they alone enable one to give an account of the heavenly phenomena. . . . Astronomy shows the necessity of recurring for the purpose of calculation and prediction to what is possible in a philosophically inadmissible sense.[56]

In this text, Strauss, just like Pines after him, reports that Maimonides was very critical of metaphysics and celestial physics ("man has no such knowledge"), and thought that only knowledge of "earthly things" is possible.

It may be noted that adumbrations of such an interpretation of Maimonides are found in Strauss's early writings. Thus, in his 1945 essay "Fārābī's *Plato*," he writes: "[Alfarabi's] philosophy does not stand or fall with the acceptance of [*substantiae separatae*] . . . [H]is concept of philosophy is not based on any preconceived opinion as to what allegedly real things are truly real things . . . Philosophy . . . is identical with the scientific spirit . . . with *skepsis* . . . with the . . . quest for truth. . . . Only by reading Maimonides' *Guide* against the background of philosophy thus understood, can we hope . . . to fathom its unexplored depths."[57] Already in 1945 Strauss knew that Alfarabi and Maimonides were not committed to Aristotelian metaphysics.

In support of his account of Maimonides's critical views on metaphysics and celestial physics, Strauss cites *Guide* "ii.22, 24; cf. ii.3, 19; iii.23." The citations of ii.3, 19, 22, and 24 are what one would have expected. In ii.3, Maimonides says that Aristotle's opinions on the causes of the motion of the celestial spheres are "simple assertions for which no demonstration has been made."[58] In ii.19, he explains that when Aristotle says in his *De Caelo* that we must study the causes of celestial motion in accordance with "the reach of our intellects ['*uqūlunā*]," he means "our incapacity to assign causes."[59] In ii.22, he asserts that everything Aristotle said about the sublunar realm is correct but what he said about the celestial spheres and the intellects is "analogous to guessing and conjecturing."[60] In ii.24, he reaffirms that Aristotle's terrestrial physics is "in accordance with reasoning" but not his celestial physics, and then writes: "[T]he causes of inference [*al-istidlāl*] regarding the heavens are inaccessible to us . . . and the general inference from them, that they indicate to us their Mover, is

[56] "How to Begin to Study the *Guide*," pp. lv–lvi. The reference to the "true perplexity" is at *Guide* ii.24, p. 326.
[57] Strauss, "Fārābī's *Plato*," in S. Lieberman, Sh. Spiegel, S. Zeitlin, and A. Marx (eds.), *Louis Ginzberg Jubilee Volume* (New York: American Academy for Jewish Research, 1945), pp. 392–393.
[58] *Guide* ii.3, p. 254.    [59] Ibid., ii.19, pp. 308–309.    [60] Ibid., ii.22, pp. 319–320.

indeed a thing whose knowledge our intellects do not reach [*lā taṣilu 'uqūlunā*]" and we must "stop at the point [*falnaqif 'inda al-maqdurah*]" at which our intellects fail.[61]

If Strauss's citation of ii.3, 19, 22, and 24 was predictable, his citation of iii.23 is surprising; for iii.23 does not treat of metaphysics or celestial physics, but only of terrestrial physics. Maimonides writes there: "[R]egarding the natural things that exist in the world of generation and corruption, our intellects do not reach [*lā taṣilu 'uqūlunā*] the apprehension of how they come into being, nor the conception of the principle of the natural force within them ... We must stop at this point [*al-wuqūf 'inda ... al-qadr*] ... This is the object of the Book of Job ... to note the inference [*al-istidlāl*] to be drawn from natural things ... so that you not err and seek to affirm that ... His governance is like our governance."[62] This passage closely parallels the passage cited from ii.24, and says about terrestrial physics what the passage from ii.24 said about celestial physics. Both passages allude to ii.19; both use the expression "our intellects do not reach"; both urge that we "stop at the point" where our intellects fail; and both refer to an "inference." In citing iii.23, Strauss hints that Maimonides's critical epistemology extends to terrestrial physics and is not restricted to metaphysics and celestial physics. This radical interpretation of Maimonides's critical epistemology goes way beyond Pines, whose remarks on "the limitations of knowledge" in Maimonides concerned only metaphysics and celestial physics.[63] Strauss, however, does not make any comments about the relationship between ii.24 and iii.23, and remains silent about the significance of iii.23.

Having duly presented Maimonides's critical ideas, Strauss unexpectedly recoils (or pretends to recoil) at "the strange remarks." It is as if he does not for some reason want to portray Maimonides as too much of a skeptic. He now insinuates that Maimonides exaggerated his critique of Aristotelian celestial physics in order to defend Ptolemaic astronomy, which contradicted Aristotelian celestial physics but gave an accurate and eminently useful mathematical account of the stellar motions.[64] This

[61] Ibid., ii.24, pp. 326–327. The reading *'uqūlunā* ("our intellects") is found in the Istanbul ms. (written in 1478); see my "Maimonides' Critical Epistemology," p. 235, n. 50. The printed editions of the Arabic text read *'uqūl insān* ("human intellects").

[62] *Guide* iii.23, pp. 496–497. The importance of this text was recognized by Rabbi Shemtov Falaquera, a philosopher well known to Strauss. See my "Maimonides' Critical Epistemology," pp. 234–235.

[63] J. Stern, *The Matter and Form of Maimonides' Guide*, Cambridge, MA: Harvard University Press, 2013, p. 345, likewise describes Maimonides's skepticism as concerning "metaphysics and cosmology," but not "sublunar natural science."

[64] Pines, Translator's Introduction to the *Guide*, p. cxi, n. 89, argued that Maimonides exaggerated his doubts about Greek science in order to impugn the doctrine of eternity.

insinuation, together with Strauss's silence regarding the meaning of his citation of iii.23, encourages the dubious opinion that Maimonides's primary commitment was to Aristotelian philosophy and physics. That such was his primary commitment seems to be presumed in Strauss's final comment about Ptolemaic astronomy and Aristotelian celestial physics. He reverts suddenly to his old Jerusalem–Athens dichotomy. Religion, like Ptolemaic astronomy, is instrumentally necessary, but philosophically inadmissible. He nonetheless mentions *en passant* that the conflict between Ptolemaic astronomy and Aristotelian celestial physics (and *not* that between Revelation and Reason) is called by Maimonides in *Guide* ii.24 "the true perplexity."

## Stopping at the Halfway Point

Strauss's chapter-by-chapter (or, more precisely, subsection-by-subsection) exposition of the *Guide* began with i.1 ("image and likeness") and ends abruptly with ii.24 ("the true perplexity"). The exposition is cut off without warning at what may be said to be the *Guide*'s halfway point. Part ii is the middle of the book's three Parts, and ii.24 concludes the first half of the middle Part's 48 chapters. It also concludes the subsection on the "Creation of the world" (ii.13–24).[65] Aryeh Tepper calls ii.24 "the peak" of the *Guide*, and opines: "[T]he true perplexity ... forms the fitting end of Strauss' essay."[66] The *Guide*, according to Tepper, progresses from "imagined perplexity" (i.1) to "true perplexity" (ii.24).[67] In any case, it is striking that Strauss's exposition covers only the first half of the *Guide*.

## Perplexity and Enchantment

Strauss concludes "How to Begin to Study the *Guide*" with an apology: "We have been compelled to put a greater emphasis on Maimonides' perplexities than on his certainties." He justifies this emphasis on two counts: first, the perplexities are less "accessible" than the certainties; and second, liberation always contains "a negative ingredient."[68] In this regard, it should not be forgotten that Strauss's exposition of the *Guide* ends with the chapter treating of the "true perplexity."

[65] See Tepper, *Progressive Minds, Conservative Politics*, pp. 26–27, 29, 42–43, 120–130.
[66] Ibid., p. 126. Cf. pp. 43, 127.     [67] Ibid., p. 126.
[68] "How to Begin to Study the *Guide*," p. lvi.

We can only be grateful to Strauss for his explications of Maimonides's perplexities. As we have seen, the perplexities are of many different kinds and not restricted to the Jerusalem–Athens dichotomy. Some of them, like the ones associated with the "twofold character" of Maimonides's explanation of biblical terms, were not noticed by modern scholars before Strauss.

# Bibliography

## Primary Sources

Al-Ash'arī, 'Alī Ibn Ismā'īl. *The Theology of Al-Ash'arī: The Arabic Texts of Al-Ash 'arī's Kitāb Al-Luma' and Risālat Istiḥsān al-Khawḍ fī 'Ilm al-Kalām*, ed. and tr. R. McCarthy (Beirut: Catholic Press, 1953).

Al-Ash'arī, 'Alī Ibn Ismā'īl. "Creed," tr. in D. MacDonald, *Development of Muslim Theology* (New York: Russell and Russell, 1965) 293–299.

Albertus Magnus. *Opera omnia*, ed. Borgnet (Paris, 1890–1899).

Averroes. *Talkhīṣ kitāb al-ḥiss wa-al-maḥsūs*, ed. H. Blumberg (Cambridge, MA: Medieval Academy of America, 1961).

Averroes. *Epitome of Parva Naturalia*, tr. H. Blumberg (Cambridge, MA: Medieval Academy of America, 1961).

Averroes. *Averroes: On the Harmony of Religion and Philosophy*, tr. and ed. G. F. Hourani (London: Lousac/E. J. W. Gibb Memorial Trust, 1961).

Averroes. *Talkhīṣ kitāb al-nafs*, ed. A. F. al-Ahwani (Cairo: Maktaba al-Nahḍa al-Miṣriya, 1950).

Avicenna. *The Metaphysics of the Healing: a Parallel English-Arabic text*, tr. and ed. Michael Marmura (Provo, Utah: Brigham Young University Press, 2005).

Avicenna. *Avicenna's De Anima: Being the Psychological Part of Kitāb al-Shifā'*, ed. Fazlur Rahman (London: Oxford University Press, 1959).

Baḥya ibn Paquda. *Torat Ḥovot ha-Levavot*, ed. and Heb. tr. J. Qafiḥ (Jerusalem: Aqiba Joseph, 1972/3).

Baḥya ibn Paquda. *Al-Hidāja 'ilā Farā'iḍ al-Qulūb des Bachja Ibn Josef Ibn Paqūda aus Andalusien*, ed. A. S. Yahuda (Leiden: E. J. Brill, 1912).

Bahya ibn Paquda. *Ḥovot ha-Levavot*, tr. Judah Ibn Tibbon, ed. A. Zifroni (Jerusalem, 1928).

Crescas, Hasdai. *Or Adonai*, ed. Shlomo Fisher (Jerusalem: Ramot, 1990).

Falaquera, Shem Tov ben Jose. *Moreh ha-Moreh*, ed. Y. Shiffman (Jerusalem: World Union of Jewish Studies, 2001).

Gersonides, Levi ben Gershom. *The Wars of the Lord vol. 2* tr. S. Feldman (Philadelphia, New York, Jerusalem: Jewish Publication Society, 1987).

Al-Ghazālī. *Al-Ghazālī on Patience and Thankfulness: Book XXXIII of the Revival of the Religious Sciences*, tr. H. T. Littlejohn (Great Shelford: The Islamic Texts Society, 2011).

Al-Ghazālī. *Maqāṣid al-Falāsifa*, ed. M. Bejou (Damascus: Maṭbaʿa al-Ḍabbāḥ, 2000).
Al-Ghazālī. *Maqāṣid al-Falāsifa* (Cairo n.d).
Al-Ghazālī. *Tahāfut al-Falāsifa*, ed. M. Bouyges (Beyrouth: Imprimerie catholique, 1927).
Giles of Rome. *Errores philosophorum*, tr. J. O. Riedl, ed. J. Koch (Milwaukee: Marquette University Press, 1944).
*Halachot Kezuboth*, ed. M. Margulies (Jerusalem: Hebrew University Press, 1942).
Isaac Abarbanel. *Perush ha-Torah* (Jerusalem: Bene Arba'el, 1964).
Isaac Arama. *Aqedat Yitshaq*, 5 vols. (Pressburg: Victor Kitseer, 1849).
Joseph ibn Gikatilla. *Sefer ha-Hassagot*, printed with Abarbanel, "responses to Saul ha-Kohen" (Venice, 1574).
Karo, Joseph. *Shulḥan 'Arukh: Oraḥ Ḥayyim* (Warsaw: A. Baumberg, 1861).
*Medieval Jewish Philosophical Writings*, tr. and ed. C. Manekin (Cambridge: Cambridge University Press, 2007).
Melloni, G. B. *Atti o memorie degli uomini illustri in Santità nati o morti in Bologna raccolte e illustrate da Giambattista Melloni* (1713–1781), ed. A. Benati and M. Fanti (Rome: Multigrafica, 1971).
*Midrash Otiyot de-Rabbi Akiva*, ed. S. Wertheimer. Jerusalem, Y. D. Frumkin, 1914.
*Midrash Tanḥuma* (Warsaw: Unterhendler, 1877).
*Mishnat Rabi Eliezer o midrash sheloshim u-shetayim middot*, ed. H. G. Enelow (New York, 1933).
Moses Maimonides. *Medical Aphorisms, Treatises 16–21*, ed. and tr. G. Bos (Provo: Brigham Young University Press, 2015).
Moses Maimonides. *Medical Aphorisms, Treatises 6–9*, ed. and tr. G. Bos (Provo: Brigham Young University Press, 2007).
Moses Maimonides. *Mishneh Torah (Code of Law)*, ed. Z. Frankel, 14 vols. (Jerusalem, 1975–2007).
Moses Maimonides. *On Asthma*, ed. and tr. G. Bos (Provo: Brigham Young University Press, 2002).
Moses Maimonides. *Haqdamot ha-Rambam la-Mishnah*, ed. I. Shailat (Jerusalem: Maaliyot, 1992).
Moses Maimonides. *Iggerot ha-Rambam*, ed. I. Shailat (Jerusalem: Maaliyot, 1988).
Moses Maimonides. *Iggerot: Maqor ve-Targum*, ed. Y. Kafih (Jerusalem: Mossad ha-Rav Kook, 1987).
Moses Maimonides. *Crisis and Leadership: Epistles of Maimonides*, tr. A. S. Halkin, with essays by D. Hartman (Philadelphia: Jewish Publication Society of America, 1985).
Moses Maimonides. *Perush ha-Mishnah*, 7 vols., ed. and Hebrew tr. J. Kafah (Jerusalem: Mosad Harav Kook, 1963–1968).
Moses Maimonides, *Le Guide des égares*, tr. and ed. S. Munk (Paris: 1856–66, repr. Paris 1960 and Osnabrück 1964), 3 vols.
Moses Maimonides. *The Guide of the Perplexed*, tr. S. Pines, with introductions by L. Strauss and S. Pines (University of Chicago Press, 1963).

Moses Maimonides. *Teshuvot ha-Rambam*, ed. and tr. J. Blau (Jerusalem: Mekitsei Nirdamim, 1957–1961).

Moses Maimonides. *Moreh Nevukhim be-ha'ataqat ha-Rav Shmuel ibn Tibbon im arba'a perushim* (Jerusalem, 1960).

Moses Maimonides. *Pirqei Mosheh*, ed. S. Muntner (Jerusalem: Mosad Harav Kook, 1959).

Moses Maimonides. *The Code of Maimonides: Book Eight: The Book of Temple Service*, tr. Mendell Lewittes (New Haven: Yale University Press, 1957)

Moses Maimonides. *Iggerot ha-Rambam: mikhtevei Mosheh ben Maimon u-mikhtevei benei doro 'elav*, ed. D. H. Baneth (Jerusalem: Meqiẓe Nirdamim, 1946).

Moses Maimonides. *Treatise on Resurrection. Arabic original and medieval Hebrew translation*, ed. J. Finkel (New York: American Academy for Jewish Research, 1939).

Moses Maimonides. *Dalālat al-Ḥā'irīn*, ed. S. Munk and I. Joel (Jerusalem: Junovitch, 1930/31).

Moses Maimonides. *Dux seu director dubitantium aut perplexorum*, ed. Augustinus Iustinianus (Parisiis, 1520).

Moses Narboni. *Be'ur Narboni*, ed. J. Goldenthal (Vienna, 1852).

Al-Muqammiṣ, Dāwūd. *Twenty Chapters*, ed. and tr. S. Stroumsa (Leiden: Brill, 1989).

Raimundus Martini. *Ordinis Praedicatorum Pugio Fidei adversus Mauros et Judaeos cum observationibus Josephi de Voisin, et introductione Jo. Benedicti Carpzovi* (Leipzig: Friederich Lanckis, 1687).

Roland of Cremona, *Summa Theologica*, Ms. Paris, Bibliothèque Mazarine, Cod. lat. 795.

Saadia Gaon. *Siddur R. Saadja Gaon*, ed. I. Davidson, S. Assaf, and B. I. Joel (Jerusalem: Rubin Mass, 2000).

Saadia Gaon. *Emunot ve-De'ot*, tr. Judah Ibn Tibbon (Warsaw, 1894).

Saadia Gaon. *Sefer ha-Yerushot*, ed. Y. Miller (Jerusalem, 1967/1968).

Thomas Aquinas. *Opera omnia*, ed. Leonine Commission (Rome: Commissio Leonina, 1882).

Ibn Tibbon, Samuel. *Ma'amar Yiqqavu ha-Mayim*, ed. M. Bischeles (Pressburg: Anton Edlen v. Schmidt, 1837).

Ibn Tumart. *Livre de Mohammed Ibn Toumert: Mahdi des Almohades*, ed. I. Goldziher (Algiers: Imprimerie Orientale Pierre Fontana, 1903).

William of Auvergne. *Opera omnia*, ed. B. Le Feron (Paris, 1674; repr. Frankfurt: Minerva, 1963).

## Secondary Sources

Abramson, Sh. *Inyanot bi-Sifrut ha-Geonim* (Jerusalem: Mosad Harav Kook, 1974).

Adamson, P. *Al-Kindī* (New York: Oxford University Press, 2007).

Adamson, P. "Knowledge of Universals and Particulars in the Baghdad School," *Documenti e Studi sulla Tradizione Filosofica Medievale* 18 (2007) 141–164.

Adamson, P. "On Knowledge of Particulars," *Proceedings of the Aristotelian Society* 105 (2005) 273–294.

Altmann, A. "The Ladder of Ascension," in Urbach, Werblowski and Wirszubski (eds.), *Studies in Mysticism and Religion Presented to Gershom G. Scholem on his Seventieth Birthday by Pupils, Colleagues and Friends* (Jerusalem: Magnes Press, 1967) 1–32.

Altmann, A. "Maimonides and Thomas Aquinas: Natural or Divine prophecy?" *AJS Review*, 3 (1978) 1–19.

Altmann, A. *Saadya Gaon: The Book of Doctrines and Beliefs, Abridged Edition* (Oxford: Phaidon Press, 1946).

Al-Akiti, M. Afifi. "The Good, the Bad and the Ugly of Falsafa: Al-Ghazālī's *Madnūn, Tahāfut*, and *Maqāṣid*, with Particular Attention to the Falsafī Treatments of God's Knowledge of Temporal Events," in Y. Tzvi Langermann (ed.), *Avicenna and His Legacy: A Golden Age of Science and Philosophy* (Turnhout: Brepols, 2009) 51–100.

Bello, C. "Averroes on God's Knowledge of Particulars," *Journal of Islamic Studies* 17 (2006) 177–199.

Berman, L. V. "Maimonides on the Fall of Man," *AJS Review* 5 (1980) 1–15.

Berman, L. V. "Maimonides the Disciple of Alfarabi," *Israel Oriental Studies* 4 (1974) 154–178.

Bianchi, L. *L'errore di Aristotele. La polemica contro l'eternità del mondo nel XIII secolo* (Firenze: La Nuova Italia, 1984).

Black, D. "Knowledge ('Ilm) and Certitude (Yaqīn) in Al-Farabi's Epistemology," *Arabic Sciences and Philosophy* 16 (2006) 11–45.

Bland, K. "Moses and the Law According to Maimonides," in Jehuda Reinharz and Daniel Swetschinski, Kalman P. Bland (eds.), *Mystics, Philosophers and Politicians: Essays in Jewish Intellectual History in Honor of Alexander Altmann* (Durham, NC: Duke University Press, 1982) 49–66.

Blau, J. *Dictionary of Medieval Judaeo-Arabic Texts* (Jerusalem: Academy of Hebrew Language, Israel Academy of Science and Humanities, 2006).

Blidstein, G. "The 'Other' in Maimonidean Law," *Jewish History* 18 (2004) 173–195.

Blidstein, Y. (G.). "On the Status of the Resident-Alien in Maimonides' Thought," *Sinai* 101 (1988) 44–52. (Heb.)

Broadie, A. "Maimonides and Aquinas on the Names of God," *Religious Studies* 23 (1987) 157–170.

Buijs, J. A. "The Negative Theology of Maimonides and Aquinas," *Review of Metaphysics* 41 (1988) 723–738.

Burrell, D. B. *Knowing the Unknowable God: Ibn-Sina, Maimonides, Aquinas* (South Bend, IN: University of Notre Dame Press, 1986).

Chiesa, B. "Dawud al-Muqammis e la sua opera," *Henoch* 18 (1996) 121–156.

Cohen, M. *Opening the Gates of Interpretation: Maimonides' Biblical Hermeneutics in Light of His Geonic-Andalusian Heritage and Muslim Milieu* (Leiden: Brill, 2011).

Dahan, G. "L'exégèse de la Bible chez Guillaume d'Auvergne," in F. Morenzoni and J.-Y. Tilliette (eds.), *Autour de Guillaume d'Auvergne* (Turnhout: Brepols, 2015) 237–270.

Dales, C. "Maimonides and Boethius of Dacia on the Eternity of the World," *The New Scholasticism* 56 (1982) 306–319.

Davidson, H. "Ibn al-Qifṭī's Statement Regarding Maimonides' Early Study of Science," *Aleph* 14 (2014) 245–258.

Davidson, H. *Maimonides the Rationalist* (Oxford: Littman Library of Jewish Civilization, 2011).

Davidson, H. *Moses Maimonides, the Man and His Works* (New York: Oxford University Press, 2005).

Davidson, H. *Proofs for Eternity, Creation, and the Existence of God, in Medieval Islamic and Jewish Philosophy* (New York: Oxford University Press, 1987).

Davidson, H. "Maimonides' Secret Position on Creation," in I. Twersky (ed.), *Studies in Medieval Jewish History and Literature* (Cambridge, MA: Harvard University Press, 1979) 16–40.

Davies, D. "Reason, Will, and Purpose: What's at Stake for Maimonides and His Followers in the Doctrine of Creation," in Anderson and Bockmuehl (eds.), *Creation ex Nihilo: Origins, Development, Contemporary Challenges* (Notre Dame: University of Notre Dame Press, 2017) 213–231.

Davies, D. *Method and Metaphysics in Maimonides' Guide for the Perplexed* (New York: Oxford University Press, 2011).

Di Segni, D. *Moses Maimonides and the Latin Middle Ages. Critical edition of Dux neutrorum I, 1–59, Inauguraldissertation zur Erlangung des Doktorgrades der Philosophischen Fakultät der Universität zu Köln im Fach Philosophie, Digitalpublikation* (Köln: Universität zu Köln, 2013).

Di Segni, D. "Traces of a Vernacular Language in the Latin Translation of Maimonides' *Guide of the Perplexed*," *Recherches de Théologie et Philosophie médiévales* 83 (2016) 21–48.

Di Segni, D. "'verba sunt Rabbi Moysis': Eckhart e Maimonide," in L. Sturlese (ed.), *Studi sulle fonti di Meister Eckhart*, vol. II (Fribourg: Dokimion, 2013) 99–135.

Diamond, J. A. *Maimonides and the Hermeneutics of Concealment: Deciphering Scripture and Midrash in the Guide of the Perplexed* (Albany: SUNY Press, 2002).

Diamond, J. "'Trial' as Esoteric Preface in Maimonides' *Guide of the Perplexed*: A Case Study in the Interplay of Text and Prooftext," *The Journal of Jewish Thought and Philosophy* 7 (1997) 1–30.

Dienstag, J. I. "Maimonides in English Christian Thought and Scholarship: An Alphabetical Survey," *Hebrew Studies* 26 (1985) 249–299.

Dienstag, J. I. *Studies in Maimonides and St. Thomas Aquinas* (New York: Ktav, 1975).

Diesendruck, Z. "Samuel and Moses ibn Tibbon on Maimonides' Theory of Providence," *Hebrew Union College Annual* 11 (1936) 341–366.

Diesendruck, Z. "Die Teleologie bei Maimonides," *Hebrew Union College Annual,* 5 (1928) 419–42

Dobbs-Weinstein, I. "Maimonides' Reticence toward Ibn Sīnā," in J. Janssens and D. De Smit (eds.), *Avicenna and His Heritage* (Leuven University Press, 2002) 281–296.

Dobbs-Weinstein, I. "Medieval Biblical Commentary and Philosophical Inquiry as Exemplified in the Thought of Moses Maimonides and St. Thomas Aquinas," in E. Ormsby (ed.), *Moses Maimonides and His Time* (Washington: The Catholic University of America Press, 1989) 101–120.

Dunphy, W. "Maimonides and Aquinas on Creation. A Critique of their Historians," in L. P. Gerson (ed.), *Graceful Reason, Essays in Ancient and Medieval Philosophy Presented to Joseph Owens* (Toronto: Pontifical Institute of Mediaeval Studies, 1983) 361–379.

Efrati, S. *The Lexicographic Chapters of the First Part of the* Guide of the Perplexed (Heb.), doctoral dissertation, Bar-Ilan University, 2016.

Eisen, R. *The Book of Job in Medieval Jewish Philosophy* (New York: Oxford University Press, 2004).

Eisenmann, E. "The Term 'Created Light' in Maimonides' Philosophy," *Daat: A Journal of Jewish Philosophy & Kabbalah* 55 (2005) 41–57.

Elders, L. J. "Les rapports entre la doctrine de la prophétie selon Saint Thomas et le Guide des égarés de Maïmonide," *Divus Thomas* 78 (1975) 449–456.

*Encyclopaedia of Islam*, second edition 12 vols. (Leiden: E. J. Brill, 1960–2005).

Eran, Amira. "Al-Ghazālī and Maimonides on the World to Come and Spiritual Pleasures," *Jewish Studies Quarterly* 8 (2001) 137–166.

Even-Chen, A. "Of the Divine Knowledge and the Rational–Emotional Experience of the Known Single, Under Providence, and the Beloved in *The Guide of the Perplexed* [sic]," (Heb.) *Daat* 74–75 (2013) 105–134.

Feldman, S. *Gersonides: Judaism within the Limits of Reason* (Oxford: The Littman Library of Jewish Civilization, 2010).

Feldman, S. "The Binding of Isaac," in T. Rudavsky (ed.), *Divine Omniscience and Omnipotence in Medieval Philosophy* (Dordrecht, Boston, Lancaster, 1985).

Feldman, S. "A Scholastic Misinterpretation of Maimonides' Doctrine of Divine Attributes," *Journal of Jewish Studies* 19 (1968) 23–39.

Fenton, P. "Les traces d'Al-Hallag, martyr mystique de l'islam, dans la tradition juive," *Annales Islamologiques* 35 (2001) 101–127.

Filthaut, E. *Roland von Cremona O.P. und die Anfänge der Scholastik im Predigerorden: ein Beitrag zur Geistesgeschichte der älteren Dominikaner* (Vechta i. O.: Albertus-Magnus-Verlag, 1936).

Flasch, K. *Aufklärung im Mittelalter?: Die Verurteilung von 1277* (Mainz: Dieterich, 1989).

Forte, D. "Back to the Sources: Alternative Versions of Maimonides' Letter to Samuel Ibn Tibbon and Their Neglected Significance," *Jewish Studies Quarterly* 23 (2016) 47–90.

Fraenkel, C. *Min Ha-Rambam le-Shemu'el ibn Tibbon* (Jerusalem: Magnes, 2007).

Fraenkel, C. "Maimonides' God and Spinoza's Deus sive Natura," *Journal of the History of Philosophy* 44 (2006) 169–215.

Freudenthal, G. "Maïmonide: La détermination biologique et climatologique (partielle) de la félicité humaine," in T. Lévy and R. Rashed (eds.), *Maïmonide: Philosophe et Savant (1138–1204)* (Leuven: Peeters, 2004) 81–129.

Freudenthal, G. "Pour le dossier de la traduction latine médiévale du Guide des égarés," *Revue des études juives* 147 (1988) 167–172.

Goldman, E. "On the End of Existence in the Moreh Nevukhim," in A. Kasher and Y. Lewinger (eds.), *Sefer Yeša'yahu Leibowicz* (Tel-Aviv: Agudat ha-studentim, 1977) 164–191 (Heb.).

Goodman, M. *Maimonides and the Book That Changed Judaism: Secrets of the Guide for the Perplexed* (Philadelphia: Jewish Publication Society, 2015).

Gopnik, A. "Could David Hume Have Known about Buddhism? Charles François Dolu, the Royal College of La Flèche, and the Global Jesuit Intellectual Network," *Hume Studies* 35 (2009) 5–28.

Green, K. H. *Leo Strauss and the Rediscovery of Maimonides* (University of Chicago Press, 2013).

Griffel, F. *Al-Ghazālī's Philosophical Theology* (Oxford University Press, 2009).

Griffel, F. "Al-Ghazālī's Cosmology in the Veil Section of his *Mishkāt al-Anwār*," in Y. Tzvi Langermann (ed.), *Avicenna and his Legacy: A Golden Age of Science and Philosophy* (Turnhout: Brepols, 2009) 27–50.

Griffel, F. "Ibn Tumart's Rational Proof for God's Existence and His Unity: And his Connection to the Niẓāmiyya 'Madrasa' in Baġdad," in P. Cressier, M. Fierro, and L. Molina (eds.), *Los Almohades: Problemas y Perspectivas* (Madrid: Consejo Superior de Investigaciones Científicas, 2005) 753–813.

Grossman, A. *Ve-hu yimshol bakh?: ha-ishah be-mishnatam shel ḥakhmei Yisrael bi-yeme ha-benayim (And He Shall Rule Over You? Medieval Jewish Sages on Women)* (Jerusalem: Zalman Shazar Center, 2011).

Guttmann, J. *Die Philosophie des Judentums* (München: Ernst Reinhardt, 1933).

Guttmann, J. "Guillaume d'Auvergne et la littérature juive," *Revue des études juives*, 18 (1889) 243–255.

Halbertal, M. *Maimonides: Life and Thought* (Princeton University Press, 2014).

Harvey, S. "Alghazali and Maimonides and their Books of Knowledge," in Jay M. Harris (ed.), *Be'erot Yitzhak; Studies in Memory of Isadore Twersky* (Cambridge, MA: Harvard University Press, 2005) 99–117.

Harvey, S. "Maimonides in the Sultan's Palace," in Joel L. Kraemer (ed.), *Perspectives on Maimonides* (Oxford University Press, 1991) 50–64.

Harvey, W. Z. "Maimonides' *Guide of the Perplexed*: An Enchanted Book of Puzzles," in Stuart W. Halpern (ed.), *Books of the People* (New Milford: Maggid, 2017) 44–48.

Harvey, W. Z. "Spinoza and Maimonides on Teleology and Anthropomorphism," in Y. Melamed (ed.), *Spinoza's Ethics. A Critical Guide* (Cambridge: Cambridge University Press, 2017) 43–55.

Harvey, W. Z. "Maimonides' Monotheism: Between the Bible and Aristotle," *CISMOR Proceedings* 7 (2013) 56–67.

Harvey, W. Z. "Les nœuds du Guide des égarés: une critique de la lecture politique de Leo Strauss," in Géraldine Roux (ed.), *Lumières médiévales* (Paris: Van Dieren, 2009) 163–176.

Harvey, W. Z. "Maimonides Critical Epistemology and Guide ii.24" *Aleph* 8 (2008) 228–230.

Harvey, W. Z. "How Leo Strauss Paralyzed the Study of the *Guide of the Perplexed* in the Twentieth Century," *Iyyun* 50 (2001) 387–396 (Heb.).

Harvey, W. Z. *Physics and Metaphysics in Hasdai Crescas* (Amsterdam: Gieben, 1998).

Harvey, W. Z. "Maimonides and Aquinas on Interpreting the Bible," *Proceedings of the American Academy for Jewish Research* 55 (1988) 59–77.

Harvey, W. Z. "Maimonides' Interpretation of Gen. 3:22," *Da'at* 12 (1984) 15–22 (Heb.).

Harvey, W. Z. "The Obligation of Talmud on Women According to Maimonides," *Tradition* 19 (1981) 122–130.

Harvey, W. Z. "A Portrait of Spinoza as a Maimonidean," *Journal of the History of Philosophy* 19 (1981) 151–172.

Harvey, W. Z. "Maimonides and Spinoza on the Knowledge of Good and Evil," *Iyyun* 28 (1978) pp. 167–185.

Harvey, W. Z. "Nissim of Gerona and William of Ockham on Prime Matter," *Jewish History* 6 (1992), 88–98.

Hasselhoff, G. *Dicit Rabbi Moyses: Studien zum Bild von Moses Maimonides im Lateinischen Westen vom 13. bis zum 15. Jahrhundert* (Würzburg: Königshausen & Neumann, 2004).

Hasselhoff, G. "Anmerkungen zur Rezeption des Maimonides in den Schriften des Thomas von Aquino," in W. Kinzig and C. Kück (eds.), *Zwischen Konfrontation und Faszination: Ansätze zu einer neuen Beschreibung jüdisch-christlicher Beziehungen* (Stuttgart: Kohlhammer, 2002) 55–73.

Hasselhoff, G. "The Reception of Maimonides in the Latin World: the Evidence of the Latin Translations in the 13th–15th Century," *Materia giudaica* 6 (2001) 258–280.

Heidrich, P. *Im Gespräch mit Meister Eckhart und Maimonides*, ed. H. M. Niemann (Berlin: Lit Verlag, 2010).

Henshke, D. "The Commandments of the Forefathers and the Commandments of Sinai: The Case of the Sciatic Nerve as a Chapter in Maimonides' Halakhic Conception," in N. Rabinovich, Z. Hever, and K. Kohen (eds.), *Mi-Birkat Moshe: Qovez maamarim be-mishnat ha-Rambam li-khevodo shel ha-Rav Nahum Eliezer Rabinovich* (Ma'aleh Adumim: Maaliyot, 2011).

Heschel, A. J. *Heavenly Torah as Refracted Through the Generations*, ed. and tr. G. Tucker with L. Levin (New York/London: Continuum, 2005).

Hissette, R. *Enquête sur les 219 articles condamnés à Paris le 7 Mars 1277* (Louvain, Vander-Oyez, Paris: Publications Universitaires, 1977).

Hofer, N. "Scriptural Substitutions and Anonymous Citations: Judaization as Rhetorical Strategy in a Jewish Sufi Text" *Numen* 61 (2014) 364–395.

Hyman, A. "Demonstrative, Dialectical, and Sophistical Arguments in the Philosophy of Maimonides," in E. Ormsby (ed.), *Moses Maimonides and His Time* (Washington, D.C.: Catholic University of America Press, 1989) 35–51.

Hyman, A. "Maimonides on Causality," in S. Pines and Y. Yovel (eds.), *Maimonides and Philosophy* (Dordrecht: Martinus Nijhoff, 1986) 157–172.

Idel, M. *Studies in Ecstatic Kabbalah* (Albany: State University of New York Press, 1988).

Imbach, R. "Alcune precisazioni sulla presenza di Maimonide in Tommaso," in D. Lorenz and S. Serafini (eds.), *Istituto san Tommaso: Studi 1995* (Roma: Pontificia Università S. Tommaso d'Aquino, 1995) 48–64.

Imbach, R. "Ut ait Rabbi Moyses. Maimonidische Philosopheme bei Thomas von Aquin und Meister Eckhart," *Collectanea Franciscana* 60 (1990) 99–116.

Ivry, A. L. *Maimonides' Guide of the Perplexed: A Philosophical Guide* (Chicago/London: University of Chicago Press, 2016).

Ivry, A. L. "Leo Strauss and Maimonides," in A. Udoff (ed.), *Leo Strauss' Thought* (Boulder: Reinner, 1991) 87–123.

Ivry, A. "Providence, Divine Omniscience and Possibility: The Case of Maimonides," in T. Rudavsky (ed.), *Divine Omniscience and Omnipotence in Medieval Philosophy* (Dordrecht: Reidel Publishing, 1985) 143–159.

Ivry, A. "Maimonides on Possibility," in Reinharr and Schwetschinski (eds.), *Mystics, Philosophers, and Politicians: Essays in Jewish Intellectual History in Honor of Alexander Altmann* (Durham: Duke University Press, 1982) 67–84.

Joel, M. *Verhältniss Albert des Grossen zu Moses Maimonides: Ein Beitrag zur Geschichte der mittelalterlichen Philosophie* (Breslau: Schletter'schen Buchhandlung, 1863).

Jospe, R. and D. Schwartz (eds.) *Jewish Philosophy: Perspectives and Retrospectives* (Brighton: Academic Studies Press, 2012).

Kaplan, L. "Hermann Cohen and Rabbi Soloveitchik on Repentance," *Journal of Jewish Thought and Philosophy* 13 (2004) 213–258.

Kaplan, L. "I Sleep but My Heart Waketh: Maimonides' Conception of Human Perfection," in Ira Robinson, Lawrence Kaplan, and Julien Bauer (eds.), *The Thought of Moses Maimonides: Philosophical and Legal Studies* (Lewiston, NY: E. Mellen Press, 1990) 130–166.

Kasher, H. *'Al ha-minim, ha-epikorsim, ve-ha-koferim be-mishnat ha-Rambam* (Heretics in Maimonides' Teaching) (Tel-Aviv: Hakibbutz Hameuchad, 2011).

Kasher, H. *"Sufferings Without Transgression," (Heb.)* Daat 26 (1991) 35–41.

Kasher, H. "Maimonides' Interpretation of the Story of the Cleft of the Rock," *Daat* 35 (1995) 29–66 (Heb.).

Kellner, M. M. *Gam hem qeruyim adam: ha-nokhri be-'einei ha-Rambam* (They, Too, are Called Human: Gentiles in the Eyes of Maimonides), (Ramat Gan: Bar Ilan University Press, 2016).

Kellner, M. M. "Philosophical Misogyny in Medieval Jewish Philosophy – Gersonides v. Maimonides," in A. Ravitzky (ed.), *Me-Romi li-Yerushalayim:*

*sefer zikaron le-Yosef-Barukh Sermoneṭah (Joseph Baruch Sermoneta Memorial Volume)*, *Jerusalem Studies in Jewish Thought* 14 (1998) 113–128.

Klein-Braslavy, S. *Maimonides as Biblical Interpreter* (Boston, MA: Academic Studies Press, 2011).

Klein-Braslavy, S. "Bible Commentary," in K. Seeskin (ed.), *The Cambridge Companion to Maimonides* (Cambridge University Press, 2005) 261–268.

Klein-Braslavy, S. "Maimonides' Interpretation of the Verb 'Bara' and the Creation of the World," *Daat* 16 (1986) 39–55 (Heb.).

Klein-Braslavy, S. *Maimonides' Interpretation of the Adam Stories in Genesis – A Study in Maimonides' Anthropology* (Jerusalem: Rubin Mass, 1986) (Heb.).

Klein-Braslavy, S. *Maimonides' Interpretation of the Story of Creation* (Jerusalem: Aḥvah, 1978) (Heb.).

Klein, S. "Maimonides' Interpretations of Jacob's Dream about the Ladder," *Bar-Ilan Year Book* 22–23 (1988) 329–349 (Heb.).

Kluxen, W. "Maïmonide et l'orientation philosophique de ses lecteurs latins," in T. Levy and R. Rashed (eds.), *Maïmonide philosophe et savant (1138–1204)* (Louvain-Paris: Peeters, 2004) 395–409.

Kluxen, W. "Maimonides and Latin Scholasticism," in S. Pines and Y. Yovel (eds.), *Maimonides and Philosophy* (Dordrecht: Martinus Nijhoff Publishers, 1986) 224–232.

Kluxen, W. "Die Geschichte des Maimonides im lateinischen Abendland als Beispiel einer christlich-jüdischen Begegnung," in P. Wilpert (ed.), *Judentum im Mittelalter* 146–66.

Kluxen, W. "Maimonides und die Hochscholastik," *Philosophisches Jahrbuch der Görresgesellschaft* 63 (1955) 151–165.

Kluxen, W. "Literargeschichtliches zum lateinischen Moses Maimonides," *Recherches de théologie ancienne et médiévale* 21 (1954) 23–50.

Koch, J. *Kleine Schriften*, vol. I (Roma: Edizioni di Storia e Letteratura, 1973).

Koch, J. "Meister Eckhart und die jüdische Religionsphilosophie des Mittelalters," *Jahresbericht der Schlesischen Gesellschaft für Vaterländische Kultur* 101 (1928) 134–148.

Kogan, B. S. ""What Can We Know and When Can We Know It?" Maimonides on the Active Intelligence and Human Cognition," in Ormsby (ed.), *Moses Maimonides and His Time* (Washington D.C.: CUA Press, 1989) 121–137.

Kraemer, J. *Maimonides: The Life and World of One of Civilization's Greatest Minds* (New York: Doubleday, 2008).

Kraemer, J. "Maimonides' Use of (Aristotelian) Dialectic," in Cohen and Levine (eds.), *Maimonides and the Sciences* (Dordrecht: Kluwer Academic, 2000) 111–130.

Kreisel, H. *Prophecy: The History of an Idea in Medieval Jewish Philosophy* (Dordrecht: Kluwer Academic Publishers, 2001).

Kreisel, H. "The Problem of 'Good' in Maimonides' Thought," *Iyyun* 38 (1989) 183–208.

Lamm, N. "Man's Position in the Universe. A Comparative Study of the Views of Saadia Gaon and Maimonides," *Jewish Quarterly Review* 55,(1965) 208–234.

Landolt, H. "Ghazālī und 'Religionswissenschaft'," *Asiatische Studien* 45 (1991) 19–72.

Langermann, Y. Tz. "Maimonides and Galen," forthcoming in Petros Bouras-Vallianatos and Barbara Zipser (eds.), *Brill's Companion to the Reception of Galen.*

Langermann, Y. Tz. "A Mistaken Anticipation in Samuel Ibn Tibbon's Translation of Maimonides' *Guide of the Perplexed* (Heb.)," *Daat* 84 (2017) 21–34.

Langermann, Y. Tz. "Sharḥ al-Dalāla: A Commentary to Maimonides' *Guide* from Fourteenth Century Yemen," in Carlos Fraenkel (ed.), *Traditions of Maimonideanism* (Leiden and Boston: Brill, 2009) 155–176.

Langermann, Y. Tz. "My Truest Perplexities," *Aleph: Historical Studies in Science and Judaism* 8 (2008) 301–317.

Lazarus-Yafeh, Hava. "Was Maimonides Influenced by Alghazali? (Heb.)," in Mordechai Cogan, Barry L. Eichler, and Jeffrey H. Tigay (eds.), *Tehillah le-Moshe: Biblical and Judaic Studies in Honor of Moshe Greenberg* (Winona Lake: Eisenbrauns, 1997) 163–169.

Lenzner, S. "A Literary Exercise in Self-Knowledge: Strauss' Twofold Interpretation of Maimonides," *Perspectives on Political Science* 31 (2002) 225–234.

Levinger, J. "Prophecy as a Universal Human Phenomenon," in *Ha-Rambam ke-filosof u-ke-poseq* (Maimonides as Philosopher and Codifier) (Jerusalem: Bialik Institute, 1989) 21–28.

Lieberman, S. *Yemenite Midrashim: A Lecture on the Yemenite Midrashim, Their Character and Value* (Heb.) (Jerusalem: Wahrmann, 1970).

Liebeschütz, H. "Meister Eckhart und Moses Maimonides," *Archiv für Kulturgeschichte* 54 (1972) 64–96.

Lloyd, G. E. R. "The Hot and the Cold, the Dry and the Wet in Greek Philosophy," *The Journal of Hellenistic Studies* 84 (1964) 92–106.

Manekin, C. "Maimonides and the Arabic Aristotelian Tradition of Epistemology," in D. M. Freidenreich and M. Goldstein (eds.), *Beyond Religious Borders* (Philadelphia: University of Pennsylvania Press, 2012) 78–91.

Manekin, C. "Review of Stroumsa, Sarah, Maimonides in His World: Portrait of a Mediterranean Thinker," *H-Judaic, H-Net Reviews* January, 2011, http://www.h-net.org/reviews/showrev.php?id=26207.

Manekin, C. "Divine Will in Maimonides' Later Writings," *Maimonidean Studies* 5 (2008) 189–221.

Manekin, C. "Conservative Tendencies in Gersonides' Religious Philosophy," in D. Frank & O. Leaman (eds.), *The Cambridge Companion to Medieval Jewish Philosophy* (Cambridge: Cambridge University Press, 2003) 304–342.

Manekin, C. "Maimonides' on Divine Knowledge—Moses of Narbonne's Averroist Reading," *American Catholic Philosophical Quarterly* 76 (2002) 51–74.

Manekin, C. "Belief, Certainty and Divine Attributes in the *Guide of the Perplexed*," *Maimonidean Studies* 1 (1990) 117–141.

Marmura, M. "Quiddity and Universality in Avicenna," *Neoplatonism and Islamic Philosophy* (1992) 77–88.

Marx, A. "Texts by and about Maimonides," *Jewish Quarterly Review* 25 (1935) 371–428.

Massé, H. "La profession de foi (*'aqîda*) et les guides spirituels (*morchida*) du mahdi Ibn Toumart," in *Mémorial Henri Basset. Nouvelles études nordafricaines et orientales* (Paris: l'Institut des Hautes-Études Morocaines, 1928) 105–117.

Melamed, A. "Maimonides on Woman: Formless Matter or Potential Prophet?" in A. L. Ivry, E. R. Wolfson, and A. Arkush (eds.), *Perspectives on Jewish Thought and Mysticism* (Amsterdam: Harwood Academic Publishers, 1998) 99–134.

Melamed, A. *Raqaḥot ve-tabaḥot: ha-mitos 'al meqor ha-ḥokhmot* (Apothecaries and Cooks: The Myth of the Source of the Sciences) (Jerusalem: University of Haifa and Magnes Press, 2010) 113–119.

Miller, C. L. "Maimonides and Aquinas on Naming God," *Journal of Jewish Studies* 28 (1977) 65–71.

Nawas, J. "Trial," in *Encyclopaedia of the Qur'ān* (Brill Online, consulted 2018).

Nuriel, A. *Concealed and Revealed in Medieval Jewish Philosophy* (Heb.) (Jerusalem: Magnes, 2000).

Parens, J. *Maimonides and Spinoza. Their Conflicting Views of Human Nature* (Chicago: University of Chicago Press, 2012).

Pearce, S. J. "The Types of Wisdom Are Two in Number: Judah ibn Tibbon's Quotation from the *Iḥyā' 'ulūm al-Dīn*," *Medieval Encounters* 19 (2013) 137–166.

Perles, J. "Die in einer Münchener Handschrift aufgefundene erste lateinische Übersetzung des Maimonidischen 'Führers'," *Monatsschrift für Geschichte und Wissenschaft des Judentums* 24 (Breslau: A. Skutsch Verlag, 1875).

Pines, S. *The Collected Works of Shlomo Pines*, 5 Vols. edited by Stroumsa et al. (Jerusalem: Magnes Press, 1979–1998).

Pines, S. "A Lecture on Maimonides' *Guide of the Perplexed* (Heb.)," *Iyyun* 47 (1998) 115–128.

Pines, S. "Maïmonide et la philosophie latine," in S. Pines, *The collected works of Shlomo Pines*, vol. V (Jerusalem: The Magnes Press, 1997) 393–403.

Pines, S. "Truth and Falsehood versus Good and Evil," in Isadore Twersky (ed.), *Studies in Maimonides* (Cambridge MA: Harvard University Press, 1990) 95–157.

Pines, S. "Some Distinctive Metaphysical Conceptions in Themistius' Commentary on Book Lambda and Their Place in the History of Philosophy," in Jürgen Wiesner (ed.), *Aristoteles: Werk und Wirkung* (Berlin/New York: Walter De Gruyter, 1987) 177–204.

Pines, S. "The Philosophical Purport of Maimonides' Halachic Works and the Purport of *The Guide of the Perplexed*," in Y. Yovel and S. Pines (eds.), *Maimonides and Philosophy* (Dordrecht: Martinus Nijhoff, 1986) 1–14.

Pines, S. "Dieu et l'être selon Maimonide: Exégèse d'Exode 3, 14 et doctrine connexe," in A. de Libera and É. Zum Brunn (eds.), *Celui qui est: Interprétations juives et chrétiennes d'Exode 3, 14* (Paris: Les Editions du Cerf [Collection "Patrimoines"], 1986) 15–24.

Pines, S. "Le discours théologico-philosophique dans les oeuvres halachiques de Maimonide comparé avec celui du Guide des Égarés," in *Déliverance et fidelité: Maimonide [Textes du Colloque tenu à l'Unesco en decembre 1985 à l'occasion du 850 anniversaire du philosophe]* (Paris: Éditions Érès 1986) 119–124.

Pines, S. "Les limites de la métaphysique selon al-Farabi, ibn Bajja, et Maimonide: sources et antithèses de ces doctrines chez Alexandre d'Aphrodise et chez Themistius," *Miscellanea Mediaevalia* 13 (1981) 211–225.

Pines, S. "The Limitations of Human Knowledge According to Al-Farabi, ibn Bajja, and Maimonides," in I. Twersky (ed.), *Studies in Medieval Jewish History and Literature* (Cambridge, MA: Harvard University Press 1979) 82–109.

Pines, S. "Jewish Philosophy," *Encyclopedia of Philosophy*, vol. IV (New York: Macmillan, 1967) 261–277.

Pines, S. "Translator's Introduction: The Philosophic Sources of the *Guide of the Perplexed*," in Maimonides' *The Guide of the Perplexed* (Chicago: Chicago University Press, 1963) lvii–cxxxiv.

Pines, S. "Studies in Abu'l-Barakāt al-Baghdādī's Poetics and Metaphysics," *Scripta Hierosolymitana* 6 (1960) 120–98.

Rahman, F. *Prophecy in Islam: Philosophy and Orthodoxy* (London: George Allen & Unwin ltd, 1958).

Ravitzky, A. "Samuel Ibn Tibbon and the Esoteric Character of the *Guide of the Perplexed*," *AJS Review* 6 (1981) 87–123.

Ravitzky, A. "Maimonides: Esotericism and Educational Philosophy," in K. Seeskin (ed.), *The Cambridge Companion to Maimonides* (New York: Cambridge University Press, 2005) 300–323.

*Religiöse Ehrfahrung: historische Modelle in christlicher Tradition* (München: Fink, 1992) 155–169.

Rigo, C. "Zur Rezeption des Moses Maimonides im Werk des Albertus Magnus," in W. Senner (ed.), *Albertus Magnus. Zum Gedenken nach 800 Jahren: Neue Zugänge, Aspekte und Perspektiven* (Berlin: Akademie Verlag, 2001) 29–66.

Rohner, A. *Das Schöpfungsproblem bei Moses Maimonides, Albertus Magnus und Thomas von Aquin: ein Beitrag zur Geschichte des Schöpfungsproblems im Mittelalter* (Münster: Aschendorff, 1913).

Rosenak, M. *Roads to the Palace: Jewish Texts and Teaching* (Providence and Oxford: Berghahn Books, 1995).

Rosenthal, F. *The Classical Heritage in Islam* (London: Routledge, 1992).

Rosman, M. *Founder of Hasidism: A Quest for the Historical Ba'al Shem Tov* (University of California Press, 1996).

Roth, N. "The Theft of Philosophy by the Greeks from the Jews," *Classical Folia* 32 (1978), 52–67.

Rubio, M. *Aquinas and Maimonides on the Possibility of the Knowledge of God* (Dordrecht: Springer, 2006).

Rudavsky, T. *Maimonides* (Chichester: Wiley-Blackwell, 2010).

Rudavsky, T. "Divine Omniscience and Future Contingents in Gersonides," *Journal of the History of Philosophy* 21 (1983) 513–536.

Saranyana, J. I. "La creacion 'Ab aeterno': Controversia de santo Tomas y Raimundo Marti con San Buenaventura," *Scripta Theologica*, 5 (1973) 127–174.

Schenker, A. "Die Rolle der Religion bei Maimonides und Thomas von Aquin," in A. Schenker, *Recht und Kult im Alten Testament: Achtzehn Studien* (Universitätsverlag Freiburg Schweiz, 2000) 178–202.

Schwartz, D. *Central Problems of Medieval Jewish Philosophy* (Leiden: Brill, 2005).

Schwartz, D. "The Debate over the Maimonidean Theory of Providence in Thirteenth-Century Jewish Philosophy," *Jewish Studies Quarterly*, 2 (1995) 185–196.

Schwarz, M. "Who Were Maimonides' Mutakallimun? Some Remarks on 'Guide of the Perplexed', Part 1, Chapter 73," *Maimonidean Studies* 2 (1995) 159–209, and Maimonidean Studies 3 (1995) 143–172.

Schwartz, Y. "Authority, Control, and Conflicts in 13th Century Paris: The Talmud Trial in Context," in E. Baumgarten and J. Galinsky (eds.), *Jews and Christians in 13th Century France* (New York: Palgrave MacMillan, 2015) 93–110.

Schwartz, Y. "Zwischen Einheitsmetaphysik und Einheitshermeneutik: Eckharts Maimonides-Lektüre und das Datierungsproblem des 'Opus tripartitum'," in A. Speer and L. Wegener (eds.), *Meister Eckhart in Erfurt, Miscellanea Mediaevalia* 32 (Berlin-New York: De Gruyter, 2005) 259–279.

Schwartz, Y. "Meister Eckhart and Moses Maimonides: From Judaeo-Arabic Rationalism to Christian Mysticism," in J. M. Hackett (ed.), *A Companion to Meister Eckhart* (Leiden: Brill, 2012) 389–414.

Schwartz, Y. "Meister Eckharts Schriftauslegung als Maimonidisches Projekt," in G. Hasselhoff and O. Fraisse (eds.), *Moses Maimonides (1138–1204). His Religious, Scientific, and Philosophical Wirkungsgeschichte in Different Cultural Contexts* (Würzburg: Egon, 2004) 173–208.

Seeskin, K. *Maimonides on the Origin of the World* (Cambridge University Press, 2005).

Seeskin, K. *Searching for a Distant God* (New York: Oxford University Press, 2000).

Seeskin, K. "Maimonides and Aquinas on Creation," *Medioevo* 23 (1997) 453–472.

Sermoneta, G. *Un glossario filosofico ebraico-italiano del XIII secolo* (Roma: Edizioni dell'Ateneo, 1969) 40–42.

Sezgin, F. *Geschichte des Arabischen Schrifttums*. 13 vols. (Leiden: Brill, 1967–2000).

Sirat, C. "Les traducteurs juifs à la cour des rois de Sicile et de Naples," in G. Contamine (ed.), *Traduction et traducteurs au Moyen Age* (Paris: CNRS, 1989) 169–191.

Sklare, D. *Samuel ben Ḥofni Gaon and His Cultural World* (Leiden: Brill, 1996).

Smith, L. "William of Auvergne and the Jews," *Studies in Church History* 29 (1992) 107–117.

Sommer, B. "Revelation at Sinai in the Hebrew Bible and in Jewish Theology," *Journal of Religion* 79 (1999) 422–451.

Steinschneider, M. *Die hebraeischen Uebersetzungen des Mittelalters* (Berlin: Kommissionsverlag des Bibliographischen Bureaus, 1893).

Steinschneider, M. "Kaiser Friedrich II. über Maimonides," *Hebräische Bibliographie* vol. VII (1864) 62–66.

Stern, J. *The Matter and Form of Maimonides' Guide* (Cambridge, MA: Harvard University Press, 2013).

Stern, J. "The Maimonidean Parable, the Arabic Poetics, and the Garden of Eden," *Midwest Studies in Philosophy* XXXIII (2009) 209–247.

Stern, J. *Problems and Parable of Law: Maimonides and Nahmanides on Reasons for the Commandments* (Albany: SUNY, 1998).

Strauss, L. "The Place of the Doctrine of Providence According to Maimonides," *Review of Metaphysics* 57 (2004) 538–549.

Strauss, L. *Studies in Platonic Political Philosophy* (University of Chicago Press, 1983).

Strauss, L. *Liberalism: Ancient and Modern* (New York: Basic Books, 1968).

Strauss, L. "Notes on Maimonides' Book of Knowledge," in E. E. Urbach, R. J. Z. Werblowsky, and Ch. Wirszubski (eds.), *Studies in Mysticism and Religion presented to Gershom G. Scholem* (Jerusalem: Magnes, 1967) 271–279.

Strauss, L. "How to Begin to Study the *Guide of the Perplexed*," in Maimonides, *The Guide of the Perplexed* (Chicago: University of Chicago Press, 1963) xi–lvi.

Strauss, L. *Persecution and the Art of Writing* (Glencoe: The Free Press, 1952).

Strauss, L. "Fārābī's Plato," in Saul Lieberman, Shalom Spiegel, Solomon Zeitlin, and Alexander Marx (eds.), *Louis Ginzberg Jubilee Volume* (New York: American Academy for Jewish Research, 1945) 392–393.

Strauss, L. "The Literary Character of The Guide for the Perplexed," in Salo Wittmayer Baron (ed.), *Essays on Maimonides* (New York: Columbia University Press, 1941) 37–91.

Stroumsa, S. *Maimonides in His World* (Princeton University Press, 2009).

Stroumsa, S. "Citation Tradition: On Explicit and Hidden Citations in Judaeo-Arabic Philosophical Literature," in Joshua Blau and David Doron (eds.), *Heritage and Innovation* (Ramat Gan: Bar Ilan, 2000) 167–178.

Stubbens, N. "Naming God: Moses Maimonides and Thomas Aquinas," *Thomist* 54 (1990) 229–267.

Tepper, A. "'Progress' as a Leading Term and Theme in Leo Strauss' 'How to Begin to Study the Guide'," in Shmuel Wygoda, Ari Ackerman, Esti Eisenmann, and Aviram Ravitsky (eds.), *Adam le-Adam* (Jerusalem: Magnes, 2016) 127–151.

Tepper, S. *Progressive Minds, Conservative Politics: Leo Strauss' Later Writings on Maimonides* (Albany: SUNY Press, 2013).

Thorndike, L. *Michael Scot* (London: Nelson, 1965).

Touati, C. "Les Deux Théories de Maïmonide sur la Providence," in *Studies in Religious and Intellectual History* (Alabama: University of Alabama Press, 1979) 331–340.

Van der Heide, A. *'Now I Know': Five Centuries of Aqedah Exegesis* (Amsterdam: Springer, 2017).

Vansteenkiste, C. "Autori arabi e giudei nell'opera di San Tommaso," *Angelicum*, 37 (1960) 336–401 and 372–393.

Verskin, A. "Reading Strauss on Maimonides: A New Approach," *The Journal of Textual Reasoning* 3 (2004).

Wisnovsky, R. *Avicenna's Metaphysics in Context* (Ithaca, NY: Cornell University Press, 2003).

Wohlman, A. *Maïmonide et Thomas d'Aquin. Un dialogue impossible* (Fribourg: Editions Universitaires, 1995).

Wohlman, A. "La Prophétie: Maïmonide et Thomas d'Aquin," *Ibn Rochd, Maïmonide, Saint Thomas ou "la filiation entre foi et raison": Colloque de Cordoue, 8, 9, 10 mai 1992* (Paris: Castelnau-le-Fez, 1994) 341–349.

Wohlman, A. *Thomas d'Aquin et Maïmonide: un dialogue exemplaire* (Paris: Editions Du Cerf, 1988).

Wolfson, H. *The Philosophy of the Kalam* (Cambridge, MA: Harvard University Press, 1976).

Wolfson, H. "Hallevi and Maimonides on Design, Chance and Necessity," *Proceedings of the American Academy for Jewish Research*, 11 (1941) 105–163.

Wolfson, H. *The Philosophy of Spinoza (2 vols.)* (Cambridge, MA: Harvard University Press, 1934).

Zonta, M. "Influence of Arabic and Islamic Philosophy on Judaic Thought," *The Stanford Encyclopedia of Philosophy* (Winter 2016 Edition), Edward N. Zalta (ed.), https://plato.stanford.edu/archives/win2016/entries/arabic-islamic-judaic/.

# Index